THE OTHER PRESENCES

RE-MAPPING THE TRANSNATIONAL
A Dartmouth Series in American Studies

SERIES EDITOR
Donald E. Pease
Avalon Foundation Chair of Humanities
Founding Director of the Futures of American Studies Institute
Dartmouth College

The emergence of Transnational American Studies in the wake of the Cold War marks the most significant reconfiguration of American Studies since its inception. The shock waves generated by a newly globalized world order demanded an understanding of America's embeddedness within global and local processes rather than scholarly reaffirmations of its splendid isolation. The series Re-Mapping the Transnational seeks to foster the cross-national dialogues needed to sustain the vitality of this emergent field. To advance a truly comparatist understanding of this scholarly endeavor, Dartmouth College Press welcomes monographs from scholars both inside and outside the United States.

For a complete list of books available in this series, see www.upne.com.

FLORIAN TATSCHNER

THE OTHER PRESENCES

Reading Literature Other-Wise
after the Transnational Turn
in American Studies

DARTMOUTH COLLEGE PRESS
HANOVER, NEW HAMPSHIRE

Dartmouth College Press
www.upne.com
© 2019 Trustees of Dartmouth College
Manufactured in the United States of America

For permission to reproduce any of the material in this book, contact
Permissions, Dartmouth College Press, 6025 Baker-Berry Library,
Hanover, NH 03755; or visit www.upne.com

Library of Congress Cataloging-in-Publication Data available upon request
Names: Tatschner, Florian, 1966- author.
Title: The other presences : reading literature other-wise after the
    transnational turn in American studies / Florian Tatschner.
Description: Hanover, New Hampshire : Dartmouth College Press,
    [2019] | Series: Re-mapping the transnational : a Dartmouth series in
    American studies | Includes bibliographical references and index.
Identifiers: LCCN 2018050396 | ISBN 9781512603484 (Hardcover) |
    ISBN 9781512603576 (Paperback) | ISBN 9781512603583 (Ebook)
Subjects: LCSH: American literature—20th century—History and
    criticism. | Other (Philosophy) in literature. | Literature and
    society—United States—History—20th century.
Classification: LCC PS228.O85 T38 2019 | DDC 810.9/005—dc23
LC record available at https://lccn.loc.gov/2018050396

5 4 3 2 1

Für Mama
Für Papa

CONTENTS

ACKNOWLEDGMENTS

The creation of this book would not have been possible without the sustained help and support of several institutions and in-dividiuals. First, I would like to express my sincerest gratitude to my indefatigable supervisor, professor Heike Paul; not only for her expert advice as well as her extraordinary encouragement to even fathom writing this dissertation, but also for having been, and continuing to be, a brilliant conversation partner and a source of inspiration. I would also like to acknowledge the support of professor Donald E. Pease, who urged me on to proceed on the ways of critical theory. Especially in the later stages of my project, Professor Wolfgang Schoberth also encouraged me to pursue my interests and, always with an open ear for initial unease, helped me delve into new fields. I would also like to thank Klaus Lösch for constructive critique during the beginning stages of my work and for helping me making my argument more concise.

Throughout the genesis of this book, Heike Paul's American cultural studies research colloquium at the University of Erlangen-Nuremberg provided an ideal environment for further specifying and polishing my argumentation. I benefited a great deal from the critical feedback of all its members. Especially Katharina Gerund and Stephen Koetzing have been most valuable conversation partners over the last years. Furthermore, I also would like to thank all professors and fellows of the interdisciplinary graduate program 1718 of the German Research Foundation on "Presence and Tacit Knowledge" for their constructive criticism and advice. As an associated member of this program, I was in the privileged position of enjoying the critical input of two equally stimulating intellectual environments. In this context, I also need to thank the German Academic Scholarship Foundation for funding me. Without this generous support, I would not have been able to realize my project.

Thank you to my awesome friends Petja Posor and Sarah Schulz, Simon Layer, Stephen and Nadine Hamilton; my cousins Felix Tennert, Karin Vogel, Michael and Jonathan Hürdler; my aunt and uncle Gisela and Peter Tennert; my uncle Wolfgang Fritsch; for their kind support, friendship, encouragement, consolation, as well as for pulling me out of my academic contexts from time to time. Mandisa Haarhoff and Roberto de la Noval—my best friend and one of the most intelligent scholars I have ever met—have been with me through all the ups and downs of a not always easy dissertation process with their continued moral support, shared wisdom, prayers, and always kind words. I would also like to thank my grandmothers Johanna Tatschner and Else Fritsch, who both passed away before I could finish this book.

The last acknowledgements are reserved for the most important people in my life, who know me better than anybody else and have been my most ardent supporters and critics. Thank you, Mama, for always being there for me, for shaping my personality, and for having made it possible for me to pursue my intellectual interests. There are no words to summarize an entire lifetime of loving support. And thank you, Papa, for always believing in me and my work even when you were worried about my future. I am so sorry, and it pains me that I could not finish this project earlier and you did not live so see its publication. I miss you a lot. I could not have had a better father. And, finally, thank you, Carmen, my love, for reading through the entire manuscript with such painstaking diligence, for being with me always, for thinking with me, teaching me, listening to me, bearing with me, edifying me, laughing with me, walking with me through difficult times, putting me in my right mind when necessary, and for always believing in me and my work. Thank you for us. Let us plunge ourselves into life together.

THE OTHER PRESENCES

(B)ORDERING PRINCIPLES: NEGOTIATING
THE PARAMETERS

As to those for whom to work hard, to begin and begin again, to attempt and be mistaken, to go back and rework everything from top to bottom, and still find reason to hesitate from one step to the next—as to those, in short, for whom to work in the midst of uncertainty and apprehension is tantamount to failure, all I can say is that clearly, we are not from the same planet.
—Michel Foucault, *The History of Sexuality, Vol. II: The Use of Pleasure*

THE QUESTION OF THE other and (cultural) difference has for a long time been of central interest in the field of American Studies. With the increasing attention to the transnational, the scope of this problem has broadened significantly, calling for a renegotiation of the stakes of otherness. One of the central epistemological challenges of this inquiry is that the very otherness of the other withdraws from the epistemic determination of scholarly discourse. Every attempt at grasping otherness with the tools provided by Western[1] thinking robs the other of its sting. Fixated within the discursive categories and frameworks of the *ratio*, the other is turned into a construct of alterity. However, this subjection is never complete, as the irreducible validity of the distinction between otherness and alterity suggests. The former never quite dissolves into the latter and vice versa: otherness can never be totally effaced. In fact, I argue that otherness remains as a specific form of presence, defying the discursive regime even (from) within, and saturating discourse with something it cannot contain within its own logic. Two interconnected questions arise: "how is this possible?" and "how is this perceptible?"

In this book, I am going to pursue these questions in the context of contemporary North American literature. This study focuses on four literary works from different cultural contexts: Anna Lee Walters's *Ghost Singer* (1988), Michael Ondaatje's *Anil's Ghost* (2000), Theresa Hak Kyung Cha's *Dictée* (1982), and Richard Powers's *Plowing the Dark* (2000). Based on this selection of texts, I will begin to develop and operationalize a way of reading that does not regard literature as an always already ideologically tainted form of representation, but rather also as a curious existential space where a presence of otherness possibly resides within discursively constructed alterity. Understanding the term "aesthetics" from its Greek root as sensual/ sensory perception, I will outline the potentials of what I would like to call "reading other-wise:" a mode of reading *from* the other, not merely *about* the other; a specifically perceptual modality that maintains an openness to the claims and concerns of the other (in literary texts).

My goal, consequently, is not to develop a philosophical system to be subjected onto the object(s) of study. Rather, my understanding of reading other-wise entails a radical revision of the Western tradition—specifically the Enlightenment legacy of the Cartesian subject/object split—in search for sidelined de-systematizing epistemological potentialities regarding the question of otherness. To accomplish this, I will draw on Bernhard Walden-fels's phenomenology with its firm insistence on thinking subjectivity from the position of the other as a first perspectival alignment. I bring together Waldenfels's thought with Jean-François Lyotard's notion of the figural, as my prime example of an overlooked potential in the Western tradition's engagement with the other, to lay out how the presence of otherness possi-bly dwells within works of literature. This will enable me to show how the texts themselves—through their specific agency as *acting* entities of other-ness and not as mere aesthetic objects—call for such a different mode of reading. Reading other-wise challenges and circumvents the epistemological violence of crude aestheticism by ousting systematic hierarchical subject/ object thinking.

In the interdisciplinary spirit of American Studies, this book integrates insights from the newly sparked debate in the humanities and social sciences on matters of "presence"—in the sense of phenomena withdrawing from *ratio*nal appropriation and exceeding the limitations of merely cognizing explication—into the discussion regarding otherness in American Studies. So far, the field has failed to fully account for the analytical possibilities granted by participating in these reflections. I claim that complementing the transna-tional paradigm with an awareness for phenomena of presence can help avoid intellectual imperialism. Regarding otherness as an ever-particular presence serves to introduce a decidedly "positive" (or, better, "posing") element into current debates of otherness in which notions of negativity dominate.

This chapter delineates my approach by negotiating the parameters of my book's endeavor. Starting with the positioning of my work in the context of *Transnational American Studies*, I will then explicate my specific take on *oth-erness*, *presence*, *aesthetics*, and *literature* to illustrate how these connect. I use each of these loaded terms according to what Jacques Derrida has termed "paleonymy," that is, "the 'strategic' necessity that requires the occasional maintenance of an *old name* in order to launch a new concept" (1981: 71).[2] Revising these terms allows me to construct the theoretical kaleidoscope for the analyses which follow. Yet, this introduction does not form a pre-determined roadmap that can be used to easily navigate a territory already completely discovered, nor does it provide a fully calibrated compass that points only into one specific direction. Ideally, it functions as a dynamic device of orientation capable of responding to ever new contexts and to adjust accordingly. The thoughts I am developing here are not to be read as a summary of quasi-empirical findings. Reading other-wise, with its pretensions of thinking around crude forms of Cartesianism, does not allow for such a procedure. Rather, rejecting the systematic closure of a simplistic cause-and-effect logic, the analyses of the literary works will (de-)systematically supplement and repeatedly redefine the (un-)concepts delineated on the following pages without ever claiming a status of completion: just as turning a kaleidoscope brings forth a new and different alignment of the same elements, the chapters which follow are going to approach similar topics from different angles to reveal other in-sights in an-other con-*figuring*. In instances where discursive closure is inevitable, for a scholarly book, I hope that the other presences still undermine it from within.

Transnational American Studies

Transnational approaches dominate the disciplinary landscape of American Studies in the twenty-first century so far. Especially the last decade has seen a major shift away from the paradigm of the nation-state toward a less restrictive, less static, and less exclusive conceptualization of the field's object of study. With the so-called transnational turn, the mono-cultural reduction of the signifier "America" gives way to more dynamic concepts which reflect the increasing plurality and hybrid polyphony of modern societies, as well as the discipline's growing internationalization (cf. Hebel 420ff.). However, this does not mean that the nation becomes obsolete altogether. By focusing on travel, crossings, and flows, Transnational American Studies rather embraces broader perspectives that situate the United States in a hemispheric, or even global, context. Transnationalist scholars employ comparative and relational approaches, and draw on multilingual cultural and literary traditions. The goal is to create "a version of American Studies that is less insular and parochial" (Rowe 2000: 2), in an effort to sidestep the pitfalls of exceptionalism that have haunted the discipline since its inception.[3]

Clearly, the multiplication of approaches with an explicit focus beyond the confines of the nation-state occurred mostly over the past 10 to 15 years. Nevertheless, the wish to shed the discipline's exceptionalist tendencies already implies that the transnationalization of the field began before the onset of the new millennium. In fact, Donald Pease has identified three overlapping phases in the turn toward the transnational which will also provide the rough historical framework for the project at hand.

Pease's first phase reaches from 1968 to the early 1980s, the second from the 1980s to 2001, and the third from the aftermaths of 9/11 until today (cf. 2011: 11f.). The last period coincides with shifting global configurations that seem to indicate the closing of the so-called American century and weaken the myth of the exceptional status of the United States (cf. Edwards and Goankar 5). The terrorist attacks on the World Trade Center and natural disasters, such as Hurricane Katrina, underscore the nation's vulnerability and loss of sovereignty. This vulnerability calls for a planetary awareness that recognizes a palimpsestic crossroads of ever-evolving and multifarious pathways underneath the arbitrary borders of the US (cf. Dimock 2007: 1; 2006: 3). Pease's second phase is already characterized by certain "forces of deterritorialization" (Giles 14). Worldwide economic infrastructural changes, President Ronald Reagan's free market philosophy, and the crumbling of the Soviet bloc after the Fall of the Berlin Wall situate the United States of the post–Cold War era within a more and more globalized commercial web. These forces require an appropriate response from American Studies (cf. Kaltmeier 6f.; Pfister 16). In this phase, developments in the humanities at large, particularly the increasing influence of postcolonial and border studies, contribute to the transnational turn. With the help of challenging theoretical concepts, such as hybridity and mestizaje, these two fields have offered powerful tools for the deconstruction of an imagined community of the nation-state (cf. Mihăilă 6ff.; Ngai, M. 59). Pease's first phase eventually locates the beginnings of transnationalization in specific extra- and intra-academic forces of the 1960s that reinforce each other in a reciprocal manner: international political and social movements, the critique of nineteenth century liberal humanist assumptions concerning the study of cultural artifacts, and the rise of what is usually termed "poststructuralist" thinking lays the groundwork for subsequent critiques of nationhood and other totalizing categories (cf. Jay 17). Transnational approaches in the current American Studies of the twenty-first century remain indebted to all these developments.

Particularly, an awareness of the importance of Pease's first period serves as a guide for the further course of this book. Paul Jay emphasizes the significance of the epistemological shift—mostly due to "poststructuralist" thinking— from focusing on issues of sameness to highlighting matters of difference; this reaches a climax in the aftermath of the events of 1968. Jay writes that "[i]f we are going to understand how and why national paradigms for the study of literature have broken down in the age of globalization, it is important that we grasp the dramatic role this shift in our attention from sameness to difference has played in facilitating this transformation" (ibid.). Consequently, what goes under the label of "poststructuralism" has been a (de)central(izing) force in the transnationalization of American Studies. However, I agree with Donatella Izzo who contends that "its intellectual potential has been left partly unexplored, its contribution too hurriedly conflated with the more urgent political needs that have driven the reconfiguring of American Studies" (603). This study, thus, re-integrates a re-vised form of what is called "poststructuralist" or "postmodern" thought into my own current transnational endeavor.

Moreover, Pease's genealogy not only functions as a rough historical frame of reference but has also guided the selection of the primary literary texts for this study. Richard Powers's *Plowing the Dark* roughly represents the third phase (although written and taking place before the incidents marking this phase, the novel foreshadows, or pre-*figures*, this latest phase's issues), Michael Ondaatje's *Anil's Ghost*, then, stands in for the second, and Theresa Hak Kyung Cha's *Dictée* for the first. By also discussing Anna Lee Walters's *Ghost Singer*, I furthermore introduce a text, which relativizes the status of the year 1968 (as well as 2001, for that matter) within the narrative of the turn toward the transnational by invoking an even larger historical scope (and, indeed, an entirely different sense of historicity, as I will show).

The plethora of studies with a transnational agenda testifies (at best) to the potential of the paradigm. Exemplary essays with titles such as "Chin-America: Intercultural Relations for a Transnational World" by Alfred Hornung, "Liberty: A Transnational Icon" by Sieglinde Lemke, and "American Studies in Motion: Tehran, Hyderabad, Cairo" by Brian Edwards indicate the abundance of this body of work. Many more scholars picked up on Shelley Fisher Fishkin's programmatic question "[w]hat would the field of American [S]tudies look like if the *trans*national rather than the national were at its center" (2005: 21) to produce valuable insights into the "crossroads of cultures" (ibid. 42) that is the United States. In her presidential address to the American Studies Association (ASA) on November 12, 2004, from which the above quotation is taken, Fisher Fishkin draws attention to this work and celebrates the transnational as a groundbreaking paradigm for the futures of American Studies, and particularly for the task of distancing the field from lingering notions of exceptionalism. She praises the advantages of abandoning the nation-state as the paradigmatic unit of analysis and, emphasizing developments transcending national boundaries instead, repeatedly proclaims that past and present injustices may be remedied by considering what American Studies has usually tended to ignore (cf. also Athanassakis 2). In her response to Fisher Fishkin's presidential address, and in accordance with Jay's emphasis of the role of difference, Mae

Ngai adds that "a focus on the transnational, with its emphasis on multiple sites and exchange, can potentially transform the figure of the 'other' from a representational construct to a social actor" (60) with its own claims and concerns. My project is sympathetic to all these promising achievements of the paradigm, but it is particularly this last aspect which provides the point of departure for my own positioning within the field. Throughout my analyses, I will extrapolate on the potential of approaching the other not as a socio-cultural construct but as an acting entity.

At this point, however, a central question arises: does the transnational turn in American Studies in its contemporary form, despite all its achievements, really constitute an appropriate framework for pursuing a mode of relating to otherness beyond mere constructivism? In other words, are the changes envisioned and lauded by Fisher Fishkin and her followers as radical as they imagine them to be? Or should it give a more radical modification of often unquestioned, tacit, and deeply rooted ideologic-epistemological assumptions? To argue for the latter, I will now move on to point out certain problems of the paradigm that need to be considered to avoid falling prey to the very dangers transnationalism seeks to circumvent in the first place. Moreover, I will map out a position from where the question of the other can be posed anew.

Introducing an essay collection on the transnational turn in American Studies, Berndt Ostendorf writes: "Transnationalism is a more encompassing, perhaps less frightening notion than globalization or Americanization, because it heralds the fading of borders and promises some sort of empowerment by transgression, both literal, epistemological, and metaphorical" (1). Nevertheless, over the past decade, optimism concerning transnationalism has not been shared by everybody. Although Fisher Fishkin's programmatic proposals have been enthusiastically embraced, several scholars also have subjected her ideas, and the shift toward the transnational in general, to a thorough critique. Most of these criticisms draw attention to similar issues that can be summarized in four interconnected theses: (1) Transnational American Studies often uncritically celebrates the cultural diversity of the United States, thereby, (2) the paradigm betrays a still remaining exceptionalist attitude and continues to reproduce it, mostly because (3) transnationalists tend to disregard the limits of their own scholarly expertise, and (4)—in their epistemological arrogance—these thinkers perpetuate an academic imperialism that turns transnationalism into a scholarly version of Manifest Destiny.

Critics like Winfried Fluck and Joel Pfister, for instance, argue that the predominant strand in Transnational American Studies has succumbed to the "romance of the intercultural space beyond the borders of the nation-state" (Fluck 2007: 26). The central irony involved in this is the fact that on the institutional level, the increasing internationalization has done little to decenter the hegemonic status of the authoritative American voice (cf. ibid. 24). Proponents of this "aesthetic transnationalism," as Fluck terms it (2011: 144), rather leave the sovereign position of the United States—on both the institutional as well as the scholarly level—unchallenged by abusing the paradigm to praise the nation's rich diversity of cultural artifacts as a consequence of intercultural encounters. Although now considered as part of a grand global web of cultural exchange, the United States remains at its center. As extreme examples of this stance, Fluck lists Angela Miller's (et al.) *American Encounters, Art, History, and Cultural Identity* and Rebecca Zurier's "Newness, Flatness, and Other Myths" (cf. 2011: 159); works that reproduce a much older, problematic variety of transnationalism, namely the one Randolph Bourne promotes in his 1916 essay "Trans-National America," where the term first appears, to consolidate the leading cosmopolitan role of the United States pertaining to the arts. The resulting notion of an intercultural space certainly does not present a suitable framework for relating to otherness.

The transnational paradigm, according to this bleak rendering, reproduces a decidedly exceptionalist logic. Bryce Traister argues that it is precisely the prevalent anxiety over American exceptionalism and the ardent desire to leave it behind that causes this constant re-perpetuation. Notions of a weak and vulnerable nation not only constitute the basic assumptions of Transnational American Studies, they already guide the striving for democracy and liberty from the early eighteenth and into the nineteenth century—values that would come to form the core of exceptionalist discourse rendered manifest in the Declaration of Independence and the Constitution. Transnationalism, Traister claims, mirrors Puritan and early Republican ideals in prophesying that the new paradigm "will release us [and obviously the rest of the academic world] from the madness and bring us safely into the 'futures of American Studies,' a time and place free from the original sin of exceptionalism" (2012: 152). The struggle for emancipation from this dire malefaction, as the aforementioned examples suggest, often plunges the discipline back into the same mire: "[a]lthough launched under the banner of an antinationalist dream, a great deal of 'post-Americanist' critique either unwittingly or unwillingly reaffirms some of the very narratives of America otherwise dismissed as nationalist ideology and politically insane delirium" and stylizes transnationalism as "our latest critical messiah" (Traister 2010: 14). Instead of decentering the founding myths of American exceptionalism, Transnational American Studies is in danger of deteriorating into just another sort of exceptionalist fantasy that re-affirms and bolsters instead of challenges and undermines the United States' (critical) sovereignty (cf. Pease 2011: 19;

Edwards & Gaonkar 23; Kennedy 574): no longer considered unique as a nation-state, America still functions as the privileged crossroads of cultures.

Regarding its epistemology, this (trans-)national form of exceptionalism becomes most problematic and, in some cases, even borders on spatiotemporal megalomania. As Hembrecht Breinig argues in a roundtable discussion, extending the discipline's object of study so as to accommodate increasingly global dimensions and attempting to analyze cultural artifacts from various linguistic, historical, and cultural contexts in the disciplinary framework "heightens the risk of overreaching the limits of one's scholarly competence" (Benesch et al. 620). Wanting too much, American Studies might achieve only very little. The broadened perspective comes with the menace of superficiality. Joel Pfister also writes that sometimes transnationalism's "critical globe trotting is too cursory and the tours are too exotic"; this leads him to ask: "How quickly and effectively can cosmopolites-in-training really learn about the many histories and cultures that deeply inform what they quote?" (17). By assuming that the intricacies of other cultures are readily accessible even in the horizon of Western knowledge, Americanists all too often display a form of epistemological superiority and arrogance which invokes the specters of Enlightenment (cf. Hong 33). Traister forcefully summarizes the implications of such an academic stance when he writes that the "encyclopedic disciplinary extension" and its "decidedly global reach" together "sound uncomfortably like the literary critical equivalent of the World Trade Organization" (2010: 16). Such an overestimation of one's own intellectual expertise and one's ability to easily transcend socio-cultural and spatiotemporal boundaries, in fact, harbors a destructive potential.

Failing to reflect in an adequate manner on the privileged status of its own forms of knowledge production (cf. Heinze 258), American Studies runs the risk of promoting an attitude of scholarly arrogance that threatens to reintroduce a form of neo-imperialism or neo-colonialism on an epistemological level. Radically critical voices even go so far as to read the transnational paradigm as an extension of the Monroe Doctrine or, ironically, complicit with the logic of the Cold War apparatus it seeks to reject (cf. Kaltmeier 3; Wiegman 580). To them, what presents itself as a Gadamerian fusion of different—often marginalized—horizons, in fact, turns out to be a violent digestion of horizons. Certainly, heterogeneity and otherness are embraced; embraced, however, within the tight hug of the discipline's own epistemological designs that remain unchallenged. Izzo describes this configuration as a "*technology of transnationalization*, effecting the translation of the new worldwide horizon of the economy into culture and transferring the old nationalistic version of American identity onto a globalized stage" (595). Other scholars share this sentiment. Timothy Clark, for instance, writes of an "institutional Americanism of critical thinking" (2005: 24) that "vitiates what ought to have been the generally globalizing scope of modern criticism and thought" (ibid. 25) and perpetuates an academic form of colonialism, "in which," as Traister adds, "the interests of the center . . . are exported to the international hinterlands for implementation" (2012: 61). Ultimately, if transnationalists retain a subliminal air of scholarly exceptionalism by ignoring the limits of their intellectual capabilities, American Studies will not achieve its self-professed goal of affirming formerly marginalized perspectives, but rather the opposite: the transnational paradigm is going to be tantamount to a perfidious epistemological parochialism that subjects otherness to its own categorizations to be able to celebrate it.

All these aspects allude to the ongoing influence of a deep-seated conviction regarding the hegemonic status of Western knowledge even in the critical project of American Studies. To disclose the full critical potential of the transnational paradigm—that is, to renegotiate the status of otherness—this sense of epistemological superiority needs to be discarded. To conceive of "'Americanity Otherwise'" (Saldivar xvi), I argue, the delimitation of American Studies' paradigmatic framework must coincide with the delimitation of its epistemological framework; otherwise, the hope for the transformation of the figure of the other will only result in the production of a more effective disempowerment.

The work of Walter Mignolo provides a useful route in this direction. In his book, *Local Histories/Global Designs*, he presents a forceful critique of Western militant epistemology and its results. In its stead, he develops a different mode of thinking which he terms "[b]order gnosis or border thinking" (19); an alternative way of approaching the phenomena of the world— informed by subaltern(ized) conceptualizations of knowledge production and founded on an "epistemological disciplinary disobedience" (xvi)—that opts for a "delinking from hegemonic epistemology ('absolute knowledge') and the monoculture of the mind in its Western diversity" (xvii). More specifically, border gnosis indicates a *"thinking from dichotomous concepts rather than ordering the world in dichotomies"* and, thereby, constitutes "a dichotomous locus of enunciation" (85) which stubbornly resists categorical fixation and rejects static hierarchies of knowledge. Border gnoseology, therefore, offers a suitable epistemological configuration from where the question of otherness may be posed anew within a transnational context.

For my overall argument, Mignolo's work will fulfill a mediating function. Mignolo's critique of "postmodern" philosophy renders border gnosis a useful tool to uncover the disregarded potential of "poststructuralist" thinking concerning matters of *presence*; in connection to his notion of decolonial aesthetics, Mignolo's concepts are helpful for discussing a possible deconstruction of the Western *aesthetic tradition*; and his understanding of *literature* as an existential space, lastly, forms an important contribution regarding the primary subject matter of this study. Due to these synergies, I will use Mignolo's concepts as an interface for anchoring the subsequent parameters of my project in the context of *Transnational American Studies*. His concepts also serve to further contextualize, demarcate, and refine my own thought beyond this context, since the very "logic" of border thinking suggests that my argument will not unfold simply within the rigid framework of disciplinary boundaries. My project seeks to problematize such boundaries and, consequently, engages in various transdisciplinary dialogues. Transnational American Studies — the way I see it — cannot remain American Studies in a traditional sense, but rather needs to be open for unusual interdisciplinary coalescences. As a first step in this direction, I will probe the potential of border gnosis in relation to the question of *otherness* by initiating a conversation between Mignolo's thinking, Bernhard Waldenfels's phenomenology and Jean-François Lyotard's distinction between discursivity and figurality.

Otherness

"[H]ow can we engage the alien [the other] without already neutralizing or denying its effects, its challenges and demands in and through the way of dealing with the alien [the other]" (2011: 4f.) — this fundamental question formulates the point of departure for Bernhard Waldenfels's recent *Phenomenology of the Alien*.[4] Although his examinations contain valuable insights pertaining especially to transnational perspectives, American Studies has so far largely ignored Waldenfels's thought. By integrating his philosophy into the project at hand, and, thereby, also the larger context of transnationalism, I hope to remedy this shortcoming. However, before I can pick up on the challenge posed by his question, a short overview of the key concepts in Waldenfels's work regarding their compatibility with Mignolo's concept of border thinking are necessary.

In his *Topographie des Fremden*, the German phenomenologist differentiates between three — sometimes overlapping — types of otherness, namely normal, structural, and radical (cf. 1997: 35ff). An otherness that remains within the boundaries of a specific order, such as that of one's neighbor next door, Waldenfels describes as normal. By structural otherness, he refers to forms of otherness within different (cultural) orders as expressed, for instance, within a foreign language or calendar. Lastly, with the term radical otherness, he draws attention to a form of irreducible otherness outside the confines of different orders of things that nonetheless has effects (from) within. It is evident that "radical" does not mean "totally absolute" in the quasi-religious sense of Emmanuel Levinas; otherness in its radical form rather always remains in a relation of reference to that which it exceeds as (extra-)ordinary. Waldenfels writes that "[t]he limit zones [*Grenzzonen*] which expand between and beyond the orders are the breeding grounds for the alien [other]" and that "[t]he alien [other] is a limit phenomenon [*Grenzphänomen*] par excellence" (2011: 8). Resisting any fixed distinction between inside and outside, but not abolishing these categories altogether, radical otherness defies easy binary reasoning and indicates a paradoxical logic of "both and neither" or "within and without" that resonates with Mignolo's call for working from the uncertainties of dichotomies (cf. 2000: 67). Similar to the (a-)logic of radical otherness, border gnoseology constitutes "a way of thinking in and from borders" (ibid. 327) which exceeds a systematic (Western) order and "overflows its disciplinary definition" (ibid. 244). Hence, radical otherness functions as a first point of contact between Waldenfels's phenomenology and Mignolo's border thinking.

Certainly, the question of the other has for long been of utmost interest to American cultural and literary studies. However, their dominant approach differs significantly from the understanding of otherness just described. The disciplinary focus—due to its political alignment—almost exclusively lies on matters of representation or, more specifically, on discursive processes of othering and their ideological implications. The goal is to engage in the ideological critique of renderings of otherness—based on differences concerning race, gender, or class—which addresses the unequal power relations and value judgments inherent in the often reproduced and reductive binary logics of "us versus them" structuring these discourses (cf. Wilden 274; Broders 12). Sten Moslund writes that "[w]hen we represent something we fix its identity, we determine it by use of the conformity of dominant codes and categories" (187). Consequently, stripped of its otherness in a gesture of epistemological violence, the other is turned into an inferior, often infantilized and demonized, socio-cultural construct of alterity. From this perspective, Americanists analyze the other as an *alter ego* that serves to delineate and reaffirm a normative self (cf. Lösch 32). In short, the other is not really regarded as other, but the product of prejudiced projections.

The criticism of discursive constructs of alterity is certainly valid and a lot of important work in American Studies has been produced in this vein. Nevertheless, as Winfried Fluck points out, "the concept of representation has its own normative base," as well; if left unchallenged, it functions as "a premise that guides all subsequent interpretive acts" (2002: 84) and precludes any other form of insight into cultural artifacts. In fact, taken to the extreme, sticking to the assumption of the impossibility of encountering the other as other, but always as a socio-cultural construct, representationalism turns a supposed weakness into a strength by attributing to discourse the absolute power to grasp and annul radical otherness. According to Waldenfels, however, "the other is *more* and *different* than that which is representable" (1999b: 149). It resists appropriation into the discursive order by defying its fixating grip; but he is quick to add: "but otherness is *never* what it is *without* all that which is representable" (ibid.).[5] When American Studies always already treats the other in literary texts as discursively constructed only, it runs the risk of promoting the same epistemological violence it seeks to criticize. The sole insistence on the capability of representation to completely contain the other entails the effective denial of the potential of radical otherness and limits the critical horizon of the discipline. In my analyses, I will, therefore, attempt to encounter the other as rendered in literary texts from the intersection of discourse's controlling impetus and radical otherness's denial thereof.

However, how should we conceive of radical otherness in the context of literary writing? Jean-François Lyotard's book *Discourse, Figure* from 1971, which has only been translated into English in 2011, helps me answer this question. Just like Waldenfels's work, Lyotard's early thinking, until recently, has been largely neglected in American Studies and harbors insights yet untapped (cf. Bamford 5). In his book, with the help of a critical examination of phenomenologist Maurice Merleau-Ponty's later thought and a modified form of Sigmund Freud's psychoanalysis, Lyotard develops the distinction between what he calls the figural and the discursive as two inherently interrelated aspects of textuality (and language in general). Thereby, he conducts a thorough critique of a limited understanding of (written) language; a criticism that is compatible with both Waldenfels's work and Mignolo's border gnosis. Vlad Ionescu's preliminary definitions paves the way for further outlining this congeniality: "while the figural designates the visual density of signs, discourse designates the regularity of any coding system that is readable and so abides by the communicative function of language" (2013: 144f.). Lyotard's notion of discourse mirrors the cohesive principles of what Waldenfels refers to as "order" and what Mignolo calls "system," whereas figurality points toward something else—or (radically) other. Eventually, carving out these correspondences between the three thinkers is also going to help me clarify my reintegration of "postmodernist" or "poststructuralist" thought into Transnational American Studies. The time of the original publication and the date of its translation situate *Discourse, Figure* neatly into two of Pease's phases of transnationalization: I will show how this type of thinking—and Lyotard's work in particular—can contribute to approaching otherness in literature beyond a reductionist form of constructivism.

Therefore, I will focus on the critique of discourse's supposed totalizing systematicity that Lyotard shares with Waldenfels. Like the character of radical otherness, the figural constitutes a disruptive force that "introduc[es] in the course of the text a depth that is not of pure signification, but that conceals and signals a kind of excess of meaning" (Lyotard 2011: 70), and consequently "always withdraws from the grasp of logocentrism" (2013: 216). Through its transgression of significatory discourse, figurality defies the logic of representation as well as any reductive instrumental notion of language as linear or communicative only (cf. Rodowick 14; Tomiche 155; Bamford 20ff.). These aspects of irreducibility further indicate the relatedness of figurality to Waldenfels's concept of radical otherness. In fact, Anne Tomiche renders this connection even more explicit when she refers to the figural as "the other of discourse that deconstructs it" (155). Lyotard's notion of figurality provides a way to understand how radical otherness *figures* on the level of discourse.

Lyotard describes how this disruption or transgression is constantly being generated in discourse by drawing on two (connected) philosophical inquires: phenomenology and psychoanalysis. In a first step, he subjects a structuralist conceptualization of language to a phenomenological critique and begins with the following observation: "Now there is a fact that our experience of speech renders incontrovertible, which is that every discourse is projected toward something it seeks to grasp, in other words, that it is incomplete and open" (30). This moment of imperfection and lack of closure marks (written) language with a sense of distance, negativity, and opacity. According to Lyotard, the workings of signification are powerless concerning this impinging of something that ever remains exterior to the signified's appropriative impetus. He argues that the "illusion of the signified" to be able to totally capture its referent as a concept of thought stems from Hegel, whose system—by "tak[ing] the word for the object, the name of the thing for its presence" (Lyotard 2011: 45)—has the pretense of being able to completely signify the referent within it. Against Hegel, Lyotard insists that this belief is simply a desperate act of disavowing a remaining outside. He concedes that "[o]nce signified, this exteriority is no doubt internalized in language; but the latter will not have lost its margin for all that, and this margin is the face that looks elsewhere" (ibid.). Consequently, for him, there remains a "slippage in the status of signification" (93), which inhibits systemic completion by always holding discourse open toward something other than itself.

This dimension of openness, testifying to the fact that (written) language does not exhaust itself within the realm of significations, Lyotard refers to as "designation" (cf. 99). It constitutes a process that paves the way for the disruptive potential of figurality from the thicker and deeper layers of language, because the designated "riddles discourse with a spatialization that the linguistic system cannot master" (Rodowick 6). As a spatial modification, designation exhibits a deictic quality that does not follow the rules of reductive principles of linguistic order and frees the referent from the levelling grip of signification. When Lyotard writes that a gesture of deixis constitutes an "*act* of showing" (2011: 38; my emphasis), he emphasizes a momentum of transitory fleetingness and uncertainty in discourse (cf. Bennington 1988: 120) or, in other words, a certain performative potential resisting total discursive stasis. This sense of incompletion, brought about through the inevitable deictic reference toward something other that must remain outside, is certainly what renders signification possible at all. However, it simultaneously denies the force of signification by maintaining an invitation to the intrusion of an exteriorizing depth into discourse (cf. Lydon 14). Emphasizing the opening potential of designation, Lyotard preliminarily concludes: "Language and its other are inseparable" (2011: 63).

In a second step, Lyotard elaborates on this inseparability with recourse to Freud's psychoanalysis. However, as Tomiche shows, Lyotard does not merely engage in a simplified, vulgarized psychoanalyzing of authors or characters in literary texts, but rather "draws an analogy between the functioning of the psychic apparatus and the functioning of the work of art [which also includes literary texts]" (161). For instance, Lyotard draws on Freud's interpretation of dreams to argue that the dynamics of the figural is similar to the dream-work, in that it deconstructs discourse by way of opening onto different forms of (un-)consciousness. It transforms rational thought into something else that cannot simply be re-cognized and makes itself felt in the form of an affect that remains out of reason's reach (cf. Bennington 1988: 80; Tomiche 161f.). It is in this way, as D. N. Rodowick argues, that "the figural incessantly inhabits and haunts the logocentric space that attempts to exorcise it" (137). Consequently, figurality assumes the ambiguous quality of what Freud has called the uncanny (*das Unheimliche*). Just as the "unhomely" character of uncanniness always remains tied to the "homely," as Freud shows with reference to the original German word *unheimlich*, the workings of the figural link discourse to an other that saturates discursivity, but that cannot be incorporated into its logic. The figure counters discourse not as counter-discourse, but as an estrangement from within.

Lyotard illustrates this by revisiting the much-discussed idea of the death drive, which Freud develops in his late work *Beyond the Pleasure Principle*. At the beginning of *Discourse, Figure* Lyotard writes: "Having given up on the folly of unity, of offering the founding cause in a unitary discourse, on the phantasy of origins, we are bound by Freud's utopia to the rule dictated by the so-called death drive, according to which the unification of the diverse, even within the unity of discourse (and not least in that of Freudian theory), is continually deferred and always prohibited" (2011: 13). Based on this description, Lyotard formulates the following explicit connection: "the principle of figurality that is also the principle of unbinding . . . is the death drive" (2011: 355). He elaborates on this via a reinterpretation of Freud's parable of the *fort/da*-game. For Lyotard, this anecdote functions as an analogical model of how reference (and the sense of negativity it introduces into discourse) works: the spool at the end of the string ultimately represents all objects, while the string itself represents referential distance (cf. 2011: 124). From the openness created by this spacing the potential of the figural springs forth. However, contrary to Freud, Lyotard does not see the death drive only as an inclination toward (self-)destruction, but also as a newly invigorating "drive for *jouissance*" (Bamford 150). Figurality implies both: the longing for desire's fulfillment and its simultaneous negation. "The figural is not simply the death of discourse," explains Geoffrey Bennington, "but discourse never quite successfully binds the figural either: desire is never quite literalised, the death-drive is what is never quite brought back to presence, the force that repeats the *fort* in the *fort/da* game" (1988: 99). The figural functions according to the (un-)logic of Waldenfels's radical otherness in that figurality, paradoxically, always remains exterior to discourse without ever completely breaking the relation to the inside of the order of things in the sense of an absolute other: the figural constitutes an-other (extra-)ordinary phenomenon.

At this point, I can braid the strands of my argument back together. In *Strangers to Ourselves*, Julia Kristeva paraphrases this sense of (extra-)ordinariness when she writes that "[w]ith the Freudian notion of the unconscious the involution of the strange in the psyche loses its pathological aspect and integrates within the assumed unity of human beings an *otherness* that is both biological *and* symbolic and becomes an integral part of the same" (1991: 181). It is the emphasis on the (extra-)ordinary—albeit in different forms—that Mignolo's concept of border thinking, Waldenfels's understanding of radical otherness, and Lyotard's notion of the figural have in common. This requires further clarification. The title of Kristeva's book, together with her paraphrasing conclusion, provides a suitable point of departure for this undertaking: "foreignness is within us: we are our own foreigners, we are divided" (ibid.) or, as I would like to add accordingly, (proper) self and (the radically) other are inherently interwoven.

Discursivity and figurality, as well as radical otherness and ipseity, or properness, form an ever-unstable non-binary relationship of simultaneous "both and neither." This relationship, therefore, does not constitute a dialectics harboring the potential of a synthesizing *Aufhebung*, but rather "a perpetual state of coming undone and being re-formed, like the interplay of colors of several kaleidoscopes" (Lyotard 2011: 32). In the moment when a specific order seems to stabilize itself, the opening dynamics of the figural disrupts it. Discourse appropriates this disruption right away into the stability of its ordering closure once more. Mary Lydon explains: "discourse and figure are given together. Not sequentially, not in juxtaposition, but together, at once, one on top of the other like two superimposed photographic images, or like the representations of the unconscious" (24). Just as there is no unbound figurality that is free of discourse's grasp, there is no discourse that is free of the figural's irruption. "Figure and discourse connive together" (Ionescu 150); that is, they "coexist with or within [each other]" (Bennington 2013: 205), always remaining in a tight but uneasy embrace.

In analogy, Waldenfels writes of coinciding movements of selection and exclusion, or shrouding and unveiling, in which radical otherness shows itself in its simultaneous withdrawal into the order of an own or proper (cf. 2008: 52; 1997: 20). To illustrate this point, he employs the metaphor of a weave, in which the other is bound to the proper, just as the proper is bound to the other. Due to this entanglement, radical otherness always remains a relational concept that never drifts into total transcendence à la Levinas in Waldenfels's thought, but always treats otherness and properness as residing in an unstable and fractured liaison of "more and less" (cf. 1997: 67). Guy Callan and James Williams mobilize a different metaphor to elaborate on this: "there is a 'chiasm' in the flesh of the world between the human self and that which is other—not absolutely other, because the flesh is the same, but sufficiently other to create the necessity to know it and interact with it, and also the space in which to do so" (43). Radical otherness remains in a chiasmic relation to an own or proper in a mutual embrace just as the figural does to discourse. That is, radical otherness outlines a relation; it does not constitute an attribute.

I stress the chiasm of the (extra-)ordinary, because, through this relation, Waldenfels's radical otherness and Lyotard's figurality can be seen as displaying the functioning principles of Mignolo's border gnosis on different levels. The figural transformation of consciousness and textuality, as explained by Lyotard with recourse to Freud, mirrors Mignolo's notion of the transformation of the old epistemological frontiers (cf. 2000: 12): "allowing for an intersection between incommensurable . . . forms of knowledge" (85), border gnosis constitutes a *chiasmic thinking* or, in Mignolo's own terms, "a critical reflection on knowledge production from *both* the interior borders of the modern/colonial world system . . . *and* its exterior borders" (11; my emphases). Proceeding from the (un-)logic of "both and neither," it perpetuates epistemic heterogeneity which de-territorializes thinking just as the irruption of radical otherness de-territorializes and negates any stable notion of an own or proper (self) within Waldenfels's phenomenology (cf. 2006: 124f.). Consequently, border thinking, as Mignolo explains with reference to Éduard Glissant's "an other thinking," rejects clarity over the unforeseeable and opacity (2000: 81f.). Engaging in "cross-epistemological conversation" (85), border gnosis aims to "question the universal location and the epistemological purity of the knowing subject" (167). Mignolo, thereby, insists on subjectivity's internal division, in which dwells a trace of irreducible exteriority and that turns, according to Waldenfels, the experience of the other into an ever-border-crossing endeavor (cf. 2006: 26). Discarding the rational stasis of Western knowledge, border gnoseology constitutes an "enactive epistemology" with an "emphasis on performance and transformation" (Mignolo 2000: 26). This again coincides with the deictic performativity of the figural that constantly opens discourse onto its other. Border thinking takes place in this opening, writes Mignolo, namely in the "cracks and fissures" of divided epistemologies (17). Lyotard argues that this "is the result of the tear, integral to language" (2011: 8), between discursitiy and figurality; a tear that lends a work of art—such as a literary text—the character of a "border zone"; that is, a "'Zwischenwelt,' or interworld" (78) as he also calls it, with reference to the artist Paul Klee. Ultimately, as all these aspects taken together indicate, Waldenfels and Lyotard illustrate how the guiding principles of Mignolo's colonial difference in *Local Histories/Global Designs*, with its split between the occidental modern world system and subalternized forms of knowledge, functions on the level of the subject (and culture) and (written) language respectively.

I am aware that scholars familiar with Mignolo's work might want to disagree with this assertion. Is it really legitimate to argue that these Western forms of knowledge production shed light on what border gnoseology is all about? After all, Mignolo explicitly states that "poststructuralist" or "postmodern" thinking—"belonging to the legacies of colonial and imperial discourses" (203)—disregards the colonial difference and remains Eurocentric in its focus. This is certainly true for some vulgarized forms of disciplinary theorizing that turn "poststructuralist" thinking, such as Derrida's notion of deconstruction, into readily applicable concepts. As Haidar Eid writes in *"Worlding" (Post)modernism*, it is not Derrida's philosophy itself, but "rather what his American followers have reached in their literal—not to say dogmatic—application of deconstruction" (35) in the wake of the so-called Yale School that lends "poststructuralism" an appearance of Eurocentrism. Therefore, it is important to point out that also Mignolo himself does not reject "poststructuralism" *per se*, but rather reminds his readers that it "was conceived not as a science or a discipline but as a critical position vis-à-vis scientific and disciplinary knowledge" (325). In her early commentary on *A Poetics of Postmodernism*, Linda Hutcheon, too, emphasizes "that the postmodern is, if anything, a problematizing force" (xi). I pick up on these reminders with my assertion of the potential of Lyotard's and Waldenfels's work to clarify what Mignolo means by border gnosis. I draw on these two thinkers from Jay's perspective concerning the first phase of transnationalizing American Studies. Seen as not having been digested in the apparatus of Western academia altogether, I agree with Hutcheon that "postmodern" thought outlines "the site of the struggle of the emergence of something new" (4); or at least something sidelined and forgotten. Therefore, I read theory in the wake of "poststructuralism" as a form of thinking which potentially brings about an opening of spaces within an epistemological landscape for the encounter with an other beyond the confines of reason; and this thinking is readily compatible with Mignolo's concept of border gnosis.[6]

It has become evident that the meeting with otherness as a disruption, in the aftermath of "poststructuralism," is characterized by destabilization, menacing negativity, and absence. Kristeva also writes that "[t]he foreigner, as it has often been noted, can only be defined in negative fashion"; but she immediately adds the question: "Negative with respect to what?" (1991: 95). It would be misleading, and also ethically questionable, to conceive of the other as absolutely negative only. The withdrawal of the other from the limitations of discourse always coincides with its simultaneous unconcealment in figurality. As Kristeva implies, the other's negativity is also a relational characteristic of "both and neither," largely dependent on our own perspective or mode of being and the world and with others, as Ute Guzzoni explicates: "The more important certainty and security become for consciousness, the more threatening everything becomes, on the other hand, that which falls out of secure order and nevertheless requests to be taken into account; that which—as other [*Fremdes*]—is not founded upon the imperturbable foundation of the certainty of the 'cogito ergo sum'" (2012: 14).[7] From a transnational perspective of border gnosis, which rejects the stability of the *ratio* and the closure of ordering systems from the outset of its reflections, the other can never be regarded as negative and absence only. Rather, a project with this vantage point needs to draw attention to the irreducible (posing or en-active) "positivity" of the other's claims and concerns or its insisting presence that continuously calls for acknowledgment.

With this insight in mind, I can now reformulate the question I raised in the previous section of this chapter: How can an inquiry in Transnational American Studies manage to take into account the presence of otherness in literary texts without falling prey to the appropriating logic of Western

metaphysics or another romanticized celebration which ultimately reproduces the very exceptionalism it seeks to shed? In the following, I will provide a preliminary answer to this question. Extending the supplementation
of Lyotard's notion of figurality, Waldenfels's radical otherness, and Mignolo's
border gnoseology, I will further develop the notion of presence to show,
then, (how) the *other presences* in works of literature.

Presences

After several decades of criticism, matters of "presence" have regained importance within the discourse of the humanities and social sciences over the
course of the last 15 years. The renewed interest in this problematic term
is mostly connected to a certain lamenting fatigue toward the predominant
mode of inquiry within the disciplinary framework of literary and cultural
studies, which Jean-Luc Nancy succinctly summarizes in *The Birth to Presence*: "A moment arrives when one can no longer feel anything but anger, an
absolute anger, against so many discourses, so many texts that have no other
care than to make a little more sense, to redo or to perfect delicate works of
signification" (6). This statement expresses a discontent with what has now
become a reductive scholarly perspective that dooms research in the humanities to answering the same questions repeatedly with little gain. In the orbit
of this *cri de coeur*, a (re)turn to questions concerning materiality, eventness,
and performance, then, begins to displace the almost exclusive focus on
representation. The goal of this measure is to open up a possibility to bear in
mind that which cannot be fixed or rendered explicit within discourse, and
consequently provide an access to different insights into cultural artifacts
of all kinds. My work has its roots in this context—as has become obvious—and matured through thorough examination and critical distancing.
I will now briefly introduce the work of the Romance scholar Hans Ulrich
Gumbrecht as a point of departure to advance my own understanding of
"presence" in connection to the question of the other.

    In his *Production of Presence*, Gumbrecht picks up on Nancy's complaint
and calls for a culture of presence which, as the work's subtitle suggests, considers what semiotic meaning cannot convey. He critiques "an *institutional*
configuration within which the absolute dominance of meaning-related
questions had long led to the abandonment of all other types of phenomena and questions" (16). To him "presence" indicates a more spatial mode
of relating to the things of the world—as, for example, still expressed in
the Catholic Eucharist, based on the belief in transubstantiation (cf. 28)—
beyond the grasp of interpretation; a way of being-in-the-world which the
Western tradition of thought has supposedly forfeited through the increasing

success of what Gumbrecht calls the hermeneutic paradigm. In this process, the impact of Descartes's thought constitutes the climax: "his name and the adjective 'Cartesian' refer to the endpoint of a century-long development on the level of *histoire des mentalités*, a development that spans the earliest manifestations of Renaissance culture and the fully unfolded state of the hermeneutic field" (33). According to Gumbrecht, the resulting hegemony of constructed meaning subdues more presence-oriented approaches to the world and its entities.

While the impulse to reestablish a mode of being and thinking that is able to relate to phenomena of presence is without question worth supporting, its premature realization harbors a significant danger. In their celebratory stance, Gumbrecht and others run the risk of creating an unproductive stalemate between asemiotic presence and semiotic discourse, as Christoph Ernst and Heike Paul have pointed out (cf. 12). The two critics refer to German media scholar Dieter Mersch, who, in his work, simply switches around the chronological order and asserts that presence precedes discourse: "It is the opening [the event of presence]; thinking and its terms that which comes afterwards" (39).[8] Gumbrecht attempts to evade this dilemma with his notion of an oscillation between presence and meaning effects (cf. 107). Nevertheless, his Weberian *Idealtypen* dichotomy between presence and meaning cultures only reinforces the impression that a form of binary reasoning, that he himself criticizes within Descartes's philosophy, still subliminally guides Gumbrecht's own theorizing (cf. 79). At worst, his discourse contains a peril similar to that of the transnational paradigm: the longing to extend the epistemological territory of Western thought into the realm of presence, free of a semiotic discursive taint, seems to come with the price of curtailing the relevance of other forms of knowing and the risk of reviving an older, colonialist impetus.

I see the prime reason for this peril in Gumbrecht's conceptualization of an oscillation between meaning and presence; a conceptualization in line with his *Idealtypen*, which mirrors the Cartesianism he seeks to reject. This central problem in Gumbrecht's account of presence, I believe, arises due to two related issues: a somewhat dubious reading of Martin Heidegger's ideas in the essay "The Origin of the Work of Art" and Gumbrecht's broadly dismissive stance toward "postmodern" philosophy. I argue that a radical reconsideration of the lessons of "poststructuralist" thinking does not entail an abandonment of presence-accustoming modes of approaching the (things of the) world, but, in fact, helps avoid the dangers inherent in Gumbrecht's (as well as others') reductionist conceptualizations of presence. I revisit the work of several key figures in what has been labelled "poststructuralist" or "postmodern" thinking in an *in-tense* manner; not to reaffirm their status as great thinkers, but rather to disclose sidelined potentials in their way of thinking. Instead of a move beyond, I propose a move back into this type of thought to uncover the overlooked potentialities—buried all too often beneath the prominence of well-known names—of an-other "poststructuralism."

This reconsideration can be approached via a critique of Gumbrecht's interpretation of Heidegger's essay; an essay which forms both the stepping stone for many "poststructuralist" endeavors—such as Lyotard's—and a central reference within the debate around presence (cf. Clark 2005: 2). Gumbrecht founds his notion of oscillation between effects of presence and meaning respectively on the relation between Heidegger's opaque concepts of "world" and "earth" through which the German philosopher describes the happening of truth as *alētheia* (ἀλήθεια). World denotes a "self-opening openness," whereas earth refers to the "spontaneous forthcoming of that which is continually self-secluding" (2011: 111). For Heidegger, these two forces ever-belong to each other. Together, they form a continuous struggle of give and take. However, reading this dynamism as a form of oscillation, like Gumbrecht does, is misleading. There is no simple movement toward the one or the other and then back again. Rather, world and earth, distinct and yet ever-inherently intertwined, make up a simultaneous movement of unconcealment and hiding within a ludic-agonistic chiasm which cannot be resolved (cf. Kern 169; Kockelmans 155). Heidegger explicates this as follows: "World and earth are essentially different from one another and yet are never separated. The world grounds itself on the earth, and earth juts through world. Yet the relation between world and earth does not wither away into the empty unity of opposites unconcerned with one another. The world, in resting upon earth, strives to surmount it. As self-opening it cannot endure anything closed. The earth, however, as sheltering and concealing, tends always to draw the world into itself and keep it there" (2011: 111). While oscillation implies two easily identifiable poles, the sense of simultaneity expressed in Heidegger's elaboration defies the distinction into such a binary. In fact, it is ironically the very urge to touch or grasp presence in its purity that reproduces the violently appropriating embrace of a militant Western epistemology. Gumbrecht seems to merely invert Hegel's notion of pristine presence as Idea into one of unblemished presence as spatial manifestation—both being readily accessible. Nonetheless, the underlying logic remains the same. Since he, unlike Heidegger, simply accepts the validity of the Western concept of semiotic meaning outlined in his book, Gumbrecht establishes presence as its opposite. Ultimately, the insistence on a pure, even unmediated, material presence that can be, in this case even literally, touched or grasped *as such* reproduces a form of metaphysical reasoning that runs counter to Gumbrecht's originally professed motivation.[9]

Despite these major reservations, I share with Gumbrecht the critique of a simplified Cartesian worldview and the initial idea "that a certain 'theoretical' move could indeed reenergize our dealings with all kinds of cultural artifacts and maybe even enable us to reconnect with some phenomena of our present-day culture that now seem to be out of reach for the humanities" (1). However, to achieve this, one may need to enter premises Gumbrecht himself is unwilling to venture into.

By first targeting and reworking the received concept of "meaning" itself, thinkers like Heidegger, and many of the "poststructuralists" after him, subject the Western metaphysical tradition to a more severe criticism than Gumbrecht's ideas allow for. As Lyotard explains, the discursive logic of signification is not autarkic, but dependent on the process of denotation that constantly invites a figural otherness into language that discourse cannot contain. Through the irruption of figurality, discourse harbors the non-explicable and unfixable within it or, in other words, a sense of presence, as Tomiche spells out when she describes the figural as "the 'presence,' within articulated discourse, of the non-articulated, the non-linguistic" (159). Thus defined, meaning without a trace of presence is an impossibility. Although it perhaps seems somewhat arbitrary to equate Heidegger's notions of world and earth with the terms discourse and figure, these two conceptual "pairs," indeed, share the same paradoxical (a-)logic of an indivisible, but never fully merging, chiastic embrace of "both and neither" in simultaneity (cf. Callan and Williams 48). Showing that presence is not simply to be regarded as outside of but rather as constituting an outside (from) within meaning, Lyotard circumvents the binary reasoning Gumbrecht wishes to, but eventually cannot, avoid.[10]

What kind of presence does the figural then invite into language if it always coincides with meaning? Did not Lyotard define figurality in terms of an opacity, a negativity, and even an absence? It is important to insist once more on Kristeva's insight that these characteristics are not to be taken as absolute but as relational. I insist that one should reformulate the question and ask: opaque, negative, and absent with respect to what? Connected to deictic acts—and in this aspect similar Gumbrecht's understanding of presence—the figural adds a spatiotemporal component to language which, in Derrida's terminology, defers meaning ad infinitum. Inhibiting the closure of the signifying process, this spatiality/temporality appears as decidedly negative when observed from the logic of discourse. The figural presents itself as negating the systematicity which it interrupts; but this does not mean that the figural represents negativity as such. It is correct that, with the irruption of figurality, discourse maintains an irreducible openness; and while this openness certainly denies any notion of homogeneous self-presence—as imagined in the Hegelian Idea—it still also *figures* as an-other presence; a presence which only ever surfaces within the relation to the appropriating grasp of signification, but always remains out of its reach, and, thereby, continuously (re-)asserts its claims and concerns. From this angle, the figural attains a positive character. Strictly speaking, however, never coming to rest, and always residing in the simultaneity of unconcealment and hiding, figurality never ossifies into a static substantive presence at all but always maintains a verbal dynamic: it *presences*.

The emphasis on this dynamism shapes my conceptualization of presence. In the following chapters, I will further unfold the notion of *presencing* in transnational literary and cultural analysis to (re-)introduce a sidelined and neglected potential of "poststructuralist" thought into contemporary American Studies. Placing the focus on that which *presences* within the (relative, or relational) absence of signification, serves to attenuate the by now habitualized, albeit misguided, assumption that "poststructuralism"— as "usually accompanied by a grand flourish of negativized rhetoric" (Hutcheon 3)—epitomizes the nemesis of all presence-based modes of approaching the world and its entities. A renewed emphasis on presence counters the jargon of negativity by showing that the disturbance of signification does not exhaust itself within the perpetual deferral of meaning. However, the disturbance also does not succumb to notions of (semiotic) purity and/or homogeneity that have for a long time characterized the Western tradition of thought. Treating phenomena of presence as a dynamic motion of *presencing* (from) within discourse serves to circumvent an unproductive deadlock between meaning and presence, which Ernst and Paul criticize in Mersch's and Gumbrecht's critical efforts. The stress on this *other* aspect of "poststructuralism" might help rekindle and bring back into current scholarship some of the formerly "liberating effect of such work" (2005: 20), as Clark puts it; an opening impulse lost underway as "poststructuralist" thought increasingly "was absorbed . . . into an essentialist, modernist and in many ways US-centric understanding of criticism" (ibid. 160). Through rereading "poststructuralism" with Jay as constitutive of the first phase of transnationalization, I also hope to do justice to Mignolo's criticism of "postmodern" philosophies and his reminder—also hinted at in Clark's remark—of the once critical agenda these modes of critical thought entailed concerning epistemologic systemic closure. I proceed from this challenging stance regarding the hegemony of Western reason, and hold that, within this variant, "poststructuralist" thought does not merely constitute a Eurocentric but rather a "Euro-de-centric" endeavor and contributes to what Mignolo calls a delinking from the *ratio* as expressed in his notion of border gnoseology (cf. 2013a: 1). The irruption of figurality ousts the illusion of a closed, centered, or unified systematicity, and keeps discourse open toward something radically other that *presences* beyond the appropriative and re-cognizing concepts of occidental epistemology.

I have already shown how Lyotard's figural functions as a dynamic pres-ence and how it coincides with Waldenfels's radical otherness. Klaus Lösch and Heike Paul describe radical otherness as a similar phenomenon of pres-ence. They refer to the unreachable and inexplicable character of the other that renders it fundamentally un-re-cognizable and only ever acknowledgea-ble implicitly. Consequently, to them, the experience of otherness has a qual-ity of a presence of absence toward consciousness (cf. 2013: 155). While this assertion is certainly not wrong, it is somewhat misleading to retain the sub-stantive forms in this context, as they suggest a static relationship between the two forces. There is no denying that the other *figures*[11] as interrupting absence regarding conscious reflection. However, Clark quotes Derrida ex-plaining that this "interruption does not interrupt the relation to the other, it initiates that relation" (Clark 1992: 134). My emphasis lies on this initiation and the (en-active) "positivity" of the other's claims and concerns expressed in it, which remain and require a response, to employ Waldenfels's terminol-ogy. The presence of otherness is not merely absence; the other never ceases to be related to that which it escapes, and, as such, ever-remains elusively present. More specifically, there is always an ongoing double movement of unconcealment and hiding—both in the sense of a "more or less." Even while withdrawing into absence, the other still *presences*; and linked to the notion of figurality, this radical otherness then also inhabits the space of the literary text.

At this point I can finally explain the ambiguities contained in the title I chose for this book. The phrase "the other presences" contains the just ex-plicated verbal meaning of presence as always singular *presencing*.[12] How-ever, it also implies plurality. There is not just one monolithic presence of otherness, but several presences. Taken together, the two overlapping mean-ings of the title—verbal singular(ity) and substantive plural(ity)—suggest that there are multiple, in each instance ever-singular, presences that con-sequently differ from one another and may also possess dissimilar modes of *presencing*. With the insistence on the plural on the one hand, and the particular on the other, I wish to avoid fetishizing or over-abstracting both the terms presence and otherness.

In conjunction with Mignolo's border thinking and Waldenfels's phe-nomenology, Lyotard's notion of figurality provides a suitable terminological (de-)framework for expressing this ambiguity. Particularly in Anglophone contexts, figurality constitutes a "poststructuralist concept" not yet worn out or oversaturated with one-sided implications of deferral, negativity, or absence.

It denotes the neglected sense of positivity in this type of thinking—that I want to draw attention to—without dismissing notions of *différance*, but regarding them from an-other angle. I consider thinking literary texts from the uneasy relationship between discourse and figure as the equivalent of border gnosis on the level of language itself. Complemented by the notion of radical otherness, it provides a way of welcoming and restituting the epistemic potentialities of what Mignolo calls "critical subaltern thinking" (2000: 95). Radicalizing his argument further, I hold that Western reason's mission of subalternizing deviating forms of knowledge is not only geared toward that which threatens the epistemic hegemony of the *ratio* from the position of a beyond—such as, in Mignolo's argument, Indigenous cosmologies—but also toward subversive epistemological forces arising from inside the Eurocentric tradition. I agree with Mignolo when he writes that "the transcending of the colonial difference can only be done from a perspective of subalternity, from decolonization, and therefore, from a new epistemological terrain where border thinking works . . . Border thinking can only be such from a subaltern perspective, never from a territorial (e.g., from inside modernity) one" (ibid. 45). However, I reject the notion that any type of thinking emerging in Europe constitutes a form of thinking that is always doomed to remain "inside modernity" and, therefore, colonialist or Eurocentric in its outlook. I believe that this is also what Mignolo has in mind when he draws attention to the initially critical attitude toward Western reason of what is now referred to as "poststructuralist" or "postmodern" thought. Liberated from the systematization under the label of "poststructuralism," which keeps them "hidden under the reproduction of Western civilization and metaphysics" (ibid. 329), Lyotard's figurality and other similar (non)concepts re-emerge as Euro-de-centric forms of forgotten subaltern knowledge that point toward an outside or epistemological otherness within the confines of occidental reasoning.

This assertion already paves the way toward the next section of this part, and to another question of central importance which I have not yet addressed: if the *presencing* of the other in literary texts goes beyond the confines of (Western) *ratio*nal consciousness, then how is one to perceive it at all? To provide an answer this question, I will move into a field nowadays often marginalized in American cultural and literary studies—aesthetics.

Aesthetics

In the preface to the English version of her book *The World Republic of Letters* the French literary critic Pascale Casanova writes that, within a transnational setting where the critical (ac)claim of the other(s) increasingly gains in significance, "it is not enough to geographically enlarge the corpus of works needing to be studied, or to import economic theories of globalization into the literary universe—still less to try to provide an impossibly exhaustive enumeration of the whole of world literary production. It is necessary to change our ordinary way of looking at literary phenomena" (xi). (Re-)turning to matters of aesthetics to develop this alternative mode of approaching literature might seem problematic in light of my agenda to develop a mode of reading other-wise. From the position of ideology critique, many scholars in the field of American (cultural and literary) Studies in particular might consider this methodological move equivalent to an infestation of anachronistic ideological assumptions they have worked hard to exterminate. This dismissive attitude stems from several convictions that form the result of a distancing from the pitfalls of (one should add, a vulgarized form of) the New Criticism: in this context, aesthetics is often seen as an immoral, repressive, elitist, and highly normative philosophical discipline preoccupied with outdated categories, such as the beautiful and the sublime. This discipline's ultimate goal is to judge or evaluate the worth of fetishized aesthetic objects in accordance with these categories to then perpetuate the illusion of transcendental or universal artistic values (cf. Ickstadt 2002: 264; Fluck 2002: 80; Claviez xx). According to this rendition, drawing on the aesthetic for unfolding a mode of relating to literary texts, which is supposed to be capable to perceive the *presencing* of otherness within them, seems doomed to fail.

However, several scholars have critiqued the premature removal of aesthetics from literary and cultural inquiry by pointing toward the somewhat limited understanding underlying this crude banishment. Fluck argues that contemporary American Studies "has *systematically* misunderstood and misrepresented the issue of aesthetics, because it has conflated the New Critical version of aesthetic value with the issue of aesthetics in general" (2002: 84; my emphasis). Focusing on questions regarding the aesthetic is, thus, always already considered ideologically flawed, because it sidelines social and political problems inherent within cultural practices and artifacts, making them disappear behind the veil of value (cf. ibid. 80). While such critique is often justified and necessary, Fluck shows—as previously mentioned—that the exclusive concentration on the ideological criticism of representation is no less dogmatic. The systematicity of judgment's evaluative logic is readjusted and not avoided: at worst, political value simply replaces aesthetic value. Heinz Ickstadt succinctly summarizes this by asserting that the theoretical "aversion [concerning questions of aesthetics] is only the flipside of a radical cultural critique which, in its attempt at purging American Studies of aesthetics by politicizing it, has, in fact, aestheticized its politics" (2002: 263). He makes clear that taking an aesthetic dimension into account does not always simultaneously entail the eradication of historical, political, or social aspects inherent in literary works and other forms of art (cf. 264f.). Consequently, rejecting aesthetics altogether, based on the reductive version the New Criticism (and its problematical Enlightenment roots) promoted, results in nothing less than the respective inverse reduction of the potential for different insights into these artifacts.[13]

What kind of different understanding of aesthetics then do the scholars in favor of aesthetics allude to and where does the potency of the aesthetic lie? What prompts scholars like Samantha Pinto in her book *Difficult Diasporas* to examine aesthetics as a mode of subversion of established categories and even Mignolo to emphasize the aesthetic as an integral aspect of border gnoseology (cf. 2000: xvi)? Mignolo renders explicit a distinction between two different meanings of the term *aesthetics* that also implicitly guides the arguments of Fluck and Ickstadt. He "distinguish[es] here esthetics (which is a philosophical discipline constituted toward the second half of the eighteenth century) from *aiesthesis* [sic], which refers to the domain of feelings, sensing, affect" (2000: xviif.). His interest in aesthetics is based upon the latter. Tracing the term back to its Greek root *aísthesis* (αἴσθησις), Mignolo begins to reveal a specifically epistemological potential of the aesthetic. Thus understood, aesthetics does not indicate categorization or judging artistic value. It constitutes a way of relating to the world and its entities which the hegemony of Western *ratio*nal consciousness suppresses; a form of knowledge which retains what he calls "'sense-sensitivity'" (ibid. xi) and, therefore, remains amenable toward multiple forms of (corporeal) sensory/ sensual perception. In his own words, Mignolo's goal is, via aesthetics, "to reinscribe in the history of humankind what was repressed by modern reason, either in its version of civilizing mission or in its version of theoretical thinking" (2000: 110). He goes beyond other critics who are sympathetic to aesthetics as an "attitude we take toward an object" (Fluck 2002: 86). For him, *aísthesis* is related to what Waldenfels calls the "becoming other of one's own experience" setting in when "it is not yet covered by rationalizations" (2008: 42).[14] Mignolo, therefore, certainly does not indulge in an irrational celebration of aesthetics which would mirror the exceptionalist attitude of "aesthetic transnationalism." Neither does he conceive of the aesthetic as being disconnected from social and political questions. Rather, from the perspective of border gnosis, the emphasis on *aísthesis* functions as a means of effectively "decolonizing aesthetics" (Mignolo 2000: xvii) and opening the Western tradition from the inside for the reemergence of subalternized modes of knowing. In short, for Mignolo, aesthetics harbors the possibility for "*a different kind of rationality*" (ibid. 187) that arises in the interstitial spaces of the old Enlightenment dichotomy between rationality and sensuality.[15]

In an essay collection entitled *An Aesthetic Education in the Era of Globalization*, Gayatri Spivak, too, affirms the significance of aesthetics within an increasingly transnational context as a form of "epistemological preparation" (2010: 1024). She introduces a theoretical maneuver that corresponds with Mignolo's take on the aesthetic and has the potential to foster the becoming other of perception that Waldenfels describes.[16]

Instead of claiming the option of dismissing the Western tradition of aesthetics entirely and putting something else in its place, Spivak calls for "productively undoing [aesthetics as] another legacy of the European Enlightenment" (2012: 1), namely in the form of a creative "'ab-use'/'use from below'" (ibid. 11). As her book's title implies, Spivak begins to undertake this constructive sabotage via a critique of Friedrich Schiller's *Über die ästhetische Erziehung des Menschen* and particularly his notion of the play drive. According to Spivak's ab-usive interpretation, the play drive does not fulfill the task of securing the capability for the appreciation of true beauty and the experience of a true freedom, but rather "takes away the absoluteness of guarantees" (2012: 21) and functions as a means for coping "with the double bind: learning to live with contradictory instructions" (ibid. 3). The deconstructive (a-)logic of the double bind does away with the systematization of difference into hierarchized binary oppositions without collapsing into relativistic indifference altogether, namely by maintaining the relation of undecidability characterized by constant flux. Spivak elaborates on this incommensurability by sharpening her notion of ab-use as follows: "Indicating both 'motion away' and 'agency, point of origin,' 'supporting,' as well as 'the duties of slaves,' it nicely captures the double bind of the postcolonial and the metropolitan migrant regarding the Enlightenment" (ibid. 3f.). Sabotaging the Western tradition of aesthetics in this way—accepting the condition of the double bind—entails a mode of thinking *from* rather than *in* dichotomies that resonates with Mignolo's border gnosis. Therefore, Spivak's notion of the ab-use of aesthetics allows me to bolster the argument that the other *presences* (from) inside (the text) and to outline further how this *presencing* (within literature) becomes perceptible. In fact, Spivak's thinking of the double bind will help me show how these two aspects are inherently inseparable.

To be able to do so, however, I first need to take a step back. The examination of Gumbrecht's thought has shown that the critique of the current debate around presence targets one specific legacy of Enlightenment: the so-called Cartesian paradigm with its split into *res cogitans* and *res extensae* or, in other words, the dichotomy between subject and object; a paradigm which, due to its location of the thinking subject as external to the things of the world, has often been identified as the origin of all binary thinking in the context of presence-based forms of relating to the world. I am, in principle, sympathetic to this criticism. However, I would like to recast it in line with what I have argued so far regarding the relevance of sidelined potentials of "poststructuralism" as a type of thought that—as is almost superfluous to mention—has also made it its central task to challenge established binaries.

Mignolo's work again proves helpful within this context. Firstly, he shares with Gumbrecht a critical stance toward this "poststructuralist" or "post-modern" thinking. Secondly, Mignolo's call for border gnoseology, too, is concerned with overcoming Cartesianism and "the distinction between the knower and the known" (2000: 18). In fact, he sees this separation as one of the prime engines of subalternization and writes: "once a correlation between subject and object was postulated, *it became unthinkable to accept the idea that a knowing subject was possible beyond the subject of knowledge postulated by the very concept of rationality put in place by modern epistemology*" (ibid. 60). In the professed goal to do away with the subject/object paradigm Gumbrecht and Mignolo agree. Nevertheless, while Gumbrecht seeks the solution by wandering astray in the ontological meadows of Heidegger's being-in-the-world, Mignolo dwells in the interstitial borderlands of subject and object. This is a crucial point, for here it becomes obvious that the two thinkers' respective critiques of what is called "poststructuralism" differ radically. Misguided by the longing for pure presence, that has, in itself, for long been the foundational hallmark of Western thought, Gumbrecht rejects "poststructuralism" and claims that going beyond subjectivity altogether is possible; but, at the same time, he reinstates the binary logic on another level with his notion of oscillation between presence and meaning. He does not seem to realize that Heidegger's existential clearing always already marks a dynamic borderland of revealing world and concealing earth, of simultaneous offering up and withdrawal, or, to be even more precise, of *presencing in meaning* and *meaning in presencing*. Subject and object are not eradicated there—only their relationship changes. Heidegger's philosophy is far more "poststructuralist" than Gumbrecht would have it. Mignolo's border gnosis on the other hand nicely captures this sense of undecidability, which shows, once more, that his critique of "poststructuralism" is geared toward its vulgarized and systematized form; a form that runs counter to its initial critical impetus. Instead of subscribing to the illusion of simply going beyond the subject/object paradigm, Mignolo's border gnosis allows for the renegotiation of their interdependence in the form of a double bind.

What exactly does this specific interrelation of subject and object entail for aesthetics in a transnational context? This relationship is connected to matters of aesthetics insofar as the distinction between subject and objects coincides with the dichotomy between rationality and sensuality. Descartes's dictum *cogito ergo sum* privileges the rational mind and categorical fixation

over the more elusive sensual perceptions of (the rest of) the body, resulting ultimately within a hierarchized binary opposition.[17] Sensibility is consequently
rendered, at best, as a lower form of knowledge. Many thinkers in the Western tradition have, ever since the establishment of the dichotomy, challenged
this degradation of the aesthetic (in the sense of *aísthēsis*).[18] However, it is
Theodor Adorno's *Ästhetische Theorie*—drawing on and yet simultaneously
distancing itself from this genealogy—that most clearly spells out the significance of aesthetics with regard to the question of the other. Adorno states:
"The more densely human beings . . . have over-woven [the world] with the
categorical net, the more they have gotten out of the habit to be astonished
about that other, cheated themselves out of the other" (191).[19] For him, then,
there is more to the world than rational categorization is able to grasp and/or
fix (cf. Seel 36). Like Waldenfels and Lyotard, Adorno holds that the epistemological impulse of reason to define phenomena exhaustively—and this pertains even to aesthetics itself as harnessed within a philosophical system—has
foreclosed what Mignolo calls sense-sensitivity. Reason effectively sealed off
the possibility of an access to the other that does not always already approach
it according to the logic of its own ordering principles. Adorno, however, also
implies that—not robbed and stored away by someone else, but by the *ratio*
itself—the possibility for a different form of relating to otherness still lies
dormant as an opening force (from) within.[20]

Luce Irigaray writes that "approaching the other requires sensory perceptions and ways to express them that our culture has neglected" (116)—
neglected, but not extolled. With the help of the subject/object split, Western
thought has (re)pressed this aesthetic dimension into the framework of a
philosophical discipline that forces sensual/sensory perception to reproduce
the same objectifying logic in the form of contemplation from a distance to
re-enframe aesthetics within the confines of reason. Although the aesthetic
was stored away as stolen goods in the philosophical basement of occidental
reasoning, it still continues to exert a sneaky influence, which unswervingly
endangers the epistemological hegemony of *ratio*nal[21] consciousness. Despite its subjugation under the yoke of cognition, an untamable sensuality
exposes the *ratio*'s own internal heterogeneity. The aesthetic persistently reminds the *ratio*nal *cogito* of its certainly disavowed, but ultimately undis-
solved, connection to the body; an inseparability which, through its recurrence, unmasks the necessarily artificial character of the subject/object split
and reveals a state of undecidable contradiction.

Spivak's "use from below" can help twist the *ratio*nal logic of the Cartesian paradigm to further uncover this hidden—subalternized—potential
of undecidability within the occidental tradition. A peculiar aporetic force

constantly reintroduced via the aesthetic, as Kristeva writes, "can make us feel that we are not in touch with our own feelings" (1991: 187). It harbors what Waldenfels calls the becoming other of perception, which again creates the chance for "an opening toward the new, as an attempt to tally with the incongruous" (Kristeva 1991: 188) or, in other words, the possibility for mode of relating to radical otherness. Creatively sabotageng the legacy of Enlightenment does not consist in the rehabilitation or celebration of (an irrational) sensuality next to reason, resolving the incoherent state of the self, and reestablishing the guarantees of a stable order. As I already argued regarding Gumbrecht's reinstatement of presence next to meaning, this move would betray an even greater—because subliminal—indebtedness to the *ratio* by introducing systemic binarism on another level. Rather, starting with the insight that otherness irreducibly resides in the self and maintaining the "*destructuration of the self*" (ibid. 188), ab-using the subject/object dichotomy means turning the Cartesian split into an enabling factor by regarding it as a border phenomenon and by thinking from the double bind of rationality and sensuality. Only then can one begin to muse with Kristeva: "Strange indeed is the encounter with the other—whom we perceive by means of sight, hearing, smell, but do not 'frame' within our consciousness" (ibid. 187).

In the context of this book, to speak of reading other-wise does *not* mean developing a systematic philosophy of a literary canon labeled "transnational" and establishing a catalogue of fixed characteristics and static ordering categories according to which works of literature can be judged or their value determined. The goal is *not* to identify a transnational aesthetic next to something like a feminist aesthetic, African American aesthetic, or the like. Instead, I am trying to describe, with the help of aesthetics ab-used, an-other mode of relating to literary texts, thinking from within the double bind of the dichotomy between subject and object; a way of approaching literature that consequently remains open for the claims of the artwork without prematurely reducing it to the status of one more aesthetic object ready for contemplation from a distance—without claiming ever to achieve this openness completely.

With Spivak's notion of an ab-use of the Enlightenment legacy of the term "aesthetics," I am also picking up on a declaration made by Iain Thomson to supplement Mignolo's notion of border gnosis. Thomson writes that "Western humanity's sense of being can only be changed historically through the creative discovery of possibilities hidden within the tradition that has come down to us" (99). At first glance, this statement seems contrary to Mignolo's claim that such a radical revolution can only arise "from the historical exteriority of Western metaphysics" (2000: 73). However, I have already illustrated that this epistemological exteriority must not necessarily coincide with a geographical one.[22] Mignolo argues that border gnoseology, in fact, means to be thinking *from* rather than *in* binaries, or, in Spivak's terminology, to maintain and engage with ever-aporetic instructions. If this is the case, then I hold that teasing out subalternized forms of knowledge from within the Western aesthetic tradition constitutes the necessary other entangled "half" of border gnoseology, without which Mignolo's ideas would fall prey to epistemological essentialism and constitute another, rather peculiar, form of Cartesianism.

Neither Gumbrecht nor other theorists of presence, it should be noted, employ the term aesthetics precisely due to its problematic Cartesian implications. According to a philosophy that supposedly has left subjectivity behind on its way to a pristine and substantive presence, the subject/object relationship, which the aesthetic necessarily indicates, can only be rejected as counterintuitive. In order not to give up on the term completely, some have replaced it with another hyphenated neologism, namely "post-aesthetics."[23] I have already voiced my suspicion concerning the focus on something like pure presence. Similarly, I want to avoid such replacement and hyphenation as it seems to me just one step away from forming yet another systematizing gesture. Rather, attempting to think from the tension of double binds, I will retain the word "aesthetics," with all its epistemic historical baggage and problematic binary implications, since they cannot simply be ignored, circumvented, or reduced, but certainly, as I attempted to show, creatively sabotaged from within. In line with Spivak, I argue that only by productively ab-using the legacy of aesthetics thus, and residing within the aporetic tension of borders, does one remain open for the unexpected and ungraspable or, to put it otherwise: the *presencing* of the other. While this might seem tedious, I see it as necessarily *in-tense*.

To wrap up this section, I want to return to the quotation that serves as its introduction. There, Casanova asserts that within an increasingly transnationalized context, the study of literature must adapt to the new situation by developing suitable approaches: "It is necessary *to change our ordinary way of looking* at literary phenomena" (xi; my emphasis). Although her call could be read as implying a decidedly aesthetic approach toward literary texts, Casanova's own argument ignores her oblique — and obviously completely metaphorical — reference to sensual/sensory perception, and then proceeds into an entirely different direction. In *Discourse, Figure*, almost 30 years before Casanova, Lyotard takes this request literally by beginning his work with the claim that a piece of literature "possesses an inherent thickness, or rather a difference, which is not to be read, but rather seen" (3). Shortly after, he elaborates on this as follows: "Discourse is always thick. It does not merely signify, but expresses. And if it expresses, it is because it too has something trapped within it [namely figurality], enough movement and power to overthrow the table of significations with a quake that produces the meaning. *Discourse too opens itself up to grazing, and not only to understanding*" (9; my emphasis). In many ways, these statements sparked the idea for this book. In the following, I will elaborate on how Lyotard's notion of grazing ties in with the project of developing and operationalizing reading other-wise. That is, unfolding the idea of grazing will enable me to further explicate how the attempt of engaging with literary texts from the dichotomous border position of the subject/object split's double bind requires an "alternative thinking of literature" (Clark 2005: 29) that does not simply subject these works of art to a pre-formed theoretic analytical grid, but is always willing to constantly re(de)fine its approach by meeting texts on eye level and equal footing. I will, then, lay out how this relates to the potential of perceiving the *presencing* of the (radically) other (from) within, and yet beyond, discursive representation(s).

Literature

Beyond pragmatic considerations with regard to the scope of this book, the reason for choosing to engage only with works of literature in my analyses is related to the central position that language—particularly in its written form—for a long time has occupied, and is still occupying today, in the intellectual history of the West. More precisely, it concerns the critique of this centrality that has entered into literary studies, mainly through the work of Derrida and the notion of logocentrism. I have argued, with repeated reference to Mignolo, that the adoption of "poststructuralist" thinking into the disciplinary framework has, more often than not, ignored the radical scope of this type of thinking. I am not trying to suggest that this integration has not brought forth any valuable work within the field. Neither do I want to imply that the critique of logocentrism is not important. Yet, I insist that, particularly concerning matters of presence, the prospect of "poststructuralism" has been significantly diminished by holding on to a largely reductive notion of language. Erroneously understanding and consequently somewhat misled by Derrida's deconstruction of a Western metaphysical conceptualization of presence as Idea, scholars have all too often and all too willingly plunged themselves into the bottomless pit of infinite deferral. They, consequently, (dis)missed the potential of *différance* not only as a critique of stable meaning and fixed truths, but as an opening force which changes the very meaning of meaning toward the unfixable; an aperture into a notion of (written) language that does not already, in its very constitution, close off the *presencing* of otherness.

Still, criticizing logocentric enterprises as well as the (mis)usages of language attached to them is worthwhile and of continued importance. To underline this relevance, I will briefly draw attention to the etymological roots of the term "literature." It derives from the Latin *litteratura*, signifying "writing" or "alphabet" and, especially within the later medieval usage, also "grammar" or "language science" as well as "written evidence," "account book," or "document." As Marion Hiller points out, all these meanings of "literature" indicate the logic of closed discursive systematicity that holds in place and objectifies language into a supposedly static and unchanging piece of writing (cf. 55f.). It is well known that written language—especially also in the US—was not only conceived of in terms of such ordering guarantees, but employed to propagate as well as promote a closure of (nationalistic) systems: Mignolo asserts that, as instruments of power, "literary practices have been, in the modern/colonial world system, linked in different ways to the coloniality of power in its colonial as well as its national versions" (2000: 223). Undeniably, this makes ideology criticism a necessary aspect of literary analysis.

Nonetheless, insisting on the exhaustiveness of this approach and the understanding of language tied to it, cultural and literary studies remain bound by the logocentric worldview they seek to denounce. The fields' "starting premise is [almost always, one might wish to add] that the text is part of a discursive network or regime which should become the object of study, because it exerts power by means of classification, representation, and exclusion" (Fluck 2002: 83). From this perspective, language is regarded as only an instrument for communicating and consolidating power. However, especially when it comes to reading literary texts, "poststructuralist" thinking does not only consist in challenging this ideological function; it also provides the groundwork, as Clark writes, "to set aside the instrumental misconception of language as a mere tool of human mastery" and to acknowledge that "language is not [only] a system of signs, i.e. tiny tools whose decoding supposedly takes place 'in' the minds of their users" (2005: 39). Derrida asserts that the ultimate goal of his critical efforts does not exhaust itself within the critique of logocentrism, but envisions and works in the direction of a more extensive modification of the occidental epistemological horizon toward the other(s) (cf. 1984: 123): it opts "to enable a fleeting or elusive access to a pre-reflective, unthematized pre-understanding of 'language' in which we already live" (Clark 2005: 39).[24] To realize that a thus altered view of language does not entail the illusion of a poetic aesthetic space entirely free of ideology, but rather creates possibilities for renewed contestation with a difference is what renders this type of thinking highly relevant for contemporary Transnational American Studies.

One possible explanation for the momentous misunderstanding of Derrida's thought lies in the counterintuitive and paradoxical notion that this enlarged understanding of language arises from inside textuality itself. I have tried to draw renewed attention to this with the help of Lyotard's *Discourse, Figure*. Consequently, next to the systematizing factor of *litteratura*, "poststructuralist" thinkers stress the untamable flexibility coinciding with this stasis, which becomes especially evident in literature's protected form as a work of art. Derrida's treatment of literary writing as a form of art differs significantly from the deconstruction of the Western philosophical tradition. He writes that "[w]hat literature 'does' with language holds a revealing power" (1992: 71); a power that Lyotard also mentions when he introduces his notion of grazing: literature gives free reign to its inherent figural-performative workings that possibly bring forth singular poetic events beyond discursive Cartesianism. In the form of these dynamic *acts*— always co-constitutive of the text next to significatory stasis—pieces of literature retain their open-endedness and harbor the potential for an alternative mode of relating to the *presencing* of the other(s); for, as such events, explains Thomson, literary texts exhibit a peculiar "agency:" they "push back against us, making subtle but undeniable claims on us" (22), namely by addressing sensual/sensory dimensions beyond the grasp of *rati*onal consciousness from within the Western tradition's own aesthetic framework.

To unfold the broader implications of this point of literature's force as an *acting* entity, I need to introduce two terms I borrow from Waldenfels that have implicitly already been part of my whole argument: response and pathos. These concepts concern the specific mode of relating to the other in its otherness. Waldenfels holds that one cannot actively search for radical otherness, for this would imply that one already knows what one is going to find. This attitude robs the other of its very otherness, its sting, and replaces it with an appropriative construction of alterity. The encounter with the radically other, however, exceeds the principles of systemic order and is always unexpected. Strictly speaking, the other can never be found. The meeting with it constitutes a stealthy foray, or unforeseeable invasion, which precedes every *rati*onal expectation and always takes one by surprise (cf. 1997: 123).[25] Waldenfels refers to this anticipation as "pathos," which he further explicates as follows: "Pathos means that we are affected *by something*, in such a way that this 'from where' is neither founded on the previous 'what', nor can it be sublated into a subsequently accomplished 'for what'" (2011:

27). Therefore, the only appropriate—or, maybe more precisely, the only possible way—of relating to otherness in its radicality is to give in to this disappropriating pathos that puts one in a position of response; a "responsiveness that allows us to recognize and encounter entities as being richer in intrinsic meanings than we are capable of doing justice to conceptually" (104), Thomson adds, and, thereby, alludes to the epistemological dimension of this equanimous mode of perception.

If Lyotard's figurality illustrates that discourse always remains saturated with radical otherness, then the notion of the figural allows for transferring Waldenfels's logic of pathos and response into the context of (how) the other *presences* in literature. This means that, through the pathos of a *presencing* figural otherness (from) within discourse, works of literature *themselves* retain the irreducible potential to stimulate the possibility for an-other—responsive—attitude of aesthetic perception, which does not at once (re-)subject the other to the preconceived framework of a contemplative objectification. Grazing, in Lyotard's sense, constitutes an example of such an aesthetic mode. It is sensible to the other's pathos and considers the becoming other of perception itself: "learning how to see [the other] is unlearning how to recognize [alterity]" (2011: 153). Taken together, all this also provides an explanation to my claim that *presencing* and its perception are necessarily intertwined and cannot be dissociated from one another.

Doing justice to the work of literature's performative pathos by giving in to an-other mode of perception entails a different relationship between literary texts and the analytic practices dealing with them. Mignolo's concept of border gnoseology again offers valuable points of departure. He writes that (literary) "[a]rt allows for abnormality" (2000: 244)—even in the confines of normalizing systems; a sanctioned irregularity through which literature can possibly function as an arena of epistemic disobedience and contribute to the restitution of subalternized forms of knowledge. Therefore, Mignolo explains his approach toward literary texts as follows: "My discussion is intended to create, through border thinking (e.g. thinking in between human sciences and literature), a frame in which literary practice will not be conceived as an object of study (aesthetic, linguistic, or sociological) but as production of theoretical knowledge; not as 'representation' of something, society or ideas, but as a reflection [sic] its own way about issues of human and historical concern, including language, of course" (ibid. 223). Similar to Derrida's work, this theoretical move does not only result in a critique of established approaches to literature, but harbors the more far-reaching epistemological ambition of slowly "transforming knowledge-as-representation into knowledge-as-enactment, and of erasing the subject/object destruction" (ibid. 126). Mignolo addresses the legacy of Enlightenment and its hierarchized binary opposition of the supposed rationality of thought and the sensuality of aesthetics that I have already discussed.

Mignolo's insistence on the epistemological potentials of literature is compatible with other recent developments in literary theory. In her book *The Use and Abuse of Literature*, Marjorie Garber, for instance, writes that literature should not (only) be read as an aestheticized object and "not as an instrument of moral or cultural control, nor yet as an infusion of 'pleasure,' but as a *way of thinking*" (7); a thinking which resists appropriative reasoning and always remains characterized by the "happy resistance of the text to ever be fully known and mastered" (ibid. 30). It is through this playful resistance of literary writing—as Lyotard and Jean-Loup Thébaud write in *Just Gaming*—that literature can become "a form by which one assumes a relation to otherness, without, however, claiming to have appropriated it" (106). Situated between discourse and figure, adds Clark, "the fate of the literary is to inhabit an elusive and incalculable space" (2005: 130); a textual borderland where the other *presences* in defiance of systemic categorization and violent discursive leveling or complete effacement (cf. also Lösch 40).[26]

My project critically resonates with what Stephen Best and Sharon Marcus, as well as others, have recently termed "surface reading," a mode of reading which indicates—in opposition to a so-called symptomatic reading, as propagated by Fredric Jameson—a strong sensibility for the material aspect of a text, the intricacies of verbal structures, as well as texts' affective and ethical potential(s). I certainly share with Best and Marcus an insistence on a non-objectifying openness toward texts as art-works (cf. 16), their rejection of a critical mastery over the text (cf. 8), as well as their emphasis on textuality's sensuous dimensions (cf. 10). Nevertheless, I do not think that a restriction to what they conceive as an entirely apparent surface is possible, or even desirable. Dismissing from the text the opaque dimension of depth as solely linked to ideological critique in the sense of Jameson, Best and Marcus assert that surface reading instead takes into account "what is neither hidden nor hiding; what, in the geometrical sense, has length and breadth but no thickness, and therefore covers no depth. A surface insists on being looked *at* rather than what we must train ourselves to see *through*" (9).[27] Drawing attention to the depth of figurality irrupting (from) inside a text, in contrast, my notion of reading other-wise outlines a mode of engaging with texts that can be reduced neither to a symptomatic reading's uncovering of maybe hidden (semiotic) meanings nor to a surface reading's description of apparently literary (material) meanings. I argue that conceiving of the possibility of (how) the other *presences* (from) within literary texts, requires a mode of reading—susceptible to the becoming-other of perception itself—that is both close and deep at the same time (and, therefore, stands in contrast to what Heather Love describes as a form of reading that is "Close but not Deep," as the title of one of her essays reads). Reading other-wise attempts to maintain the tension between depth and surface.

Moreover, I agree with Mignolo that the *ratio*nal Western tradition of thought still does not regard (aesthetic) literary knowledge as equal to philosophical insight and that, in many ways, the ongoing scientification of literary studies has fostered the increasing devaluation of the field's primary subject matter. Mignolo explains: "The problem is that the restrictive rules operating in cultures of scholarship are based on the belief that literature is fine, but doesn't constitute serious knowledge; and that is a consequence of both the imperial difference (e.g., science vs. literature) and the colonial difference (e.g., literature vs. folklore)" (2000: 222). Nevertheless, not being able to contain the subversive potential of the sensual/sensory within its system of aesthetics as a branch of philosophy or modern disciplinary framework, the *ratio* still shelters the momentum for a change (from) within; an epistemological modification which can be initiated by way of Spivakian ab-use of the Enlightenment's legacy, stressing the pathos of literary texts, in order to envision "a dehierarchization of the hierarchy between philosophy and art" (Claviez 154). Mignolo quotes a trio of Martiniquais writers — Jean Bernabé, Patrick Chamoiseau, and Raphael Confiant — to assert that this possibly leads to "the *resuscitation* of consciousness" (2000: 245; my emphasis) — and not to its mere dismissal. Literary texts present themselves as up to the task, because via retaining an extended notion of language beyond instrumentalist reduction, albeit without rejecting this quality altogether, literature forms a "difficult crossroad of heterogeneous contradiction" (Kristeva 1984: 84), residing in and openly displaying the chiasm of discourse and figure: instead of remaining bound by a limiting *ratio*nal philosophical logocentrism, literary works of art call for coping with the contradictory tension of the double bind between knowledge as both representation *and* enactment.

My privileging of literature in this book is not based on the assumption that literary texts are essentially the privileged site for the *presencing* of the other to occur or somehow more fit for operationalizing reading other-wise than other media. As I stated at the beginning of this section, my reason for choosing literature as my primary subject matter is mostly of historical nature and concerns the central, and often ambiguous, epistemological status of the (written) word in Western thinking. My argument regarding the other presences as well as the attached call for an alternative mode of perception, however, could well be undertaken in similar studies with a primary focus on photography, film, or even the multimedia of the internet. An example that points in this direction is D. N. Rodowick's *Reading the Figural, or, Philosophy after the New Media*. Rodowick successfully integrates Lyotard's notion of the figural into the debate surrounding new electronic, televisual, and digital media. Still, as one of the oldest media of fixing difference in the Western tradition, literature seems a suitable starting point for my project of thinking how to read other-wise.

At this point, let me reiterate that my work distances itself explicitly from crude forms of aestheticism and from what Fluck has called "aesthetic transnationalism" with its still exceptionalist tendencies. Nothing could be further from my overall goal than to uncritically celebrate the multiculturalism of contemporary North American literature that supposedly reflects the grandness of the United States. In fact, as has become clear, my take on aesthetics does not allow for this kind of easy aesthetic categorization. Instead of a philosophical system of judging the (ideological) value of aesthetic objects, aesthetics ab-used constitutes a form of sensory/sensual perception that is not bound to art as a *ratio*nally closed order, but rather implies a potentially everyday activity that disrupts this very systematicity, holding it open toward the radically other. While I am certainly not claiming that art is the only space where the *presencing* of the other takes place, I still hold that literature as a form of art—due to its approved abnormalities—retains an irreducible aesthetic force (as defined above) that is sidelined in strictly pragmatic discourses and other everyday affairs. My work views literature (and other artistic media) not as the sole and exclusive but as a (at first) most likely and/or capable locale for renegotiating the question of the other in a(n everyday) transnational context.

My choice to focus on texts written in English requires some qualification, too. In her presidential address to the ASA, Shelley Fisher Fishkin states that the transnational turn in American Studies is supposed to bring about a critical awareness for the voice of the other by recognizing the significance of "American literature written in languages other than English" (26). One might expect that a study propagating such a thing as reading other-wise would heed this call and include non-English texts into its analytical corpus. A look at my chosen examples, however, shows that this is not the case. The titles I selected for analysis are all (for the most part) written in English. Does this mean that I am rejecting Fisher Fishkin's contention concerning the importance of other literatures? Certainly not; the reason for limiting this study to English texts is rather an attempt of expressing epistemological humility and an understanding that analyzing literature written in other languages requires more than just a reading knowledge of these languages (and the cultures attached to them). With my focus on works in English,

I try to avoid overstepping my own academic expertise. I believe that the suggested selection, as it is, offers a breadth of cultural implications which is highly challenging without adding further complications in the form of multilingualism.[28]

Furthermore, I agree with Jay, as well as Brian Edwards and Dilip Gaonkar, who argue that the very quality of literature in English is subject to change within a situation of ongoing globalization, and that subversive elements increasingly can be (and always could have been) found within it (cf. Jay 25; Edwards and Gaonkar 16). Another quotation from Mignolo's *Local Histories/Global Designs* illustrates this quality of internal heterogeneity, or linguistic (extra-)ordinariness, which displaces monolithic notions of the English language as only a tool of (epistemological) colonization and (cultural) imperialism:

> In the domain of literature . . . one can write in English and still add to it the density of Spanish/Latin American memories, as Latino/as are doing in this country. English in postpartition India doesn't carry the same memory as national English in Britain; in the same way that English spoken in England by Third World immigrants doesn't carry the same cultural and ideological weight as the King's English. In other words, what the current stage of globalization is enacting is (unconsciously) the uncoupling of the "natural" link between languages and nations, languages and national memories, languages and national literature. Thus, it is creating the condition for and enacting the relocation of languages and the fracture of cultures. (2000: 292f.)

Of course, this also applies in other contexts, such as—in the case of this book—Native American writing, different postcolonial scenarios, and other immigrant experiences (although such labels are being questioned in the readings that follow). All these examples attest to the fact that English can no longer be regarded as a national language only. Through its own colonial and imperial history, (national) English has exposed itself to and become susceptible for the intrusion of *other* elements it cannot fully contain; subversive factors which turn English into a fundamentally transnational language. I would like to conclude this brief legitimation of my corpus with Spivak's (maybe too) optimistic take on the role of contemporary English: "If . . . some of us engage in ab-using the enabling violation of our colonial past to converse with each other, we may be able not only to turn globalization around, but also to supplement the necessary uniformization of globalization with linguistic diversity" (2012: 28). If my project constitutes a however small contribution to this major transformation, its goal has been more than fulfilled.

Reading Other-Wise

At the beginning of this introduction, I critically positioned my work within the field of Transnational American Studies. I held that, to disclose the promising potential of the new paradigm regarding a renegotiation of the question of the other beyond the ordering principles of the nation-state, a still lingering sense of Western epistemological hegemony first needs to be jettisoned. Mignolo's notion of border gnoseology with its focus on subalternized knowledges presented itself as a suitable approach and roadmap for this critical endeavor. In connection with Waldenfels's radically other and Lyotard's distinction between discursivity and figurality, I then developed a notion of otherness that resists discursive closure or significatory fixation without ever absolutely transcending its systematizing grasp; a form of otherness that always remains an (extra-)ordinary presence (from) within. Drawing on sidelined potentialities of "poststructuralist" thinking to link the question of the other to the humanities' renewed interest in matters of presence, I critically demarcated my understanding of a plural and/or verbal *presencing* (within or through meaning) from substantive conceptualizations that run the risk of establishing a gridlock between presence and meaning and reintroducing stable dichotomies on another level. I turned to aesthetics to show that perceiving (how) the *other presences* in literature requires what Waldenfels calls a becoming other of the perception itself. With the help of Spivak's notion of productively ab-using the aesthetic's Enlightenment legacy by way of thinking from the tension of the double bind, I contended—supplementing border gnosis—that the possibility for reinvigorating sense-sensitivity also resides buried within the Western tradition as a subalternized epistemological potential. This claim, eventually, brought me back to Lyotard's thought and to the specific potentials of literary texts as (en-)active textual agent that, through its figural pathos, stimulates a responsive engagement with its artwork; an engagement beyond attesting an infinite deferral of meaning that, by way of reading other-wise, remains open to (how) the other *presences* irrupting (from) within literary works of art, as the following chapters are going to unfold.

In "Ghosts in the Archive," I initiate a dialogue between Diana Taylor's concepts of archive and repertoire as well as Anna Lee Walters's novel *Ghost Singer* with the help of Derrida's notion of spectrality. Offering another perspective on archival matters, I do not only revisit so-called "poststructuralist" notions of historicity but enter into an ongoing discussion within American Studies. Lisa Lowe holds that "the archive is ... a way of referring to epistemological parameters for knowing, reading, and making legible"

(2015: 87). Drawing on Taylor's conception of the repertoire, I introduce an epistemological potential beyond archival fixity. I attempt to show how reading other-wise necessarily entails an epistemological reconceptualization regarding notions of historicity and thinghood. I am going to do so with the help of Walters's narrative. Dealing with the treatment of Native human remains and artifacts, *Ghost Singer* raises questions concerning the possibility of modes of perception and temporality beyond the limitations of objectifying epistemology and aesthetics. As itself an act of what Gerald Vizenor has called *native* survivance, the novel constitutes a live repertoire where the other *figurally presences* as spectrality; that is, in a form that challenges the fixed boundary between static archive and live performative repertoire.

In the part entitled "Being-Two with the Other," I then explain the consequences concerning notions of relationality between human beings in the envisioned epistemological de-limitation by drawing on Luce Irigaray's concept of being-two. In short, I read this concept as a circumscription of an irreducible being-bound to the other that bears strong affinities to Waldenfels's notion of radical otherness. I also use Irigaray's being-two to further critique the phallogocentric monocultural universalism identified by Mignolo. I argue that being-two, as a specific mode of relationality with the other, can help to avoid reading Mignolo's notion of pluriversalism as a simple multiplication of universalisms in the form of a one-plus-one-plus-one logic. In the second half of the part, I show how Theresa Hak Kyung Cha's *Dictée* performatively en-acts this new form of relationality through a specific ab-use of the Western tradition based on a what I describe as affective *écriture féminine* beyond counter-discursivity that considers the bodily workings of the figural.

In "Dwelling in the Borders," I conduct an (ab-)usive reading of Martin Heidegger's notion of attunement in connection to Alexis Shotwell's concept of sensuous knowledge to unfold what can be called "attuned sensuousness" as an embodied, localized, and non-Cartesian mode of engaging with phenomena or being-in-the-world that does not culminate in nostalgic notions of home, but circumscribes a(n) (un-)homely tension between place and planet. These concepts are then further elaborated in dialogue with Michael Ondaatje's *Anil's Ghost*. I will show how the narrative performs a process of sense-sensitization with a focus on the relevance of the haptic. Tying this back to the elaboration of (un-)homeliness developed in the first chapter, I stress the novel's transnational potential by focusing on the connection between aesthetics and politics in the context of the human rights investigation at the center of the plot. I argue that *Anil's Ghost* rejects a (subliminally) Western-dictated form of transnationalism and, instead, outlines the necessity of an *a-topic* (not utopic) border dwelling characterized by simultaneous awareness for particularity and planetarity.

Lastly, in "Precarious In-Dividuality and the Other," I will negotiate the relationship of simulation and presence as another fundamental epistemological issue by initiating a dialogue between Jean Baudrillard and Richard Powers's *Plowing the Dark*. In this part, mirroring the structure of the part on Taylor and Walters, I will draw on Baudrillard's philosophy and link it to Judith Butler's conceptualization of framing and precariousness. Thereby, I am also going to elaborate on my take on the continued relevance of "poststructuralist" and/or "postmodernist" thinking. In contrast to Haidar Eid's damning assertion that "(post)modernism continues the proceedings of colonialism and modernity, pushing the project to 'civilize' and 'humanize' the 'Other' towards its (post)modern endgame: to absorb and consume the 'Other'" (61), I will reaffirm my own claim regarding the opening potential of this mode of thought: I will show how both Baudrillard and Butler call for a revised form of aesthetics to unfold a mode of sociality that is not founded upon a monadic modernist conception of the individual, but rather resides in what could be termed a form of precarious existential sameness, wherein radical otherness always remains *presencing* as an irreducible social actor. In my analysis of Powers's narrative *Plowing the Dark*, I will explain how this necessarily coincides with notions of virtuality and/or simulation and the foundational epistemological assumptions regarding the nature of reality which undergird these notions. Ultimately, once again mirroring the chapter on Taylor and Walters, and problematizing surface reading's renewed "accent on immersion in texts without paranoia or suspicion about their merit or value)" (Best and Marcus 16), I am going to dis-close how the novel itself circumscribes a precarious figural virtuality that harbors the potential for an apprehension of radical otherness.

Entering In-Tense Dialogues

In his *Poetics of Relation*, Édouard Glissant writes that "[w]e 'know' that the Other is within us and affects how we evolve as well as the bulk of our conceptions and the development of our sensibility" (27). Beginning from the always already irreducible entanglement of self/other, this book offers an open(ing) invitation to read other-wise. As such, it cannot simply subscribe to the established methodologies in the humanities of going about things. The principles of Western academia ask for a coherent argument that will be gradually unfolded through logically connected steps. While my book certainly does not just dismiss such an approach and is going to *enact* what is necessary to qualify as an academic text, it is going to do so with a certain *twist*: in an on-*going* attempt of contributing to a dehierarchization of philosophy or theory, and art or, here, literary texts, my project engages each work of literature with the works of several thinkers. Unfolding—or enfolding—its own poetics of relation, the book, thereby, has both enter into critical, mutually complementing, dialogues. Each part is going to out-line a relationality between one thinker and one work of literature.[29] In these dialogues—not organized according to a linear teleology, but rather resonating with one another—the parameters of reading literature other-wise after the transnational turn in American Studies are going to be further negotiated, approached from different angles, additionally modified, and supplemented. As *dia-logues*, arguing from an *in-tense dichotomous locus* of theory and literature, the chapters will attend to the *pathos* of the texts to be discussed. The arising *responses* always already *figure* in the make-up of this book: in *ritualistic* fashion, each part is going to *ab-usively* (re-)iterate the same twofold structure within a *counter-turning* circle, where concepts recur in a *spectral* nexus with a difference, to attune the reader to the inher-ent *reversibility* of Western discourse(s). I pick up on Irigaray's assertion in *The Way of Love* that

> we, Westerners, are accustomed to applying our attention to and con-fronting ourselves with a still coded meaning, often forgetting the poietic, rhythmic, melodic, more generally carnal requirements which ought to take part in the elaboration and the passing on of the sense. In order to talk to the other, to listen to the other, to hold a dialogue between us, we have to again find an artistic, musical, touchful way of speaking or saying and of listening able to be perceived in a written text, then not reduced to a simple assistance for remembering meaning or to some code to be respected. (2002b: xx)

Consequently, one could also use a different verb to de-scribe what this book will do: it is going to *pose*; it is going to *pose* a challenge to said princi-ples of academic argumentation and will not im-*pose* a fixed categorical grid over objects to be analyzed, but rather com-*pose* dialogical readings of texts and, thereby, ex-*pose* the insufficiency of relying on such fixations to dis-*pose* of them as far as this is possible.

I would like to ask the reader to accept my invitation to enter into a pact with my book: to follow its *textual performance*, to move along, and to *see* what it has to *show*. And I would like to reiterate this invitation once again in the somewhat more demanding words of Irigaray: "I ask the reader of the text to accept the invitation to listen-to in the present, to enter into dialogue with a thought, with a way of speaking, and to give up appropriating only a content of discourse in order to integrate it among knowledge already gained" (2002b: x). Reading other-wise ever-begins where appropriation ceases.

PART ONE

GHOSTS IN THE ARCHIVE: NEGOTIATING HISTORICITY AND SURVIVANCE WITH DIANA TAYLOR AND ANNA LEE WALTERS'S *GHOST SINGER*

What is called poetry or literature, art itself (let us make no distinction for the moment) — in other words, a certain experience of language . . . — is perhaps only an intense familiarity with the ineluctable originarity of the specter.
— Jacques Derrida, *Specters of Marx*

IN "CROSSROADS OF CULTURES," her programmatic address to the American Sociological Association (ASA), Shelley Fisher Fishkin lauds transnational scholarship as a fundamental shift in the disciplinary framework with far-reaching consequences for the future of American Studies and its pursuit of exorcising haunting notions of exceptionalism. In a manifesto-like fashion, Fisher Fishkin introduces each of her arguments with the same invocation. "As the transnational becomes increasingly central to American studies" (22, 2005), she repeatedly prophecies, past and present injustices may be remedied by considering what American Studies has tended to ignore.

This revision of the discipline's perspectival outlook potentially harbors spatial as well as temporal modifications of its scope. On the one hand, Fisher Fishkin claims, "we will probably make more of an effort to seek out the view from *el otro lao*" (23), for instance, when it comes to military conflicts with US involvement. On the other, it also means that "we may well seek to recover chapters of the past that have eluded any archive despite their importance" (25), such as immigrant documents and other marginalized literatures in languages other than English, to fill the gaps in the files of historiography. The introduction raised the question whether these changes can really be considered as deeply profound as Fisher Fishkin and other transnationalists would have it, or whether the subjunctive qualifiers "probably" and "may," in fact, allude to more than just a relative uncertainty concerning the future development of the provisioned reforming efforts, namely to a lingering notion of the very exceptionalism transnational scholarship seeks to displace. This part, supplementing Donald Pease's three phases of transnationalization, is going to further pursue this critical query by alluding to possible temporal and spatial modifications of the paradigm, and its notion of the archive yet largely unfathomed in current debates within American Studies.

Despite the sheer breadth of criticism regarding the field's increasing transnationalism, there still remains a curious gap. Over the past decade, nearly all branches of the discipline have offered significant critical contributions to the so-called transnational turn. However, there seems to be a strange silence regarding a Native American voice in the discourse of the transnational; a silence which scholarship has only recently attempted to explain.[1] For Hsinya Huang, Philip Deloria, Laura Furlan, and John Gamber, the reason for this absence lies in the very spatial and temporal implications so praised by Fisher Fishkin and others. In a collaborated essay, they write that "while the dominant idea concepts [*sic*] concerning the transnational weight our thinking toward the global, there are internal national communities . . . that point in more complex directions" (8). This does not mean that Native Americans simply wish to hold on to the paradigm of the nation-state; they are drawing attention to a different dimension of transnationalism, which is often ignored in the dominant discourse surrounding it. The authors make clear that "[f]rom a Native perspective, the US has always been transnational, due to its relationships with sovereign Native nations within its borders" (1). Contrary to Fisher Fishkin's idea, then, this Native point of view suggests that the transnational cannot simply become more central to anything in the future. As Shari Huhndorf writes, "[t]he transnational viewpoint in Native American studies makes possible a critical analysis of the ways in which colonization has reshaped Native societies, culture, and modes of resistance, as well as an examination of the challenges that indigeneity poses to global capitalism, empire, and the colonial nation-state" (3). That is, the transnational Indigenous perspective, rather, has always been working internally and continues to function as a decentralizing force inside the United States' national project.

Disregarding the Native American presences forming this internal transnationalism and simultaneously reaching beyond the confines of national and natural borders, therefore, runs the risk of perpetuating the logic of a Manifest Destiny on an intellectual level. The gesture of centralizing the transnational within American Studies mirrors the operations of crude national expansionism, leaves the superordinate principles organizing it unquestioned, and subliminally reintegrates exceptionalist thinking into the paradigmatic turn toward the transnational. As Walter Mignolo writes: "From the project of the *Orbis Universalis Christianum*, through the standards of civilization at the turn of the twentieth century, to the current one of globalization . . . , global designs have been the hegemonic project for managing the planet" (2000: 23). To draw attention to and avoid this danger, the following part situates the project of developing an alternative mode of relating to literary texts in the form of reading other-wise within the context of what can be called the United States' internal transnationalism as a point of departure. The analyses in this part will show that successfully uprooting American exceptionalism requires not only a change of perspective and an inclusion of forgotten archives, but rather a profound modification of entire ways of perception and an openness toward different understandings of historicity as well as conceptions of the archive. For Mignolo, with the onset of what he calls the hegemony of the occidental modern/colonial world system, Western concepts of history and time "became the essential 'connector' of colonial and imperial differences throughout the globe" (2011: 168), since they contributed to a classification of cultures as either modern or primitive, and, in extension, promoted the quick dismissal of Indigenous epistemologies: "The Western notion of time supports 'history' and 'science' to acquire a hegemonic force and to develop a comparative point of view that allows for the erasure or devaluation of other forms of knowledge" (172). A radical re-vision of occidental historicity is called for. To this question of seeing and time, as this part argues, literary writing can offer an important contribution.

The part is subdivided into two interconnected main chapters. The first chapter engages in a critical dialogue with Diana Taylor's *The Archive and the Repertoire*, which constitutes a significant first step toward a revision of Western conceptualizations of the historical past. Taylor's performance studies background allows her to tackle transnationalism from a different angle. She stresses the role of (apparently) transitory performative practices regarding the transmission of history across the Americas, which established Eurocentric historiography, with its focus on static documents, has traditionally dismissed as insufficient historical evidence. This coincides with a polemical critique of the hegemonic role of language and writing in Western cultures in general. Next to the archive of written texts, she aims to (re-)establish what she calls the repertoire of live and embodied memory as an equally valid mode of relating to the past.

To fruitfully integrate Taylor's concepts into the discussion of transnational Native American presences within the borders of the United States, a thorough critique of her attitude toward language and textuality is necessary; a critique undertaken mainly with the help of Jacques Derrida's concepts of iterability and singularity and based on Jean-François Lyotard's connection between discursivity and figurality. A short overview of the role of writing since the first encounter between European settlers and the Indigenous population of the Americas paves the way for pointing out the inseparable reciprocity and interpenetration of archive and repertoire. The analysis picks up on Taylor's discussion of notions of haunting in performative practices, which contains a hint toward this reciprocal relationship. Although she claims that her understanding of spectrality is central to her argument, it only appears quite marginally within her book. Granting this aspect a stronger position and connecting it to Anishinaabe scholar Gerald Vizenor's idea of an "aesthetics of survivance" will testify to the compatibility of writing and Taylor's repertoire. Eventually, this chapter argues that Indigenous literature not only provides a counter-discourse to hegemonic Western narratives, but potentially stimulates an alter-Native mode of (historical) (re-)vision; *videlicet*, a form of seeing that allows for a different experience of historicity by considering the workings of the repertoire within the archive.

The second chapter of the part's critical dialogue is devoted to the analysis of Anna Lee Walters's novel *Ghost Singer*, which not only illustrates, but, more importantly, helps further unfold the main arguments. The narrative revolves around Native American spirits haunting the Smithsonian Institute in Washington, DC. These ghostly apparitions stem from a collection of Indigenous human remains and artifacts stored in the attic of the museum. Walters's text suggests that the archival space houses something it cannot fully contain. The filed and stored materials give rise to a live spectral repertoire. *Ghost Singer*, thereby, does not only offer a commentary on the illegal and impious modus operandi of Western science. Drawing on Native American cosmology, it also alludes to qualities of supposedly dead and static artifacts beyond the limitations of an objectifying Western epistemology and aesthetics.

The analysis first examines the institution of the museum as an extension of a unilateral colonialist mode of seeing that has guided occidental reasoning in the Americas since the times of the so-called Conquest of America. The narrative increasingly breaks down this monolithic lens by juxtaposing differing Anglo and Native points of view. It is in the interstices, created by this cross-cultural multiperspectivalism, at the edges of clear vision, that an alternative perception, defying the appropriative logic of an imperialist gaze, becomes possible. Through this vision at the curvature, as Lyotard terms it, the spectral performance of Native spirits appears (from) within the archive, blurring the boundaries between material and immaterial as well as dead and (a)live. The part then investigates how, by alluding to the enmeshment of archive and repertoire, *Ghost Singer* renders visible traces of *presencing* Native survivance. Contrary to the logic of Western historiography, the narrative emphasizes a sense of remaining presence and historical *revenance*, in which the past is not simply a matter of the past, but *presences* from afar in a spectral nexus.

In 2003, *American Quarterly* published an article by Osage scholar Robert

Warrior on a convention of the ASA, where he writes the following: "I want Native American studies to have a provocative presence in American studies, challenging old and new orthodoxies and demanding attention to the still-present realities of the foundational history of this continent. To borrow an image from Hortense Spillers, we need to be a poltergeist shaking the tables at meetings like this one" (686). By pairing Diana Taylor's study and Anna Lee Walters's novel, the following part aims to draw attention to the ongoing importance of these uncanny Native presences, particularly in the context of the potentialities of reading other-wise. Quoting Warrior's work, Huang and her colleagues write that "Native writing and Indigenous scholarship continue to unsettle a history that in the minds of many dominant intellectuals is 'already complete'" (Warrior qtd in Huang et al 2012: 4). This part lays out how American Indian writing indeed challenges occidental historiography by functioning as a spectral repertoire (from) within and simultaneously beyond the limits of archival discursivity.

EN-ACTIVE TEXTUALITY

THE CENTRAL AIM OF Taylor's work is first to expose and then to depart from "the historic role of writing introduced by the Conquest" (2003: 17) to "challenge the preponderance of writing in Western epistemologies" (16). She aims to achieve this by introducing the concept of the repertoire of ephemeral practices next to the archive of stable documents. However, one needs to understand what exactly Taylor is critiquing. Thus, it is appropriate to sketch out briefly the significance of written language in colonial endeavors. Drawing attention to the modifications of the (mis)uses of writing, it will become evident that Taylor's instrumentalist conception of textuality entails unproductive contradictions concerning her notions of archive and repertoire, as well as the significance of written documents for the Indigenous population of the Americas.

Writing and Manifest Manners

Ever since the publication of semiotician Tzvetan Todorov's seminal study *The Conquest of America*, the fundamental role of language, and particularly writing, has been the subject of numerous analyses of early intercultural encounters in the so-called New World. Todorov conceives of "the process of discovery and conquest as simultaneously a question of power and an epistemological struggle, waged on battlegrounds that were as much semiotic as military fields" (Damrosch 516). In both areas of conflict, Europeans had the upper hand. While Native Americans fought with axe, bow, and arrow, and were restricted to the spatio-temporal limitations of oral communication, the invaders had access to advanced weaponry and the superior representational technology of the printing press. In fact, for Todorov, the latter ultimately constitutes the prime reason for the Westerners' success in defeating the Indigenous population. He concludes that "everything happened because the Mayas and the Aztecs lost control of communication" (61). Printed documents allowed for accelerated intellectual exchange across large distances. Through writing, the Europeans discovered, conquered, and effectively Christianized the Americas. Over the period of subsequent colonization and the establishment of European nation-states, written language would remain an effective device of dominance.

Todorov has been criticized from various angles, primarily for reproducing a racially inflected essentialist discourse of the character of Native Americans structured around a reductive binary logic that deems them inherently inferior to the European *Conquistadores* (cf. Root 217f.). This very criticism, however, somewhat ironically, testifies to the validity of Todorov's fundamental claim. Written representations have indeed exerted a semiotic power that—after more than five centuries—continues to inform and shape Western perceptions of the Indigenous peoples of the Americas. The *grand récit* of the Judeo-Christian tradition had long validated the status of writing as expressing authority, being able to produce supposedly fixed accounts of true history, and to set down binding laws. Acting upon the conviction "of the existence of an organic link between writing and an ideological-religious system," the colonizers "did not hesitate to consider the Indigenous systems of notation inventions of the devil" (Lienhard 81). They denied Native pictography the status of proper writing—a mistake even Todorov still perpetuates (cf. 80)—and declared oral traditions defective and the mark of lacking civilization. Stephen Greenblatt writes in *Marvelous Possessions* that Europeans were, at least in their own eyes, able to legitimately set up a discursive web of "appropriative mimesis" (99) that aimed for the epistemic extermination of Native American culture through (re-)naming, conversion, and recording.

According to Greenblatt, writing functioned as a means of coming to terms with the otherness of the Americas and its peoples. Faced with the incalculable wonders of the New World, "the Europeans themselves struggled to bring as much of their experience as possible under the control of discourse" (64). Instead of attempting to confront the cultural differences of Native Americans with a certain openness, the colonizers drew on the rich archive of intercultural encounters in the Western tradition. Informed by such writings as Herodotus's *Histories*, Marco Polo's travelogues, or chronicles of fifteenth-century expeditions to Africa (cf. Lienhard 79), they projected their preconceived notions on the tribes. Thereby, the invaders integrated Indigenous societies into a Eurocentric discursive worldview that provided "a glass through which [already] Columbus looks to find what he expects to find" (Greenblatt 88). This becomes most apparent in the discoverer's premature misnomer "Indian." In the Natives, Columbus and his successors only rediscovered, or recognized, prior constructs of cultural difference that enabled them to maintain their sense of superiority. More than an ideological instance of justification for claiming territories, writing constituted a tool for exercising control over the existential status of Native Americans (cf. Rabasa 51). Western representations of the "Indian" forever altered the reality of Indigenous people across the entire hemisphere.

The preconditions of European settlement within the area of what was to become New England differed in many ways from the Spanish situation. However, not least due to the shared Christian conviction apropos scriptural authority, the status of writing in the creation of mythological discursive structures supporting the colonial endeavor and infantilizing Native cultures remained the same. In *Regeneration through Violence*, his seminal account of the myth of the frontier in early English settler societies and into the first century after the founding of the United States, Richard Slotkin draws attention to the centrality of written language in the context of the Puritan project. Preceding Todorov's efforts by more than 10 years, he writes that "[p]rinted literature has been from the first the most important vehicle of myth in America" and the English "were much inclined toward the writing and printing of books and pamphlets and the creating of elaborate metaphors proving the righteousness of their proceedings" (19), all to the detriment of the Indigenous population, as Puritan providence reveals. In John Winthrop's vision of America as a *"vacuum domicilium"*—a virgin land in wait of European cultivation—Native Americans did not figure as more than a curiosity, nuisance, or both. Cotton Mather described them as minions of the devil and, therefore, less than human (cf. Bataille 3). The American Adam is certainly not a Native in these early Anglo writings.

The ensuing history of representations of Native Americans in the United States is one of further dispossession and European takeover. Early Indian war narratives and tales of captivity set the stage for a gradual discursive appropriation. The stereotypes stemming from these texts, vacillating opportunistically between positive and negative, were further refined and became anchored in the American imagination, the romantic fiction of the nineteenth century. James Fenimore Cooper's novel *The Last of the Mohicans* serves as a prominent example. In the figures of Chingachgook and Magua, respectively, the author produced the epitomes of the heroized noble and demonized ignoble savage. Furthermore, the work's title alludes to the trope of the "vanishing race." Just like the Spanish invaders before, Anglo-Americans considered the Indigenous population primitive and past-oriented, in the process of being crushed under the wheel of civilization, and consequently doomed to utter extinction (cf. Porter 50). However, Supreme Court decisions, as in the case *Johnson and Graham's Lessee v. M'Intosh* from 1824 and the Indian Removal Act from 1830, attest that this vanishing was actively pursued and not at all a natural process.[1] These legal documents paralleled notions of the Native as a vanishing figure in American literature. They retroactively installed a discourse of legitimation for past and future expropriation under the Manifest Destiny of complete westward expansion (cf. Cheyfitz 110ff.). Considered as dematerializing into the evanescence of the mists of history, the American Indian could be appropriated as a literary figure and simultaneously dispossessed in the legislation of a rising nation.

Although hegemonic Anglo-American discourse, with the help of modern technologies, such as photography and film, has continued to misrepresent Natives to the present day, the events during the twentieth century—particularly the watershed period of the 1960s—have changed the situation of the Indigenous population. Political activism within the context of the Civil Rights Movement led to investigation into the conditions of Indians. The population level had reached an all-time low around the turn of the century, but was rising again throughout the following decades. Despite heavy decimation, Native Americans were far from vanishing. On the contrary, groups like the National Indian Youth Council, or the controversial American Indian Movement (AIM), and the Alaskan Federation of Natives (AFN) strove to abolish Termination policy, which opted for the assimilation of Indians into the US mainstream population, or, in other words, the complete disappearance of Natives. Following the *Declaration of Indian Purpose* by the American Indian Chicago Conference in 1961, they called for self-determination instead of forced cultural integration (cf. Porter 57f.). These efforts successfully built up pressure for reform that ultimately resulted in an ongoing improvement of the circumstances Natives found themselves in as a consequence of centuries of colonization.

The influential work of Slotkin, Greenblatt, and Todorov certainly stand in the wake of the political developments of the 1960s. However, the postmodern critique of master narratives brought about further significant change regarding the representation of the Native population beyond critical re-readings of European texts. This is particularly the case in the context of (literary) writing. Scholarship considers, for instance, the publication of N. Scott Momaday's landmark novel *House Made of Dawn* in 1968, as the beginning of a veritable renaissance of Native literatures—including oral traditions. Nevertheless, as Vizenor does not tire to point out, "Native American Indian literature is not a newcomer in the course of literary resistance to dominance. Natives have resisted discovery and dominance for centuries, from first stories of touch and breach of trust" (2009: 8). With the *Cherokee Phoenix*, the tribe of the Tsalagi established the first Indigenous newspaper in 1828, and Pequot writer William Apess published the first

Native autobiography in 1829. The so-called Native Renaissance not only paved the way for the publication of future Indigenous literature, but also engendered the recovery of previously ignored Native writings.

Taylor is certainly correct to note that "early colonial writings [as well as their modern extensions] are all about erasure, either claiming that ancient practices had disappeared or trying to accomplish the disappearance they invoked" (2003: 41). Nonetheless, early Native American texts also show that writing did not only function as a tool of dominance and control, but also as a mode of resistance. On the one hand, Native Americans indubitably figure as always already vanishing in European texts. Vizenor writes in *Fugitive Poses* that, due to the imposition of preconceived notions of alterity, the colonizers constructed a homogenized image of the Indigenous people completely divorced from reality. Vizenor refers to this as the simulation of the *indian* (cf. 1998: 26). One the other hand, Native Americans have, from early on, countered this imaginary fabrication by appropriating the technologies of (Western) writing for themselves. Originally introduced by missionaries as "a practical method of confirming and disseminating European values, Natives often used [Western] literacy for their own purposes— including at times, as a means of reaffirming an identity that was very much in opposition to that imposed by missionaries" (Hackel and Wyss 201). Written language, therefore, eventually provided a subversive medium for articulating and/or expressing Indigenous worldviews, and not only the proliferation of European culture.

American Indians' use of writing certainly poses a challenge to traditional suppositions about the authoritative pretensions of the Western archive and stimulate social reform (cf. Rainwater xiv). Nevertheless, restricting the narratives by such authors as N. Scott Momaday, James Welch, and Anna Lee Walters to the status of a political discourse places Native literature on the same level as all Western discourse(s) and executes Termination policy on literary grounds, for it assumes that Native American writers simply adopted a static Western system. Taylor's critique runs the risk of falling prey to this attitude. She claims that "[i]t is only because Western culture is wedded to the word, whether written or spoken, that language claims such epistemic and explanatory power" (2003: 24). The importance of oral traditions in the cultures of Indigenous peoples testifies to the fact that the first half of this statement is misleading. However, the second part alludes to a significant problem. Is language only about epistemic and explanatory power, or can it also perform other-wise? By extension, do Native authors then simply install a counter-discourse in the archive of absence introduced by the Conquest, or do they rather question Western notions of the archival process altogether? Does American Indian literature merely provide corrective stories of Indigenous history or does it contest European notions of historicity in general? How do Native American modes of relating to the world allude to a force of writing beyond Western conceptualizations of meaning and signification?

The work of Vizenor provides a point of departure for discussing these questions in connection to Taylor's work. Vizenor claims that Native American literature differs from what he calls the "manifest manners" (1999: 4) of the Western "literature of dominance" (23) not only insofar as Indigenous writing perpetuates corrective narratives to Anglo stereotyping, but also—in a sense to be clarified—essentially. For him, there is a distinctive mode of Native literature that he calls "the aesthetics of survivance" (2009: 3). He explains that "[n]ative survivance is an active sense of presence over absence, deracination, and oblivion; *survivance is the continuance of stories, not a mere reaction*, however pertinent. Survivance is greater than the right of a survivable name" (85; my emphasis). Vizenor's insistence on continuity indicates an understanding of the past that differs significantly from the efforts of Western archival practices. The simulation of the *indian*, he writes in *Fugitive Poses*, results from "the 'archive fever' of preservation, and the cause of narrative dominance" (1998: 50). Bernadette Rigal-Cellard is somewhat mistaken, nonetheless, when she argues: "For Vizenor writing freezes the world as it freezes events, as it chronicles the present to turn it into the past" (34). He does not leave it at that. According to Vizenor, there always remains a trace of native presence. The simulation of the *indian* is never complete. The archive houses something it cannot ever fully contain: "The *indian* archive is *institutive* and, at the same time, the conservation and deconstruction of an elusive native presence in literature and history" (2009: 18). In Vizenor's specific version of "postmodern" reasoning, the erosion of Western master narratives brings forth a *presencing* of the other (from) within discourse and the reappearance of a supposedly vanished past.

Archive and Repertoire

The title of Taylor's *The Archive and the Repertoire* appears to suggest the acceptance of the binary opposition between a superior archive of written documents and other storable evidence and a repertoire of oral traditions of ephemeral quality. The colonizers robbed Natives of their voices and subjected them to Western epistemological categories. Taylor aims to challenge this malady. Instead of the archive, she wants to (re)emphasize the performative quality of the repertoire that "allows for an alternative perspective on historical processes of transnational contact and invites a remapping of the Americas, this time by following traditions of embodied knowledge"

(2003: 20). Despite the allure of a transnational dimension involved in her endeavor, sentences like these create the impression that Taylor's approach consists in simply reversing the hierarchy of authority between the archive and the repertoire to produce a counter-history based on the analysis of corporeal practices.

That Taylor's position is somewhat more nuanced than her polemics implies in multiple instances throughout her book becomes apparent when she describes the relationship between archive and repertoire more closely. The qualifying adverbs in her introduction of the two terms allude to a critical stance toward simple dichotomies: the archive is made up of "*supposedly* enduring materials (i.e., texts, documents, buildings, bones)" and what she calls the repertoire consists of the "*so-called* ephemeral" realm "of embodied practice/knowledge (i.e., spoken language, dance, sports, ritual)" (19; my emphases). She does away with some common myths surrounding the notion of the archive, such as its unmediated character or resistibility to change and/or manipulation (cf. ibid.). Taylor also dismisses prejudices concerning the repertoire by emphasizing its capacity of storing and transmitting knowledge, albeit in a dynamic fashion, which permits the tracing of traditions and influences (cf. 20). Instead of reproducing a static opposition between archive and repertoire, Taylor works toward its deconstruction.

In an article published a year after *The Archive and the Repertoire*, Taylor reiterates a crucial point she already made in the book itself, namely that "[t]he repertoire and the archive work in tandem, transmitting knowledge in different but usually complementary ways" (2004: 372). The repertoire does not reflect an outdated irrational model of a mythic past, but a vital force continuing to shape modern cultures. It is not, and has not been, restricted to Indigenous communities: the colonizers made use of the repertoire when they rammed the flag into the ground and recited the accompanying speeches of appropriation (cf. 56). Even though Western discourse certainly disavowed the epistemological significance of the latter, archive and repertoire have always been existing in a state of interaction, Taylor explicates that the relation between repertoire and archive is not to be conceived as sequential, nor as true versus false or archaic versus modern—the relationship is not binary but all too often plunges into a binary, where the archive constitutes a hegemonic stance and the repertoire an anti-hegemonic challenge (cf. 22). Archive and repertoire, however, do not form the hierarchized poles of a static binary logic, but equal counterparts in an agonistic struggle. Archive and repertoire form a chiastic embrace of reciprocal reinforcement.

In Taylor's work, the reciprocity between the two dimensions comes somewhat too short. Her strong emphasis on the significance of embodied practices to create an awareness for different modes of relating to the world, and specifically the past, is laudable and constitutes a groundbreaking success. But Taylor does not disregard archival knowledge completely. By introducing the paradigm of what she calls "scenario"—instead of sticking to the centrality of the text—she rather aims to combine theoretical concepts borrowed from literary studies, such as plot and narrative, with an "attention to milieux [*sic*] and corporeal behaviors such as gestures, attitudes, and tones not reducible to language" (2003: 28). If Taylor emphasizes the archival powers of the repertoire, a study (uneasily) situated within literary studies, such as the present one, is going to focus on the force of the repertoire within the archive of written texts. *Reverting* Taylor's logic through an ab-usive twist, mainly via Vizenor, Lyotard, and Derrida, this part problematizes several aspects of her work, for instance the "nondiscursive" (6) character of the repertoire, as well as her notions of liveness and embodiment. Which implications arise if one thinks the enmeshment of archive and repertoire even more radically?

A crucial aspect for arriving at such a radical thinking requires the detour of working through Taylor's relationship to (written) language. Ironically, the very authority of the text she wishes to challenge also continues to (in)form her entire endeavor. The conception of the repertoire rests on a certain understanding of the constitution of texts. In a conversation with Marianne Hirsch and Barbara Kirshenblatt-Gimblett, Taylor explains that "a literary lens leaves out many discursive and nondiscursive practices, acts of communication and transmission" (1503). But what is this "conventional literary sense" (2006: 69) of textuality and its analysis she repeatedly criticizes? Taylor's account of (written) language is solely tied up with questions of meaning, structure, and communication; in short: an instrumentalist conceptualization. She writes that "[t]he dominance of language and writing has come to stand for *meaning* itself. Live, embodied practices not based in linguistic or literary codes, we must assume, have no claims on meaning" (2003: 25). For Taylor, (written) language is limited to communicative discourse, signification, and understanding. The insight that language is not restricted to these dimensions and that modern linguistics, if taken as exhaustive, cripples language by putting it in fixed confines is not new (cf. Heidegger 2006: 165).[2] That is why Lyotard insists in *Discourse, Figure* that "a model of discourse enclosed or obsessed with closure . . . must be stripped of its originary imperative if it wants to speak from within itself what otherwise, in all its 'eloquence,' it cannot succeed in speaking" (2011: 53). Taylor, however, holds on to this narrow sense of (written) language nonetheless.

She follows a different strategy of coming to terms with textuality, with contradictory consequences regarding her notion of supposedly nondiscursive performative practices. While Taylor may not construct a complete binary opposition between archive and repertoire, she certainly locates them in a relationship of analogy. Even though she wants to unhinge the centrality of language in Western epistemology, Taylor's model of the repertoire appears, contrary to her own assertion, thoroughly discursive in nature, when she explains that performances also function according to their own codes and structures (cf. 2003: 21). She concludes that "[t]he repertoire, on a very practical level, *expands* the traditional archive used by academic departments in the humanities" (26; my emphasis). If the interrelatedness of the two systems is restricted to this extension, then Taylor falls prey to her own critique, for her methodology also seems to remain problematically infested by its literary legacy (cf. 27). A simple expansion of the archive certainly cannot be her motivation. In that case, she would be actively participating in what she wants to leave behind: "the imperial ambitions of literary studies" (1498), as Kirshenblatt-Gimblett formulates it in the already quoted discussion. It is this strategy of assimilating the repertoire to the archive that puts Taylor's work in danger of reproducing Termination policy on an epistemological level.

Her attested relationship of analogy between the archive and the repertoire breaks down when, as Taylor herself writes, "[e]ach system of containing and transmitting knowledge exceeds the limitations of the other" (2003: 173). This simple sentence deconstructs the very notion of containment. As the archive opens to the repertoire—and *vice versa*—in a reciprocal embrace, the systematic character of both epistemic dimensions begins to crumble. Taylor acknowledges this, at least regarding the concept of the repertoire, as she eventually, and contrary to her initial claim, draws attention to its "discursive workings" (ibid.). This, once again, raises questions about the character of knowledge and transmission not addressed in her work. If the repertoire can take on the discursive qualities of the archive, then cannot also the archive enact those of the repertoire? Rather than doing away with Taylor's contradictions, thinking along these critical lines pushes them even further, but turns them into productive paradoxes that help avoid the danger of reproducing terminating epistemological gestures. It also assists in clarifying the relation of the repertoire to the categories of knowledge and meaning, not simply as a contributing extension, but also a modifying excess.

Taylor's understanding of the challenging potential of performance in relation to the workings of the archive also requires elaboration. She writes that "[p]erformance carries the possibility of challenge, even self-challenge, within it" (15). But how is one supposed to think this when she simultaneously denies a binary structuring of hegemonic archive and anti-hegemonic repertoire (cf. 22)? This remains unclear as long as Taylor's own account with her analogous conceptualization of archive and repertoire suggests that challenge only happens within the same epistemological horizon. Focusing on the relationship of complementarity of the two concepts more radically instead alludes to a dynamics of contestation that is both inside as well as outside, and defies a simple binary reasoning. The interrelatedness of archive and repertoire implies that writing is not merely complicit with Western hegemonic discursivity, but inherently heterogeneous. Both are "inseparably enmeshed yet radically different" (Bamford 23) from one another. Discourse always already harbors the challenging potential of performance within it (and *vice versa*), but developing this thought requires a step Taylor's work does not to take. Rather than a departure, it calls for a return to the text to describe the workings of the repertoire within the archive.

Writing and Native Survivance

Taylor condemns writing to play the role of a tool of absentification. Concerning the Native peoples of the southern hemisphere, she asserts that "[t]he 'lives they lived' fade into 'absence' when writing alone functions as archival evidence" (2003: 34). However, the treatment of texts as documents of evidence only is already a restriction in service of Western epistemological hegemony. "The rules of evidence and precedence are selective by culture and tradition, and sanction juridical practices over native presence and survivance" (2009: 87), writes Vizenor. Implicitly, Taylor downplays the significance of writing for the Indigenous community as an important domain for the continuous expression of cultural potency and resilience (cf. Porter 40). Her attitude is not uncommon. According to Vizenor, "[t]ragically, many readers consider native literature as an absence not a presence, a romantic levy of the enlightenment" (2009: 8). One might wonder whether he would count Taylor among these readers. She clearly disregards the possibility that texts, and especially those with the qualifier "literary," can do more than just function as a means of documentation. Of course, they never shed this quality completely. Writing always remains tied to some form of institutionality—be it politics, the law, economy, or even religion—and may be misused as ideological device. But literary writing in particular has a strange status as an institution, as Derrida explains in his interview with Derek Attridge. There, the French philosopher states that literature comprises "the institution which allows one to *say everything*, in *every way*" and concludes: "It is an institution which tends to overflow the institution" (1992: 36); and therein lies its strength. In the subversive excess which transgresses institutional borders, writing potentially safeguards "a native literary presence and survivance" (Vizenor 2009: 36), namely as an eruption of the repertoire from within the declarations of archival absence.

This sense of overflow yields significant consequences for Taylor's notion of liveness that is central to her argument. The repertoire, she writes, consists of "[l]ive, embodied practices" (2003: 25), "transmitted 'live' in the here and now to a live audience" (24), and "because it is live, exceeds the archive's ability to capture it" (20). This, again, does not necessarily indicate a binary logic as long as one takes into account the possibility of an excess from within archival texts. In that case, the workings of the repertoire function as instances of the figural in Lyotard's understanding, introducing "an event where the rigid signifying order is disturbed" (Ionescu 150). The infusion of this dynamism, albeit disavowed in hegemonic discursivity, always already compromises the archive's own power of epistemic fixation and challenges purely discursive concepts of textuality. What agents of the archive consider an unwanted and defective aberration, the remonstrators of the repertoire would embrace as an undeniable, impeccable enhancement. Both belong together: "the grammē is simultaneously calculation, determination and letter, [as well as] indeterminacy" (Stiegler 1998: 257). Written language is never merely a conglomerate of static characters on a blank page, constructing just as stable meanings. In particular, the strange institution that goes by the name of "literature" does not refute the undecidability inherent in the figural force of the repertoire within it. What theater scholar W. B. Worthen writes in defense of dramatic texts also applies to other writings, in this context especially Native literature with its strong connections to oral traditions: instead of simply forming fixed representations which ultimately neutralize liveness, "those texts are always in motion, thinking about and with performance"; they potentially constitute a "living event" (20) of literary survivance.

A short detour via Kiff Bamford's book *Lyotard and the Figural in Performance, Art and Writing* can help further clarify this aspect. As the title suggests, the author also integrates Lyotard's notion of figurality into the discussion of performance studies. Bamford provides a convincing argument regarding the chance of events arising through "acts of writing" (Attridge 1992: 2) by focusing on the documentation of performance art. In contrast to Taylor's negative assertion concerning the recording of the repertoire's workings, he claims that the performative "'event' could be as likely to occur in the gap opened by the non-representative aspects of its documentation . . . and consequently it brings into question the privileging of 'liveness'" (34). Insisting on the irruption of the figural as a nondiscursive force (from) within discourse which challenges the logic of signification, Bamford contends that archival documentation is never complete. Rather, it creates or continues a situation where meaning, to some extent, always remains undecidable and unstable. The questioning of epistemic ossification, which is the goal of many performance pieces, Bamford concludes, also continues in the form of their archival extensions (cf. 30).[3] The function of writing does not exhaust itself in the consolidation of signification and its communication, but can also play a role of performative amplification by alluding to and executing the ephemeral qualities of the repertoire within the archive: "The act of writing about performance and its documentation is itself a continuation of that performance and its documentation" (167). Taylor, however, is reluctant to consider such a possibility regarding her understanding of the relationship between liveness and textuality.

As Bamford's sources imply, the adherence to a mode of approaching writing—and literary texts in particular—that endures signification's instability and embraces more elusive qualities, is not a novel phenomenon. So-called "poststructuralist" thinkers like Derrida and Lyotard, arguing in the vein of Heidegger, have repeatedly stressed the event character of literature and challenged a simplistic conception of temporality concerning the transmission in a *hic et nunc*. In fact, when Derrida speaks of a "poetico-literary performativity" (1992: 55), he explicitly establishes a connection between the archive of literary writing and the elusive action of the repertoire. It is this poetic potential which yields the possibility for the occurrence of literary events. Like Heidegger, Derrida's understanding of eventness is tied to his reading of the ancient Greek term *poiēsis* (ποίησις) as a creative *act* of bringing forth or a *play* of unconcealment (and hiding), although a contaminating one that destabilizes any notions of pure discursivity. Consequently, he argues that "[w]hat literature 'does' with language holds a revealing power" (71) that differs from the use of textuality in the militant epistemology of the West expressed in the Conquest and its aftermath. There, the central aim "is to absorb the event, to recuperate the Other into the Same" (Lyotard 2011: 17).[4] The eventness stemming from the revelatory potential of literary writing, on the contrary, implies a moment of suspension of this absorbing momentum and a pharmacological challenge—in Derrida's sense of *pharmakon*—to the established semiotic order. As "an active, creative force" (2009: 24) confronting the colonial concealment of native presence and its flattening into the simulation of the *indian*, Vizenor's notion of survivance is also inherently related to this figural-poetic process. The event "reveals in language a voluminosity by diverting it from its informational function" (Lyotard 2011: 287) so that discourse expresses something that is external—or *other*—to its own order, and yet resides within. Literary *poiēsis* can create an eventness which, instead of depending on a situation of liveness, (re-)invokes a nondiscursive here and now within the text where a native presence may unfold.

The idea that the repertoire, despite its quality of liveness, can function as a source of memory adds another layer of complexity to its temporal dimension. How is it that the repertoire manages to store the live, and in what way is this tied to the notion of (re)invocation? The answer to this question, once more, lies in thinking the reciprocal relationship between archive and repertoire. Derrida attempts to do this with the help of the notions of iterability and singularity, which themselves are tied to his understanding of the performative. Taylor only refers to these briefly when sketching the development of performance studies from J. L. Austin and Derrida to the work of Judith Butler only to declare eventually that "[i]n this trajectory, the performative becomes less a quality (or adjective) of 'performance' than of discourse" (2003: 6).[5] Taylor's limited conception of writing that does not allow for its modification through the figural character of the repertoire also precludes her from further considering the ideas of singularity and iterability as valuable assets for the discussion of liveness.

In fact, the connection between iterability and singularity constitutes a key element for understanding the temporality of the repertoire vis-à-vis the archive. To Derrida, "[t]he uniqueness of the event is this coming about of a singular relation between the unique and its repetition, its iterability" (1992: 68). In his essay "Signature Event Context," Derrida defines iterability as the possibility of a singular event to become perceptible at all: it must be repeatable, imitable, and recognizable or signifiable, even beyond the death or disappearance of acting entities (cf. 1988: 8). Consequentially, it functions as a rupture of an event's presence by introducing a sense of absence. This absence makes possible what it simultaneously limits and denies: liveness. "There is no pure singularity which affirms itself as such without instantly dividing itself" (1992: 66), asserts Derrida. Even so, one needs to emphasize that iterability does not completely negate singularity, but rather retains it in the form of a trace that continues to *presence* in the absence of its original context (cf. Pada 85). Both form a primordial chiasm: presence is always already infested by absence just as absence is always already saturated by presence. That is why Derrida sums up singularity in the formula "*each-time-only-one time*" (2005: 11) or "each time in the same way and each time differently, one more time, at another date" (1992: 67). Just as archive and repertoire, presence and absence, singularity and iterability do not form binary oppositions but co-(in)determine each other.

Taylor, too, stresses the importance of repetition, albeit with a significant difference: "Multiple forms of embodied acts are *always present*, though within a constant state of againness. They reconstitute themselves, transmitting communal memories, histories, and values from one group/generation to the next" (21; my emphasis). Taylor's focus on the liveness of embodied practices and her insistence on the equation "writing = absence" results, again, in the danger of reproducing the logocentrism she wishes to subvert. That this verdict is not a matter of hair-splitting logomachy becomes apparent in sentences such as the following: "even though the embodiment changes, the meaning might well remain the same" (20). The price of holding on to the live almost seems to culminate in a return to stable meaning, which would ultimately only reaffirm a Western epistemology by claiming the same powers for the repertoire. Derrida's notions of singularity and iterability, on the other hand, imply that performative practices are never fully present to themselves and that their liveness depends on the possibility of absence. Nevertheless, this relative lack of the live does not constitute a deficit, but enables the gain of the archival function of a memory storage, in which the past *figures* as something that always also remains to come (cf. Attridge 2004: 64). To be able to act, the repertoire requires the archive; but in reverse, the archive also needs the repertoire that (re-)introduces a sense of presence. Absence and presence are always in play and their separation is a violent gesture.

Taylor is mistaken if she really believes that Derrida's analysis of discourse, or Butler's and Lyotard's for that matter, eventually only serves to bolster the centrality of discursivity in a militant epistemology which eradicates all difference. Such "concepts" as singularity and the figural constitute attempts to allude to decentering forces of "something undecipherable or unsignifying" (Derrida 2005: 38); in short: an uncontainable otherness. Taylor's critique of textuality seems to miss the central insight that "there is simply no way to go to the other side of discourse. Only from within language can one get to and enter the figure. . . . And one can get to the figure without leaving language behind because the figure is embedded in it. . . . The figure is both without and within" (Lyotard 2011: 7). As a singular event simultaneously inside and outside of discourse, the figural harbors the possibility for encountering the other beyond predetermined constructions of alterity and cultural difference a hegemonic West has been re-perpetuating since the Conquest: "a sense of presence and distinctive identities in the very midst of these many contradictions and contingencies" (Vizenor 2009: 164). This calls for an understanding of writing that goes beyond its mere instrumentalization in the service of the epistemico-colonialist endeavor of a Western nation-state denying the *presencing* of the native within it.

Next to and connected to her privileging of liveness, Taylor's polemic against textuality primarily stems from her insistence on the importance of corporeal practices or embodiment. Her self-professed goal consists in "revalorizing expressive, embodied culture" (16). It is here that the discussion of Taylor's repertoire in relation to the archive of (Native American) literatures becomes most problematic but, at the same time, also most pro-ductive. The central question is whether it is possible to treat literary writ-ing as expressive embodiment, too. This seems, at best, counterintuitive. It might come as a surprise, then, that in *Discourse, Figure*, Lyotard attempts just that. Therein he writes "[d]iscourse is always thick" and "[i]t does not merely signify but *expresses*" (9; my emphasis). For him, this is a vital func-tion of writing, although one that is constantly being subdued, for "[t]he other function—communication—requires the almost total exhaustion of the *Wortkörper* [literally: the word-body]" (76). In Taylor's account, this communicative function of writing reigns supreme. Expression, for her, is limited to the realm of performance. Lyotard's project in *Discourse, Figure*, however, is to reclaim this bodily expressive quality for (written) language, and he does this also by way of his notion of figurality, in which writing retains the dimension of gestures, movement, and matter (cf. Bamford 18). The aim of drawing attention to expressive embodiment is something the French philosopher shares with Taylor, only that to him, it is also an inher-ent quality of writing. Lyotard indicates that the revaluation of embodied, expressive culture must go beyond the mere recognition of the validity of the repertoire alongside the archive.

To clarify how language can perform in the embodied fashion of the rep-ertoire through the archive, a closer look at the role of the body in Taylor's thought is necessary. When she lists dancing, singing, gesturing, and speaking as instances of the repertoire (cf. 2003: 20), then the body *figures* as the ma-terial basis enabling these ephemeral practices. All of them imply some sort of (possible) motion that writing supposedly lacks, as Taylor implies. Empha-sizing the role of designation in the workings of language and highlighting deictic acts in words like "here" or "I," as well as in the inscription of dates, which all *point toward* some time, thing, or person, Lyotard—supplementing Derrida's notion of the dynamics of *différance*—shows that texts also exe-cute certain movements (through and beyond signification). Taylor does not consider this and seems to confuse the relative stasis of the text, as printed on paper, with a stasis of writing in general. However, it is this supposedly immobile material arrangement of letters that enables the more elusive acts of writing, and in this way is very similar to the function of the body in the repertoire. While the text's body might not move, its performances differ with every reading or *grazing*, to hold on to Lyotard's term. If Taylor were to insist that the printed letters on the page move in order for her to accept the performative character of writing, then one could counter that, for this demand to apply in reverse, bodies involved in practices of the repertoire also disassemble or dismember themselves. For Taylor, it is impossible for a completely static body to be able to perform. If one strictly follows through her argument, a body that ceases to be able to move ceases to be a body, and turns into archival material and nothing more.[6]

Taylor bans the text from the culture of expressive embodiment and establishes the repertoire in analogy to the archive. Still, in showing that the repertoire can also function as a mode of transmitting memory, she indicates that there are no clear-cut boundaries between the two dimensions. But she does not grant the archive a similar potential for modification via the repertoire as *vice versa* and ignores the performance of the text (itself). This relative one-sidedness within her approach, something she herself condemns (cf. 8), indicates a lingering Cartesianism which betrays Taylor's very own indebtedness to Western metaphysics and its central dichotomy of *res cogitans* and *res extensae*: "a mind-body/sensate-rational distinction" (Shotwell 136). The exclusion of the text from the realm of embodied practices plays into the *ratio*'s tendency to oppose matters of the mind to the things of the world, which entails reason's estrangement from the body as another external entity. She builds her critique of textuality on this perspective, establishing the repertoire as equal to the archive. The logic of the latter itself remains unquestioned. Basing her work on this strangely metaphysical worldview, however, is what makes *The Archive and the Repertoire* appear unproductively contradictory in several instances. Taylor wishes to avoid the construction of a binary opposition between the two modes of memory transmission, but achieves this by retaining a binary conceptualization of (written) language that locates texts as always already in opposition to the things of the world.

As its role throughout the Conquest and its modern extensions attests, it is undeniable that language can exert significant power over the beings and things of the world; a potential that, after centuries of misappropriation, may create the impression that language exhausts itself in this violent function. Nevertheless, particularly literary writing shows that there is more to language than its epistemological misuse suggests. Derrida celebrates the poetic acts of texts as follows: "Experience of Being, nothing less, nothing more, on the edge of metaphysics, literature perhaps stands on the edge of everything, almost beyond everything, including itself" (1992: 47). In his essay "The Most Interesting Thing in the World," Jonathan Culler points out that Derrida does not here privilege a specifically literary essence, but rather describes a non-thetic experience literature may bring forth, which renders possible a non-metaphysical mode of relating to the world (cf. 10). Here, the Heideggerian thread within Derrida's notion of the potential of literary writing is most evident, but also particularly worn out. The performance of *poiēsis*, to Derrida, is never a setting-to-work of truth as it is for Heidegger, but always an elusive "poematic experience" that may lead into a certain "down-to-earthness" (1995: 312); a specific form of an epistemological (re-)humiliation—stemming from Latin *humilis*, literally an "earthing"—plowing the Cartesian *cogito* back into the soil whence it arose. Literature, therefore, heralds a reintegration of the *ratio* as residing among the *other things* of the world. At this point, Lyotard's work, extending Derrida's, again establishes the connection to language's embodied quality: "To argue that words treated poetically recover the power to bring us in agreement with things would mean that language is essentially like a world or a body. Like a body, because through significations language ushers us into an ante-reflexive relation analogous to that through which the body unites us with rhythms, colors, and lines" (Lyotard 2011: 287). Taylor's metaphysical lens concerning the character of writing prevents her work from taking this nondeterminative character of writing into account. She does not grant a text the ability of the dynamic functions of a body, which may create a singular literary event.

Still, the question remains of how exactly one is to conceive of the relationship between textuality and embodiment. Taylor herself provides a useful hint toward a possible answer. She herself, however, does not follow this direction, although it literally turns out to be a matter of life and death. In a later chapter of *The Archive and the Repertoire*, she explains that her "view of performance rests on the notion of ghosting" and elaborates: "Performance, then, involves more than an object . . . , more than an accomplishment or a carrying through. It constitutes a (quasi-magical) invocational practice" (2003: 143) and is connected to notions of haunting and spectrality. These notions challenge the homogeneity of liveness and embodiment (and of fixity and signification). Just as Taylor connects the repertoire to notions of haunting, Derrida writes in *Archive Fever* that "the structure of the archive is *spectral*" (1996: 84). Consequently, spectrality *figures* as what links and, at the same time, divides archive and repertoire, albeit not as a third dimension, but rather as the dynamicism of the dynamics of the reciprocality between the two realms, which renders them inherently (in)distinguishable. The specter implies spatio-temporal transgression. It cannot be confined in one fixed space: it walks through closed doors, defies linear temporality, and poses a challenge to the pastness of the past by *still presencing* from afar.

What kind of body, then, does a ghost have or does it possess a body at all? It certainly used to have some sort of body, but what role does that corporeality still play? Can the static and dead body still perform, or does it turn into archival remains and nothing more, as Taylor apparently would have it? Kiff Bamford writes that in the specter, "materiality is shot through by an immateriality, entwined like discourse and figure" (146). This alludes to a lingering link between the ghost and its body, performance and textuality.

Accordingly, Derrida speaks of "a paradoxical incorporation" (2006: 5), which, in spectrality, conjugates the supposedly opposed: presence and absence; tangible and intangible; furtive and fixable; visible as well as invisible all appear in an irreducible embrace. If the repertoire does not merely imply (a)live, and if the archive does not only consist of fixity and death, then one can ask with Bamford: "When does performance end?" Does writing merely capture and annul the live? "Or does this also provide the space-time for a hauntology" (161)? Certainly, with the collapse of life and death into a "life-death" (Bennington 1988: 99), the distinction between embodiment and writing also crumbles. The body (of the text), then, potentially becomes the paraphernalia for the iterable invocation of singular *revenant* presences in a poetico-figural *hic et nunc*.

Here, the argument can now return to Native American literature and Vizenor's notion of the aesthetics of survivance. With the discussed concepts in mind, it is possible to define the Anishinaabe scholar's concept of a native presence even within the archival simulations of the *indian* as a literary-performative event. Vizenor, in dealing with dictionary entries, emphasizes the specifically hauntological character of survivance as an afterlife beyond death, (en-)actively remaining within existence or perseverance (cf. 2009: 99f.), and not simply the tragic aesthetic victimry of lost identities, melancholic nostalgia, trauma, vanishing, and absence. "Natives are in the world of the book" (164), he writes, not as dead archival remains, but as un-dead specters of native presence haunting the institution of literature. Building on Taylor's notions of the archive and the repertoire with an emphasis on her understanding of ghosting, one can argue that, read or *grazed* as poetic performance, Native American writing "conjures up and makes visible not just the live but the powerful army of the always already living" (2003: 143); such literature defies Western conceptualizations of temporality and establishes a sense of historicity where the so-called Native American Renaissance rather *figures* as a Native American *Revenance* of those deemed dead.

NATIVE AMERICAN REVENANCE

THE FOLLOWING ANALYSIS OF Anna Lee Walters's novel *Ghost Singer* will show that texts potentially figure as a live spectral repertoire and will help develop further the concepts discussed in the previous section and to integrate them into the context of an aesthetics of survivance. It will also situate them into the overall project of the question concerning the other presences and reading other-wise. Taking Native literature into account calls for an acceptance of a modality of relating to the things of the world, which, as Derrida puts it in the Exordium to *Specters of Marx*, "supposes that justice carries beyond present life or its actual being-there, its empirical or ontological actuality: not toward death but toward a *living-on* [sur-vie], namely, a trace of which life and death would themselves be but traces and traces of traces, a survival whose possibility in advance comes to disjoin or dis-adjust the identity to itself of the living present as well as of any effectivity. There is then *some spirit*. Spirits. And one must reckon with them" (2006: xx). It is from within the interstices of life and death, of a temporality in-between, that an-other mode of being(-in-time) becomes possible; interstices that may open up through the in-tense dialogue between critical thinking and literary writing. As this chapter seeks to unfold eventually, reading other-wise circumscribes an interstitial mode of reading which heeds (how) the other presences within spectrality beyond the confines of static Western archival historicity.

Vision: Sensation at the Edge of Western Epistemology

At the center of Lee Walters's novel is an institutional manifestation of the archive. In *Ghost Singer*, the structure of the museum functions as a spatial metaphor for an archival logic and, connected to it, the specifically Western lens for looking at the beings and things of the world. The story revolves around Native American remains and items housed in the Natural History Building of the Smithsonian Institute in Washington, DC of the late 1960s. Strange incidents begin to happen that affect everybody who comes into contact with the collection. Negotiating differing conceptions of possession, history, and materiality, *Ghost Singer* tells the story of how an inter-tribal group of Native Americans and several Western researchers try to come to terms with the appearance of a spectral figure in the museum. Taking place in a pre-NAGPRA (Native American Graves Protection and Repatriation Act) situation, where "the dominant society is free to commodify Indian artifacts for the sake of historical study, profit, or plain amusement" (Aigner-Alvarez 49), the objects are reduced to the status of archival material to be handled at will, filed and stored away in boxes and drawers, or put on display without sensitivity for American Indian concerns. In the *Archive and the Repertoire*, Taylor also describes the space of the museum as historically one of the quintessential instances of the workings of the archive:

> Museums have long taken the cultural Other out of context and isolated it, reducing the live to a dead object behind glass. Museums enact the knower-known relationship by separating the transient visitor from the fixed object of display. Like discoverers, the visitors come and go; they see, they know, they believe — only the deracinated, adorned and 'empty' object stays in place. Museums preserve (a particular) history, (certain) traditions, and (dominant) values. They stage the encounter with otherness. The monumentality of most museums emphasizes the discrepancy in power between the society that can contain all others and those represented only by remains, the shards and fragments salvaged in miniature displays. (2003: 66)

The museum represents the manifest manners of a hierarchical, unidirectional process of producing meaning by introducing and (re-)perpetuating "a particularly powerful way of seeing" (Tillett 90), which opts for the discursive containment of time in space. In the novel, this gaze of "ethnographic surveillance" (1998: 145), as Vizenor terms it, consequently renders Native American culture as an extinct curiosity right next to ancient fossils and reproduces the trope of the vanishing or vanished race.

When Taylor writes that visitors of museums often behave like the colonizers, she explicitly emphasizes the continuity of a visual mode that already had guided the intercultural encounters during the times of the Conquest. Tzvetan Todorov takes this a step further and describes an entire historical configuration. He writes that the establishment of the first museums and production of early anthropological accounts on the way of life and manners of foreign peoples during the fifteenth century coincides with significant modifications in Western sensory perception, namely the development of the central perspective (cf. 109). In its vulgarized form, this mode of seeing integrates the perceived into a mathematical grid which aligns the world along centralized axes and forcefully subjects otherness to its system. Lyotard refers to this as a "Euclidian bias" (2011: 155): the strategy of a *bridling of the gaze is the condition for the geometrization of the field of vision*" where "[t]*he only possible convention is to prefer the straight to the oblique, the simple to the complex, the identical to the dissimilar, the one to the multiple*" (188). The museum in *Ghost Singer* represents the putting into operation of a reductive stance toward all phenomenal entities; an epistemological configuration structuring the world by subjugating it under the authority of an imperial mode of vision that becomes apparent in the observer/observed split characteristic of anthropological and museological discourse (cf. Tillett 87). Catherine Rainwater goes so far as to suggest that, in this context, "the concept of the museum itself may point to Eurocentric blindness to realities of the Other" (124) and forms an extension of medieval prejudices. The institution upholds the hegemony of a colonial mindset, disregarding and downplaying other viewpoints as irrelevant, irrational, or both.

There is also another option of how the archive guides the gaze. The problematic Native American collection in the text is not on display for the public at all. The text, thereby, suggests that the museum also has the power to simply hide certain (arti)facts. The narrative depicts "the academic [realm] as the disseminator, of a specific cultural viewpoint, clearly choosing what should be seen and how" (88), which, according to Rebecca Tillett, results in the "perceptual inability to see beyond academia's narrow definition of 'history'" (93). The limited view becomes more restricted still through the selection of that which may be seen and that which must not be seen, because it is incompatible with the founding mythology of the US nation-state. In the novel, some artifacts have the potential to draw unwanted attention to the more unpleasant aspects of Western epistemology as well as historiography that would (mostly) ignite Indigenous anger, for "other groups were more educated and tolerant" (Walters 44), as the museum worker Geoffrey Newsome thinks. The controversial items—consisting, for example of medicine bundles as well as other paraphernalia, "a necklace of twenty human fingers" (42), pairs of Navajo ears, an arrangement of skulls, scalps, and an entire mummified body—are securely stored away in boxes, cabinets, and drawers in the attic of the Smithsonian. The archival logic of the museum assumes total control over its materials, disavowing the disagreeable and constantly reestablishing a predetermined monolithic point of view.

In an interview with Rhoda Carroll, Walters replies as follows when asked what she would like to say to prospective readers and students of her work: "I would tell them to experience another view of the world besides the one they've always known. There's magic in doing this, and enrichment. I hope that my stories reflect another perspective that is rewarding to receive. And last of all this: We as humans don't have to know all there is about everything. If we did, there would be no magic, no wonder, no joy in discovering what and who we are" (72). *Ghost Singer* builds on Walters's conviction concerning different modes of relating to the world and challenges the homogeneity of the colonial gaze institutionalized in the archival space of the museum. By juxtaposing several narrative perspectives with the help of different focalizers and their respective stories, and other (minor) characters, the novel exposes the insufficiency of the Western perspectival monopoly and the hegemonic epistemological horizon tied to it. Dorothy Graber writes that, throughout the text, "Walters consistently privileges complex and multilayered indigenous perspectives over the dominant culture's rationality—a rationality that ultimately proves itself completely ineffectual in the face of generative indigenous spirituality" (13). However, Walters does not merely create a binary opposition between Native viewpoints and a homogenous Anglo perspective. She also draws attention to the internal differences of the latter. As Heike Paul has shown, Walters's use of multiple narrative angles consequently enables the novel to contrast different attitudes toward the encounter with the (culturally) other (cf. 2012: 108). By putting these points of view into dialogue, *Ghost Singer* emphasizes their interrelatedness, deconstructs notions of homogeneity on either side, and encourages the experience of different worldviews.

The text does not simply constitute a counter-discourse to the dominant culture's ideological restraints either, but also traces the perspectives of individuals on the Native and the Anglo side, as well as their interferences. As representative of the colonialist gaze of the archive, the already mentioned Geoffrey Newsome considers contemporary American Indians essentially uneducated; he is "thoroughly disgusted by [their] appearance and presence" (46) and becomes "emblematic of academia's propensity to downgrade and dismiss alter/Native knowledges and worldviews" (Tillett 89). Geoffrey's task is to construct a coherent narrative out of the artifacts in the attic according to the historiographical rules of Western reason and the modern nation-state. To reach this goal, he subjects them to "his rough and careless handling" (44); he even puts on the finger-necklace. Newsome also personifies the central irony and double standards of the museum's archival logic, for although his job is a result of the historical intrusion of the Conquest, he himself gets angry when he notices that someone has "enter[ed] *his* space and violate[d] his territory, without his approval" (42).

Newsome's colleague Donald Evans holds similar views: as living anachronisms unfit for modern civilization, "American Indians were curiosities to

him, people who should have become extinct by all rules of the game" (91).
Evans dismisses Indigenous wisdom as mere superstition. This becomes especially apparent in his conversation with the Creek/Cherokee tribal official
George Daylight, who attempts to explain that the collection housed in the
museum cannot be possessed according to Western notions of ownership:
"To *own* it, one must be able to make use of it" (125), George says, for these
items "were *created to be extraordinary*" and "like people, these creations
have characteristics and a nature . . . this nature, and their power are embodied in that creation" (127). Donald only derides Daylight's view on the
artifacts in a condescending manner as irrational "hocus-pocus" (128). The
encounter of the two men constitutes one of the first of many instances of
clashing epistemologies in the novel.[1]

Another central confrontation, developing over the course of the novel,
occurs among another three individuals. Having met in Washington, DC,
where both are doing research on Diné culture, the young Navajo Willie
Begay introduces the white historian David Drake to his grandfather, the
storyteller Jonnie Navajo. The tribal elder is supposed to help Drake with his
planned book on Navajo history by providing the Indigenous perspective,
which the historian—unlike Newsome and Evans—is genuinely interested
in and keen to include into his project. In this configuration, Willie is torn
between two conceptualizations of the world, namely the traditional one of
his ancestors and the ratio-scientific one of Western historiography. From
this hybridized perspective, he tries to mediate between Drake and Jonnie
as a translator. When David keeps asking "Why is he telling us all this?"
(30) regarding Jonnie's stories, Willie realizes that language is not the only
barrier, but that Drake's archival understanding of history radically differs
from Jonnie's, which is based on an oral tradition. David's initial openness
toward Native wisdom stems from the expectation that it is fully compatible with the logic of Western thought and will simply form a quantitative
modification of knowledge, while it actually necessitates a qualitative one.

By putting these perspectives next to each other, Walters suggests that
there is not only a plurality of equally valid viewpoints, but, in fact, a variety
of entirely different ways of seeing. The novel illustrates this with the help
of the characters of Jonnie Navajo, George Daylight, and also the medicine
people Anna and Wilbur Snake. The latter explains the matter to his nephew
Russell as follows: "We doubt that there's anymore to his life than what we
seen. You know, Sonny, sometimes too we can't see very good either—poor
eyesight. We're pitiful, Sonny. We try to know the whole universe, but we
set our minds when we're like pups and learn to see only certain things.
Maybe "cause us peoples is scared sometimes—scared to look for something more, but even more scared to find it and accept it" (201). Walters's

novel, therefore, does not provide an easy solution to cultural conflict in the form of a happy pluralism, but draws a more challenging picture: "the mysteries in *Ghost Singer* are multi-dimensional and interrelated" and "many of those mysteries remain unsolved" (Fiesta 370); the narrative calls for a deeper engagement. It suggests that experiencing another view of the world, for both Natives and Anglos, requires a modification of one's perceptual mode, a change of perception which harbors the potential to glimpse the dynamic workings of the repertoire constantly interrupting and disturbing the ossifying gaze of the archive.

It is through this alternative way of seeing that the event of native *presencing* becomes discernible (but never fixable) from the simulation of the *indian*. A connection between sensory perception and the event has also been established by Martin Heidegger. He builds on the etymological relatedness of the German term for "event"—*Ereignis*—to the German word for "eye"—*Auge*—and argues that experiencing an event always implies *er-äugen*—glimpsing (cf. Seubold 302). The connection to Vizenor's aesthetics of survivance becomes apparent once one reads it according to the Greek sense of *aísthēsis*, meaning (sensual/sensory) perception. The Anishinaabe scholar's sense of aesthetics, however, implies an excess that can also be found within *Ghost Singer*, for "Walters represents 'Indian' reality as vaster and more spiritually sophisticated than the conventional white man's materialist vision allows him to see" (Rainwater 50). Consequently, it is a mode of perception that does not reduce the term "vision" as only related to the sensory apparatus or referring to particular designs for the future but takes into account the third option: the experience of an extraordinary apparition. Anything else would imply a certain deficit, as Anna Snake muses within the novel: "according to her people's way of thinking, something would have been wrong with her if she didn't see beyond this world. It would mean that her senses didn't work, and that she, in a way, was handicapped by her own lack of sensitivity" (Walters 143). The aesthetics of survivance stresses this beyond that resists *ratio*nal appropriation and surpasses the rules and boundaries of Western reason, deeming them insufficient and blinding toward the perception of native presence.

This modified gaze poses a challenge to the geometrical Euclidian vision privileged by the colonizers. The alternative mode of seeing does not operate along the clear-cut lines of the centralized perspective, but rather within the diffuse "field of vision which focalized attention represses" (Lyotard 2011: 154), located at the margin of Western epistemology's horizon. In *Ghost Singer*, the medicine man Wilbur explains that "sometimes peoples stands on the brink . . . where everyday things don't matter none. In fact that brink, that edge, it's everywhere. Right here on the edge you can reach out and feel something else you can't get a hold of in this everyday world, some *other* thing that don't have no end to it" (143; my emphasis). With Lyotard, one can refer to this seeing as one that does not form a "clear vision (foveal zone)," but the vision at "a vast peripheral fringe of curved space" (2011: 154) around the focused field of sight. There the perceived constantly withdraws "and any attempt at *grasping* it loses it" (155). Vision at the curvature maintains the otherness of that which appears and, because it is only ever seen implicitly at the edge of perceptual clarity, simultaneously remains elusive, resisting identification. This is fundamentally different from the prejudiced imperialist view of Columbus and his successors, who projected their preconceived notions on the things and beings of the so-called New World, only seeing what they thought they already knew from elsewhere. The mode of vision described by Wilbur requires a different (in)sight: "Learning how to see is unlearning how to recognize" (Lyotard 2011: 153). The novel attempts, for Anglos and for Natives themselves, to stimulate such a discernment that engenders the possibility for experiencing a different sense of temporality and history as *Ereignis*.

The text, however, does not only allude to a different mode of seeing through diegesis, but through specific visual devices of language. Walters's strategy of not providing easy explanations to the issues raised is connected to these devices. Tillett analyzes the sensory qualities of the novel's employment of punctuation and points out that particularly "[t]he punctuation of the final line of the text, ellipsis, visually marks—and forces the reader to *see*—the significance of *Ghost Singer*'s topic, and its lack of resolution" (106). In several instances Walters also uses italics to underline another dimension of her text. Toward the end of the narrative, for example, Jonnie Navajo says "[t]hat we exist, that *we are here*, this is the one thing that cannot be refuted" (246). In this sentence, the deictic utterance is stressed. The three words stick out from the rest, potentially referring to—or, more specifically, designating—a figural-poetic *hic et nunc* beyond the confines of the novel. The already discussed juxtaposition of multiple viewpoints constitutes a more nuanced device still, for within the interstices opening at the edges and brinks of the different angles, the questioning of the museum's centralizing archival gaze becomes a part of the stylistic level of the text as well and alludes to an extradiegetic vision at the curvature of the militant epistemological logic introduced by the Conquest. On both levels of *Ghost Singer*, content and form, this perceptual mode renders visible, for better or worse, the traces of native survivance housed but uncontainable in the institution of the museum. It is there, in the archival remains, where the spectral repertoire of the other *presences* and stares back.

Haunting: Presence at the Intersection of Life and Death

There are ghosts in the archive, haunting the Smithsonian. The source of this uncanny presence is the controversial collection of Native human remains and artifacts. Everybody exposed to these items—both Anglo and Native—is affected by the visitations. The museum employees in charge of the relics begin to see things invisible to Western everyday perception. Jean Wurly, David Drake's sister, is the first character in the novel to report this: "I can't explain it . . . , but there *are Indians there. I've seen them.*" (5). In the archival absence of supposedly dead matter, native survivance remains, defying the selective museological gaze and bringing forth a different shade of reality and the more unpleasant aspects of history. In *Archive Fever*, Derrida writes that "hauntedness is not only haunted by this or that ghost . . . but by the specter of truth which has been thus repressed" (1996: 87). The ghosts in the novel allude to the disavowed atrocities committed by the colonizers and their successors. Read as a counter-discourse, *Ghost Singer* suggests that the logic of the archive and its handling of Native objects is complicit with these acts of cruelty and forms a problematic continuance. The past atrocities of slavery, genocide, and colonialist exploitation continue through the imperial-capitalist connection of profit and death—in both metaphorical and material manner—in the form of practices of possessing, interpreting, collecting, and selling Native American artifacts and remains (cf. Graber 13). For the invaders—ever since the first encounters—American Indians have been always already archival. Infantilized and dehumanized, Europeans have treated the Indigenous peoples first as (useful) curiosities and later as (valuable) specimens for scientific research. The militant Western epistemology kills Natives while still alive, reducing them to the status of ready-to-hand objects and (re)moving them at will. The spirits in the museum contest this objectification and displacement through their uncanny, or in this case literally un-homely, presence.

The focus on American Indian relics is not an arbitrary topic but constitutes a central controversy in the history of Anglo-Native relations. Walters's novel was written and takes place before the passing of the so-called Native American Graves Protection and Repatriation Act (NAGPRA) in 1990, which constitutes a response to the tension around the question of ownership and repatriation of Indigenous human remains and artifacts in European possession (cf. Archambault 7). For the first time, this Congressional statute grants the Native population a say in this matter and enables tribes to reclaim remains, funerary items, and sacred objects of cultural significance that rightfully belong to and had been taken from them through illegal means.[2] *Ghost Singer* describes how the collection at the Smithsonian is the result of repeated looting of Indigenous ruins, the desecration of burial sites, and

bounty hunting. A letter Donald Evans finds in one of the boxes testifies to
the ignorance concerning and the commodification of Native items:

> *Get what you can for this Indian stuff. It should be worth something in $.*
> *Try a museum first. . . . I don't know what the red stones are, but they came*
> *outta a woman's grave in Nebraska. Those people are extinct. . . . We dug up*
> *the jewelry near the Oklahoma/Louisiana line ourselves. We had a lot of this*
> *stuff, but our kids often played with these and broke a lot of them. . . . Daddy*
> *ran across the ears in New Mexico and won them in a poker game about*
> *1890. . . . I sure could use the $ if you could sell all this junk. It's been in the*
> *attic for years.* (93)

This account is not entirely fictional. For Western science, the ends have long
justified the means, also concerning the acquisition of new "specimens."
The salvage anthropology of the nineteenth century repeatedly organized
rather macabre harvesting sessions (cf. Sommer and Krüger 29). In 1867,
for instance, the United States surgeon general Madison Mills ordered the
exhumation of Native bodies and artifacts from fresh graves and/or their
removal from battlefields (cf. Simpson 27).[3] Most of these eventually ended
up in the filing cabinets of the Smithsonian Institute, where presently, more
than 20 years after the passing of NAGPRA, over 18,000 human remains
(not counting other relics) are stored (cf. Cryne 102). This fact testifies to
the actuality of Walters's novel and suggests that the attitude toward Native
culture has not changed significantly. Evans's only concern after reading
the note is that he still needs to catalogue the objects in the specific trunk.
Nothing strikes him as disrespectful or impious. *Ghost Singer* portrays the
anthropologic archival vision as blind toward Indigenous concerns.

Indeed, Walters's story illustrates that American Indian epistemology differs radically from Western reason, also in the context of questions regarding
life and death. Native wisdom grants human remains as well as artifacts a
special status. They "act as cultural bridges to the tribes' past and allow
them to preserve ancestral traditions for the future" (Talbert 200), and,
therefore, require proper treatment, as George Daylight also attempts to
explain to Evans. The medicine man Wilbur elaborates that "[a] lotta old
peoples thinks that nothing ever dies" and these items "is wondrous things"
(Walters 201). He, thereby, draws attention to the fact that in many Native
cultures, neither artworks nor human remains are considered lifeless matter,
but sacred entities with an affective presence (cf. Fontein 215). This view
differs significantly from the objectifying practices of Western aesthetics
and science. Moira Simpson explains that, in a way difficult to accept and
honor within the limits of the *ratio* and its inherent Cartesianism, in Native
cultures' cosmological conceptualizations of the world "they [remains and

artifacts] are not only important sacred objects; they are animate, living beings" (30).⁴ Not respecting the life of these items leads to dire consequences for everyone involved. In *Ghost Singer*, Jean Wurly is the first to commit suicide after having been exposed to the haunting presences within the museum, followed by her colleague Geoffrey Newsome. In this context, Julia Cryne writes that "[i]t is commonplace belief across multiple Native American groups that the disturbance of the dead (either by desecration or grave-robbing) forces the spirits of those individuals to wander without rest" (101). Particularly in the eschatology of the Navajos, the tribe around which the plot of the novel revolves, the deceased are said to return to locate and reclaim missing parts and belongings (cf. Pensley 52). Similarly, Walters's Native specters resist the powers of archival absentification.

The story surrounding the Native human remains and artifacts in *Ghost Singer* allude to the inseparability of Taylor's concepts of material archive and immaterial repertoire. By taking spectrality and haunting into account, she writes, "[n]ew performances . . . rise out of . . . archival remains" (2003: 154f.), challenging Western notions of liveness and embodiment. This also applies to the Smithsonian's collection in the novel. The ghostly repertoire, there, consists of haunting gestures leaving handmarks on the door (cf. 94), disincarnated voices singing Native songs out of nowhere, spectral apparitions of spirit people (cf. 6f.), and several other supposedly inexplicable incidences. These examples imply what Derrida has called "a supernatural and paradoxical phenomenality, the furtive and ungraspable visibility of the invisible, or an invisibility of a visible X, that *non-sensous sensous*" (2006: 6). In Walters's narrative, the figure of the ghost singer, the specter who is responsible for the suicides at the museum, personifies these contradictory qualities. When Donald Evans encounters the angry spirit, completely naked except for a piece of cloth wrapped around his ankle, he perceives "an unusual sensation" and can "feel the presence of a living breathing person" (130), albeit at first unseen. The situation then vacillates between different phenomenal states as the ghost singer materializes and inaudibly bangs on one of the storage cabinets, but then is able perform the act of sweeping everything from Donald's table and even picking him up and throwing him back on the ground, only to eventually disappear once again. Throughout the course of the entire narrative, this (extra-)ordinary specter—both material and immaterial, embodied and disembodied—while himself being able to grab and grasp, remains inherently ungraspable, his motivations unclear, and his identity unknown: "The mystery of the ghost singer is larger than life both literally and figuratively, and his mystery is never resolved" (Fiesta 371). The Native spirit's spectral repertoire resists fixation in the straightjacketing filing system of the archive, *presencing* (from) within it.

The Indigenous spirits in the archive, however, do not only haunt Anglo-Americans, but also Natives. The spectral presences begin to affect the young Diné Willie Begay, too. While doing research at the museum, he accidentally comes across an entire Navajo scalp with ears still attached and emanating the smell of living persons. Shocked, he attempts to get rid of the oily feel of the piece, but it sticks to his fingers and will not come off (cf. Walters 50). According to his native culture's beliefs, touching the dead equals the breaking of a taboo that potentially results in "ghost sickness" (Aigner-Alvarez 55). After the incident, Willie begins to suffer from this malady and episodically breaks out into hysteric fits, crying and yelling in Navajo. (cf. Walters 54f.). Apparently, "[o]nce physical contact with the dead has been established, the humanity of the remains and the manner of their death and collection can neither be denied nor avoided" (Tillett 102) by Begay. Holding the scalp within his hands has enabled Willie painfully, or even forcefully, to relate to the pain of his ancestors. The specters grant the young Native American a glimpse from their view on the things of the world. His perception starts to change. The roles are reversed, and he begins to see the archival gaze fixed upon the other in the visages of the Western scholars surrounding him at the Smithsonian: "Willie realized that the figures, the dark vestiges in the room, had turned toward him. They wore no expressions on their faces. Only their eyes were clear little lights. They looked like demons. Their terrible eyes lit the room and hurt Willie like stinging cactus needles when they looked at him. He covered his eyes with his hands to shut out the demons. He leaned over on the table, threatening to collapse" (Walters 82). The ghostly performance grappling Begay evokes what Taylor describes as "a moment of revisualization" (2003: 144), namely of the violent colonialist vision regarding American Indians as a vanished race. Tillett confirms this when she writes that this scene constitutes "a comment not only upon the history and reverberations of Federal Indian relations, but also upon the dangers and repercussions of an anthropological/museological view of the dead" (102). In *Ghost Singer*, nobody is exempt from the risks and pitfalls of Western epistemology—neither the Natives nor the Anglos themselves. The novel suggests that both (internally heterogeneous) groups need to learn how to consider the vision of the other at the curvature of the colonialist foveal zone.

This diffuse mode of seeing other-wise goes beyond the limits of Western rationality, challenging the insistence on stable boundaries between life and death. The experience of the blurring intersection between two supposedly distinct existential states within the uncanny presences of the specters at the museum also plagues Evans. Just as Willie finds help in the sacred songs of his ancestors, Donald is forced to seek the help of Natives, despite his condescending prejudices. Eventually, Wilbur Snake, together with his wife as well as several other members of his family, conducts a ceremony for the scientist and his girlfriend in the archival space of the Smithsonian's attic, using paraphernalia like those stored in the museum to invoke the apparition of native specters. What Taylor states in her discussion of hauntology and performance also applies in this context: "[t]he sumptuousness of the ceremony performs the sacrilization of the remains [from the Euro-American perspective] theoretically antithetical to performance. The *remains* . . . take on a life of their own" (2003: 142). The ceremony constitutes a chance for Donald to learn to see things differently, to properly perceive this specific form of liveness, and to accept the elusive undead presences withstanding direct (visual) appropriation.

This necessitates a certain sensory epistemological humility, wherefore Wilbur advises the Anglo participants: "When the man [the ghost singer] comes 'round here, don't look right on him. Watch him only out of the corners of your eyes" (Walters 215). The medicine man asks them to make room for the ephemeral workings of the repertoire within the archive. This opening up of sensorial space enables the "spectral asymmetry" of the vision at the curvature, where "[t]he spectral *someone other looks at us*, [and where] we feel ourselves being looked at by it" (Derrida 2006: 6). Here the other is not subjected to the closure of museological colonialist seeing. This perceptual mode requires posing what Derrida has called the question of life-death, which "open[s] onto a dimension of irreducible *sur-vival* or *surviving* [survivance]" (ibid. 185). When Evans momentarily fails to maintain this questioning state, when he does not bridle his archival gaze, and turns toward the ghost singer, the latter's uncanny visual anticipation reveals — within a spectralized moment of being face-to-face with the undead other — the resisting force of native survivance in a set of haunting eyes: "Donald turned to the figure beside him and looked into its face, the hate-filled eyes. Donald's teeth started to chatter again" (Walters 216). In *Fugitive Poses*, Gerald Vizenor writes that in "[t]he eyes are the stories of [Native Americans'] wounded bodies" (159), even if housed within the archive: there also *remains presence*. Insisting on the always already enmeshed state of repertoire and archive, Walters's novel alludes to the traces of native survivance at the intersection of life and death.

In the reciprocal chiasm of archive and repertoire, this active sense of a *presencing* over absence also transgresses the limitations of the institutionality of literature. Particularly when keeping in mind the concluding insights of the previous section concerning the extradiegetic potential of diffuse vision, it becomes apparent that *Ghost Singer* does not simply constitute a counter-discourse to the atrocities of the colonial past (and present). Through discursive means, the text points beyond the confines of representation and discursivity into a spectral "reality." Within the fixating impulse of the *ratio*, this is difficult to accept, as Taylor also writes: "Maybe because it's so hard to get a handle on, *spec-ere* (to see) that phantoms, fantasy, and performance have traditionally been placed on the opposite side of the 'real' and 'historical'" (2003: 141). Presenting and situating her story in the form of a novel, at first, seems to indicate a compliance with the rules of Western epistemology and literature on Walters's side. Her narrative is certainly understandable and works within the long-established genre of the ghost story. As such, it forms a legitimate example of literary writing's discourse, safely stored in the archive of fiction—according to occidental reasoning. However, as has been shown, in Native American cosmological worldviews, artworks do not simply constitute objects of dead matter but live sacred entities. Language especially is said to possess "the power . . . to transform, to move mountains" (Denetdale 45), and, therefore, able to bring forth the ephemeral workings of the repertoire within the archive. In an interview with Matthias Schubnell, the Kiowa writer N. Scott Momaday expresses this point as follows: "I think that language is sacred. I have been for a long time interested in the power of language. I think we don't know nearly enough of the power of language. We don't understand how powerful words are or can be. In our daily lives, we tend, I think, to disregard language in that sense, we don't try to understand it in terms of the sacred. We think of it as communication rather than as spiritual expression or a vehicle for the sacred" (45f.). According to this perspective, Walters's text becomes more than a novel; it turns into a literary act of native survivance, resisting what Vizenor has called the "causal narratives of museum consciousness" (1999: 129f.) that guide the archival gaze of surveillance.

The location of *Ghost Singer* within the ghost story genre, then, turns out to be a cunning and ironic strategy. By complying with and not entirely denying the *ratio*'s rules, the narrative, like the trickster figure "coyote who played dead" (Walters 246), retains the traces of a native presence in spectrality: it functions as a literary fugitive pose similar to the Natives within the theater of Western photographs. The text explicitly *acts* as a ghost story only to implicitly draw attention to survivance within the archive, which "sows havoc and generates effects of meaning deriving neither from signification nor from syntax, but from sight" (Lyotard 2011: 273), ultimately making *Ghost Singer* a both "haunted and haunting novel" (Tillett 87). With the help of the discussed perceptual strategies, Walters opens up Western discourse from the inside to the possibility of relating to Native conceptualizations of the world, which also enables a different perspective on Indigenous remains and artifacts and their inherent qualities as well as their abusive treatment, especially before NAGPRA. In the disrupted gaze of the archive, the workings of the repertoire resurface (from) within; in the diffuse vision at the curvature of Western epistemology, a spectral native survivance *presences* that points toward a different sense of temporality and a form of history beyond the separation of archive and repertoire.

Historicity: Survivance in the Chiasm of Archive and Repertoire

Taylor writes that this alternative mode of perception, what she calls "[s]*pec-ere*, to see, is possible only through a history of [performative] spectacles and ghosts" (2003: 144), which clashes fundamentally with a purely archival Western conceptualization of historicity that considers Native Americans nothing more than an effectively vanished race ready for scientific exploitation. "Spirit peoples don't know time, don't care nothing 'bout clocks" (76), Wilbur Snake explains in the novel, contesting the static simulation of the *indian* introduced by the militant epistemology of the Conquest. Encompassing and re-vising a period of more than 130 years of Euro-Native relations, the main plot revolving around the Native ghost in the 1960s is itself repeatedly haunted by the horrors of the past, such as the genocidal Conquest, the Spanish and Mexican enslavement of the Navajo, and US-American Termination policy (cf. Tillett 85). The novel, in general, negotiates the collision of the Indigenous oral traditions' performativity with the discursive nature of European documented history. Walters's novel creates a complex configuration of intersecting and diverging temporalities which increasingly collapse into a spectral nexus.

   The text does not merely form a counter-discourse which opposes Native oral traditions to Western historiography as an alternative historical narrative, but rather emphasizes the fundamentally differing understandings of (the relationship between) past, present, and future. As the Diné historian Jennifer Nez Denetdale writes, "[i]n the stories about the past, the primordial time comes alive as storytellers reiterate accounts of events that led to the establishment of the world, how the boundaries of Navajo Land were set and how the People learned the rules for proper living" (43). Instead of forming fixed accounts of bygone times ready for the dust-filled shelves of the archive, oral story-telling constitutes a poetic effort of emphasizing and invoking the dynamics of the continuity between the tribal past and present (cf. 140). Denetdale, quoting anthropologist Keith Basso, concludes that "to tell stories is to 'speak the past into being,' to summon it and give it dramatic form so we can participate in our ancestors' quest for survival and the need to create a sense of community and kin" (157). For Native communities, the ambiguous character of the stories' performance—both, in the sense of their *own per-formantive force* as well as their *being performed* repeatedly within the circle of the tribal collective—constitutes active acts of survivance.

The traditional *ratio*-scientific attitude of Western historiography is in-compatible with such an understanding of historicity, as Walters's *Ghost Singer* demonstrates. Despite having been interested in the Navajo perspec-tive on the past since his early childhood, the Anglo historian David Drake eventually falls prey to the pitfalls of Western logocentrism that Taylor crit-icizes in her work. Disappointed by the uselessly "scanty and generalized" (78) accounts available on the history of the Diné, Drake is all the more amazed by the detailed accuracy of Jonnie Najavo's story-telling (cf. 162). At the same time, this fascination, coupled with his question why there were no accounts of this from the Indigenous side, again betrays David's lasting ignorance regarding Indigenous cultures, as well as a deeply rooted convic-tion of the authoritative character of (supposedly) static archival sources and "the absolute legitimacy and veracity of written history" (Tillett 94). Realizing the scope of the differing conceptualizations of historicity in Na-tive American culture and Western science, Drake gives in to the reasoning of his colleagues. Just as the museum employees Newsome and Evans, they derogatorily refer to Indigenous wisdom as "sentimental hogwash" and dis-miss it as the irrational "romanticism" of uneducated and illiterate peoples. They argue that "without records, there is no history" (Walters 225). David understands that seriously taking a Native viewpoint into account would have to result in far-reaching modifications of his discipline and the episte-mological hegemony of Western historiography in general. In his conclusion regarding his academic project, *ratio*nal pragmatism beats an initially radical ambition: "In the long run, David had decided, his professional reputation was a life-and-death matter. This project was not worth the risks after all. When he had a 'real Navajo history' in his possession, he could reject it in its entirety or in part, and he could even alter it to suit his needs. He would take care to be objective, fair, and thorough. He couldn't think of anyone who could do a better job" (228). This decision underscores the importance of Diana Taylor's critique of the absolute supremacy of written documents. *Ghost Singer* portrays the Anglo way of writing history as an extension and persistent (re-)affirmation of the archival impetus of a colonialist mindset. Ironically, Drake's resolution, then, literally turns out to be an-other issue of life and death: he rejects the significance of Native repertoire's liveness over the authority of a lifeless archive.

In this sense, Walters's text goes beyond the so-called postmodern challeng-ing of conceptualizations of historiography and/or historicity as described, for instance, in Linda Hutcheon's notion of "historiographic metafiction" (92). In line with this concept, the text's performance asks, as Hutcheon puts it: "What is the ontological nature of historical documents?" (93). *Ghost Singer* shares a rejection of a clear separation of (historical) fact and fiction, but it develops this notion beyond the confines of metafiction. Although challenging established notions of historicity and historiography, Hutcheon describes historiographic metafiction as residing still in the limits of archival reasoning: "It refuses the view that only history has a truth claim, both by questioning the ground of that claim in historiography and by asserting that both history and fiction are discourses, human constructs, signifying systems, and both derive their major claim to truth from that identity" (93). *Ghost Singer*, on the other hand, as a live spectral repertoire not bound by a static discursivity, challenges the epistemological limitations of Hutcheon's assertion via its insistence on an ongoing revenance of the past even within archival remains. The novel's performance is not restricted to challenging the problematic notions of Western historiography's supposedly objective, neutral, impersonal, as well as transparent character (cf. Hutcheon 92)— although it certainly does that, too, as the story around Drake makes clear. As an act of survivance, the text's ironic ex-*posing* of Western notions of temporality opens onto a spectral nexus wherein "the textualized remains (documents, archival evidence, witnesses' testimony) of that past" (ibid. 96) defy the objectification of archival fixation: instead of dealing with archival remains, in *Ghost Singer*, the archive remains alive.

Walters's narrative in its totality calls for an openness on either side of the supposedly incompatible conceptualizations of temporality. *Ghost Singer* does not promote a spiritual Native American mode of relating to history over a calculated Western one. What she criticizes about the latter is an epistemological stance which suffers from a superiority complex that had already been guiding intercultural encounters during the Conquest, rendering colonialism an ongoing reality for Native Americans even today (cf. Denetdale 21). According to Rainwater, "Walters suggests that mechanical time diminishes our sense of personal power when we assume that the past is beyond our control and outside of our responsibility, and that the future is a clean slate where no ghostly messages from the past may appear" (122f.). One could even go so far as to argue that the Western understanding of time with its emphasis on the irretrievable pastness of the past, in its most extreme form, turns into a strategy of disavowing historical responsibility altogether.

Nevertheless, insisting on spectral recurrence or *revenance*, Walters's story suggests that the repression of past atrocities is never entirely successful. Not only does she, thereby, stress the existence of American Indian ghosts haunting the archival space of the Smithsonian, she also draws attention to Anglo historiography's very own specters, constantly resurfacing—albeit never recognized as such—in the subliminal re-perpetuation of a colonialist worldview. Dismissing every other perspective as always already inferior, Western epistemology creates a static binary opposition between its truth claims and that of the other(s). "According to a Western logocentric and Cartesian-Newtonian understanding of the academy, sciences, and humanities," as Kerstin Knopf confirms, "Indigenous knowledges have been viewed as primitive, folkloric, anecdotal, unscientific, amethodological, insignificant, and lacking scientific rigor and objectivity" (179). Western and Indigenous knowledges are viewed as inherently incompatible. In the novel, Jonnie Navajo realizes this and says: "It seems like we are told that we can choose one source of knowledge or the other, but we are discouraged from having both, because it seems that the two don't go together. Some day we are going to have to do something about this" (Walters 138). *Ghost Singer* picks up on Jonnie's radical demand. Instead of playing along with a binary logic and simply elevating the Native repertoire to the same epistemological status, the text constitutes an attempt of working against this containing mindset by constantly pointing toward the primordial chiasm of repertoire and archive which harbors survivance.

Seemingly contradictory, Walters's narrative alludes to the reciprocal reinforcement between performative and discursive forms of relating to the past, primarily by inscribing specific (Western) dates into the story. At first glance, the structure of the text implies a linear progression of time. The individual chapters follow a straightforward chronological order, clearly demarcating past and present. However, the (spectral) events of Native *presencing* on the level of the plot simultaneously undercut this occidental temporary logic, breaking with distinct temporal boundaries and introducing a different sense of time. Making a similar point in her analysis, Rainwater describes the situation in *Ghost Singer* as follows:

> Sacred or 'unitary' time is encoded in the novel together with mechanical time . . . The narrative opens with a preface concerning key historical events of June 1830, proceeds through thirty-three chapters taking place in 1968 and 1969, and ends with an epilogue recording events from the fall of 1976 [*sic*]. . . . These events . . . are so directly connected to the Jacksonian Era atrocities that the past appears actually to impede the forward flow of time that is measured by clocks and western-style calendars. (119)

The dates certainly serve to situate the narrative in a historical framework ripe with connotations of (post-)colonial cruelties. Therefore, the text potentially opens up the impeding discourse of counter-history. At the same time, the narrative works beyond Rainwater's purely semiotic argument. In what can be termed a Spivakian ab-use of Western temporality, the poetic inscription of the chosen dates does more than present the simple reverse ignorance of an opposing account of the past: *dated* (i.e. pointing toward historical events) but not dated (i.e. simply past), *Ghost Singer* rather invokes a haunting continuance or *living-on*.

The spectral character of this unpredictable historical continuance remains unclear as long as one does not keep in mind the plot revolving around the Native spirits haunting the Smithsonian Institute, as well as the sacred character of American Indian remains and artifacts connected to it: "[i]n *Ghost Singer*, the past is present in these ghosts and artifacts, and it commands attention" (118), writes Rainwater. Therefore, to illustrate how Walters's narrative points toward the primordial chiasm of archive and repertoire through the poetico-figural inscription of dates, it is again necessary to proceed with the analysis of the work of art beyond a Cartesian split between *res cogitans* and *res extensae*. This is because, as an act of storytelling, *grazed* through the diffuse vision at the curvature of Western reason, Walters's haunted and haunting narrative actively participates in what Taylor calls a spectral history of ghosts (cf. 2003: 141) and constitutes a performative spectacle of survivance, where the past continually (re-)*presences* as still or again to come.

It is imperative, at this point, to return to Derrida's notions of iterability and singularity to illustrate their link to this practice of poetically inscribing dates into a work of literature. In his essay "Shibboleth," the French philosopher writes that "[t]he date must conceal within itself some stigma of singularity if it is to last longer than that which it commemorates" (2005: 20). This is to say that although a date designates the singular eventness of a *hic et nunc*, it needs to be(come) iterable to be legible at all. Thereby, the date simultaneously effaces its singularity, which nonetheless *presences* from within this effacement. Absence and presence—past and present—converge in the date, wherefore, as Derrida continues, it becomes "a future anterior: it gives the time one assigns to anniversaries to come," and as such, "gives access to the memory of the date, to the to-come of the date, to its proper to-come" (25), namely through acts of invocation.

These performative spectacles go hand in hand with another process. According to Derrida, "the inscription of a date (here, now, this day, etc.) always entails a kind of signature: whoever inscribes the year, the day, the place, in short, the present of a 'here and now' attests thereby his or her own presence at the act of inscription" (16). In *Ghost Singer*, this process of signing is not that of an individual, but, as the already quoted figural statement *"we are here"* (246) indicates, forms the collective signature of an entire community. The performance of the narrative thus signed constitutes what Vizenor calls a "storied presence of native survivance" (2009: 87). As such, it transgresses Western historiography's evidential rules, challenges the boundary between fact and fiction, and consequentially alludes to a paradoxical order of truth that withdraws from discursive appropriation, but nonetheless haunts discourse from the inside. Derrida describes this spectral dynamic of the date as follows: "If the date that is mentioned, commemorated, blessed, sung, tends to merge with its recurrence in the mentioning, commemorating, blessing, and singing of it, how then can one distinguish, in a poetic signature, between the *constative* value of certain truth (here is when it took place) and that other order of truth which one would associate with poetic *performativity* (I sign this, here now, at this date)? Is a date true? What is the truth of this fiction, the untrue truth of this truth?" (2005: 47). In this fashion, inhabiting the mutual embrace of discourse and figure, the temporality of the to-come—singular and yet iterable—that characterizes the poetically inscribed date, brings forth an ir*rati*onal (dis)order of truth, which does not deny the continual eruptions of the repertoire's ephemeral spectral apparitions in the supposedly stable accounts of the archive's written (hi)stories.⁵

Consequently, *Ghost Singer* emphasizes spectral continuances over the irrecoverable pastness of the past by poetically inscribing specific dates not only into Native, but also Anglo cultures. The Indigenous spirits haunting the museum certainly tell their story of survivance, but in so doing, they also unmask the West's own specters in the attic of its epistemological archive. Beginning her narrative in the June of 1830, Walters unmistakably establishes a link to the infamous Indian Removal Act signed by President Andrew Jackson and issued in the same year. Furthermore, the date also situates the novel in the less well-known context of the Mexican slave raids on Navajo settlements ever since the 1820s. The text begins with a concrete instance of Native absentification, namely the abduction of one of the twin children of Jonnie Navajo's great-grandfather, Tall Navajo. Throughout the entire narrative, the family does not manage to retrace the fate of their missing ancestor. Constituting a retroactive American Indian signature next to Jackson's, *Ghost Singer* here offers a compensating account of tragic wisdom on the topic of the Indigenous population's bilateral Spanish and English enslavement. For a long time Western historiography had been "skipping over [this episode] carelessly" and only given it "casual and doubtful" (Walters 78) treatment. More importantly though, the meeting of the two Western nations' interests on Native ground in the narrative testifies to the ongoing effects of a physical epistemological violence introduced over 300 years before during the times of the Conquest, culminating in the collection of human remains and artifacts in the Smithsonian. Although the *presencing* Indigenous spirits there speak of their own survivance, showing that removal has not been complete, they also bear witness to the fact that what had begun under the manifest manners of one nation of oppressors effectively continues under the hegemony of another, albeit in a different form: the specters of colonialism are haunting the archives of Western culture until today and it is thus that the date 1830 still resides in the temporal mode of *living-on*.

The ghostly scenario becomes even more apparent in the second inscribed date, 1968, which has often been referred to as the peak of Western civil rights efforts across the Atlantic. In her interview on the novel with Carroll, Walters explicitly points to the importance of the year in the context of the Indian movement (cf. Carroll 69). Beyond that, however, the date also marks the 100th anniversary of the Navajos' military defeat at the hands of the Anglos and their subsequent removal to the limited space of the reservation Bosque Redondo, known as *Hwéeldi* in the Diné language. In fact, most of the action in the novel takes place between Jean Wurly's suicide in August 1968 and Jonnie Navajo's death in the fall of 1975. The duration of the main plot consequently mirrors the entire first reservation period from 1886 until 1875, only a century later (cf. Denetdale 3). Instead of merely celebrating the achievements of civil rights campaigns, *Ghost Singer* here, again, insists on the continuance of a militant epistemology. The narrative most clearly expresses this in Anna Snake's commentary after having visited Lincoln memorial in Washington, DC: "You told me that that man we visited today, the one with the hollow eyes, put an end to slavery, huh? But I'm afraid that our people are still being bought and sold, even though they are dead — and have been dead for hundreds of years! Even worse, some of the people are not whole. They remain in bits and pieces, and yet these pieces are also being traded, bought, and sold, like so many sheep! When does it stop?" (Walters 207). The concluding question particularly points to the continued reality of epistemological violence, which Native Americans are still facing from occidental reasoning. Even though the 1960s bring about significant improvement concerning the situation of the Indigenous population, the novel stresses the extensions of the Conquest.

This becomes evident also in the narrative's hint at the Vietnam War. Discussing the collection in the attic of the museum, George Daylight explains to Willie Begay that "[t]here's savagery here alright, no doubt 'bout it. It's always been here. We perpetuate it. Willie, right now, it's probably over in Saigon. They're probably taking ears and scalps over there. And then there's a more subtle touch. . . ." (81).[6] Daylight indicates that open physical savagery is only the precursor of a more iniquitous civilized barbarism that objectivizes Native Americans in the name of scientific reason without regard for their dignity. In the context of the novel, the figural inscription of the period between 1968 and 1975 invokes both the hope of increasing change of the Indigenous population's situation to the better, as well as, once again, a direr perspective: the connection between the atrocities of the Conquest, their extensions in the nineteenth, and their enduring reality in the twentieth century. As the three dots of the ellipsis at the end of George Daylight's comment imply, the further course of this development, reminiscent of Max Horkheimer and Theodor Adorno's dialectic of Enlightenment, remains unforeseeable and unresolved in the text.

Ghost Singer does not provide a conclusion for the issues raised in the narrative. Its ending does not bring closure to another chapter in the archive of Native Anglo relations. Quite the contrary is the case. As the sensory-figural gap at the end of George Daylight's explanation implies, the novel's aesthetics of survivance points toward the chiasm of archive and repertoire. Glimpsed through the alternative mode of perception at the curvature of Western reason, the text designates a non-Cartesian time and "space where text and world intersect in an 'open mind'" (Rainwater 120). By interweaving Indigenous and Western accounts of (hi)story into a spectral continuum, the novel maintains the tension between a certain hope and disillusionment instead of offering simple solutions.

On the one hand, the apparitions of the spirit people at the museum express the tragic wisdom of Native survivance: "They may come home yet. I have seen such things in my lifetime" (Walters 247), Jonnie Navajo says, underscoring the persistence of an active *presencing* that calls for the return or repatriation of the removed. On the other hand, there stands the repeated unwillingness of Western reason to comply with the necessary modifications of its epistemological hegemony. Just as David Drake gives in to the *ratio*nal advice of his colleagues, Donald Evans and his girlfriend Elaine eventually repress the happening of the ceremony in which they witnessed the force of spectral survivance: "It was as if they'd ripped the experience of that night right out of their minds" (239). Apparently, *ratio* prevailed.

If one assumes that *Ghost Singer* ultimately paints a rather pessimistic and static picture of a stalemate, one misses that what the novel attempts to bring forth is a dynamic reciprocity that favors neither the one nor the other attitude. It does not re-impose the hierarchies of binary reasoning. Longing for complete closure would equal a falling back into archival logic which denies survivance, just as striving for absolute openness would equal a relapse into performative absurdity which dismisses the validity of writing altogether. The novel's repeated poetic acts of invoking the past through the inscription of dates draw attention to the fact that it requires a continual and repeated effort instead of a fixed resolution for archive, on the one hand, and repertoire, on the other hand, to be working hand in hand. Closure and continuance intersect in a history of Native American *Revenance*, where the past is never simply past, but *presences* as so many spectral-singular events of a future anterior. Only within the tension of this embrace can one patiently work toward a justice to come.

The beginning of this part's analyses diagnosed a relative absence regarding the Indigenous voice in the discourse of the transnational turn in American Studies. The reason mainly lies in the temporal and spatial focus of the paradigm-shift, as Robert Warrior writes: "Native critics do not engage with transnationality because its major proponents, in spite of broader inclusivity, remain in the end more interested in what is beyond their borders ... than the transnationalism produced by colonialism within its borders" (2009: 123). Shelley Fisher Fishkin's idea of Transnational American Studies, for instance, with its primary outlook beyond the nation's borders, largely ignores the internal dimension of transnationalism. This disregard betrays a continued "willed ignorance of this nation to face its colonialist past and present" (2009: 326), writes the Native scholar Amy Lonetree, enrolled citizen of the Ho-Chunk Nation. Any serious transnational endeavor in the context of the United States, therefore, needs to be aware of and/or critically address the situation within, to not reproduce the violent gestures of a militant epistemology. Only then can it move on beyond the confines of the nation without reproducing an exceptionalist logic.

With the paired discussion of Taylor's *The Archive and the Repertoire* and Walters's *Ghost Singer*, this part has shown how the consideration of this internal transnationalism calls for an openness toward modifications of Western notions of historicity. Starting with a revision of Taylor's critique of the hegemonic role of written language concerning the transmission of memory in the Americas since the Conquest, the first chapter worked toward a notion of writing that does not operate along the axis of a binary opposition between static unchanging archive and live ephemeral repertoire. Founded on Lyotard's insistence on the importance of figurality in written texts, the analysis criticized the performance scholar's reductive and instrumentalist understanding of textuality. Employing Derrida's concepts of iterability and singularity, and with the help of Vizenor's notion of native survivance, the analysis deconstructed Taylor's specific understanding of liveness and embodiment in relation to the repertoire. By drawing attention to the event-ness and expressive corporeality of literary texts, the discussion explicated how the concepts of archive and repertoire are always already interrelated, forming a relationship of reciprocal reinforcement. As becomes evident especially in Native writing, the repertoire repeatedly erupts from inside the archive and vice versa.

The analysis of Walters's novel in the second chapter simultaneously illustrated and further expanded this argument. Exposing the museum as a *pars pro toto* of an entire perceptual mode of framing others, the text juxtaposes the viewpoints of (culturally) different focalizers in order to allude to a vision at the curvature of occidental epistemology in which ghostly apparitions show themselves.[7] Posing a challenge to the disrespectful treatment of human remains and artifacts at the hands of Western anthropology within the attic of the Smithsonian, *Ghost Singer* draws on Native American cosmology to emphasize the sacred character of such objects. The possibility of a live spectral repertoire arising from the archived material invokes a sense of presence at the intersection of live and death. The discussion, then, showed how the narrative itself only poses as and, in fact, becomes more than merely an instance of a particular genre in the institution of literature. It rather constitutes a figural-literary act of Native *presencing*. Via the poetic inscription of dates, Walters's novel eventually works toward a different form of historicity. Collapsing Anglo and Western temporalities into a spectral continuum, *Ghost Singer* neither denies the haunting specters of United States' colonialism, nor an active native survivance in the chiasm of archive and repertoire.

The Native American voice testifies to the United States' internal transnationalism. Taking this dimension into account calls for a revised understanding of the event-ness of literary texts and the altered relationship between past and present connected to it: the *other presences* from within. Only with this in-sight in mind can one dare move beyond the nation's borders.

PART TWO

BEING-TWO WITH THE OTHER: NEGOTIATING RELATIONALITY AND MIMICRY WITH LUCE IRIGARAY AND THERESA HAK KYUNG CHA'S *DICTÉE*

At some point, on our way to a new consciousness, we will have to leave the opposite bank, the split between two mortal combatants somehow healed so that we are on both shores at once and, at once, see through serpent and eagle eyes.
—Gloria Anzaldúa, *Borderlands/La Frontera*

IN THE PREVIOUS PART, reading Anna Lee Walters's *Ghost Singer* with Diana Taylor's work as a form of live embodied repertoire of survivance, I began to outline a notion of performance based on the figural corporeality of language. I quoted Taylor's comment on the development of performance studies from Austin, via Derrida, to Butler where she asserts that, in this critical vein, the term "performative" turns into a quality of an almost all-encompassing discursivity (cf. Taylor 2003: 6). This is certainly true, to some extent, for the early Judith Butler of *Gender Trouble*—maybe somewhat manacled in Foucauldian moorings—who regards performativity as discursive process. Nonetheless, even in the book that marked her academic breakthrough, Butler critiques the gendered hierarchy of the Cartesian separation of the mind and the body, argues that this separation implicitly assigns mind to masculinity and body to femininity, and, therefore, warns of an uncritical reproduction of the split between rationality and sensuality (cf. 2007: 17). She does not simply sideline the body, even in her early work. In subsequent publications, Butler is at pains to clarify her thought on the relationship between discourse and corporeality. *Bodies that Matter*, where she critically engages with the more bodily oriented approaches to language prevalent in French feminism—particularly the work of Luce Irigaray—constitutes the first longer elaboration of Butler's take on the distinction of mind/body and, in extension, language/materiality. In fact, she there describes the relationship in a manner that is strikingly similar to Lyotard's conception of the entanglement of discourse and figure. Butler writes of a chiasmic entanglement of language and materiality in which both are mutually dependent and never completely different and yet always nonidentical, exceeding one another, and never collapsing into each other (cf. 2011: 38). She regards the split of mind from body, and language from signification, as problematic, since it forecloses certain aspects of (bodily) knowing that cannot be contained within a *rati*onal framework. More precisely, she argues that this separation entails a leveling of otherness: "To posit materiality outside of language, where that materiality is considered ontologically distinct from language, is to undermine the possibility that language might be able to indicate or correspond to that domain of radical alterity [otherness]" (37). All this testifies to the fact that Butler's thought concerning the role of the body is not as straightforward as some of her readers have taken it to be. It does not dissolve in the indifferent relativity of radical constructivism, as Taylor seems to believe Butler's work to do.

Butler's thought on the relation of discourse to corporeality, indeed, has shifted over the years to emphasize an irreducible affective potential of the body. In the introduction to her more recent essay collection *Senses of the Subject*, she spells out the central role of the corporeal in relation to language: "So though we might say that bodily signifying precedes speech, we would be mistaken to think that it vanishes with the speech act, or, indeed, with the written text. In its absence, the body still signifies. Descartes tried not to know this" (2015b: 15). For Butler, the body, in its exposure to other bodies, is a site through which a self is always already implicated in others, and vice versa.[1]

With this perspective, although still critical of her work, she comes closer to the French feminism of Irigaray than some of her American readers would like to admit. Butler ties the *rati*onal *cogito* back to its disavowed corporeality so as to show that "the subject, as flesh, is primarily an intersubjective being, finding itself as Other, finding its primary sociality in a set of relations that are never fully recoverable or traceable" and, as a consequence, that "[t]his view stands in stark contrast both to the Freudian conception of the 'ego,' understood as the site of a primary narcissism, and to the various forms of atomistic individualism derived from Cartesian and liberal philosophical traditions" (169). As body, a self is never entirely at home with it-self alone (to paraphrase Waldenfels here). As also another one of her latest books confirms—namely *Notes Toward a Performative Theory of Assembly*—Butler's stress on the intersubjective has her theorize performativity other-wise. She now conceives of it as "chiasmic relation between forms of linguistic performativity and forms of bodily performativity. They overlap; they are not altogether distinct; they are not, however, identical with one another" (2015a: 9). Or, maybe even more precisely, in her more recent work "performativity functions as a chiastic relation between body and language" (137). It is in this radical sense of an-other performativity that the figural corporeal potentials of language are now going to be further investigated via a return to the (disregarded and/or misunderstood) insights of French feminism.

"We do not yet know how to look or listen to the other as subject. We still ignore the possibility of giving up a centered gaze, a fixed sight, a renunciation which would leave space and air around and within the other" (2000: 42)— writes Irigaray in *To Be Two*. Extending her early work on sexual difference, for which she is still better known, the Belgium born feminist philosopher has more recently turned explicitly to the question of the other. Her persistent search for more sensory and/or sensual modes of approaching the other and a language that can express an encounter which does not rob otherness of its sting are entirely in line with the project of thinking aesthetics otherwise. Her thought draws attention to a vital aspect that so far has only been implied: the relevance of sexual difference. For Irigaray, the forgetting and/or sidelining of certain forms of perception as well as expression is a result of the fundamentally paternalistic bent of a Western tradition which has, for centuries, repressed women's voices and insights in its phallocratic and phallogocentric epistemological horizon and reduced them to the deficient status of a commodified objects (cf. 1996: 76). Irigaray holds, that to arrive at non-levelling modes of relating to the other, it is the patriarchal hegemony over Western thinking that needs to be thoroughly challenged.

However, while most scholars in American Cultural Studies would undoubtedly agree that questions related to gender and sex are of utmost significance in the context of renegotiating occidental epistemology, they would probably not be convinced that Irigaray's thinking is the appropriate way to go about this matter. Why return to this philosopher, whose *oeuvre* already more than 25 years ago has been regarded in the Anglo-American academy as "little more than a heroic and inspiring but ultimately rather utopian manifesto" (Whitford 1991: 10)? Has she not been repeatedly accused of various forms of essentialism and for downplaying the relevance of issues of ethnicity, race, and class, and reproduced a Eurocentric way of thought which a transnational focus absolutely needs to avoid? Such objections are certainly not far-fetched. Especially to questions of cultural difference, postcolonialism, and her latent Eurocentrisms, Irigaray herself has not given enough thought (cf. Deutscher 146). Nonetheless, and maybe paradoxically, her work still harbors invaluable potentials also—or particularly—regarding this area. Hanneke Canters and Grace Jantzen are only two critics who more recently have pointed out that Irigaray's "concepts and strategies can be extended beyond the ways in which she used them" (135). Penelope Deutscher affirms this and, simultaneously, provides the cue for this part's drawing on Irigaray's work when she writes: "The Irigarayan project on cultural difference can be fruitfully re-imagined or refigured by readers insofar as it could alternatively follow a structure closer to her approach to sexual difference" (148). Instead of subscribing to Irigaray's seeming reproduction of a romanticized binary reasoning in works such as *Between East and West*, this part will read her more recent thought on how to relate to otherness, as well as particularly the notion of "being-two," considering her earlier deconstructive work on "mimicry" and "speaking (as) woman" or "womanspeak."

Irigaray's philosophy underscores this book's insistence on the validity of "poststructuralist" thought: as Spivak has already pointed out in an essay from 1981, Irigaray's work (as part of French feminism) provides "politicized and critical examples of 'Symptomatic reading' not always following the reversal-displacement technique of a [simplistic, vulgarized] deconstructive reading" (177); a form of reading that does not plunge into the negativity of endless deferral, but outlines the possibility for a different kind of positivity beyond the confines of Western epistemology.

A conversation partner for Irigaray's philosophy is Theresa Hak Kyung Cha's *Dictée*.[2] This ever-genre-defying multilingual art-work, interweaves several different cultural, historical, as well as medial contexts and weaves them into a textual performance. Originally published in 1982, and at first largely ignored because of its oblique experimental character, *Dictée* has by now become a seminal text within Asian American Studies—not least due to the influence of Elaine H. Kim and Norma Alarcón's essay collection *Writing Self/Writing Nation*, published in 1994, which is entirely dedicated to Cha's piece. Again, for some scholars, this return to a text which has already been thoroughly analyzed over the past 20 years appears, at best, anachronistic. Nevertheless, more recently several critics have drawn renewed attention to aspects of *Dictée* that, so far, have been sidelined by the sheer plethora of politically inclined analyses. This pertains mostly to the text's corporeal dimensions; that is to say, precisely those dimensions that French feminism would have been equipped to examine. But the handful of early commentators who employed such a perspective have been almost forgotten, because of their lack of political sensibility. Keeping in mind Spivak's assertion quoted above, though, this chapter argues that an-other look at *Dictée* through the lenses of Irigaray helps trace out several profound challenges regarding the supremacy of occidental patriarchal *ratio*nality that the text dis-closes. Consequently, reading *Dictée* and Irigaray's thought together is beneficial to both: what Hyo Kim calls Cha's "intercultural embodied writing" (2013: 136) can be analyzed in more detail via Irigaray's philosophy, just as *Dictée* can function as alleviating supplement concerning Irigaray's ascribed subliminal

Eurocentrism: within a *dia-logue between two*, *both together* point toward a mode of embodied relationality with otherness which exceeds static discursivity and is relevant beyond the boundaries of this chapter.

In the first chapter of this part, Irigaray's ideas will be integrated into the overall theoretical blueprint of this book. This will be done, first, by way of reading her critique of occidental patriarchy alongside Walter Mignolo's criticism of the modern/colonial world system. This will reveal how both point toward a similar rejection of the Cartesian paradigm, and the mind-body split it entails, as the prime epistemological instrument of colonizing domination that levels all entities and phenomena in-differently—that is, also women—to a status of passive *res extensae*. For Irigaray, however, this levelling never succeeds entirely: (the other) woman retains a repressed—or what Mignolo would term subalternized—knowledge, which exceeds patriarchal systematicity from inside; she remains as a Euro-de-centric force that potentially opens a new relationality with otherness. The part then moves on to further describe this relationality as a border gnostic relationship of being-two, which first requires a revisiting of the frequent accusations of essentialism thrown at Irigaray's work. Drawing on Waldenfels's thought, it will then be shown that—in a decided critique of radical constructivism—Irigaray does not dismiss "essence" entirely, but thinks it radically other-wise, namely as dynamically fluid relationality of being-two where subjectivity can neither be reduced to homogeneous or also fragmented unity nor extended into happily in-different pluralism. Being-two ultimately *figures* as a dichotomous locus of enunciation that always remains in responsive touch with the other. The last section of chapter three relates Irigaray's strategy of mimicry to Spivak's creative sabotage or ab-use to further elucidate the epistemological relevance of "poststructuralist" thought for engaging with radical otherness by reading other-wise. This provides the foundation for connecting *parler-femme* to Lyotard's notion of the figure as both transcending the established order of discursive representation, with womanspeak adding a decidedly corporeal factor to this excessive impetus. Lastly, Irigaray's caress—that is tied to this corporeality—can be evoked to clarify Lyotard's concept of grazing as a sense-sensitized mode of relating to literary texts other-wise.

Chapter four begins by analyzing the role of language in *Dictée* between colonizing tool and emancipatory mode of expression to illustrate how the text does not remain in a merely counter-discursive framework, but abusively mimics Western thinking and interweaves it with epistemological potentials beyond the *ratio*. It will be shown how *Dictée*'s fragmentary collage character forms a textual repertoire that brings forth a *poiētico*-performative incantation of resilience. In a second step, the specific subjectivity enacted within the art-work is going to be analyzed as an instance of de-colonial being (at least) two in dia-logic relationality with invoked women from dif-ferent cultural backgrounds, who become part of the textual ritual as the speaker channels their voices. The analysis will show, how *Dictée* constantly enacts a bodily touching upon others and a sense of community uncontaina-ble by national frameworks also reflected on the formal level as the art-work per-forms a fluid passage between two ever-speaking lips. The last section of chapter four further builds on the previous insights and is, then, going to pursue the text's specific corporeal qualities. It is going to read *Dictée*, with Irigaray, as itself enacting an embodied dichotomous locus of enunciation; a locus that can be provocatively described as a moist vaginal space: a figural space where the integrated visual elements do not form a Hegelian gallery of static images, but are perceived other-wise, namely by way of their dynamic affective quality that requires a released response. That is, it will be argued that *Dictée* has the potential to stimulate modes of seeing/touching beyond phallocratic objectification that possibly enable encounters with *presencing* otherness.

DIA-LOGIC CARESS

WHEN MIGNOLO WRITES IN *The Darker Side of Western Modernity* that "[r]*eversing* the terms of the conversation will not work, mainly because doing so remains within the same rules of the game and play, yet under inferior conditions" and that "[c]*hanging the terms of the conversation* is, instead, the decolonial project, through border gnosis and border/decolonial thinking" (206), then he himself provides the suitable point of entry for relating Irigaray's thought to his own. The legitimacy of establishing a connection between these two dissimilar thinkers is further consolidated when Mignolo in *Local Histories/Global Designs* quotes Norma Alarcón writing the following: "The subject (and object) of knowledge is now woman, but the inherited view of consciousness has not been questioned at all. As a result, some Anglo-American feminist subjects of consciousness have tended to become a parody of the masculine subject of consciousness, thus revealing their ethnocentric liberal underpinning" (2000: 119). These are all thoughts that appear, in slightly different forms, in Irigaray's thought as well.

Coloniality and Patriarchal Hegemony

Drawing on and re-contextualizing feminist insights—mostly those of Gloria Anzaldúa—in the transnational realm of border thinking, Mignolo emphasizes a deep-seated complicity between processes of colonization, androcentrism, as well as Eurocentric epistemology. He writes that Western imperial expansionism—fueled by authoritarian notions of a Christian Father-God—coincided with the establishment and/or reification of a hierarchal heteronormative complex with global dimensions in which patriarchal structures develop a passive and submissive concept of "woman" to regulate and normalize sex and gender relations in the colonies (cf. 2012: 18). The colonialist power structure of Western modernity as well as its undergirding epistemological horizon were controlled and shaped by the firm hands of white heterosexual men. As the "gatekeepers of Western and modern knowledge" (ibid. 45), it was—and continues to be—male intellectuals who set the standards within the modern/colonial world system. Faced with this masculine domination of epistemology, the intervention of border thinking includes a call for reevaluating the relevance of gender and sexual difference with a particular regard to matters of knowledge production.

It is this concern for the epistemological relevance of sexuality which, therefore, finally underscores the validity of relating Mignolo's thought to Irigaray's feminist philosophy. Ever since her immensely influential doctoral dissertation *Speculum of the Other Woman* from 1974, Irigaray's thinking has revolved around the fundamentally patriarchal bent of the Western tradition—to her ranging, at least, from Plato and Aristotle to Freud and Lacan (cf. Berry 229)—and its consequences for the status of women. In short, according to Irigaray, the masculine influence on occidental reasoning has been so pervasive that the category "man" has not only functioned as the guiding principle against which all phenomena had to be measured, but also predetermined the possible modes of relating to the world and its entities. In *Speculum*—and throughout other earlier works—Irigaray reads especially Freud's ideas as indicative of an entire male genealogy in which the phallus functions as "the yardstick of the same" (1985a: 28) and where "woman" is reduced to a contradistinctive semblance of masculinity: within this "*economy of the Same*" (1985b: 74), sexual difference (as well as any other form of difference) is always already filtered through the flat mirror of patriarchy. The phallocratic system, with its insistence on the maleness of the self, leaves room neither for the genuine (sexual) difference of "woman," nor for encounters with otherness in general that are not predefined against patriarchal norms (cf. Moi 64; Deutscher 138). This effectively results—to again invoke Irigaray's own terminology—in "an absorption of the other into the self in the intestine" (1993: 101) of "man." Just as Mignolo, she "sees an analogy between a masculinist culture of the same and white Western hegemony" (Ingram xvii); an analogy that calls for radical modifications of established epistemology.

For both Irigaray and Mignolo, such a modification has to begin with the deconstruction of Western universalism or "zero point epistemology" (2012: 122), as the latter calls it. In *I Love to You*, Irigaray writes that the whole occidental "tradition is marred by an original sin: to have mistaken the reason of man for the universal" (147); again bolstered by (an appropriation of) patriarchal Christian doctrine and authority, this assumption condenses in the establishment of subjectivity as one homogeneous masculine whole, albeit disguised as apparently neutral and objective, and ultimately

extends into the desire for an all-embracing (that is, "catholic" in the strict
sense of the word) unified political horizon (cf. Zakin 179). Irigaray, therefore, concludes that "[t]he whole of Western philosophy is the mastery of
the *direction* of will and thought by the subject, historically man" (1996:
45), which coincides with "annihilating the alterity [otherness] of the other"
(ibid. 110) and eradicating dissimilarity within the systemic framework of
self-sameness. With the help of abstract universalism and the (illusory) elevated position (or zero point)[1] it grants, "monolithic man" (Joy 53) projects
a phallocratic rule of the One—an absolute, violent, tyrannical dominion
(cf. Irigaray 2000a: 43, 71, 78)—on the entire world and subjects all phenomena to the symbolic order of his categorical grid; an epistemic structure of
which the modern nation-state is just one manifestation (cf. Fermon 123).
One *logos*, one *ratio*, one subjectivity: this mono-logic has guided all modes
of being in the world in the West's universalist philosophical horizon—with
devastating consequences for everyone who deviates. "Annexing the other, in
all his/her dimensions and directions, in order to capture him/her, captivate
him/her," Irigaray asserts, the rule of the One constricts otherness within an
epistemic "garment that first and foremost paralyzes the other's movement"
(1993: 195f.), namely through levelling in discursive constructs of alterity.
Consequently, the issue of how to circumvent and/or undo the phallic principle of oneness can be considered as one of the most pressing issues of contemporary societies which find themselves within ever more transnational
relations; an issue not exclusively for feminist thinkers, but for all those who
are concerned with the articulation of various forms of difference—whether
they be racial, sexual, religious, or otherwise (cf. Cheah and Grosz 15). As
such, coming to terms with the phallic mono-logic is also relevant for a project invested in pointing toward the other presences within discourse.

Both Irigaray and Mignolo, however, expose the sheer immensity of the
task of working toward an adequate articulation of difference or radical
otherness—primarily through their shared emphasis on the inherent connection between the representational apparatus and the reductive modes of
occidental knowledge production, namely *ratio*nal understandings of seeing
and touching. Due to this connection, the two thinkers argue, the concept
of representation is always already complicit with the phallic logic of the
modern/colonial world system through which patriarchal power ensures
the continual commodification of the other (cf. Miller 2007: 106; Mignolo
2012: 307). For Irigaray, this mechanism operates by way of a dissociating
conception of remote gazing and an objectifying notion of grasping, which
implies the same ocular-centric distance and reduces the potentially affective
proximity of the tactile to the stasis of (supposedly) straight visibility (cf.
1993: 175, 125). Mignolo mirrors this indictment when he writes that the

Western *ratio* represses all forms and qualities of sensing which deviate from "the epistemology and aesthesis of the zero point" (2012: 80). Gaze and grasp, Irigaray continues, thereby, are focused on achieving ideal discursive fixation and closure where the opaque "multiplicity of the other . . . begins to resolve itself into a system of intelligible relationships" (1985a: 358): maintaining the hegemony of the mono-logical masculine subject, phallogo-centric discourse engenders woman's "consignment to passivity: she is to be the beautiful object of contemplation" (1985b: 26) without any agency of her own in the representational framework of the zero point.

Long before Gumbrecht and Mignolo, Irigaray (as well as other femi-nists) targeted the thought of Descartes as a central milestone that reinforces the established epistemological configuration of patriarchal hegemony in the West: a critique of the Cartesian split between mind and body, subject and object, has occupied her thought since *Speculum*. For Irigaray, it is this separation that is responsible for the "ascetic ellipsis of the body" and its rejection of the epistemological relevance of the "senses that are still natural and, therefore, uncontrollably open to impressions from silent, forbidden matter" (1985a: 185); from the position of *ratio*nal consciousness, these impressions are regarded as irrational and deficient. Irigaray sees the reason for this dissociation of mind and body, sensible and intelligible, not as an arbitrary epistemic gesture, but as the central strategy of Western patriarchy to erase women from the representational apparatus and, thereby, to disa-vow man's own dependence on an engendering body. Descartes's paradigm serves to bolster the Platonic assumption that truth requires no material support; it denies the active role of the mother's body and relegates the (female) body to the status of a passive repository (re)producing sameness (cf. ibid. 240) to masculinize *mater*-iality and to ensure the transcendence of the Father's *cogito* (cf. Whitford 1991: 106). Irigaray argues that this rejection of (female) corporeal sensuality eventually results in the notion of an "abstract and solipsistic universe" (2000a: 32) that occidental reason projects onto the world as the only definitive *ordo mundi*. She anticipates and resonates with Mignolo's critique of Cartesianism as a fundamental element of the modern/colonial world system. He writes that by positioning knowledge exclusively in the mind and sidelining affects, emotions, and de-sires, white Europeans regarded themselves as gatekeepers and harbingers of universal insight whose *ratio*nal conceptualizations of the (things of the) world was valid for the entire planet (cf. 2012: 142). Consequently, read with Irigaray and Mignolo, the mind/body split appears as the prime epis-temic instrument for preserving the patriarchal power of the male subject and its colonial hegemony.

As such an instrument of domination, the Cartesian paradigm does not distinguish between different phenomena of otherness, and subjects them to the same impetus of colonization. Penelope Deutscher emphasizes that in asserting women's status as a merely passive object, "Irigaray argues that women have, in a sense, been colonized" (146), too. In fact, Irigaray makes the correlation unmistakably clear when she, in an outrageous enumeration, writes that women are treated as just another form of otherness—next to savages, children, and the insane (cf. 1985b: 124)—to be possessed and taken advantage of. Masculine "desires that prefer the possession of territory" (1985a: 140) imagine woman—and here she invokes Freud's famous expression—as another "dark continent of dreams and fantasies" (1985b: 141) to be invaded/penetrated and exploited/abused. The same colonial logic that produces chattel slavery conceives of woman as on the level of inarticulate materiality or inanimate things and treats her as a ready-to-hand resource at the free disposal of *rational* male mastery (cf. Lehtinen 50; van Leeuwen 120). Pointing out affinities between Irigaray and Frantz Fanon, Penelope Ingram confirms this when she writes that "the racial body, like the sexed body, is caught in the network of matter, representation, and signification" (Ingram 17) of a phallic economy which turns all forms of otherness into controllable objects.

The phallogocentric representational system casts woman as negative and/or foil for demarcating a positive male subject. Within this logic, "woman . . . can only come into being as the inverted other of the masculine subject (his *alter ego*)" (Irigaray 1985a: 129); an *alter ego* bearing all the disavowed characteristics that pose a threat to the *rational* principles of Western patriarchy's epistemological horizon: materiality, sensuality, and opacity. Effectively robbed of the power to articulate herself or declared nonsensical and mad in cases where she tries, Irigaray argues, woman "is left with a *void*, a *lack* of all representation" (1985b: 42). Speaking with Waldenfels, this means that—via the process of discursive transformation into an oppositional object—women are stripped of any potential for genuine otherness, and female difference only ever appears as inferiority and absence toward and opposing negation of the transcendental signifier that is the phallus (cf. Grosz 342; Moi 63). Woman is cast as both *outside* the representational order and yet contained *within* the system of male discourse.

Regarding the United States, Mignolo describes this containment as resulting in a form of "interior subalternity" (2000: 176); and this is precisely where a productive merging of border gnosis and Irigaray's thinking can begin, for she argues that the phallocratic order never totally succeeds in binding woman in her otherness, her sensuality. Women might be harnessed and hidden away within *rational* systematicity, but—as argued in the first chapter concerning aesthetics—can never be effaced completely: although "aim[ing] to overcome the sensible in/by schematism and categories; by disinterested contemplation of natural beauty" (1985a: 212), the paradoxical interiorized exteriority of women constitutes "a *hole* in men's signifying economy" (ibid. 50) with subversive momentum: a place that "might leave scars in the memory. Reminders, rejoinders. Passages, and hemorrhages, between sensible and intelligible" (ibid. 299). Women are in a position of "*disruptive excess*" (1985b: 78) with the potential to undermine the phallic hegemony from the inside and, as such, to turn a stifling constriction into a locus of feminine empowerment. When Mignolo writes that "border epistemology emerges from the exteriority (not the outside, but the outside invented in the process of creating the identity of the inside, that is Christian Europe)" (2012: 20), and if the phallo-logic location of women can be described as such an invented inside, then it is justified to read women's repressed epistemological relevance as a form of subalternized knowledge within the Western tradition.

It is from this position of interior excess that Irigaray vouches for "[a] revolution in thought and ethics" (1993: 6): an epistemic revolution that insists on the transformative potential of what the phallic economy designates as lack; more precisely, a revolution which radically renegotiates the very meanings of subjectivity and *mater*-iality as established by patriarchal thought. Irigaray explains that "the issue is not one of elaborating a new theory of which woman would be the subject or the object, but of jamming the theoretical machinery itself, of suspending its pretension to the production of a truth and of a meaning that are excessively univocal" (1985b: 78). She thinks that the desired change of Western epistemology can be achieved by way of focusing on the very disavowed relevance of the sensual that, if not conceived as oppositional to rationality, can pry open the illusion of closed systematicity and mechanisms which define otherness according to preconceived categories (cf. 1993: 185). In this Irigaray agrees with Waldenfels, who holds that sensuality and rationality are irreducibly bound to and cannot be thought apart from each other (cf. 2000: 349). She also argues in line with Mignolo's call for a development of sense-sensitivity by insisting that "[b]y training the senses in concentration we can integrate multiplicity" (1996: 24) which otherwise is levelled in the Rule of the One and its discursive logic of sameness. This means that Irigaray's work aims to initiate a process of learning (how) to think other-wise; for embarking on an epistemological endeavor where the opacity of the sensual is not opposed to phallomorphic notions of clarity but enables the possibility for conceiving of a different kind of "positivity."

In her critique of phallogocentrism, saming, and hom(m)osexuality, Irigaray's focus, therefore, lies entirely on woman's subversive potential regarding the masculine order. Unlike for several Anglo-American feminists, therefore, for Irigaray, it is not enough for women to work toward equality without questioning who determines what counts as equal. She holds that the battle for women's equality remains complicit with the ideological apparatus she wishes to recalibrate—a view Irigaray again shares with Waldenfels and his argument that the supposed neutrality of the legal subject is subliminally andro- and/or phallogocentric and begins with the veiling of its patriarchal locus of enunciation (cf. 1997a: 68f.). Jean-Joseph Goux goes so far as to call this "the ultimate ruse of masculine supremacy" (182). Wishing for such an equality is tantamount to succumbing totally to the levelling logic of semblance where "[l]icense to operate is only granted to the (so-called) play of those differences that are measured in terms of *sameness*" (1985a: 247). This, however, is not to say that Irigaray does not support women's rights struggles *per se*, but only that women's longing for political recognition must not result in an assimilation to established phallocratic categories (cf. Schor 65). It requires a far deeper critical engagement.

According to Irigaray, the realization of true equality calls for a culture of genuine—that is to say, non-hierarchical—sexual difference which takes into account woman's *radical otherness in relation* to man. Therefore, she does not simply aim to invert the relationship between patriarchy and a reinstated matriarchy. Although she believes that recovering female genealogies has a crucial antidotal function (cf. Joy 92), Irigaray argues that a mere inversion brings about the exact opposite of the desired outcome:

> The reversal—which would signify also an overturning, a reversal in relations of power—would still be played out within the same, that sameness put into place by the economy of the *logos*. In order to prevent the other—not the inversed *alter ego* of the "masculine" subject . . . but that other, woman—from being caught up again in systems of representation whose goal or teleology is to reduce her within the same, it is of course necessary to interpret *any process of reversal, of overturning*, also as an *attempt to duplicate the exclusion of what exceeds representation*: the other, woman. (1985b: 156)

The central argument characterizing Irigaray's *oeuvre* is *the necessity of thinking relationality itself radically other-wise*—that is, not in the phallogocentric Rule of the One—and, coinciding with it, the need for developing "an alternative sociality" (Bergoffen 162) of sexual difference where irreducible otherness prevails. However, just as this new thinking does not imply inversion, it also does not suggest that one should just try to leave behind patriarchal discursivity altogether. Such a move results only in another reproduction of a phallic logic that yearns for transcendence. Irigaray stresses that reconceiving of relationality requires *thinking from a position*

of simultaneous interiority and exteriority; to situate oneself within the borders of said patriarchal discursivity and to challenge their fixity (cf. 1985b:
122). Following Irigaray, to conceive of relationality other-wise, one needs to
think *from* a position of relationality; *from* the ambiguity of an in-between
that the phallic *ratio* deems unfit for an adequate expression of subjectivity
(cf. Bloodsworth 76). Rather than opting for inverting or abandoning male
logic, one needs to think *from* the relationality of a dichotomous locus of
enunciation of subalternized (female) otherness which cannot be contained
within it.

In contrast to Mignolo's assertions of "poststructuralism's" intrinsic
Eurocentricity, Irigaray's work—with her revised notion of the positive—
contains a decisive Euro-de-centric impetus which is inherently relatable to
border gnosis, as several scholars have underscored. Keenly observant of
the "limits of the various Western political and academic feminisms, of the
need to broaden their scope, both horizontally across cultures and verti-
cally within specific cultures" (1998: 76), as Gail Schwab writes, Irigaray's
work bolsters the overall argument of this project concerning the opening
force of "poststructuralist" thinking with regard to Western systemic epistemology. Her work goes beyond reductive understandings of "poststructuralism" and deconstruction predominant within Anglo-American contexts.
It is, therefore, somewhat misleading when Cathryn Vasseleu writes that
"[r]ather than radicalizing certain themes in deconstruction, Irigaray is attempting both a deconstruction and a feminist position which is irreducible
to the terms of deconstruction" (15). To Irigaray, this feminist position and
deconstruction are inherently interwoven. Her radical "innovation" which
surpasses reductive notions of everlasting deferral is her insistence on a new
kind of "positivity" enabled by the dynamics of deconstruction itself. That
is why Naomi Schor holds that "Irigaray's production of a positive theory
of femininity is not an aberration . . . , rather the logical extension of her deconstruction of the specular logic of saming" (66). Both belong inseparably
together. It is in this way, Nicole Fermon adds, that, despite the lack of material consciousness often attested to her thinking, Irigaray's ideas possibly
provide "ways to understand and alleviate violence done to all women as a
result of global fiscalization" (122)—particularly when it is read in relation
to Mignolo's thought: as a form of border gnosis, one can read Irigaray's
insistence on a new relationality as an ongoing working toward "models
of conviviality that Western cosmopolitanism suppressed" (2012: 270);
toward decolonial models that function via "communal principles" (ibid.
275) and that "promote communal futures" (ibid. 254) beyond national
boundaries. The following section will further develop this affinity between

Irigaray's insistence on relationality and Mignolo's border thinking eventually via Waldenfels's phenomenology of the alien.

The Rule of One and Being-Two

Before turning to Irigaray's new mode of relationality, however, it is necessary to take a step back and address a particular form of criticism which has been brought against her work from the very beginning: especially for Anglo-American feminists, Irigaray's fundamental insistence on sexual difference and her focus on the female body reeks of essentialism and the very type of reasoning feminist thought wishes to overcome in the first place. There is no need to digest the entire debate all over again; a summary of the criticism will suffice. According to Schor, it manifests itself in four, usually intersecting, variants: liberationist critiques dismiss essentialism in favor of constructivism; psychoanalytically inclined linguistic critiques, similarly, see essentialism as ideological effect of the imaginary; philosophical critiques expose essentialism's complicity with *ratio*nal Western metaphysics; and, lastly, feminist critiques reject essentialism as denying material circumstances related to race, ethnicity, class, as well as nationality (cf. Schor 60–62). But can Irigaray justifiably be considered guilty of all this considering that—as has been shown—from the very outset, her thinking has been concerned with a deconstruction of the modern *ratio*'s Hegelian "economy of 'presence,'" (1985a: 41) with its "imposition of rigid forms," of "inflexibility," and strategies of "fixing and freezing" (ibid. 234)? Most certainly not. It is counterproductive when scholars—as most recently Virpi Lehtinen (cf. 39)—emphasize the *pre-discursive* character of Irigaray's notions of sexual difference; if not treated carefully, these statements only serve to fuel the critiques of essentialism and further shove her into a drawer she does not really belong in. Irigaray's critical desire, as Maggie Berg rightly puts it, is "to retrieve woman not from discourse . . . but from determinism" (65). Pre-discursive, for Irigaray, means before the absolute reign of phallogocentric discursivity, not prior to and/or free of discourse as such. Her focus on essence needs to be understood from this perspective as well. It is certainly true that Irigaray does not discard essentialism *per se*; more radically, she argues that "essence may not be the unitary, monolithic, in short, essentialist category that anti-essentialists so often presume it to be" (Fuss 101). With this clarification, the many accusations of essentialism thrown at Irigaray are effectively neutralized and debunked as stemming from a failure to think essence as not always already bound by the supposed closure and "usurping solipsisms" (Schwab 1998: 81) of a petrifying masculine phallocentric discourse. Irigaray urges her readers to think essence and discursivity decidedly other-wise: not as forming a binary opposition but rather an inextricable entanglement where both attain a different character than within the hegemonic categorizations of the Rule of the One.

Irigaray turns the tables on her critics and unveils the phallocraticism at the roots of their constructivist positions. She shows that avouching a solely constructed character of the world without considering the possibility of the "pre-given of my body" (2000a: 34) reproduces occidental notions of epistemic superiority. As Alison Stone writes, ignoring this potential pre-givenness—that is, a body's dynamic state as not (yet) incorporated into phallic systematicity—adds to "reinforcing conceptual hierarchies between culture and nature" (2006: 13) instead of bringing about profound changes. Constructivism operates within the established opposition between nature and culture rather than exposing its artificiality. Consequently, Irigaray suggests that constructivist thought is uttered implicitly from a position of culture supposedly outside of nature; a position which is based on the tacit premise of thought's ability to conceptually contain and control all phenomena. Claiming that everything is constructed appears as in no way different from claiming that everything can be defined in its essence: both betrays an equally totalitarian logic that appropriates or distorts—through an apotheosis of wo/man—the privilege and authority of a Father-God for securing epistemic hegemony and employing it for political goals and, therefore, remains deeply informed by a corrupted Western Judeo-Christian worldview. Ingram confirms this and points out that by giving in to constructivist ideas, apparently à la Butler, completely, "we risk reinstituting static and fixed representations" (39) characteristic of patriarchal phallo-semblance: "[a]s a model for resistance, Butler's theory is inadequate because it operates in a closed circuit. The subject can resist only within the interpretative categories already in place" (102). A radical constructivist argument is only tenable when pitted against the romantic notion of untainted nature. However, despite such a notion having been projected onto her again and again, Irigaray herself never entertains such nostalgic romanticism. Instead, she argues that, learning from non-occidental horizons of knowing, one should work from the irreducible (cosmological) connection of nature and culture—essence and discourse—that can give rise to the epistemologically transformative possibility of re(dis)covering repressed *poiētic* modes of spatially and temporally relating to the world (cf. Miller 2011: 52; Stone 2003: 61; Joy 144f.); relational modes which do not strive for control but maintain an openness for (woman's) otherness.

If one remains within the critical framework of constructivism and does not work toward such a new relationality, Irigaray further elaborates, one is in danger of eventually supporting "a critique of patriarchy that might prove nihilistic" (2000a: 39)—a view she again shares with Waldenfels. Particularly within the US-American context, some constructivist critiques appear to be complicit with a specific form of nihilism stemming from a rugged individualism. In its phallocratically inflected pursuit of happiness, of the realization of a Self's fullness and only this Self's fullness alone, this nihilism regards all that is other and hinders the endeavor of Self-realization as to be effectively neutralized—even if it be "one's" body in its apparently opposing materiality. Exposing the objectifying mechanisms of phallic discourse, but simultaneously operating within this same logic that regards everything as controllable, constructivism never attempts to criticize discursive rules, categories, or delimitations. Consequently, it participates in the further objectification of the body—even in subversive attempts—treating it as ready-to-hand matter to be manipulated at will (by Western power/knowledge). In *Das leibliche Selbst*, Waldenfels aptly describes constructivism's complicity with the phallic economy of sameness as follows: "The constructivist logos, the code, the program, the cultural rule are neutral like the traditional logos. The constructivist logos is sexless" (2000: 362).[2] Elsewhere he clarifies that—based on such a form of neutrality—this epistemological stance results in nothing less than an introduction of a reissued technologically enhanced Cartesian dualism (cf. 1997a: 76) and static essentialist notions of ideal individual subjectivity that are tied to it. At worst, radical constructivism fosters a nihilistic individualism that effectively masks patriarchal hegemony behind a revolutionary passion, all the while silently drawing its impetus from this very phallocratic epistemic superiority.

To think other-wise, Irigaray conceives of discourse and essence as forming an irreducible relationship of multifarious fluidity. As several scholars have pointed out, Irigaray's emphasis on the multiple character of the feminine (body) significantly alleviates charges of established notions of essentialism brought against her, for it introduces a kind of plurality which is incompatible with and can never be entirely absorbed by the patriarchal Rule of the One (cf. Schor 76; Stone 2006: 6f.; Xu 82). In her book *Marine Lover*, Irigaray herself writes: "She does not set herself up as *one*, as a (single) female unit. She is not closed up or around one single truth or essence. . . . And she does not oppose a feminine truth to the masculine truth, because this would once again amount to playing the—man's—game of castration. If the female sex takes place by embracing itself . . . it ceaselessly becomes other, no stability of essence is proper to her" (1991: 86). However, it is vital to keep in mind that, at the same time as defying assertions of static essences, this plurality unlocks (new or forgotten) epistemological

horizons for thinking a different kind of essentialism. Irigaray's female multiplicity should, therefore, not be thought as an "unhealthy fragmentation,
'shards' and 'scattered' remnants,'" as Stone aptly clarifies, "but [as a] positive openness to change, to others, to relationships, and to varied sexual
impulses" (2006: 121f.); This type of multiplicity is always "flowing, fluctu-
ating" (Irigaray 1985b: 112); it is certainly "always in relation of excesses or
lack vis-à-vis unity" (ibid. 117), but also pointing toward the positivity of a
non-unitary dynamics (cf. 2000a: 37; 2002a: 148). In other words, instead
of simplistic one-sided resolutions resulting in the reestablishment of static
systemic order(s)—no matter whether in the phallocentric guises of constructivism or essentialism—Irigaray's thinking in-volves both discursivity
and essentiality in a dynamic liquidity that dis-solves the static binaries of
Hegelian Ideal self-same presence within the ever-fluid momentum of *presencing* radical otherness. Hanneke Canters and Grace Jantzen succinctly
summarize this as follows: Irigaray's profound renegotiation of the relationship between discourse and essence "is as far from the [one is tempted
to add misguided] rigid binary opposition of Anglo-American philosophical
logic as could be imagined. The creativity necessary for mutual relationship
requires plurivocity and movement, willingness to live with ambiguity and
to find in it resources for the future" (153).

   It is worthwhile for this chapter's argument to (re)turn to Irigaray's and
Mignolo's critiques of occidental notions of universality in more detail, for
it is from here that the former's work can be most fruitfully integrated into
the broader project of reading other-wise. Both thinkers begin with a similar
premise: for Irigaray, the deconstruction of Western philosophy is tied to
the female multiplicity just described. Mignolo puts a particular emphasis
on plurality, too. Therefore, in a way, Irigaray speaks for him as well, when
she writes that her aim is "to open up another era in our culture, an era in
which the subject is no longer one, egocentric and potentially imperialistic,
but which rather respects differences" (1996: 47). The two thinkers target
traditional conceptualizations of the subject that work according to the hierarchical binary logic of A/not-A with the help of which "throughout the
history of Western philosophy man has thought of 'the other' as 'not the
same as himself': female, black, non-Western, without formal education,
slave. Not-A" (Canters and Jantzen 36). Within this system, Mignolo writes,
but "[t]wo choices are given to the anthropos [all non-Western human be-
ings]: to assimilate or to be cast out" (2012: 82). In rejecting this, Irigaray
and Mignolo strongly agree. However, their actual approaches toward this
issue at first appear fundamentally different. On the one hand—apparently
contrary to her initial impetus—Irigaray argues that to overcome patriarchal rule what she calls the being-two of sexual difference needs to function

as the new global universal. On the other hand, Mignolo's project to displace a levelling universality reaches toward what he calls "[p]luriversal global futures" (ibid. 89) where otherness is not reduced to a phallic sameness. Their positions seem mutually exclusive. Nevertheless, what looks like a gross contradiction, in fact, can be turned into a mutually beneficial combination.

But what causes this *prima facie* incongruity in the first place? The answer lies within Irigaray's understanding of multiplicity. As mentioned above, she thinks multiplicity "based on the plurality of sexual difference" (Peebles 234); a plurality that is incompatible with patriarchal reasoning. Irigaray further argues that straightforwardly focusing on plurality and multiplicity as opposed to ideal *ratio*nal unity is misguided: "I do not believe that to question the universal subject starting from the multiple is sufficient," she explains in an interview, "because the multiple can always be equivalent to a multiple or a sub-multiple of men" (2000b: 145). This is to say that critics who—due to Irigaray's insistence on the multiplicity of woman—hope to purge her thinking entirely from any traces of essentialism and integrate her into an Anglo-American framework that merely celebrates plurality over unity are gravely mistaken; Irigaray considers such a position as complicit with the logic of phallic semblance where "the multiple is [nothing but] the one in its self-willed dispersal into unrelated atomistic singularities, many others of the same" (Cheah and Grosz 6). In fact, it is precisely such a celebration which leads ever deeper into the loss of genuine relationality. According to Irigaray, this notion of one-plus-one-plus-one-plurality is what reduces woman to the fixed status of an arbitrarily substitutable commodity and what attributes to each man the individualist sovereignty of the One (cf. Zakin 174). The questions arising from this within the context at hand is this: what kind of multiplicity underlies Mignolo's understanding of pluriversality?

Throughout his work, Mignolo has devoted himself to what he calls delinking from Western epistemic sovereignty—and pluriversality has recently become one of his central concepts to achieve such a radical epistemological opening. In de-centering the hegemony of occidental reason, he writes, pluriversality constitutes a politico-epistemological organizational principle "beyond the magisterial power and monotopic inspiration of any abstract universals, from the Right or from the Left" (235). Instead, Mignolo offers decolonial options; that is, he focuses on subalternized knowledges as alternative modes of relating to the things of the world. This project's ventures into the possibility of reading other-wise—as will have become evident throughout its chapters—is, in principle, sympathetic to this argument. However, when considering Irigaray's warnings concerning multiplicity, it becomes necessary to ask whether Mignolo's move beyond a monotopic magisterial power or inspiration into pluriversality only results in what Irigaray calls "an aggre-gate of one + one + one . . ." (1996: 101). Put differently, does Mignolo's thought foster the illusion of a happy multiculturalist pluralism whose mode of (non-)relationality stems from an individualist dissociation and care-free indifference? More precisely, does pluriversality constitute maybe just an-other manifestation of "a politics of multiculturalism . . . merely overturn-ing the Platonic model, emphasizing the many over the one without chal-lenging the mimetic relation that remains between them" (Chanter 219)? If so, then Mignolo's de-colonial options would actually be but an inverted re-colonization hidden behind epistemological dispersal that continues to function in a ruggedly individualist horizon.

Mignolo is well aware of this problem; he states explicitly that pluriv-ersality should not be thought in analogy to the commonplace notions of liberal pluralism (cf. 2012: 71f.)—and this inconspicuous statement consti-tutes the first hint toward a much deeper compatibility with Irigaray's think-ing than assumed so far; a compatibility which becomes even more evident in the following elaboration: "Pluriversality (or diversality, in the sense of diversity and not in the sense of dichotomy) is not the rejection of universal claims. It rejects universality understood as abstract universal grounded in mono-logic. A universal principle grounded in the idea of the diversal (or pluriversal) is not a contradiction in terms, but rather a displacement of conceptual structures" (ibid. 234). In this passage, Mignolo, like Irigaray, draws attention to the necessity of a new kind of universalism; how it is to be conceived, however, remains largely unclear. Here, at last, combining Mignolo's concepts with Irigaray's emphasis on the universality of sexual difference brings forth a powerful theoretical alliance. What she has in mind is "a relationship between [at least] two that is not always already overde-termined by the one" because she holds that until such a relationality is not re(dis)covered, "there is no possibility of genuine multiplicity or difference" (Chanter 118). The scarce cues Mignolo himself offers regarding the uni-versality of the pluriversal show that aligning his thought with the French feminist is not at all far-fetched. He writes that "[f]or a world composed of multiple worlds we need not have abstract universals and empty signifiers, but *connectors*," and that pluriversal thought always needs to be "*at least bi-directional*" (2012: 235; my emphases). This mirrors what Irigaray sug-gests when she writes that from the position of sexual difference, "the logos becomes dialogic" (1996: 124) and universality fundamentally relational, fundamentally other-wise. This is to say that this kind of universality op-erates from the insight that "we are always already tied, in all dimensions of subjectivity, to others and to the world whether we choose to be related or not" (Lehtinen 19). Taken together, Irigaray's and Mignolo's thoughts ultimately coalesce into what can be referred to as a *dynamically relational pluriversality*. As such, intermingling the two thinkers clarifies the former's notion of universality and saves the latter from reproducing the one-plus-one-plus-one-logic of phallocratic sameness.

It is possible to unfold how such a relational horizon positively alters engagements with otherness by reading Irigaray's notion of being-two alongside Waldenfels's phenomenology. Where Mignolo speaks of the necessity of (at least) a bi-directionality, Irigaray writes that a relational "[b]eing *we* means being at least *two*" (2000: 35); although an *uncountable* "two which is irreducible to the One" (ibid. 59) and *indivisible into two ones*—a division of the two only results in the dissociating incompleteness of halves. For Irigaray, this ir*rati*onal reasoning is connected to the repressed (or subalternized) epistemological valence of woman: a luminosity of the feminine beyond the calculative ideals of phallic Enlightenment (cf. 1985b: 207) with the subversive potential to bring forth from inside the supposed closure of Western thought "an/other woman [*une autre*], irreducible to the masculine subject" (1995: 9); to bring forth "the other as a woman" (1996: 60) not as the other of the same—that is, a not-A—as Morny Joy clarifies by quoting Drucilla Cornell's *At the Heart of Freedom*, but rather as "a kind of radical otherness to any [masculine] conception of the real or reality" (44). Thereby, she provides the key term and cue for clarifying Irigaray's (new) relationality of being-two with Waldenfels's own understanding of an "*otherness* [*Fremdheit*] *of the other sex*" (2000: 359)[3] and for elaborating on its relevance regarding notions of *presencing*.

The potential connectibility of Waldenfels and Irigaray has already become apparent in the blueprint-chapter where the title of Irigaray's essay "How Can We Meet the Other" has been read as paraphrasing the central point of departure of the former's *Phenomenology of the Alien*. The most suitable way of beginning to further develop this initial congeniality is to draw attention to congruencies between the relationality of being-two and the motion of pathos and response: conceiving being-two as characterized by an openness for *affective* qualities of otherness, Irigaray's concept strongly resembles Waldenfels's dynamics. In her book *An Ethics of Sexual Difference*, she re(dis)covers this epistemic attitude within Descartes's concept of wonder and interprets it as a mode of engaging with phenomena outside—or (maybe) prior to—the *rati*onal comprehension of the *cogito*: "a sense of the other that is not projective or selfish" (1993: 111) but remains sensitive and attentive to that which "is never situated or expected" (ibid.) and always catches one by surprise. For Irigaray, being-two is "neither active nor passive" and "never reducing the other to a mere meaning, to my meaning" (2000: 9); it is always responsive to the pathos which stems from a non-appropriable and "irreducible nature of *the other's presence*" (1993: 211; my emphasis). In Waldenfels's terms—thought within the momentum of pathos and response—Irigaray's being-two is a matter of singular performative encounters of radical otherness: it turns the phallic system of predication that asks the question "what *is* sexual difference?" (implying essential stasis) into a thinking other-wise that asks the question "how does the other sex *presence* (each-time-only-one-time)?" (implying essential fluidity) (cf. 1997a: 66; 2000: 356). Consequently, what Waldenfels thinks as a double asymmetry of mutual entanglement irreducible to equivalence or sublation into higher unity (cf. 2000: 356; 1997a: 69f.) constitutes, for Irigaray, a new (or at least repressed) kind of (feminine) "reciprocity—to affect/to be affected—irreducible to the normative oppositional or hierarchical split of subjectivity between activity and passivity" (Athanasiou and Tzelepis 2008b: 13). Thinking sexual difference as being-two (in irreducible relationality) means nothing less than thinking sexual difference as *presencing* radical otherness.

With the notion of fluid essentiality, Irigaray helps attenuate emphases on the negativity of the other and—again picking up on Kristeva's fundamental question—shows that (female) otherness is negative only with respect to a phallogocentric representational system (cf. 1985b: 217f.). Fluidity entirely alters the significance of negativity from a Hegelian instrument of working toward an elevated synthesis that levels difference in a supposedly elevated unity into a dynamic force that constantly reminds the One of its limited mastery in the face of the other's uncontrollability (cf. Joy 83, 96). However, as Krzysztof Ziarek stresses, for Irigaray, "it will not suffice to see the other differently through the changed perspective of the negative already operating within the subject" (2007: 66): in fluidity the very meaning of the negative changes. There, Irigaray writes in her book *I Love to You*, the negative is both that which ensures the non-substitutability of a "you are irreducible to me, just as I am to you" (1996: 103) and "that [which] enables me to go towards you" (ibid. 104) and to enter "into a presence that is attentive and restrained, focused and available, open and reflective" (ibid. 146) rather than marked by phallocratic mastery and control. Several scholars have pointed out that, as such, negativity "is given a more positive designation" and "becomes a living exchange" (Joy 96); in fact, instead of a negativity based on One-sided subjectivity, the motion of fluid *presencing* dis-solves the potential of the negative in an irreducible entanglement with an affirmative positivity (cf. Athanasiou and Tzelepis 2008a: 109); an-other positivity that does not regard the lacking closure of the Self as statically negative, but as the beginning of the dynamic relationality of being-two.

In line with Waldenfels's notion of the radical otherness, Irigaray writes that this beginning stems from recognizing "the other as other not only in one's own country, in one's own home but also in oneself" (2002a: 147). This means, being-two sets in with intrapersonal otherness, or, as Catherine Peebles explains: Irigaray's conceptualization of sexual difference is based on the premise of the "interiority of the other as the very beginning of the self" (233). The masculine Rule of the One tries to erase this dimension by containing it in *ratio*nal structures. Woman, due to her specific multiplicity, however, retains a sense of internal heterogeneity. Realizing that otherness is always already an inseparable part of her, woman does not regard it as a threat to homogeneous closure or the return of repressed trauma, but as enabling gesture beyond negation toward intimate proximity with others (cf. Ziarek 2007: 53, 58); a fluid proximity where notions of self and other dis-solve in reciprocal embracing, albeit without forming a homogeneous unity; that is, dis-solving in what Waldenfels calls a "process of in- or exclusion" (1997a: 69),[4] or what Irigaray herself refers to as a playing at the limits of selfness: "still outside, but already within" (2000:4). Repudiating illusions of closed-off Selfhood, woman is not *one — is* not at all — does not deny radical intrapersonal otherness, but *always already presences in-between self and other.*

Building on the connection of Waldenfels's phenomenology and Mignolo's border gnosis established in the first chapter, it is possible to conceive of Irigaray's (repressed) femininity — situated in-between being-two — as unfolding (or enfolding) a dichotomous locus of enunciation, and, as such, answers Mignolo's call for "a new epistemological subject that thinks *from* and *about* the borders" (2000: 110). This becomes particularly apparent when Irigaray thinks of woman as "a threshold that is always *half-open*" (1993: 18) or as indefinite "point of passage" (ibid. 75): uncontainable by a crude either/or-logic, she always *presences* as "both one and the other" and, at the same time, "neither one nor the other" (1985a: 165). As a subalternized type of knowledge hidden away but never eradicated by the *ratio*, Irigaray's feminine constitutes a mode of border thinking which re(dis)covers (from) within the phallocentric horizon the epistemic potential of mobile mucosity and touching interstitiality (cf. Joy 46). In other words, Irigaray's notion of embracing relationality features a decidedly Euro-de-centric potential; a potential to clarify that Mignolo's pluriversal "break with the monocultures of the mind" (2012: 247) needs to be conceived as a responsive engagement with other epistemological horizons — as relational pluriversality — instead of a re-instantiation of the Rule of the One through an indifferent dispersal into multiple dissociated sameness. Ultimately, combining Irigaray's relational philosophy with Mignolo's border gnosis and Waldenfels's concept of radical otherness helps to rid her thought of accusations brought against her regarding an apparent blindness concerning material circumstances and alleviates charges of her sidelining of other forms of difference. As the next section is going to illustrate, her notion of fluid essentiality in being-two turns into an even more helpful supplement for reading other-wise when pointing out how it interconnects notions of an-other reading, seeing, and touching.

Parler-Femme *and Thinking Other-wise*

To draw attention to this interconnection, an issue needs to be addressed which has, so far, only been carried along implicitly: how does Irigaray arrive at her non-phallic notion of woman if the Western tradition is masculine through and through? How is what she calls *parler-femme*—that is, speaking (as) woman—possible in a discourse which is inherently phallogocentric? Or, more precisely, how does she manage to re(dis)cover the repressed feminine potential in the phallic economy? The answer to these questions lies in Irigaray's notion of *mimétisme*—usually translated as "mimicry:" a wittily subversive strategy, as Whitford writes, that critically engages with male thought by making use of the location of woman as "'in exile', or 'unhoused' in male sexuality, male discourse, and male society" (1991: 150) in order "to dismantle [phallocraticism] from within the foundations of western metaphysics" (2008: 80). It is also through the notion of mimicry that conceiving of Irigaray's repressed femininity as a decidedly Euro-de-centric form of "poststructuralism"—or, as a subalternized mode of knowing in Mignolo's sense—can be further legitimized; especially through relating *mimétisme* to Gayatri Spivak's understanding of creative sabotage or ab-use. The latter even alludes to this affinity herself when, despite her reservations toward Irigaray's thought—as evinced, for instance, in her early article "French Feminism in an International Frame" (cf. 1981: 177f.)—Spivak writes: "I have spent half a lifetime learning to learn from what is diagnosed to be 'from below.' And I have understood that to be Luce Irigaray's insistence" (2008: x), too (when she is at her best, that is). Moreover, with its critique of the Cartesian "conquest of reason over embodiment" (Zakin 185) and its call for circumventing the subject/object split, Irigaray's thought also relates to Lyotard's stress on a mode of reading which considers the figural. In fact, Irigaray's mimicry will help connect the (in-)distinction of discourse/figure to the relationality of being-two—a move which will, as in the case of Mignolo's pluriversality, shed new light on both Irigaray's as well as Lyotard's thought, and forms a significant contribution to this book.

Irigaray's playful mimicry functions along similar lines as Spivak's ab-use of *ratio*nal Enlightenment's conception of the aesthetic to retrace hidden-away epistemological potentials. For Irigaray, the masculine systemic closure based on the Cartesian paradigm is nothing but a self-deluded ruse (cf. Canters and Jantzen 15); the harnessing of woman as a commodified container for the reproduction of sameness in the ordering principles of a phallocratic private sphere is never complete. Indeed, it is this very attempt of containment which introduces women into the phallic discursive economy as a decidedly subversive momentum that, consequently, always arises from the inside, "inasmuch as they are in a position external to the laws of exchange, even though they are included in them as 'commodities'" (Irigaray 1985b: 85): mimicry ab-usively operates from a position of internal exclusion. Thinking *from* this incendiary locus—and not a position of utter subservience or phallic exploitation—Irigaray insists women take on the ascribed feminine role voluntarily to relieve it of the chokehold of phallic epistemology by way of thwarting acts of playful repetition with a difference (cf. ibid. 76); a disabling impetus effectively turned into an enabling gesture (cf. Fermon 133). This is to say that via mimicry, women neither remain in the phallic system of representation by accepting static masculine notion of female passivity, nor by appropriating a hegemonic male concept of activity. Woman remains in-between. Irigaray's mimetic ab-use proceeds by "uncovering hidden meanings within [phallocentric] texts coupled with a simultaneous process of working towards a new way of thinking and of relating to each other" (Canters and Jantzen 47); by a creative sabotage which turns male discourse's strategy of fixation against itself and points toward a *haunting* female presence uncontainable in systemic closure (cf. Zakin 185)—all in an effort to dis-close non-hierarchal modes of relating other-wise.

Like Spivak's ab-use, Irigaray's mimicry does not use a vulgarly instrumentalized form of deconstruction that one-sidedly opposes phallocratic hegemony by only working toward the same privileges in inversion or toward dissociation and rejection: both goals remain complicit with the operating mechanism of the logic of sameness. Irigaray insists that "[t]he feminine is not called to carry out the task of constructing a world which is similar to man's: a violent, uncanny world, which exists through the domination of nature, of animals, of other humans" (2000: 72). That is, woman is not to access phenomena merely as a *rational cogito* based on the Cartesian separation of subject and object; this is also reflected in Irigaray's mimetic mode of reading traditional male-encoded texts: her attention to the "*ellipses* and *eclipses*," or "*blanks* in discourse," and texts' "*silent plasticity*" (1985a: 142) suggests a certain kind of non-objectifying treatment. As Athena Athanasiou and Elena Tzelepis put it, Irigaray's mimetic criticism does not reproduce phallic violence of appropriation and mastery: "It is not a cognitive commentary but rather a performative engagement" (2008b: 2) that responds to a text's sensual pathos so as to bring forth a reciprocal "philosophy that performatively resonates with the abject and fugitive other in Western discourse; a philosophy that affectively opens the possibility for the [non-phallic] discourse of the displaced other at the limits of intelligibility" (ibid. 3). Seemingly only mirroring male reasoning but, in fact, (en-)actively transforming it through this very process into a care-ful engagement with (the things of) the world, Irigaray's mimetic ab-use of the Western tradition does not strive for static one-sided distinctions, but relationality in being-two.

This process of transformative mirroring becomes most apparent in *Speculum*. There, in her influential reading of Plato's cave allegory, Irigaray illustrates how the distanced and objectifying gaze of male contemplation ultimately fails when it regards woman, or, perhaps more precisely: the evocation of the vaginal speculum serves to expose how instrumentalizing phallic modes of sensory perception cannot stop potentials of an-other mode of *vision* beginning to disrupt male systematicity from within. Due to the form of the female body, the speculum's mirror is not flat but curved; its gaze not distanced but *in-touch*. With its (ironically mimetic) adaption to women's corporeality, this device—although phallus-shaped—does not grant the straightforward contemplative vision of phallocratic semblance (cf. Jones 2011: 39). Contrary to its original purpose, it cannot function according to a logic of focused and centralized gazing but results in the distorting images of a concave mirror. As Philippa Berry explains, in Irigaray's thought, this curved mirror becomes a peculiar burning glass: mimicry overturns the speculum's dilating impetus into a deconstructive *touch* which opens the limited horizon of phallocentric reasoning, and—contrary to Western oculocentrism—delineates the obliquely dark *mater*-iality of (the other) woman not as lacking, but rather as an-other kind of positivity (cf. 234f.). Berry concludes: "through her [the other woman's] burning glass the subject-object division of seer and seen, masculine and feminine, spirit and matter, same and other, objective knowledge and personal experience is momentarily undone" (240). Through mimicry, Irigaray turns the violent visual abuse of phallogocentric epistemology into a transformative creative ab-use that outlines the possibility of seeing and touching other-wise.

Here, Irigaray's ideas can be tied to Lyotard's notion of figurality. According to Rachel Jones, it is both philosophers' (de-)central goal "to trace the way that our existence—as material, phenomenal beings—is rooted in our dependence on that which is radically other to ourselves" (2012: 141). And for both, this endeavor is tied to a re-vision of an occidental concept of (written) language as levelling representational tool. Through mimetic ab-use, Irigaray targets the inherent phallomorphic structure of the Western discursive apparatus and exposes the limiting determinism of its systemic logic of sameness (cf. Berg 54, 55); not, however, to do away with discourse

altogether, but rather to dis-close how it always already remains tied to
something it cannot statically fixate with its ordering principles: "The problem is that of a possible alterity [otherness] in masculine discourse—or in
relation to masculine discourse" (1985b: 140). This also goes for Lyotard's
work. In fact, he and Irigaray both conceive of radical otherness as an exteriority (from) within language. Furthermore, when Irigaray suggests that
speaking (as other) woman requires "going back through the dominant discourse" (1985b: 119), she directly mirrors Lyotard's assertion that "there is
simply no way to go to the other side of discourse" (2011: 7) but through
language again, albeit other-wise: a re-visionary process that, through paying a renewed attention to an affective *plasticity*, *thickness*, and *depth* of the
figure within discourse, "entails altering [othering] language itself" (Berg
55). In her controversial essay "When Our Lips Speak Together," Irigaray
herself reformulates this as follows: "Depth, for us, is not a chasm. . . . Our
depth is the thickness of our body, our all touching itself. Where top and
bottom, inside and outside, in front and behind, above and below are not
separated, remote, out of touch. Our all intermingled" (1985b: 213). Regarding radical otherness, where Lyotard stresses the figural, Irigaray, again,
invokes female corporeality.

This emphasis on female body parts has been read as an essentializing
tendency which reproduces phallic thought. It is important to point out here,
once again, that it is misleading to insist on a pre-discursive character of femininity or speaking (as) woman (cf. Lehtinen 49, 192). Linking Irigaray's *parler-
femme* to Lytard's conception of language between discourse and figure can
be of assistance to clarify this. It is certainly true that Irigaray provides ample
room for misunderstanding, for instance, when she writes that "we must go
back to a moment of prediscursive experience, recommence everything, all
the categories by which we understand things, the world, subject-object divi-
sions" (1993: 151). This, at first glance, seems to confirm the charges of essentialism. Nevertheless, the second part of the sentence (as her entire *oeuvre* in
general) suggests that discourse is not to be left behind altogether and that it
is a determining phallic systematicity that is to be overcome; a systematicity
where, as Irigaray writes elsewhere, "discourse would be for man that other
of nature" (1993: 113) and, based on this, in which "discourse still defends
its untouchable status" (ibid. 112). She does not want to invert the phallic
logic and elevate or erect a pre-discursive (feminine) materiality as the equal
counterweight to disembodied (male) rationality; neither does she want to
play out a sense of pre-discursive presence against semiotic meaning. As Ingram succinctly puts it, with her invocation of female corporeality—strongly
resonating with Lyotard's figurality—Irigaray seeks out "the possibilities for
thinking matter not prediscursively but prerepresentationally" (Ingram 2);

that is to say, she strives to re(dis)cover a "capacity to signify otherwise" (ibid. 69), namely "beyond the prevailing representative economy" (ibid. 4). In fact, Ingram herself explicitly establishes a relation between the work of Irigaray and Lyotard: "The figural operates precisely at the level of signification (even though Lyotard himself does not use the term) beyond or separate from representation" (20). She continues to explain that, like figurality, "[i]t is not that those material [female] bodies aren't subject to discourse; it is that they resist subjection through their failure to represent, and in doing so reveal the imperfection of these power/knowledge regimes themselves" (105) without, however, ever leaving a certain (dis-closing) form of discursivity behind altogether.

It becomes clear that Irigaray's femininity does not simply equal Lyotard's figurality—both (non)concepts defy such one-sidedness that only reproduces a logic of oppositional sameness. Mimetically ab-using her ascribed position of interior exclusion in phallic systematicity, woman maintains an epistemological attitude that considers the signifying force of the figural as a recursive excess arising from within discourse. Irigaray writes that, *parler-femme* "necessarily entails an *other* economy of meaning" (1985b: 131); an economy that does not operate along the subject/object axis or according to rules of discursive closure but instead in-volves within meaning excessive nearness and open proximity (cf. ibid. 134, 153); a speaking/writing which—emphasizing, for instance, verbal dynamics, relational prepositions, and deictic gestures (cf. 1996: 125)—circumvents the traditional schematics of predication. Irigaray's speaking (as) woman privileges expressive dia-logical exchange over mono-logical propositional declarations to infuse (written) language with a dis-solving fluidity: "[w]hen the copula no longer veils the abyssal burial of the other" (1993: 129), the fixating static "is" of Being transforms into a form of dynamic figural *presencing* that *(re-)embraces/(re-)induces* the phallic "sclerosis of discourse" (ibid. 135) *with/in* the moisture *between* ever-*touching* lips. This embrace neither constitutes a containing absorption nor a levelling digestion of otherness in a closed systemic horizon, but a form of playful border gnosis where rationality and sensuality/discourse and figure/man and woman appear as always already irreducibly entangled in non-oppositional being-two.

Irigaray's *parler-femme* does not work within the limits of the phallic representational economy. Critiques discarding her ludic invocation of the female body also (dis)miss that "the father's language camouflages and/or petrifies the mother's body, denying its claim to generative power" (Zakin 178), by subjecting it to bio-logistic discursive commodification whose specular regime identifies neatly separable and fixable (body) parts which then represent woman as the lacking *alter ego* of man. However, Irigaray does not regard language as an instrument of representation only, which excludes corporeality from its discursive scene. Her specific ab-use of imagery should not merely be seen as substituting phallic metaphors with vaginal ones. She writes that this imagery is "not susceptible to com-parison. To use such terms serves only to reiterate a movement begun long since, that is, the movement to speak of the 'other' in a language already systematized by/ for the same" (1985a: 139). More than just comparative substitution, to borrow from Mignolo's work, Irigaray begins "to articulate new politics of knowledge rather than new contents" (2012: 58), namely one in which the body is not objectified by the *cogito* into a static *res extensa*. Instead of a discursive containment of corporeality in representational closure, Irigaray's ironic mimicry, with its designation of labia, hymen, and vaginal opening, constitutes a performative *in-vocation* of the (female) body into language.[5] Ingram confirms this when she writes that speaking (as other) woman "is gestural, corporeal, proximate. It is performative, not constative. It cannot be captured or defined. It is in process. It is given" (xi). Consequently — to rephrase a previous insight — not constructed in phallic discursivity and its rigid essentialisms, but conceived as dynamic *presencing* through fluidity in being-two, the creative sabotage of *parler-femme* does not subject material-ity to cognition, but rather outlines an-other thinking where sensuality and rationality remain *in-touch* and always *figure* as double-bind.

Now it is possible to tie back the argument to Irigaray's critique of the central role and epistemic function of vision and touch within the occidental philosophical tradition concerning the question and treatment of otherness. Her "new *poetics*" (1993: 5) is primarily concerned with reconfiguring these established forms of relating to the things of the world. Irigaray's particular approach toward them has already been implied in the description of her mimetic ab-use of the vaginal speculum: she aims to develop modes of seeing and touching beyond the Cartesian paradigm which "requires a reconsider-ation of the split between body and thought" or, more precisely, it calls for a realization "that being has yet to be referred to in terms of body or flesh" (ibid. 86). Instead of deriving seeing and touching from the hierarchized split of cognition from corporeality, resulting in the conceptualizations of gaze and grasp, which penetrate and fixate otherness in place and rob it of its sting, Irigaray seeks to free sensual/sensory perception from its heavy *ra-tio*nal yoke; for her, re(dis)covering the repressed epistemological potentials of a sensuality doubly-bound with consciousness constitutes a significant step regarding a genuine engagement with the other in h/er otherness. In "How Can We Meet the Other," Irigaray herself expresses this as follows: "Meeting with the other demands memory and surprise, fidelity to a past and openness to a future, but also a participation of the body, of feelings and of mind. . . . Cooperation between the body, heart and mind is needed, and it requires an artistic process. The other cannot be entrusted only to a passive memory or only to a mental concern" (118). In Irigaray's philosophy, meeting with the other requires learning to respond to its affective—that is, touching—pathos. It calls for perceiving radically other-wise.

Throughout her entire *oeuvre*, Irigaray has time and again pointed out that rendering such an encounter with radical otherness possible in Western cultures "requires a change in our perception and conception of *space-time*" (1993: 7). In her reevaluation of vision and touch, she ties the success of this fundamental change first to a renewed attention to the (de-)centrality of the tactile. Irigaray even holds that "we have lost the sense of touch" (2000a: 100) due to the vulgarization of tactility into the mere fixation of the grasp which treats corporeal proximity with the distance of objectivizing aesthetic contemplation; therefore, it is necessary to "rediscover bliss, the wonder of attentive perception, the happiness of sonorous flesh" (ibid. 4), and to discard the notion of bare matter to be (mis-)handled at will. Instead of an appropriation by grasping, Irigaray consequently introduces what can be termed a *freedom in caressing* and elaborates: "The caress is an awakening to intersubjectivity, to a *touching between* us which is neither passive nor active; it is an awakening of gestures, of perceptions which are at the same time acts, intentions, emotions" (2000: 25; my emphasis); that is, a relational mode of touching which is responsive to the (bodily) pathos of the other (as other) and which always occurs in-between the non-hierarchical reciprocity of being-two. This free and released epistemic stance characteristic of the caress is what characterizes Luce Irigaray's account of perceptual modes in general. In her book *An Ethics of Sexual Difference*, she writes that "[t]o remain within perception means staying out in the *open*, always *attuned* to the outside, to the world. Senses always alert" (1993: 141; my emphases). Speaking with Waldenfels's philosophy, Irigaray holds that perception itself must undergo a becoming other-wise, namely from phallic discursive containment to the relational releasement of the caress. For her, it is possible through such an ab-usive process—which in Mignolo's terms can be called a (re-)development of sense-sensitivity—to dis-solve the patriarchal discursive stasis and *to get in-touch* with radical otherness *presencing* beyond projection and/or preconception.

However, how does Irigaray's preoccupation with the caress fit in with a project that takes its point of departure from Lyotard's assertion that textuality "possesses an inherent thickness, or rather a difference, which is not to be read, but rather seen" (2011: 3)? The answer again is found within Irigaray's creative sabotage of the speculum, for at its curved mirror touch and vision coincide. In fact, beginning with her revised sense of touch, she ultimately

ab-uses the *rational* connection between seeing and touching in the forms
of gaze and grasp to point toward a repressed deeper connection between
the sensory and the sensual. In stark contrast to the dictates of Western centralized vision, the view granted by the phallic instrument, ironically, is "[a]
look that is too close to make use of a certain perspective, of discrimination,
distancing, or mastery"; *by always touching the (female) body*, it provides
"a carnal look" (1993: 153) that has the potential to tie the disembodied
cogito back to its disavowed corporeal prerequisites: sense-sensitized openness toward the touch of the other results in "a new way of looking" (Ziarek
2007: 65) which also "enables a revision of the seeing/knowing doublet
fundamental to the historical development of Western/European cultures"
(ibid. 67). Thinking sensory/sensual perception beyond the subject/object
split, Irigaray renders vision as no longer instrumentalizable by *rational* consciousness in the form of a mere data bearer for objectifying intellection (cf.
Vasseleu 14, Olkowski 42). In fact, where seeing and touching realign once
more in fluid bodily proximity, phallocratic definitions of gaze and grasp
begin to falter as the eye, reminded of its corporeality (that is, re-bodied), no
longer functions as a window to a disembodied soul, and *ratio*nality starts
to relinquish its dis-sociating position of epistemic superiority. *By always respecting the other*, Irigaray's carnal look turns into a type of sense-sensitized
border gnosis which (re-)translates the corporeal reciprocity of the caress
into the realm of visuality, and thereby outlines a dichotomous locus of
in-between-ness. As such, the (ab-used) vaginal speculum's curved "vision
is a mode of the tactile" (1993: 175); a vision that is not characterized by
the levelling flatness of (s)emblematic discourse, but rather by a "carnal at-
tentiveness" (1996: 124) to the affective thickness, depth, and volume of
ever-ungraspable figural otherness. It becomes obvious that with its critique
of the contemplative centralizing gaze and its focus on curvature and varie-
ties of plasticity, Irigaray's carnal vision is inherently relatable to Lyotard's
own re-vision of Western modes of gazing that has been described in the
part on Taylor and Walters. Indeed, in light of mimetic ab-use, the tactile
quality implied by the term "grazing," which Lyotard uses to clarify his particular notion of seeing, can be thought as in-volving the sensuality of the
caress: seeing texts' difference beyond *rational* projection means remaining
in-touch with otherness.

   To conclude this section, it is worth emphasizing again that "such a touching and moving can also happen through words and writing" (198), as Lehtinen writes. In Irigaray's philosophy, language and corporeality are always
already connected; and their separation is a mere phallogocentric fallacy:
insisting on the "crossing between body and word"—or, ab-using Christian
doctrine, "the word being flesh and the flesh word" (2000: 12)—Irigaray

asserts that one needs to "give up the idea that a true word can be foreign to our bodies" (ibid. 106). Discourse, too, is always susceptible to the ca-ress's sensuality. Like Lyotard's notion of the figural, it manifests itself in the deictic qualities of language. Irigaray explains that "[t]he caress is a gesture-word which goes beyond the horizon or the distance of intimacy with the self" and, therefore, *figures* as "a gift of intention and of word addressed to the concrete presence of the other" (ibid. 26); more precisely, a fluid *pres-encing* in being-two which remains irreducible to static essentialism and/or discursive fixity. Ultimately, Irigaray's thinking calls for an "endless liv-ing engagement with the living text" (Canters and Jantzen 27)—a type of "carnal knowing" (Joy 52)—which maintains an openness for the figural dis-closure of the patriarchal representational order; a released openness stemming from the impetus of playful mimicry, with the potential also to re(dis)cover (repressed) alternative modes of relating to other forms of dif-ference, as well as the material circumstances to which these are bound, sur-passing the horizon of sexual difference. The next chapter will now probe this potential with Theresa Hak Kyung Cha's *Dictée*.

MOVING THE SPIRIT-HEART

CANTERS AND JANTZEN EXPLAIN that, for Irigaray, "[a]ccording to her own theory it is crucially important that women develop engaged communication amongst themselves"; they continue that, at the same time, she herself, however, does not seem to heed this requirement: "yet in her writings the voices of women are effectively silenced, and there is as little evidence that Irigaray is listening to them as there is that Freud or Lacan or Heidegger took women's voices seriously" (127). Canters and Jantzen hold that Irigaray can, therefore, be accused of reproducing the very tradition that has marginalized or repressed female thinkers since its beginnings (cf. 128). This is certainly a valid critique. However, what if one takes Irigaray's call for relationality in being-two seriously also concerning her own writings? Have not Canters and Jantzen precisely done what Irigaray has always hoped for, namely, as women, engaged with her and her thought in a fecund critical conversation, and, thereby, enacted such a relationality? Luce Irigaray is not one; also her thought only ever-unfolds between two. This part—as well as the project at hand as a (w)hole—seeks to re-spect this dia-logic alignment. Consequently, as this analysis transitions to its second chapter, one should keep in mind that this does not simply imply a moving from one closed unity to the next according to the phallic logic of the one-plus-one-(plus- . . .). This short *interstitial passage* is supposed to indicate that both chapters belong irreducibly to each other and are rather to be seen as an ongoing conversation between Irigaray's thought and Cha's art, re-spectively engaging with each other in a Euro-de-centric *poiētic* encounter of being-two.

Shamanistic Invocation

Dictée—already the title of Theresa Cha's work alludes to the central theme around which the text revolves: the uses and abuses of language.

More precisely, Cha renegotiates the relationship of employing language as a colonialist tool of paternalistic indoctrination on the one hand and drawing on language as a *poiētic* means of resisting such patronization on the other. This section investigates the specific modality of this negotiation as an-other instance of mimetic ab-use. On the one hand, as Serena Fusco explains, "Cha presents the forceful removal of Korean language during Japanese colonial rule in Korea" that, in extension, "has its counterpart in the forceful neglect of one's mother tongue as a consequence of immigration to the United States" (184): the text undeniably points out how imperialistic authority effects the (ex)termination or loss of the (m)other's language. On the other hand, however, *Dictée* neither indulges in tragic victimry and simply accepts such bereavement as entirely successful nor gives in to obtrusive hegemony altogether. In the spirit of Mignolo, Naoki Sakai stresses the text's decolonial quality. She argues that "it feigns to speak the readers' language" (26), but simultaneously alters it—not least through repeated infusions with other languages—to dis-close "English as an element for heterogeneity where a nation and a language do not correspond to each other at all" (20). *Dictée* re(dis)covers excessive epistemic potentials stemming from within and still uncontainable by the framework of colonialist systematicity itself and, thereby, challenges phallogocentric notions of discursivity.

Cha's literary engagement with discursive coercion becomes apparent from the beginning of the text: the first untitled section starts with two dictations in the colonial and/or imperial languages French and English: "Aller à la ligne C'était le premier joir point /Elle venait de loin point ce soir au diner virgule / les familles demanderaient virule ouvre les guil-/lemets Ça c'est bien passé le premier jour point / d'interrogation ferme les guillemets . . . Open paragraph It was the first day period / She had come from a far period tonight at dinner / comma the families would ask comma open / quotation marks How was the first day interroga-/tion mark close quotation marks" (1). Then, it introduces a *diseuse*, a(n unidentified) female speaker, who tries to speak but at first only manages to produce "[b]ared noise, groan, bits torn from words" (3). Finally, the passage recounts her (uneasy) participation in the Catholic sacrament of the Eucharist—all interspersed with several more grammar and translation exercises (cf. 8f.; 14f.). The indoctrinating implications inherent in this section have already been discussed extensively in the scholarship surrounding the text. For Anne Cheng, as for many others, "[t]he language lesson . . . denotes a colonizing and disciplinary act" (1998: 126). These scholars focus on how *Dictée* draws attention to discursive mechanisms, rules, and regulations for submitting otherness to the epistemological horizon of occidental knowledge and for thereby maintaining and perpetuating the supremacy of Western reason (cf. Kang 2002: 220ff.; Duncan 162). Reminiscent of Irigaray's notion of male sameness, Lowe has referred to the repeated instances of colonialist instruction as "a process by which all students are iterated and abstracted as uniform"; a violent process which the *diseuse* resists due to her failure to imitate: she remains "unfaithful to the original" (1994: 39). Similar arguments have also been made regarding the role of Catholicism. Stella Oh argues that "Cha uses Catholicism to represent the oppressive powers of political, cultural, and religious colonization" (9) founded upon the discursive hegemony of Christianity; powers to which *Dictée* opposes an "antiphonal answer" (11): "By replacing the male-centered Trinity with her own trinity composed of Yu Guan Soon, Joan of Arc, and Saint Thérèse of Lisieux, Cha deliberately breaks down the patriarchal relationships that privilege male authority and power" (7). For all these critics, the text's way of dealing with coercion through language is to construct a counter-discourse to patriarchal efforts of ideological interpellation.

Scholars have tended to interpret *Dictée*'s subversive strategy as conditioned by the impact of postcolonial trauma and ensuing feelings of insecurity, inadequacy, and incapability. Karyn Ball, for instance, reads the text's particular form—with its generally nonlinear structure, its use of nonstandard or pidginized English, frequent spelling mistakes, and fragmentary style—as reflective of "an immigrant's assimilation into another culture as an expropriation and obsolescence of a national imagery, as a perpetual anxiety feeding an unsure linguistic competence" (162). For her, and for other interpreters, a sentiment of loss prevails throughout *Dictée*; it is seen as representing a protracted repetition-compulsion: its narrative incoherence, a-chronological disorder, and general resistance to straightforward categorization testify to the inassimilable and unspeakable effects of traumatic experience(s) (cf. Cho 42). Further stressing a sense of lack and/or deficiency, Ball describes the *diseuse*'s articulatory attempts as "clumsy repetitions of the catechism" (176); and—more drastically still—Stephen Joyce regards her speech as "scurrying anxiously behind broken words and grammar, showing glimpses now and then but never daring to speak openly" (197). According to these interpretations, *Dictée*'s counter-discursive unmasking of occidental colonization always remains bound to notions of absence, dispossession, and victimization.

Cha's text certainly contains such a quality. Nevertheless, exclusively concentrating on notions of coercion, lack, and negativity is reductive and misses fundamental potentialities of *Dictée*'s strategy. Strictly speaking, it is even slightly misleading to conceive of the text merely as counter-discursive, for it does not simply remain within or reproduce the logic of occidental domination in inversion. The following analysis will side with other scholars who have also stressed this point. It is important to insist with Sakai on the text's cunning feint concerning colonizing indoctrination and regard

Dictée as an instance of "desistance rather than oppositional resistance" (37). Sakai has argued that critics of the text often disregard that the processes of instruction in *Dictée* fail to fully establish colonial hegemony; they are unable to level the *diseuse*'s otherness altogether through terminating assimilation (cf. 35). Instead, Sakai continues, "*Dictée*, skillfully and aggressively, mimicks [*sic*] the learning of foreign languages" (36); more than just being unfaithful to the original, the artwork creatively sabotages patriarchal epistemic instruments for its own *poiētic* purposes. *Dictée*'s desisting resistance does not lie in an erroneous repetition of any supposed original, for the text does not recognize such an originality of occidental patronization in the first place. It exhibits, as Sue-Im Lee writes, "a deliberate policy of incorrect and inadequate usage" (2002: 244) only if conceived from within the confines of discursive systematicity. Eric Hayot has pointed out that employing the term "failure" to account for *Dictée*'s ab-use of colonial languages remains stuck in a thought that leaves instrumental notions of discourse unchallenged; a type of thinking which has succumbed to romanticized notions of unchanging originality and/or illusions of discourse's closure (cf. 615, 633). Evocative again of Kristeva's central question regarding the negative, Elizabeth Berila aptly gets to the point: she writes that "what 'breaks' conventional form depends on how conventional form itself is defined" (32). *Dictée*, however, does not heed such definitions or conventions or regard them as valid and, therefore, does not simply oppose them. When one reads Cha's text solely through a counter-discursive matrix characterized by loss or mourning, one misses how it engages with colonizing patriarchal coercion radically other-wise, namely by drawing on epistemological horizons exceeding the limitations of the Western *ratio*.

Instead of succumbing to colonialist attempts of assimilating indoctrination, the *diseuse* in the first section, in fact, "mimicks [*sic*] the speaking" (Cha 3) of the imperialist intruders to initiate an emancipatory process or "a process of resifting and reaccentuating" (113), as Shelley Wong has called it. More precisely, her mimicry is not an obedient reproduction but an ab-usive transformation by way of in-fusion with non-Western knowledge. Several scholars have noted that—similar to Walters's novel *Ghost Singer*—*Dictée* entertains notions of the holiness or sacredness of language that differ radically from Western instrumentalist conceptions. Michael Stephens, for example, asserts that "it's simple, jagged pattern, the short sentences, the steady accumulation of words and details and emotions" turn the text into "a chant" which regards "[s]peech as mystical utterance" (199): colonialist lessons are re-cast into ritualistic incantations of deliverance (cf. Park 213; Martin 191, 198f.); the *diseuse* appears as "a *moodong* (a shaman)"

(Stephens 210)—a role reserved exclusively for women in traditional Korean culture (cf. Kim 1994: 26). The en-chanting quality of the text becomes particularly evident in numerous italicized paragraphs interrupting the language exercises; paragraphs which grant a view behind the feint into the ab-usive motivation of her learning: "*She would take on their punctuation. She waits to service this. Theirs. Punctuation. She would become, herself, demarcations. Absorb it. Spill it. Seize upon the punctuation. Last air. Give her. Her. The relay. Voice. Assign. Hand it. Deliver it. Deliver*" (Cha 4). By way of her "sibylline and shamanistic labor" (Park 215), the *diseuse* inculcates the static rigidity of *rati*onal discourse with fluid dynamic: "*Moisture. Begin to flood her. Dissolving her. Slow, slowed to deliberation. Slow and thick.*" (Cha 5). Lessons that are supposed to effectuate a levelling integration into the imperialist culture and epistemology of occidental patriarchy, through shamanistic sabotage, become an enabling gesture for the disruption of the colonial project.

These shamanistic elements shed an entirely different light on the function of Catholic sacramentality in *Dictée*. Instead of opposing religious indoctrination—as Oh has it—the text also ab-uses the Christian ritualistic formulas to re(dis)cover and tease out forgotten and/or sidelined epistemic potentials (from) within the Western tradition itself. The *diseuse* participates in catechistic recitals to be able "[t]*o conspire in God's Tongue*" (Cha 17) and to enhance it with radical otherness; a strategy which Lowe refers to as an "eloquent adulteration of the catechism" (1994: 58). Although insisting on the validity of "strategic . . . attacks on the prevailing form of domination in terms of that domination," Lowe draws even closer to this chapter's line of argument when she asserts that Cha's art-work brings about a "reappropriation of 'other' artifices" and, therefore, that "it may also be interventions from standpoints of alterity [otherness] to the structure in dominance which enable the displacement of that dominance" (ibid. 57). *Dictée* operates decidedly other-wise: instead of constructing a counter-discursive oppositionality, it weaves Christian elements into its shamanistic incantation in a syncretistic manner without fearing the contamination of originality. An important example of this is the role of the novena or the number nine as a structuring principle of the book: it indicates both a ritualized form of Christian devotion as well as a mystical number in Korean shamanism (cf. Stephens 197). Evan Chambers rejects simplistic attestations of a solely colonizing character of Catholic theology within the text, too. He argues that it "has spiritual elements that need to be viewed outside of those structures" (142). This pertains especially to notions of the subject, language, and its relation to corporeality. "*To scribe to make hear the words, to make sound the words, the words, the words made flesh*" (Cha 18), the *diseuse* utters and, thereby, draws attention to a non-Cartesian worldview inherent within the biblical foundation of the Eucharist in the gospel of John of Patmos. Stephen-Paul Martin confirms that "[t]he tradition that Cha's rhythms abolish is the masculine tradition of abstract eviscerated thinking" (192): within the patriarchal tradition that has erected its epistemic hegemony on the binary oppositions of mind and body—rationality and sensuality—*Dictée* re(dis)covers a mode of relating to phenomena where both are viewed as always already irreducibly intertwined.[1]

This perspective alleviates another aspect that contributes to the impression of the *diseuse*'s passivity regarding the colonizing efforts and even proves it to be a fundamental element of her ab-use. When "[s]he allows others. In place of her. Admits others to make full. Make swarm. All barren cavities to make swollen. The others each occupying her" (Cha 3) and "allows herself caught in their threading, anonymously in their thick motion in the weight of their utterance" (4), then this does not constitute a disempowering submission or increased loss of agency, as Patti Duncan would have it (cf. 145). Such a reading, once again, remains within the confines of a patriarchal discursivity where the intrusion of otherness is always already seen as a threat to phallocentric order and notions of homogeneous subjectivity.[2] The question arises who these others are: is it the colonizing intruders or maybe someone else besides? The answer is again connected to the notion of ab-use. The occupation by others in the art-work is certainly ambivalent. On the one hand, it indubitably testifies to the negative effects of colonization; on the other, however, it simultaneously alludes to different potentials: the *diseuse* invites/invokes *figures* from inside the Western tradition who at the same time remain in a relation of excess to patriarchal principles, such as the Greek poet Sappho, the Christian mystic Thérèse of Lisieux, Joan of Arc, as well as Demeter and Persephone—that is, someone else inside. She relates these to other *figures* from without occidental culture who similarly defied patriarchal power—as, for instance, the Korean freedom fighter Yu Guan Soon and Cha's mother Hyung Soon Oh—effectively integrates their resistance into the patriarchal Western tradition, and outlines a transnational dimension that questions the very binary logic of inside/outside.[3] The ambiguity of the invitations is intentional—disabling impetus once more turns into enabling gesture: "She relays the others. Recitation. Evocation. Offering. Provocation. The begging. Before her. Before them" (Cha 4). Instead of forming a passive receptacle for paternal in-semination, she initiates an ab-usively creative dis-seminating fecundity through the "permission and acknowledgement of [excessive] difference(s) within her" (Kang 1994: 78); or, as Mayumo Inoue phrases it: the speaker "welcome[s] numerous *ghosts of history* and inaugurate[s] their recipients, both of whom constantly undergo transformations and, therefore, resist[s] all forms of capillary subjectivation" (64f.; my emphasis). As a *moodong*—for whom "[s]peaking is not only using sounds to communicate with" but also constitutes "the act of being possessed by and becoming of, at least momentarily, transformed into the mystical other" (Stein 119)—the *diseuse* functions as a medium for sidelined political epistemological potentialities beyond Western discursive closure.

That the speaker's voice is not entirely her own, therefore, also does not only indicate a colonialist silencing of the other's language. While the text certainly, to some extent, bemoans a loss of a mother tongue, its mourning does not adhere to phallogocentric notions of discourse. Lowe has pointed out that *Dictée* does not remain stuck in the search for an ideal language prior to colonial intrusions, as it simply does not entertain such romanticized notions of originality (cf. Kang 1994: 85); instead, Lowe asserts, the speaker ab-uses the imperial languages "to forge a new composite voice, a discontinuous voice" in order to "construct an alternative, though fragmented and indirect, relationship of the subject to that 'first language'" (1994: 48f.)—an invaluable insight.[4] Nevertheless, as her insistence on fragmentation makes clear, Lowe, too, reads the *diseuse*'s speech only from a counter-discursive perspective. However, and contrary also to Elaine Kim's reading, the text does not simply diametrically oppose notions of phallic wholeness—which are characteristic both of Korean as well as American culture—with a sense of female fragmentation (cf. 1994: 5, 9). What appears as fractured, dissonant, and cacophonous noise from the perspective of the phallic Rule of the One, in fact, composes a de-colonial multivocity comprised of a transnational choir of (ghostly) women. This is to say that *Dictée*'s shamanistic language of mourning functions other-wise. It is related to the Korean concept of *han*, which Jennifer Cho describes as an "irreducible, intergenerational feeling of communal grief" (39), albeit one that does not remain steeped in defeatism: according to her, this feeling contains a positively subversive potential.[5] In coining the neologism "mel-*han*-choly"—by which she means "a cultural and racialized permutation of melancholy"—Cho outlines a force that "can burst open seemingly closed historical discourses of the US from the inside" (40). Instead of grieving over an irretrievable past, the en-*han*-ced language of *Dictée*'s shamanistic in-vocation brings forth a spectral *presencing* of the deceased. In other words, the search for the mother tongue in Cha's art-work is not a desperate looking for a forgotten national language, but the continuous re(dis)covery of a language that does not operate according to the phallocratic order: "The mother tongue is amorphous" (Sakai 21) and not rigidly fixable; the mother tongue, in *Dictée*, is a polyphonic and communal speaking which remains ever related to radical otherness beyond the spatio-temporal systematicity of Cartesian reason.

The text's fragmentary and nonlinear style surely attests to the impact of colonization, but it does so in a counterintuitive manner: it points toward a possibility of taking into account forms of subalternized thought which "require that we step beyond the body of knowledge we in the West rely on and often hierarchize as 'the best'" (Kim 1994: 22). Within the art-work, this especially pertains to the supposedly inferior status of pidginized language and the stereotypical notions of Asian (American) identity usually tied to it in Western contexts (cf. Lee 2002: 236). Instead of focusing on its systemic linguistic deficiencies, Elana Spandri invokes Mary Louise Pratt's take on the pidgin to highlight the qualities of contact, contaminating mutuality, and intersectional negotiation that also characterize colonial encounters or transactions (cf. 20). In *Dictée*'s shamanistic sabotage, this aspect of contact takes on a particularly radical quality. Hyo Kim writes that its "linguistic violations are attempts to frame embodied experiences that would otherwise be foreclosed, if not elided altogether, within the discursive limits of Standard English" (2013: 132). Already the text's epigraph—which invokes a quotation attributed to the Greek poet Sappho—attests to this: "May I write words more naked than flesh, / stronger than bone, more resilient than / sinew, sensitive than nerve" (n.pag).[6] This prepended dictum contains a pretense concerning *Dictée*'s language that differs significantly from the repeated ascriptions of deficiency: through its simultaneous renegotiation of the division between speech and the body, and its in-vocation of a possible communion with spectral otherness described above, the text's ritualistic incantation transforms the pidgin elements into a shamanistic *con-tact* language which challenges the fundamental categories of modern Western reason; a language that "puts to the test the very epistemological *conditions of enunciation* at the basis of the narrative and narrated material of the text" (Fusco 181f.). An oppositional criticism that remains in the logic of phallic discursivity, however, falls short of this radical re-vision of the epistemological foundations of Western thought.

The uneasiness with which scholars have attempted to categorize the art-work testifies to this epistemological re-vision. Genre classifications of the text range from autobiography, memoir, and documentary to novel, prose-poem, and epic, as well as numerous combinations of these types. Next to the more "literary" aspects, the text also includes several "non-fictional" elements, such as letters, newspaper excerpts, and passages from historiographical works from different cultural contexts (cf. Kim 2008: 171f.). *Dictée*'s specific style, therefore, resists easy subsuming under established Western genres. Its multilingual dimension contributes to this resistance: the text integrates both English and French, as well as instances of Korean, Chinese, ancient Greek, and Latin into its ritualistic formula. Furthermore, and just as importantly, it draws on multiple medial forms, such as reproductions of paintings, photography, calligraphy, facsimiles; other handwritten notes, maps, diagrams; and contains various references to cinematography. Due to its stylistic peculiarity, counter-discursive critiques render Cha's art-work as a suture of diverse fragments in an intertextual collage, inter-medial montage, or inter-cultural bricolage which strategically transcends genre boundaries and alludes to the limits of representation (cf. Eileraas 89; McDaniel 81; Sakai 25, 37): "a complex discontinuous weave" with "an aesthetic of fragmented recitation and episodic non-identity" (Lowe 1994: 37). These are certainly accurate descriptions; but the text does more than that. In fact, *Dictée*'s kaleidoscopic integration of diversified modes of expression aptly operationalizes what Lyotard means when he asserts that texts are "not [only] to be read, but rather seen" (2011: 3). Fusco underlines this. She writes: "*Dictée* questions both the literary status of a text and, in a wider sense, the linguistic (or discursive) one" (178); that is, its shamanistic in-vocation does not stop at the discursive limits of (Western) phallic colonialist binarism or patronizing systemic fixation, but rather points toward the possibility of excessive figurality.

The different medial elements are a significant aspect of *Dictée*'s textual ritual. They contribute to the *moodong*'s incantation as a spectral amalgamation of word, image, and body. In contrast to the argumentation of existing scholarship, it is, therefore, not enough to describe the text's montage or collage as constituting a self-representational archive containing different forms of evidence which bear witness to the postcolonial trauma of Korea (cf. McDaniel 72; Cheng 1998: 121). *Dictée* does not function according to occidental notions of the archive. As Laura Kang argues, the art-work brings forth alternative modes or methods for relating to the past which challenge the occidental historiographical regime where the voices of the other are silenced or erased altogether (cf. 1994: 80f.). According to Wayne Stein, the text's in-vocation transcends *ratio*nal conceptions of spatiality and temporality and has a very specific character: "*Dictee* is no ordinary book; instead, it can be viewed as an elaborate Korean ritual of exorcisms, a 'kut'" (118), that remains attentive to the spectral *presencing* of the past. As a *kut*, Cha's art-work does not reduce the integrated elements' figural depth or plasticity in discursive closure (cf. Park 226). Rather, it engages with them in a shamanistic "textual performance" (Sakai 39). An important example of this is the *hangul* (Korean script) inscription—a photograph of an anonymous wall-carving—functioning as *Dictée*'s frontispiece. According to Elaine Kim, it reads "mother, I miss you, I'm hungry, I want to go home" (cf. 1994: 10);[7] it can be seen as the initiation of the text's ritual and constitutes the magic formula around which the art-work's conjuration unfolds. Although only appearing once at the beginning, it characterizes *Dictée* in its entirety: integrated into the shamanistic process—and consequently more than only indicating lack, absence, and desperation—the Korean phrase and its incentive remains as "a ghostly underground presence" (Park 227) throughout the book's re(dis)covering performance. As one example of the text's numerous medial elements, the integration of the frontispiece into the ritual suggests that, instead of storing dead archival matter testifying to an irrevocable past, *Dictée* draws on its montaged components—in Taylor's terminology—as a live textual repertoire to in-voke *other* modes of relating to historical material circumstances.

As a spectral shamanistic repertoire, Cha's art-work does not adhere to Western notions of temporality: "*Let the one who is diseuse . . . Let her break open the spell cast upon time upon time again and again*" (Cha 123). The text's nonlinearity, again, only appears as defective when thinking from inside a closed framework of archival historiography. In contrast, Trinh Minh-ha writes, defending *Dictée*'s treatment of the past, "storylines heavily (if not exclusively) based on chronology and on external retrievable facts (the one privileged path to the gate of Approval) prove to be limiting and at times, despairingly inadequate" (109): working according to the phallic logic of crude Cartesianism, namely by treating all phenomena as *res extensa* to be handled at will, such histories entail a reduction of corporeality's generative potential and relevance to the process of remembering the past within its representational order; the same order that levels otherness to a construct of alterity and brackets women's contribution from its epistemological system. "In its rethinking of representation," Wong explains, "*Dictée* takes issue . . . with the idea of a universal history (such as that which necessarily grounds a concept of the representative man)" (105); it takes issue with a teleology based on the Christian imagination of the coming kingdom of a Father-God. The art-work challenges a fundamentally phallogocentric concepts of history and/or temporality—which also Kun Jong Lee confirms by asserting that "Cha's nonlinear narrative of modern Korean history ultimately reflects her critique of patriarchy in Korean historiography" (2006: 84)—as a form of relating to the past that disregards voices of others in its hegemonic narratives. Reformulating Wong's insights, one can say that the text infuses into the rigidity of "monumentalist historicism" (Wong 121) the corporeal dynamism of the (other) women in the form of "female as surplus" or fluidity in "excess of what was presumed in the original": the text embraces "[t]he presence of a surplus or excess [which] necessarily skews the operation of representation" (122) from inside. *Dictée*'s multi-medial ritual dis-closes potentials that the phallocratic archive can never fully contain.

Ultimately, the radical shamanistic re-vision of Western epistemology in Cha's *Dictée* is a fundamentally performative one which ab-usively

articulates and enacts—within its *poiētic* process of in-vocational re(dis)
covery—a specifically feminine locus of enunciation; a female position
which constitutes a de-colonial manifestation of what Irigaray calls *parler-
femme*. It is as such that, in Juliana Spahr's words, the art-work "demonstrates how women and minorities have more options than either evasion
through silence or compromise through appropriated discourse" (39). In
line with Irigaray's mimetic challenge to occidental phallocratic hegemony,
Spahr elaborates, *Dictée* engages in an "active, creative response that generates meanings and does not merely connect preexisting references" (29). To
clarify how Cha's text achieves this, the next section will now examine in
more detail the specific modality of *Dictée*'s enunciative position of speaking (as other) woman concerning its ab-usive engagement with phallic system and will draw attention to the far-reaching ethico-political implications
this entails.[8]

Lips in Dia-Logue

How to describe the subject position enunciated in *Dictée*? This question
has been at the center of the critical commentaries surrounding the oblique
text. Particularly readings that emphasize an autobiographical element
in the art-work have struggled to identify a single subjectivity—that is,
Cha's subjectivity—guiding the seemingly fragmented narration. The often-
quoted beginning sentences of Elaine Kim's influential essay "Poised on the
In-Between" bespeaks this tendency and the befuddlement that goes with it
as expectations are not met: "The first time I glanced at *Dictée*, I was put off
by the book. I thought that Theresa Cha was talking not to me but rather to
someone so remote from myself that I could not recognize 'him'" (1994: 3).
The autobiographical lens automatically assumes a congruence between
narrator and author or, at least, the existence of a unitary "I" who wishes
to communicate h/er life story. Kristina Chew also writes along these lines
and believes that *Dictée* enacts a "highly personal voice" or, more precisely,
"a uniquely Asian American voice" (62). What, however, if the very preconceived assumptions causing these interpretive attempts are themselves
fundamentally misguided and the art-work's subjectivity functions radically
other-wise? Sue Kim asserts, "[n]owhere in the novel are we told that the
'narrator' is named Theresa or that there is even a singular narrator" (2008:
164). The *moodong*'s shamanistic in-vocation of others suggests something
entirely different: within the textual ritual, rigid boundaries between individuals do not exist. Therefore, the text does not present a single voice at
all—neither unitary, nor discontinuous, nor fragmented. Instead, as already
implied above, by "always channeling others" (Park 218), the *diseuse* enacts

a peculiar "communal voice" (Kim 2008: 166). Through the creative sabotage of the Christian Eucharistic communion of spirit and flesh, *Dictée*
brings forth a locus of enunciation which—although stemming from within
the occidental tradition—does not fit the patriarchal notions of an ideal and
homogeneous subjectivity: the *diseuse*'s *auto*(-biography) *is not one* but a
constant communal touching upon others.

This sense of mystical communality determines the multivocity of the
art-work which, consequently, is irreducible to counter-discursive notions
of fractured subjectivity or dissociating plurality. It is certainly correct to
note that *Dictée*'s sabotage of patriarchal thought begins with ab-using the
very term "*diseuse*," which usually—in its phallic inflection—denotes "a
woman who is skilled in speech and who performs *monologues*," being
"spotlighted as a sole speaker" (June 36; my emphasis); as Trinh Minh-ha
asserts: "she is many" (107). Nevertheless, the speaker(s) neither challenge(s)
the patriarchal concept of subjectivity merely by way of insisting on internal heterogeneity—reflected by the polysemy of "*diseuse*," meaning at once
"fortune teller, seer, speaker, and scribe" (Duncan 159)—which implicitly
still holds on to the idea of a single subject, albeit in opposition; nor does
the in-vocation of other women simply constitute the multiplication of the
masculine lyric "I" according to the logic of one-plus-one-plus-one which
likewise reproduces the phallic economy, namely by constructing completely
exchangeable entities: it is simply insufficient to describe the art-work as
merely "a collage of many authors" (Kang 1994: 93). Elaine Kim, too, eventually observes that "[t]here are indeed multiple subjectivities in *Dictée*, but
the text challenges theories of the self that would ignore the cultural, racial,
and global *relations from which a writer speaks*" (1994: 22; my emphasis).
That is, *Dictée*'s shamanistic sabotage recovers the term "*diseuse*" from the
patriarchal Rule of the One and its representational regime to outline a forgotten feminine mode of speaking where multivocity does not mean a form
of happily in-different pluralism.

Instead of such indifference, the narrative modality of the art-work is
characterized by pluriversal border gnosis. This means that from the ritualistic perspective, when the text evokes the "Tertium Quid neither one thing
nor the other" (Cha 20), this is not to simply designate "a hybrid, nuanced,
'unfaithful' voice" (Lowe 1994: 47) which once again only "articulates a
voice in opposition" (38). It is correct that the *diseuse*(s) do(es) not adhere
to one national or linguistic representational regime, but this does not indicate a sense of non-belonging: it questions the very meaning of belonging
as defined by patriarchal systematicity; a phallic systemic logic in which
belonging entails a levelling of otherness "that seeks to remake its subjects
in the image of the One, the same, or the *propre*"(Eileraas 108).[9] The evoked

plurality of the *tertium* is irreducible to this economy of semblance. This means that it does not represent just another systemic option—another *one*. As Sue Kim writes, "the aesthetics of the text reject the representational logic of multiculturalism" (2008: 168) where the nation-state remains the guiding framework of identification—even if by way of negation. Instead, *Dictée*'s shamanistic in-vocation (per-)forms a dichotomous locus of enunciation: the *moodong* is "[s]peaking from the interstices, *She* inhabits a borderland, a space situated at the borders of the text, the borders within the text and between the text and the 'real' world" (Fusco 194). That the text does not entertain the notion of a one-plus-one-plus-one plurality becomes particularly apparent in statements such as the following: "Nation against nation multiplied nations against nations against themselves. Own. Repels her rejects her expels her from *her* own. Her own is, in, of, through, all others, *hers*" (Cha 88). The *diseuse*'s belonging, *her* own, is not defined by a *propre* that is dictated by the Law of the Father: in, of, and through others, hers is a decidedly *relational* belonging that always remains open for the (spectral) *presencing* of radical (and excessive) otherness (from) within.

Consequently, speaking *with* Irigaray, the subject position (en-)actively unfolded within the art-work of *Dictée* can be characterized as a de-colonial form of being-two. "As a self-aware feminist and ethnic text, *Dictée* breaks with the Western, male-centered tradition of self-representation" (Fusco 180); a tradition that positions at its phallogocentric core the notion of an ideal homogeneous subjectivity. In Cha's text, however, the subject is never one: instead, "*figuring* identity as *both* internally fractured *and embedded in other persons*, discourses, and histories" (Kang 2002: 219; my emphases), *Dictée* ousts masculine subjectivity's notions of a narcissistic self-representation/realization; in line with Irigaray's thinking, the text highlights reciprocal relationships between women. In one of the recurring italicized shamanistic chants of the textual ritual (that evokes the myth of Demeter and Persephone), *Dictée* emphasizes the *diseuse*'s relational plurality: rendering interpretations focusing on autobiographical tendencies yet more complicated, the in-vocation "*Let the one who is diseuse, one who is daughter*" is preceded by another: "*Let the one who is diseuse, one who is mother*" (133)—in the female speaker, the voices of mother and daughter are spectrally intertwined. Moreover, when Minh-ha points out a non-coincidental mirroring of Theresa Hak Kyung Cha's name in the name of St. Thérèse of Lisieux (cf. 120), then she suggests that this reciprocal entanglement is not restricted to parental relations alone. More than merely constituting (another) exchangeable counter-discursive female subject(s), *Dictée*'s *diseuse*(s) shamanistic channeling of multiple voices unfolds a relationality of being (at least) two with (the) other(s) in spectrality.

This form of relationality is also apparent in the text's in-vocation of the nine ancient Greek muses. Functioning as the book's chapter heading, the mythical women are integrated in *Dictée*'s creative sabotage of the novena into the *moodong*'s syncretic ritual: Clio—history; Calliope—epic poetry; Urania—astronomy; Melpomene—tragedy; Erato—love poetry; Elitere— lyric poetry; Thalia—comedy; Terpsichore—choral dance; and Polymnia— sacred poetry.[10] As such, Minh-ha notes, "the writing of *Dictée* is also a writing *dictated* by at least nine muses" (119), and not only by the colonizers. The specific way in which the art-work conjures them illustrates that also the quality of the dictation differs from Western indoctrination. They are called forth twice in the beginning section. First, reminiscent of Hesiod's *Theogony* and/or Homer's *Odyssey*, the calling reads: "O Muse, tell the story / Of all these things, O Goddess, daughter of Zeus / Beginning wherever you wish, tell even us" (7).[11] When this formula is repeated two pages later, however, it is stripped of these patriarchal implications: "Tell me the story / Of all these things. / Beginning wherever you wish, tell even us" (11). Therefore, the in-vocation does not suggest an assimilation into a Western framework, but a re(dis)covery of an-other potential (from the) inside; it simultaneously *figures* as critique of a levelling or instrumentalization of women's voices within Western discourse (for instance in the *Theogony*) as well as indicator of the different—relational—modality of narration brought forth by shamanistic channeling of others (cf. Lee 2006: 83). Unlike Hesiod, who commands his text with an authoritative patriarchal voice (cf. ibid. 82), *Dictée*'s *diseuse* does not impose her-*self* so as to construct "an autonomous and absolute subjectivity, a conscious I who speaks rather than one who is spoken of" (4), or to produce just another disempowered "compilation of multiple fragments of voices" (2), as Oh would have it. Throughout the book's nine chapters, the muses ensure that the *diseuse* never speaks alone—i.e. *mono*logically. The speaker engages and remains with/in a continuous reciprocal *dia*-logic irreducible to calculative reasoning: "not one, not two either" (108), but "another kind of *twoness*" (Minh-ha 112) which resists division into a one-plus-one(-plus-one- . . .) enumeration. Speaking *with* the muses, the text's enunciation *always* unfolds as being (at least) two.

Dictée's engagement with occidental phallic mythology functions along the lines of Irigaray's mimetic examinations that "are partly interpretation (the negative moment), and partly alternatives which act as holding devices to prevent the immediate reinstallation of the male imaginary configuration" (Whitford 1991: 103). It is accurate that Cha's text subverts masculinist renderings of women and stresses female agency (cf. Lee 2006: 94; Kim 1994: 16). However, *Dictée* does not opt to merely invert existing power structures, but to perform a more fundamental epistemological change. It is misleading when several critics suggest that the art-work aims for the erection of a counter-discursive "gynocentric pantheon" (Eileraas 110) or the creation of a collection of oppositional female voices converging in Cha's unitary authorial power (cf. Lee 2006: 95; McDaniel 75). *Dictée* does not reproduce patriarchal thought by retaining such notions of centrism; the drawing on figures like Yu Guan Soon, Joan of Arc, and Thérèse of Lisieux does not serve to establish an equal(ly phallic) feminine pantheon next to a masculine one. Strictly speaking, such supposedly emancipative options are merely forms of phallocratic parallelism. Instead, it is helpful to agree with Elaine Kim and "view *Dictée* not as an 'either/or' but rather a 'both/and' text" that— in Euro-de-centric manner—creatively ab-uses patriarchal mythology: mimetically moving "inside and outside at the same time" (1994: 23), Cha's art-work outlines a dichotomous locus of enunciation which dis-solves the systemic order of a phallogocentric *ratio* not by simply inverting it, but by insisting on border thinking.

This border gnostic dis-solution pertains to *Dictée*'s stance toward nationalism and national identity, as particularly the chapter about the story of Cha's mother—"Calliope—epic poetry"—reveals. As Lowe points out (albeit again with a strong insistence on oppositionality), the relationship of daughter and mother also serves to subvert nationalist narratives and criticize phallocentric nation-building (cf. 1994: 49). Directly engaging with the mother through second person narration, the *diseuse*(s) first recount(s) the story of Hyung Soon Oh's flight into exile in China to escape Japanese occupation:

> Mother, you are eighteen years old. You were born in Yong Jung, Manchuria and this is where you now live. You are not Chinese. You are Korean. But your family moved here to escape the Japanese occupation. China is large. Larger than large. You tell me that the hearts of the people are measured by the size of the land. As large and as silent. You live in a village where the other Koreans live. Same as you. Refugees. Immigrants. Exiles. Farther away from the land that is not your own. Not your own any longer. (45)

Dictée emphasizes that, despite the departure from Korea, her "MAH-UHM, spirit has not left. Never shall have and never shall will" (ibid.). In his interpretation of this passage, Joyce argues that this evocation of the "spirit-heart" (Cha 46) serves to draw attention to Hyung Soon Oh's "Koreanness" (cf. Joyce 161): for him, it is a decidedly "national MAH-UHM" (163) that preserves an untainted, fixed, and genuine identity.[12] There is no question that the art-work stresses the mother's resilience in the face of imperialist intrusion, as the text makes unmistakably clear: "Mother inseparable from which is her identity, her presence" (Cha 49). Nevertheless, reading this as an instance of rigid nationality appears as misguided when considering that the speaker(s) also describe(s) the mother thus: "You move. You are being moved. You are movement. *Inseparably. Indefinable. Not isolatable terms*" (51; my emphases). The dynamics in-volved within this passage must not necessarily be seen as a result of Japanese invasion only; the focus on the MAH-UHM also implies the more affective aspect of "being moved," namely as a mode of movement that remains beyond phallogocentric notions of *ratio*nal fixation. As Berila argues, "the text's experimental aesthetics perform the experience of in-betweenness to challenge constructs of nation and national identity as neatly defined" and "problematize the colonizing violence that results from narrow categories of belonging and exclusion of the nation-state" (33). This becomes evident in the last part of the chapter which describes the process of being recognized or naturalized as a(n) (American) citizen. The art-work presents it as a form of violent assimilation into the phallic Rule of the One where identity is but a matter of archival stasis and semblance: "The eyes gather towards the appropriate proof" (57), otherwise "they treat you with indifference" (56)—for the nation-state, "[y]ou are *one same* parti-cle" (57; my emphasis). Hyung Soon Oh's MAH-UHM, however, does not work according to nationalist one-plus-one-. . . .-fixation; her spirit-heart *presences* within the *movement between two*: in the relationality of mother and daughter in-voked by the textual repertoire.[13]

Dictée engages with phallic nationalism and the myths upon which it is founded by way of per-forming a modality of "*entre-femmes*" (Whitford 1991: 12); for, it is as such that its enunciative position operates other-wise. Martin asserts, "[t]he muses in *Dictee* rarely speak in ways that create the closure that typifies masculine thinking"; the art-work acknowledges other forms of relating to it and "provides instead a language or 'rhetoric of rhythm' that *affects* us in ways we cannot at first define" (200; my em-phasis); ways undefinable by phallic reasoning. In contrast to Cartesian-ism, *Dictée*'s relational dia-logic, always *touching* upon others, does not dichotomize, but outlines an interstitial space between mind and body. As elaborated in the last section, the text is irreducible to phallic concepts of discursivity and constitutes "a kind of ultimate sensual act" (Stephens 206). As such, it is somewhat problematic to distinguish between reflection on the art-work's (postmodern) form and examination of its (postcolonial) content, because, in *Dictée*'s *poiētic* repertoire, these static oppositions do not apply (cf. Kim 2013: 131; Inoue 68). The distinction between form and content is an extension of the Cartesian paradigm and, therefore, functions within an epistemological horizon that the text exceeds by remaining open to the other's spectral *presencing* in figurality: it enacts "a process of *embodiment of the voice*" (193) or, even more to the point, a "performative *coming into being* of the plural voice as maternal body" (196). That is, *Dictée*'s relational dia-logic between women also alludes to fluid (inter-)corporeal dimensions of textuality itself.

In drawing attention to the dynamic (and/or) bodily qualities of the art-work, the present analysis seeks to shed light on a neglected area in the scholarship surrounding *Dictée*. Hyo Kim recently has argued that the way "the text experiments with the connection between body and language" constitutes "an under-theorized feature of Cha's text" and elaborates: "[c]ritics often allude to but have yet to foreground this dimension of *Dictee* as being important to its overall poetics" (2013: 128). This negligence appears to be partially due to a(n implicit) disagreement on this matter within the scholarship surrounding the art-work: in contrast to several critics who have repeatedly (at least) insisted (if not elaborated) on the relevance of the body in *Dictée* (cf. Lowe 1994: 47; Wong 117; Duncan 136; Frost 183; Sakai 30), other scholars have identified a status of disembodiment or a representational absence of corporeality within the text (cf. Cheng 1998: 119; Lee 2002: 243). However, Hyo Kim makes a strong case for continuing to investigate the role of corporeality — also regarding material contexts. She connects the bodily dimension to the commonly asserted in-between-ness and/or interstitial plurality of (the) subject(s) in *Dictée* and argues that hyphenated identity, here, neither marks an impurity that pollutes supposedly homogeneous concepts nor outlines a simple synthesis but circumscribes a site of embodiment where a self becomes vulnerable in the face of the other(s) (cf. 2013:129). In fact, she even asserts further that "*Dictee*'s embodied poetics also recalls *écriture féminine*'s critique of the disembodied subject of traditional humanism" (ibid.). What follows will build on this insight as corroborating the validity of reading Cha's art-work *with* Irigaray's thought.

Dictée's figural interrelation of blood and ink serves as a point of departure for investigating elements of performative embodiment within *Dictée*. "Urania — astronomy" starts by describing a scene of giving a blood sample which picks up on the subversion of phallic hegemony begun in the directly preceding chapter on Cha's mother. The art-work illustrates how patriarchal categorization ossifies the liquidity of blood in its discursive grid to make blood function as an indicator of fixable identity: "No sign of flow / Sample extract / Specimen type" — the goal is a "containment" (Cha 64) of fluid dynamics. *Dictée*, however, via shamanistic chants in italics, starts to outline how the containment is never entirely successful: "*Should it appear should it happen to appear all of a sudden, suddenly, begin to flow begin to collect begin to spill over flow flood should it happen to*" (ibid.). The text's dia-logic exposes the containing impulse as a strategy to ensure patriarchal supremacy by harnessing potentially threatening epistemological potentialities; but the fluidity *entre-femmes* dis-solves the phallic scheme: its "[s]*tain begins to absorb the material spilled on*" (65) another, twice-repeated, chant reads. This dis-solution also concerns the phallocentric extension of this scheme into a supposed maleness of discourse as static, rigid, and fixed. *Dictée* relates the fluid quality of (female) blood to the liquidity of ink to show that, also regarding discursivity, a phallic containment is never completely successful. There is "[s]omething of the ink that resembles the *stain from the interior*" (ibid; my emphasis); this is to say that ink—and, later in the chapter, also rain (cf. 67–71)—here, serves as figure-image of "[l]anguage's liquidity" (Min-ha 114; cf. Inoue 70). In *Dictée*'s ab-use, discursivity remains ever-"'stained' by the feminine" (Eileraas 113), and the phallic strategy of containment turns out as or into an (in-)voluntary (re-)invitation of an unsystematizable sensuality into its system.[14]

This re-infusion of fluid sensuality is not restricted to the chapter "Urania—astronomy," but, retro- as well as proactively, characterizes *Dictée*'s repertoire in its entirety. This becomes particularly apparent later in the art-work, namely in "Terpsichore—choral dance," described by Joyce as the text's most oblique chapter as it consists of a stream of seemingly disconnected utterings by the *diseuse(s)* (cf. 190). While these utterings might seem disjointed if read solely within the context of this single chapter, they do, in fact, reveal other connections when seen in the context of feminine fluidity. The chapter picks up on an image of a rocky, barren wasteland offered, even prior to the already mentioned frontispiece, on the very first unnumbered page of *Dictée*. In "Terpsichore," employing mournful en-*han*-ced language, the speaker(s) in-voke(s) a situation where this desolation, which "[s]tands now, an empty column of artery, of vein, fixed in stone" (Cha 161), is still moist with fecund fluidity: "Liquid and marrow once swelled the muscle and bone, blood made freely the passages through innumerable entries" (ibid.). This mourning, again, does not signify resignation, but rather the potential for an ab-usive reworking or redefinition (cf. Cho 39)—here through a reimbuing with "bodily dynamism" (54). In yet another incantation, the text enacts this process. Transcending established analytical categories, it interweaves signification and materiality: "*Stone to pigment. Stone. Wall. / Page. / To stone, water, teinture, blood*" (Cha 162). By way of this chant, then, "[a] new sign of moisture appears in the barren column that had congealed in stone. *Floods the stone from within*, collects water as to a mere, layering first the very bottom" (Cha 161; my emphasis); a moisture which was contained and now, nevertheless, flows from inside the barren rigidity, as another photograph, at the beginning of the following chapter makes clear. It again depicts a wasteland, but this time with *two* dissipating stone columns which seem to reveal human bodies underneath the petrified surfaces (cf.

Cha 166). *Dictée* precisely mirrors Irigaray's argument that the "father's language camouflages and petrifies the mother's body, denying its claim to generative power" (Zakin 178). Joyce succinctly observes the full implications of this performative rendering and reads the barren rock as patriarchal rule and the water in the stone as the voices of in-voked women channeled by the *moodong* to re(dis)cover repressed fluid fecundity which occidental thinking fears (cf. 193). Consequently, this passage of *Dictée* shows that, in fact, its textual *kut* enacts a process of fluidizing static patriarchal epistemology.

Returning once more to "Urania—astronomy" can now help trace out another corporeal aspect of this fluidization. After the rendering of the blood donation, the chapter is made up of a poem printed in both French as well as English facing each other. Not least due to the frequent recurrence of the image of the rain (cf. 66f.), this bilingual dual poem further stresses the text's dynamic "movement / line / after line" (Cha 73) or "mouvement / lignes / après lignes" (72). In fact, this section's imagery, together with its layout on facing pages, illustrates perfectly the kind of movement that Sakai describes as *Dictée*'s "work of *passage* from one language to another" (26; my emphasis): a movement *between* (at least) two. As Duncan asserts, *Dictée* often "rel[ies] on spatial and visual epistemologies" in its "reclamation of liminal and interstitial space" (164). The poem in "Urania" is, thus, not the only instance of this. With the dictation in both English and French, a similar form of doubling serves as the beginning of the art-work. Considering these spatial and visual dimensions, again, changes also the quality of other *passages* throughout the book.

An even more explicit example of this spatial visuality are two instances of two largely printed Chinese characters, again on facing pages: translated, the first pair reads "woman" and "man" (cf. 26f.) and the second says "mother" and "father" (cf. 54f.). Readings, such as Wong's (cf. 126), which see in this a critique of imperial influences on Korea without considering the formal dimension, miss *Dictée*'s interstitial mode of enunciation. Sakai explains that Chinese characters have been part of the cultural repertoire of East Asian countries for centuries and cannot be read as only an effect of colonization; in the text's ab-usive ritual, they function other-wise: "they are registered for their graphic visuality" (26) or figural potential.[15] The specific calligraphic quality of the letters—the *thick* lines and uneven margins caused by brushstrokes—simultaneously preserves both the dynamics of (hand-)writing and draws attention to its inky liquidity. As Nicole McDaniel argues, "in discussions of images and graphic narratives," the placement of the Chinese characters, forces one to "read these two pages together—and try to reconcile them in some way—or physically turn the page" (78); an impulse that the allusion to fluid motion underscores. This is to say, instead of opposing "man" to "woman" or "father" to "mother," *Dictée*'s repertoire has them embrace in the sensual dia-logic of being-two—literally as one turns the page. By way of its figurally en-*han*-ced language which entails certain "shape-shifting qualities" (Cho 39), the book itself continuously undergoes a process of "fluid metamorphosis" (Inoue 70), making its specific corporeal quality become ever more apparent.

The chapter "Erato—love poetry," further enacts this dia-logical figural embodiment. Playing again with the spatial visual configuration of the text, it interweaves passages from the diary of Thérèse of Lisieux and the experience of watching a film. The passages describing the movie and the Catholic saint's life respectively are again placed on pages facing each other, but with a slight variation: not opposed in parallel fashion, but offset, so that there always remain blank spaces between the text passages.[16] In one instance of these passages, on the left page it reads: "It is the husband who touches. Not as husband. He touches her as he touches all the others. But he touches her with his rank. By his knowledge of his own rank. By the claim of his rank. Gratuity is her body her spirit. Her non-body her non-entity. His privilege possession his claim. Infallible is his ownership. Imbues with mockery at her refusal of him, but her very being that dares to name herself as if she posesses a will. Her own" (112). On the facing page, the supplementary text adds the following contour: "She forgets. She tries to forget. For the moment. For the duration of these moments" (113). Joyce is, therefore, again correct to note that, here, "[m]eaning will not lie in any of the texts [alone] but in the relationship that emerges between them" (153). The gaps in the textual arrangement are only filled through the process of turning the pages. The movement reveals the specific dia-logic relationality of the two accounts as they once more get back in *touch* to per-form an in(di)visibly embracing textual body—a corporeal dichotomous locus of enunciation, ever touching (upon) others. As "Erato" suggests, unlike the hierarchized and undifferentiated grasp of phallogocentrism, the text's (en-)active embrace per-forms a mutual caress between two that, nevertheless, remains open toward the other in its radical otherness. When considering *Dictée*'s figural dynamics and moisture, the enacted interstitial locus can be *seen* as "an eroticized site of narrative connection and exchange" (Cho 54); as "an orifice expressive of desire for narrative contact and community" (56). Cha's art-work *figures* as a moist bodily *passage* between two lips always already speaking together: a vaginal space.

Vaginal Space

Conceived as the fluid passage between two lips through shamanistic ceremony, the text itself—in its irreducible materiality—does not only represent a spectral/corporeal repertoire, but (en-)actively *brings forth* and *becomes* the very dichotomous locus of enunciation *entre-femmes* that the
art-work continually in-vokes. Referring to the merely metaphorical "'slip-
periness' of the book" (Kang 1994: 76) does not go far enough: Cha's text
itself per-forms a moist "amorphous space" (Inoue 80) that defies notions
of static and one-directional signification as defined by the phallic order
of representation (cf. Cheng 1998: 122) by insisting on an excessive force.
Here, also Inoue explicitly draws on Lyotard's work to describe *Dictée*'s specific "paradiscursive energy" (74), or the dynamic "*figural* presence" (72), of
its words and images even within phallogocentric systematicity. This energy,
Elisabeth Frost adds, insists on "ambivalent intersections of the symbolic
and the material" (183) beyond the Cartesian paradigm. Saturated with figurality, the art-work's vaginal space outlines a fecund dichotomous locus of
enunciation where image and word both function radically other-wise and,
eventually, point toward (repressed) ethico-epistemologica potentials beyond the confines of (the) patriarchal (Western) tradition(s).

The two enveloping black pages at the beginning and the end of the book
constitute an important example of such ambivalent intersections of the symbolic and the material. These pages play a significant role in the art-work's
performance that has been ignored by critics of the text: they contribute to the
figural transformation of word and image in/to *Dictée*'s vaginal space. Only
Minh-ha has commented on this feature. Considering Cha's background as a
filmmaker, she writes: "The work ends the way it begins—with a film still and
with black—moving from bordered to non-bordered pages that close in on
all white then on all black, until the white comes to the fore and what is left is
the empty page framed by black: the papery version of a film screen" (109).
Put differently, for Minh-ha, the black pages serve as indicator of the text's
dynamic cinematographic qualities. This is an important—albeit partial—
insight; which needs to be *viewed* in light of the analysis of the previous
section. Keeping in mind the image of the phallic barren wasteland and the
frontispiece that directly follow the black page at the beginning, the enveloping pages can be *seen* as turning the entire book into a cave-like structure.
Furthermore, remembering the process of fluidizing patriarchal sclerosis initiated by the art-work's repeated shamanistic chants, the black pages *figure*
as moist insides of two lips speaking together. Thereby, *Dictée*'s ritualistic
process effectively mirrors Irigaray's mimetic ab-use of Plato's "Allegory of

the Cave": rather than a mere film screen, the two enveloping black pages circumscribe a curved *corporeal-dynamic* projection chamber.

In this vaginal cinema, *Dictée*'s montaged (photographic) images function other-wise. As part of the art-work's live textual repertoire that defies the fixating grasp of archival closure, they remain irreducible to *ratio*-aesthetic objectification. The pictures in *Dictée* are for the most part not accompanied by descriptions of what they actually depict: images of Cha's mother (cf. Cha 44), of Thérèse of Lisieux (cf. 93), and of a student revolt in the context of the Korean Independence Movement (cf. 122) — to name just three examples — are de-void of captions or footnotes and reject "the desire for documentation" (Cheng 2001: 142). Shamanistic syncretism further contributes to this impression of non-identification: another photograph shows the execution of three Korean peasants — standing next to each other with outstretched arms shaped like a cross-piece — by a group of Japanese invaders; a scene that is also reminiscent of the Crucifixion at Calvary (cf. Cha 39). Although acknowledging this rejection of documentation and infusion of inter-textual un-decidablity, most critics who commented on *Dictée*'s visuality, nevertheless, read it as constituting a collection of visual representations; albeit an unconventional one: "It is constructed almost like an archive itself, full of grainy black-and-white photographs" (Cheng 2001: 143). Eileraas, for instance, refers to the images' withholding of clear documentary evidence as the "creative use of misrecognition" (91), which helps *Dictée* oppose the norms of patriarchal hegemony, and/but "denies the opportunities for intimacy typically afforded by the genres of autobiography and the family album" (92). She concludes that Cha's text "reinvents the family album as a study in dislocation, discomfort, and estrangement" (91). Other scholars have noted also that *Dictée*, by way of this particular employment of visuals, challenges the terminating nationalist impetus that is connected to the notion of the photo album; an impetus which regards images either as evidence of national identity or as tokens of the Ideal static presence of history ready to be consumed at will, as Cheng argues with reference to Susan Sontag (cf. 2001: 146). And it is correct that *Dictée* does not adhere to such a phallogocentric systematicity; but it is misleading to regard this as coming at the price of forfeiting intimacy. The contrary is the case. If grainy "visual images in *Dictée* subvert the discursive functions of journalistic photographs or diagrams, pushing the text . . . toward materiality" (Frost 184), then Cha's text (en-)actively repudiates intimacy as defined by an exploitative phallic economy: the art-work does not operate according to the principles of a Hegelian gallery of images where pictures can be one-sidedly consumed — in dis-sociating contemplation — as stable objects to be handled at will that ensure the absolute supremacy of Western knowledge (cf. Soppa 46). *Dictée* dis-closes the archive to re(dis)cover (from) with/in a dis-location of documentary stasis the possibility of a reciprocal intimacy in being-two.

This requires further clarification. In the first section of this analysis, it was argued that the images and photographs are part of the art-work's spectral repertoire that defies occidental notions of chronology and teleology. The visual elements in *Dictée* turn into a haunting *presencing* or spectral recurrence of the past. Remaining in the fluid dia-logic relationality *entre-femmes*, the photographs of women (and the other visuals) do not reproduce a Western conceptualization of seeing and time that reduces memory to the Hegelian process of *rati*onal (re)cognition; they do not construct "a gallery of the portraits of women" (Lee 2006: 79) which adheres to a phal-locratically in-different pluralism. As a cinematographic performance, Joyce rightly observes, the art-work rather stresses the relational dynamics of the Kuleshov effect that says that meaning always arises *between* (at least) two shots (cf. 199). The principle applies to the calligraphic Chinese characters on facing pages, as well as to the image of the barren wasteland and the one showing two eroding stone statues, or also the photograph of Thérèse of Lisieux and the close-up of the actress Maria Falconetti playing the protagonist in Carl Theodore Dreyer's film *The Passion of Joan of Arc* (both framing "Erato—love poetry"). *Conceived* within the text's vaginal projection chamber, this relational dynamic now attains a decidedly bodily quality that "enable[s] the past to *affect* those living in the present" (Kim 2013: 138): it transforms memory into an embodied sensuous experience which transcends the limits of *rati*onal fixation and remains in *touch* with the perceived (cf. Park 237; Joyce 156). Through *Dictée*'s shamanistic repertoire, corporeal fluidity, uncanny spectrality, words, and images, all coalesce into a textual whole to bring forth the potential of a hauntingly affective relationality.

"So far," Joyce claims, "no one has tried to see *Dictée* as a whole to see how the different parts fit together," which, for him, is "a weakness ethical criticism is always open to because the goal is primarily to use the text (or pieces of the text) to advocate for a better future" (136). Scholars who focus on the text's subversive impetus concerning patriarchal rule in its various (dis)guises, he holds, miss half of what the art-work has to say, for it at the same time questions the Western modus of this subversion. However, his specific insistence on the text's wholeness (and the polemic against political criticism which accompanies it), has Joyce analyze *Dictée*'s nine chapters individually and chronologically. He himself effectively reintegrates them into *rati*onal teleology and, thereby, also again reduces half of the text's potential. But the art-work's (ideological) challenge and (corporeal) wholeness must not (necessarily) be divided: creative mimicry interweaves both within a dia-logic of being-two. As Frost writes, "if in *Dictée* Cha negotiates modes of signification . . . she also seeks to recuperate the corporeal in the face of constant re- and de-constructions" (191). In other words, approaching the text with Irigaray's thought—reading it as a vaginal space—helps illustrate how *Dictée* has deconstructive ethico-politcal critique and a certain positive potential coincide as/in "a female whole that . . . is not closed off" (1993: 105): every element which is part of the shamanistic performance remains "defined by *depth* and *interiority*, by its *presence* in a general *atmosphere* which contains slight *differences that it does not organize into a system*" (Hayot 608; my emphases).[17] Hence—unlike Joyce, who again fixates *Dictée* within phallogocentric systematicity—regarding the text in its *figural-vaginal (w)holeness* risks neither (re)producing "schematic and fossilized identities," nor contributing "to a general sclerosis of discourse" (135). Joyce "approaches the female other carelessly" (Irigaray 1993: 210), namely by binding *Dictée*—as well as its (female)—in a *ratio*-categorical grid. However, when allowing for its *figuring* as fluid *passage*, the art-work invites the reader to remain in *touch* with the other without robbing it of its sting. This means, as a vaginal space, *Dictée*'s shamanistic performance draws attention to the ethico-epistemological stakes involved in our "understanding of our relationships to the books we read and the world in which we read them" (Kim 2008: 176); it raises the question of how to conceive of and/or enter into a non-reductive and responsive relationship with radical otherness.

   The nation-state as defined by patriarchal hegemony does not constitute a suitable space for such relationality in *Dictée*. Joyce admits as much.[18] Nevertheless, and despite his critique of occidental thought, his own deduction remains stuck in a *ratio*nal epistemological horizon when he suggests that the art-work "posits not the fluid, multiple Self of Western postmodernism but an essentialist version of the national spirit" (160). There is no separation of essence and fluidity in *Dictée*'s art-work. However, unable to think "postmodernism" and "essentialism" simultaneously, Joyce concludes that "Cha thus depicts an essential Self and Nation that is at odds with artificial constructs of citizenship and State" (ibid.). Although he draws attention to the influence of French feminism on Cha's work, Joyce does not seem to take this into account and, therefore, misses that, in *Dictée*, "essence" *figures* other-wise: its dichotomous enunciative locus outlines a corporeal relationality of always already being (at least) two and, as such, "discloses the space of 'in-between', a space for 'community' for subjects in transit, a community that cannot be contained in or by a nation" (Sakai 36). This means, Cha's *Dictée* neither promotes a simplistic "postmodernism" of multiple and/or fragmented (one-plus-one-plus- . . .) subjectivities, nor does it seek to rehabilitate traditional occidental notions of ideal Being based on Cartesian binarism. Via shamanistic *womanspeak*, the art-work brings forth a space where the MAH-UHM—the spirit-heart—always retains also a bodily dimension (cf. Park 240), which, instead of tying subjectivity to a Self-containing Law of the Father, responds to the ever excessive pathos of radical otherness. *Dictée em-bodies* (an ethical) relationality to things and entities beyond the subject/object split rather than (re)perpetuating dis-sociating fragmentation; it unfolds an irreducible modality of always already being-in-the-world-with-others that, through repeated in-vocations of (spectral) women from various cultural and/or historical backgrounds, takes on a specific de-colonial quality (cf. Ingram 85; Eileraas 114; Spahr 26; June 37). As vaginal space, *Dictée* outlines the possibility of a fluid transnational community based on the (ab-usive) communion of spirit and flesh.

The art-work's figural-vaginal (w)holeness suggests that what to phallic thought appears as a mere "hole," in fact, harbors a potential for thinking "wholeness" other-wise. This becomes particularly evident in *Dictée*'s numerous evocations of the void (cf. Cha 3, 69, 161). From the perspective of the phallocentric tradition, the void (of the vagina) is considered as indicating absence and/or loss. This is also true for the myth of Demeter and Persephone, upon which the text draws to circumscribe the (severed) relationship of mother and daughter. In the story, the void of the underworld, where Persephone must reside after her abduction by Hades, signifies the separation of the two women. Through another syncretistic move, *Dictée* re-enacts the initiation ceremony of the Eleusinian cult. There, initiates were led into a cave to experience the separation of the two women first hand (cf. Stein 122; Siegle 242). The art-work functions in a similar manner, albeit with a shamanistic twist: transformed through a *poiētic* process of fluid *in-corporation* into the text's repertoire, the void, or cave, constitutes "an almost utopian space where the reader/viewer can find pleasure in escaping from the conventional demands of narrative and from the constraints of ideology and discourse" (Nguyen 155).[19] The void's negativity, as also Chambers clarifies, is dependent on the patriarchal position from where it is uttered: the void seems negative toward static discursive closure, but, as vaginal space, it "can also be interpreted as a positive, empowering position" (128), namely as a space for thinking other-wise.[20] In-volving readers in vaginal fluidity through a shamanistic rite of *passage*, *Dictée*'s en-*han*-ced language certainly has them undergo a sense of Eleusinian desperation with a postcolonial bent; but only to lead the readers eventually to a space for the radical dis-closure of subalternized knowledge(s).

Within the vaginal space per-formed by the text through figure and discourse, *ratio*nal consciousness does not reign supreme. "If my words have meaning," suggests Irigaray, "it is because they touch the other from the starting point of my perception, and having touched me and touching the other, they organize a possible dwelling for these perceptions" (1993: 172). The same applies to Cha's *Dictée*. In the text's spectral repertoire each word is not only a sign to be read, but "an affect-word that is entangled with and in another culture, language, and history" (Kim 2013: 132); each word is not only a static signifier to be cognitively processed, but a figural "word-image [which] is seen, heard, smelled, tasted and touched" (Minh-ha 116). What, at first, may appear as failing or fragmented speech, in fact, serves as guide into an elsewhere in perception or, maybe more precisely, a perceiving other-wise (cf. 117ff.). Laura Kang is certainly correct when she asserts that *Dictée*'s ab-usive employment of language is "accompanied by the search for an equally revolutionary manner of seeing, hearing and reading" (1994: 95f.); namely, a mode of perception which does not impose preconceived *ratio*nal concepts and categories onto all phenomena, but remains open to their affective pathos and engages them in released responsiveness. Irigaray writes, "we must ask the question of the other as touched and touching" (1993: 157)—by way of its figural-vaginal (w)holeness, the art-work (en-)actively *stimulates* such a process of sense-sensitization regarding radical otherness.

The art-work invites readers to *enter into* the re(dis)covery of excessive epistemological potentials: as a vaginal space, Cha's *Dictée* (en-)actively "*incorporates* the reader's experiential engagement with the text" (Wald 215; my emphasis), although it initially leaves open the mode of the readers' entering. As Spahr notes, the text shows "that postmodern works can both emancipate and decolonize reading," namely "[b]y destabilizing reading practices that seek to conquer or master" (24). Nonetheless, it appears slightly misled when she further argues that "*Dictee* forces the reader out of linear, absorptive reading practices and into vertical, circular, inter- and intracultural ways of reading" (25). Critical readings like Joyce's illustrate that—despite its obscurity and/or obliquity—the text does not entirely "refuse to offer a teleological moment of interpretive mastery" (Cho 43). Several critics claiming otherwise notwithstanding (cf. Duncan 152), the phallic option of consuming penetration remains. While *Dictée* wishes to set into motion an ongoing reflection on "reading's colonizing powers" (Spahr 32), it does not *force* its readers to do so. The textual body resists confinement in hegemonic patriarchal order (cf. Cho 50), but only by simultaneously desisting from it; that is, by not merely inverting its phallic epistemic violence. The art-work indeed "implicates us in our very *desire* to know and see through reading" (Cheng 1998: 13), but it does not try to predetermine the mode of how this desire is to manifest itself. In Irigaray's terms, *Dictée* offers a chance that "consciousness finds itself embroiled willy-nilly in the rape of the other" (1985a: 222). And still, the relationality that Cha's text outlines cannot be one-sidedly imposed: it seeks to embrace readers performatively in its dia-logic of being-two, and, as such, its relationality is a matter of remaining in the reciprocal dynamics of pathos and response. This means, too, that this relationality always must retain the character of an open invitation. However, this is not a deficit. In fact, it is precisely due to this hopeful openness of its invitation to "*a process* of mutually active collaboration" (Kang 1994: 78), albeit ever under threat of being passively consumed again, that *Dictée* can unfold its epistemological potential and point toward sense-sensitized modes of reading other-wise.

Through its figural corporeality, *Dictée* illustrates that the care-less (mis)handling of its enacted vaginal space in only *ratio*nally objectifying readings equals a repeated epistemic rape. By (ex)posing (itself) as a "site of storytelling, of recovery and of *human contact*" (Kang 1994: 97; my emphasis), *Dictée* unmasks modes of analysis which attempt to wrap the art-work into a totalizing straightjacket of a single theory to subject it to discursive closure as fundamentally reductive (cf. Lowe 1994: 37, 54); the same, however, goes for analytical approaches which, although stressing the text's resistance to theoretical straightjacketing, repeat a similar kind of totalizing instrumentalization in reverse, namely by reading *Dictée* as only oppositional. All such readings deny the fecundity of the text's generative *mater*-iality (which always already exceeds phallogocentric discourse), as they ultimately subsume the art-work—albeit, granted, in dissimilar ways—under the same mono-logical grasp or gaze which treats all phenomena as *res extensa*: a *ratio*nalized analytical grip lacking in sensuality that regards textual corporeality merely as lifeless matter and fixates otherness within its dis-sociating central vision. Figural *passages*, such as the embracing text segments in "Erato—love poetry" or, once again, the Chinese characters on facing pages, can be *read* as instances of fragmentation and alienation in opposition to *ratio*nal homogeneity and closure; but—within the process of turning the book's pages—they can simultaneously also be *seen* and *touched* respectively as a fluid "split [that] is experienced bodily, as something sensory that is felt" (June 36). This is to say, similar to Irigaray's thought, the art-work unfolds itself "in a poetic, allusive style so that the reader can make something of it only by actively engaging with it" (Canters and Jantzen 125); a type of engagement that calls for a "[c]ooperation between the body, heart and mind" (Irigaray 2011: 118), and not only unidirectional reduction to *ratio*nal cognition that violently (re)presses *Dictée*'s open dia-logical space back into a uni-form phallic grid.

Cha's art-work ab-uses this vulnerability to epistemic penetration by gaze and grasp to unfold a possibility of mutual caressing to arise (from) within phallogocentrism (itself); a mode of relationality where otherness is not merely perceived as a threat to discursive closure, but also as harboring "a promise, an ethical imperative, *and an opening onto a new aesthetics*" (Eileraas 117; my emphasis). By *in-corporating* the haptic or tangible experience of the book, the mentioned figural *passages* of *Dictée*'s emphasize an irreducible "impact on the body and the physical senses" (Martin 196). This impact is always connected to the reading process and patriarchal *ratio*nality may well repress its significance but is never able to fully dispose of. Though hidden in the basement of *ratio*nal systemic closure, there remains inherent in distanced contemplation a trace or *sense* of corporeality that ties the *cogito* (back) to an "indeterminacy of the body in touch" and, thereby, outlines "an erotically constituted threshold" (Vasseleu 12) upon which all thought and perception are (unwittingly) based. The art-work unconceals a fundamental scandal at the heart of patriarchal supremacy: that it has managed repeatedly (and successfully) to disavow and, simultaneously, harness—or, more precisely, to disavow by harnessing—the epistemological validity of unsystematizable corporeality. While phallocratic hegemony, via Cartesian *ration*alization, pretends to be able to treat aesthetic perception as a dis-sociating "kind of surface eloquence" (Martin 190), *Dictée* re(dis)covers (from) within this pretention a "metabolic intelligence" (194) which dis-closes a mode of sensuality that is always at the same time both *close and deep*; a (willfully forgotten) kind of sensuousness which opens up "new ways of seeing and engaging with existing representation" (Eileraas 117). When/where grasp and gaze are reminded of their erotic corporeality, aesthetic perception becomes a reciprocal process *between* (at least) two.

Ultimately, *Dictée*'s vaginal space *figures* as dis-closure regarding the pathos of radical otherness. Instead of containing difference inside the patriarchal discursive order, the art-work per-forms a *passage*—both "within-without, without-within" (Irigaray 1993: 160)—where "[t]o remain within perception means staying out in the open, always attuned to the outside, to the world" (141). Being per-formed between lips in a fluid dia-logic, *Dictée*'s corporeal "dis-closure is both a perpetual opening and a communicative gesture" (Vassseleu 125): a non-reductive communion which invitingly embraces the other in released response. Insisting on *Dictée*'s figural-vaginal (w)holeness does not mean "allegorizing the physical enclosure of the book as object into the final closure of a coherent and delimited self, making the unity of the text-as-book testify to the completion of another story of ethnic Americanization" (Hayot 607); as a vital aspect of the shamanistic spectral repertoire, *Dictée*'s physicality does not offer such static confinement. It rather brings forth an "embodied poetics" (Kim 2013: 141) and, thereby, participates in the playful *stimulation* of "a sensuous, embodied process involving the dynamic interplay between affect and thought" (134). Cha's textual ritual enacts a relational space between sensuality and rationality where the other *presences.*

After the photograph of the dissipating stone columns, the last chapter of *Dictée*—"Polymnia—sacred poetry"—evokes the myth of Princess Pari, "the ancestress of Korean shamanism" (Lee 2006: 92), albeit with a decisive twist: instead of obtaining medicine to cure her parents from a supernatural male being, the princess in the text's rendering receives the medicine from another woman. The creatively sabotaged story becomes an allegory of the art-work as a (w)hole (cf. Joyce 195). However, due to the chapter's clear narrative prose, Joyce proclaims that the text's project has failed; that after the highly cryptic section "Terpsichore," with its experimental language, the last chapter is not able to articulate its purpose properly and seeks refuge in the shelter of myth. The deconstruction of Western concepts of identity, history, memory, as well as art, leave the *diseuse(s)* speechless: "Once the tools are destroyed, the diseuse is left with no way to achieve her desires, merely that the reader can achieve them for her" (Joyce 198). Such a reading remains entirely within the horizon of occidental epistemology. However, Stephens emphasizes that "[s]acred poetry is not only myth; there is the ritual as well, and this last section is rounded out by such ritual" (210). The same ab-usive shamanistic ritual, that had first initiated the mimetic sabotage of colonial languages, now per-forms the ab-usive twist of the phallogocentric bent in the Princess Pari myth. Thereby, the text refers to the beginning of *Dictée* at the same time. The text circumscribes a space of transformative cyclicality that continuously deconstructs and renegotiates meanings and reconstructs new meanings from these deconstructions as an ongoing gesture of *survivance* (cf. Oh 19). Unlike the traditional teleological impetus of Western thought, which Joyce seems to reproduce, *Dictée*'s shamanistic ritual simply does not strive toward a statically fixed goal but calls for remaining within the fluid circulation of the *passage* where the spectral others *presence* in being (at least) two.

It is from this moist dichotomous locus of enunciation that reading otherwise can set in—even from within the hegemonic phallocratic epistemology; a type of reading that does not distinguish between "man" and "woman" by way of binary opposition and instead opts for a (re-)fluidization of "male" and "female" that resists final systemic closure. Thinking other-wise trans-*figures both* to start treading upon "the path of an amorous knowledge"

(Irigaray 2000: 55) where *both*—also discourse and figure, rationality and sensuality, mind and body—always already belong irreducibly to each other, "linked ('both at once') in a kind of creative and fertile partnership" (Whitford 1991: 25). This sense-sensitized mode of thinking and knowing, however, can never be simply fixed as a static goal to be achieved; it can only be repeatedly *circumscribed*, remains processual, and, as such, requires a continued, relentless effort: *being-two with the other* calls for ever moving in "a circle within a circle, a series of concentric circles" (Cha 175).

PART THREE

POETIC DWELLING IN THE BORDERS: NEGOTIATING ATTUNEMENT AND SENSUOUSNESS WITH MARTIN HEIDEGGER AND MICHAEL ONDAATJE'S *ANIL'S GHOST*

[T]he true question of *touching* and, in general, of literary and artistic *sensibility*, the true question of *aesthetics*, is yet to be posed, or very nearly so, so long as bodies are signifiers above all . . . are there bodies in literature that do not constitute a sign?
— Jean-Luc Nancy, *Corpus*

DUE TO HER APPARENT desire to "*have a fling with the philosophers*" (1985b: 150), Luce Irigaray has often been accused of a certain complicity with the very tradition she seeks to challenge. However, as the previous chapter has shown, her flinging does not indicate a willful submission to patriarchal dominance, but rather an ab-usive mimetic dia-logue that does not simply claim to be able to shed the impact of centuries of masculine hegemony with a critical(ly indifferent) shrug. Irigaray does not merely oppose her thought to the tradition which, in a certain sense, has first made it possible. Assumptions of simply being able to leave something behind risk repeating the Rule of the One; and this also pertains to the aim of ridding American Studies of exceptionalism, and thus my point of departure for this study: the possible complicity with neoliberal globalization has been a serious threat endangering the endeavor of transnationalizing American Studies from the very beginning. This raises several questions: is the transnational paradigm merely a way for Western academics to cope with their own dissatisfaction regarding the cultural and disciplinary situation they find themselves in? Is it only geared toward a scholarly self, trying to underscore the humanities' relevance in the twenty-first century where the institution of the university is more and more turning into a business? In other words, does the transnational turn truly bolster the claims and concerns of the other(s)? Or is it merely a logical consequence of capitalist market logic? What is at stake if transnationalizing American Studies is not supposed to turn into an extension of Manifest Destiny and a reaffirmation of the militant epistemology it stems from? Not having the potential of the transnational paradigm turn

into another form of militant messianism requires more than just delving into
new or forgotten (dark?) territories beyond the nation-state's borders. In her
ab-usive mimicry of the male-inflected Western intellectual history, Irigaray
has found a different way of going about, or rather around, things, which will
also guide the argument that follows.

This part argues that one vital element for answering the questions just
raised above is, first, the revision of conceptualizations of how one "is"
within an increasingly globalized world. It will be argued that an existential mode is required which resides in local particularity as well as global
universality at once; a mode of being which is willing to readjust again in
every new singular encounter with beings and things, and—through these
encounters—realizes its en-velopment within a planetary habitat. Only such
an existential comportment can keep transnationalism, despite—or maybe
precisely due to—its good intentions, from turning into one more manifestation of a neoliberal intellectual colonialism on a global scale. To outline the
possibility of such an existential mode, this chapter is going to initiate a critical dialogue between Michael Ondaatje's postcolonial novel *Anil's Ghost*
and the later thought of Martin Heidegger.

In the field of cultural studies, the very mention of the name Heidegger
is often tantamount to anathema. To render plausible why implied critical
readers from this (and other) background(s) should not also prematurely
condemn what follows (and, indeed, this entire project) as politically flawed,
a preliminary explication on how Heidegger is to be integrated into the
argument of this chapter is necessary.

The reasons for a cautious treatment of Heidegger's thinking are without
a doubt valid and usually pertain to the philosopher's relationship with National Socialism and how it may or may not be connected to his thinking.
Therefore, the fundamental question arises of how to deal with Heidegger's thought.[1] Often, the answers in academic discourse have been divided
into diametrical opposites of sympathetic apology on the one hand, and
utter condemnation on the other.[2] However, here, this part again follows
Irigaray's insight. Instead of merely offering one more biased position, the
following analyses seek to avoid such polarization and attempt to engage
with Heidegger's work in another way, namely—in accordance with one of
the overarching themes of this book—by way of (playfully mimetic) ab-use;
and in a similar fashion as Irigaray herself treats him in *The Way of Love*:
"Faithful to the teaching of Heidegger *in a way* but shifting the emphasis
into a frame or a space in which Heidegger did not venture, those of the
meeting with an other" (xii; my emphasis).

The repeated emphasis on the word "way" in this context is intentional, for
it is here that a creative sabotage can productively ab-use one of Heidegger's

own favored terms for the purposes of reading other-wise. This sabotage is inspired by Ute Guzzoni's approach in *Der Andere Heidegger*. She argues for going along with Heidegger's thought to simultaneously depart from it. In her preface, she outlines this paradoxical logic thus:

> Or we can *regard* the work of Heidegger *as a way or path*, a way containing ever-new experiences of thinking that both point ahead or remember what is behind: from his early engagement with the philosophers of the beginning previous century, via the engagement with Aristotle and Kant, and, eventually, his engagement with a plethora of *thinkers* of the tradition of the history of being as well as selected *poets*, all the way to his intense work of his last decades on what is today; what he, on the one hand, thought as the *Wesen* of technology, and, on the other hand, as interplay between world and things. That Heidegger travelled on a way or path of thinking is not to be understood as a mere metaphor [this is to be kept in mind throughout this entire chapter]. He himself had often reflected on the proceeding of his thought. It led him to ever-new views and perspectives and, in the strict sense, never came to an end, but points beyond itself" (2009: 7)[3]

For Guzzoni, this walking along the lines of Heidegger's philosophy does not consist in trying to merely provide a sterile factually and historically "correct" interpretation thereof (however, she also does not deny the necessity of careful analysis), but pursuing the possibilities opened by this thought. Her own ab-usive strategy is to read Heidegger against his own grain (cf. 11, 15). She subjects his formulations to "a certain shift in meaning" so as to draw attention to how "he implicitly responded to questions and thought in ways whose relevance and range he himself did not altogether realize anymore" (16);[4] directions which Heidegger himself might even have considered as erring or going into the wrong direction.[5] The creative sabotage of this part's line of argument follows Guzzoni's path and will trace out or lure forth (sometimes) implicit potentials inherent in Heidegger's terminology. Consequently, with Mariana Ortega, another critic who has recently dared to venture into the problematic work of Heidegger, this part—indeed, this entire project—enacts a seriously playful "rethinking, a reorientation of his work" (5) toward other potentials as the most severe criticism of Heidegger's political affiliation. This chapter shares Ortega's sentiment: "I have jokingly said to friends who ask me why I pay attention to Heidegger at all that I wish to shatter Heidegger's account of *Dasein*—to see all the different directions in which Heidegger's views [which are, thereby, effectively no longer his own but derive from his thought] can be taken rather than staying confined within the borders set up by Heidegger's text and those who interpret it—but I am serious" (ibid.). When the German language casts the sense of erring and moving in the wrong way in one noun as *Abweg*—literally indicating an "off-way" or deviating "from-way"—then it offers an elegant option of terminologically linking this supposedly negative meaning with the productive implications of ab-use, namely by recasting it as *(Ab-)Weg* (the insertion of the dash constitutes a performative *act* that again mirrors and twists Heidegger's philosophical practice). Moving on the *(Ab-)Weg* neither avoids nor courts Heidegger's work. While acknowledging his philosophy's potentials concerning its radical critique of Western metaphysics, pursuing this path always also keeps in mind its dangers. Moving on the *(Ab-)Weg* does not aim at saving Heidegger's work from critical rejection; instead it subjects his thinking to a specific form of salvaging to not give away fruitful insights. To invoke the German language once again, the walking along the *(Ab-)Weg* can be expressed with the verb *umgehen*, which means "to avoid," in connection to the preposition *mit* (with) also "to deal with," as well as, literally, "to walk around," "circumvent," or "to walk along." Repeating the performative *act* above once again, turning it into *(um-)gehen*, the verb retains these different shades of meaning within their simultaneity; a simultaneity that suggests an entanglement of avoidance and engagement. Ultimately, this sense of entanglement which constitutes the chapter's strategy of dealing with Heidegger by way of creative ab-use culminates in the following German formula: "(Mit) Heidegger auf dem (Ab-)Weg (um-)gehen." This procedure is necessary not least due to the enormous influence of Heidegger's thought on postmodern and left-wing thinkers like Foucault and Derrida as well as countless US-American critics inspired by their work, who are dealing with questions of otherness, identity, and difference (cf. Eubanks and Gauthier 143; Wolin 411ff.).[6] If one is not willing to dismiss entirely all work that has been built on this critical tradition, such an approach seems suitable to (re-)think Heideggerian concepts while also maintaining an awareness for the grave dangers inherent in extremism on either end of the political spectrum. As will become increasingly apparent when walking the subsequent line of argument, the embarking onto this ludically ab-usive *(Ab-)Weg*, in fact, anticipates the further course of the argument and is already situated in the very midst of it. As such, this disclaimer is to be kept in mind as a critical con-tour for what follows.

This (ad-)venture of integrating "Heidegger's philosophy" into current transnational thinking is also bolstered—maybe surprisingly so—by imminent postcolonial scholar Homi Bhabha. He introduces his seminal essay collection *The Location of Culture* with the following epigraph: "A boundary is not that at which something stops but, as the Greeks recognized, the boundary is that from which *something begins its presencing*" (1). This quotation is taken from Heidegger's article "Building, Dwelling, Thinking" and alludes to those potentials within the infamous philosopher's thinking yet undeveloped by himself and, therefore, ready for a creative (ab-)use. As J.P. Riquelme explains, Bhabha himself pursues a similar strategy: such central terms in his work as "location" and "dwelling" are borrowed from Heidegger; borrowed, however, with a twist, for Bhabha does not just reproduce but "[b]y taking terms from Heidegger and putting them to new uses, he mimics Heidegger without being quite the same" (552), and unhinges the terminology "from its apparent moorings" (543). Bhabha's perspective may contribute to conceiving of the possibility of something like "postcolonializing" Heidegger.[7] Timothy Clark asserts: "Why not delimit Western thinking [with Heidegger] by opening a dialogue with the thinking and languages of non-Western civilizations? After all, no one more than Heidegger has criticized at so deep a level the bases of Western thought and life, making him, before the term was even invented, a major thinker of 'globalization'" (2002: 86). In fact, when Cecil Eubanks and David Gauthier diagnose in Heidegger's work an incessant critique of the Cartesian subject/object split and a strong emphasis on the ontological significance of the local, then the thinker appears as an intriguing reference for transnational endeavors beyond Eurocentric epistemology and as another critic of global projections that remain stuck within nation-statist (or static) logic: "For Heidegger, the universal cosmopolitan state is the product of the metaphysical mode of thought that is unique to the West. Or perhaps, it is more accurate to say that the universal cosmopolitan state is the product of the *end* of Western metaphysics" (133). Focusing on the idea of poetic dwelling as an alternative mode of being-in-the-world in connection to his specific understanding of the boundary—which is also related to a particular understanding of what Bhabha calls "unhomeliness"—Heidegger's thought can be fruitfully incorporated into the project at hand as one more supplement of the critical parameters operationalized so far.

Initiating a dialogue between Heidegger's work and the literature of Michael Ondaatje is also not as far-fetched as it might seem at first glance. The novelist's work, too, "can be seen as shedding light onto the dark spots of modernity understood in its philosophical sense" (25), writes Annick Hillger. She adds that, with his repeated emphasis on sensuality and corporeality, Ondaatje stresses "the suppression that *aesthesis* [sic] has undergone in modern epistemology" (29) and outlines "the special nature of poetic knowledge" (30) beyond *ratio*nal systematicity. These aspects turn *Anil's Ghost* into an ideal choice for unfolding the significance of an ab-used notion of Heidegger's poetic dwelling in the context of reading other-wise.[8]

The part will carry out this dialogue between philosophy and literature in two chapters. The first will realize the ab-use of Heidegger's thought in three interrelated steps. Picking up on passages from the part on this project's (b)ordering principles, chapter five will elaborate on Heidegger's concept of a struggle between world and earth as a more suitable foil for unfolding the dynamics of *presencing* than Gumbrecht's conceptualization of the relationship between meaning and presence. Pointing out the pitfalls in the latter's work—particularly regarding questions of gender, race, and class—the first section is going to critique the notion of oscillation and point out the compatibility of Heidegger's *counterturning* with Mignolo's border thinking and Waldenfels's radical otherness. In further distinction to Gumbrecht (including his notion of reading for *Stimmung*) and considering Heidegger's critique of the Western aesthetic tradition, the second section will tease out the potentials of Heidegger's particular understanding of attunement, namely by reading it with what Alexis Shotwell calls "sensuous knowledge." Implying an embodied, localized, and non-Cartesian mode of engaging with phenomena, attuned sensuousness will be (ab-usively) connected to Heidegger's *Besinnung* (mindfulness) in the sense of *Be-Sinnung* (the addition of senses) to describe it as a mode of sense-sensitizing relevant for transnational perspectives. The third section links the ab-usive concept of attuned sensuous knowledge with Heidegger's concepts of human (un-)homeliness and dwelling (through literature and beyond) by picking up on his reading of *Antigone*. It connects to the second chapter of the part (chapter six) by elaborating on and extending Lyotard's concept of grazing as a mode of poetic and sensuous dwelling in the border *Bezirk* (precinct) of discursive world and figural earth.

The sixth chapter's analysis of Ondaatje's *Anil's Ghost* continues and further concretizes the ab-use of Heidegger's thought again in three interconnected sections. The first of these sections illustrates how the literary text's (art-)work(ing) mirrors the *counterturning* epistemological struggle of world and earth—first on the level of the protagonists through negotiating local knowledges with Western science, but, then, also on the formal level by collapsing teleological and a-chronological narrative elements. The second section further probes the entanglement of world and earth by focusing on different modes of perception, particularly the haptic (as a form of sensuous knowledge) and the alternative notions of truth stemming from these (cf. Sanghera 90). First again concentrating on the interaction of major characters in the novel and, afterwards, once more considering specific formal features of the text, it will be explicated how the narrative enacts a sense-sensitizing process. The chapter shows how the reading process itself turns into an attuned act of sensuous (haptic) g(r)azing that partakes in the narrative's poetic performance. The last section will, ultimately, tie the analysis back to the notion of (un-)homeliness developed in the fifth chapter to emphasize the transnational potential unfolding in the novel. Specifically addressing the connection between aesthetics and politics in the context of the human rights investigation at the center of the plot, the argument is going to show how the text—through its potential as a poetic *Bezirk*—rejects a (subliminally) Western-dictated transnationalism and, instead, outlines the necessity of a border dwelling defined by simultaneous awareness for particularity and planetarity.

AB-USIVE DEVIATIONS

TO OFFER A FIRST characterization of said simultaneity's modality in relation to this project's focus on the other presences and to pave the way for the subsequent sections, the argument is now going to turn to the critical renegotiation of Gumbrecht's notion of oscillation in contrast to Heidegger's understanding of a *counterturning* motion; a(n un-)concept that assists in further refining and clarifying the notion of *presencing* and will remain important throughout what follows and beyond this part.

Oscillation and Counterturning

With the publication of *Production of Presence* in 2004, Hans Ulrich Gumbrecht established himself as one of the major proponents of presence-based epistemology within contemporary academic discourse. Weary of the dominant trends in the humanities, he seeks to draw attention to aspects of artifacts that literary and cultural studies have foreclosed due to the modalities of their approach (cf. 1). For Gumbrecht this is the outcome of larger historical developments. He argues that, through an epistemological process beginning with the Renaissance and reaching a climax in the philosophy of René Descartes with its differentiation between *res cogitans* and *res extensae*, occidental thought has ascribed to the human mind a privileged position that is still in place today; a vantage point from which materiality is reduced to the status of a mere object subjected to the judgment of reason (cf. 33). Critical of the Cartesian subject/object paradigm, Gumbrecht's focus on matters of presence highlights the relevance of spatial sensual modes of relating to the (phenomena of the) world: "Something that is 'present' is supposed to be tangible for human hands, which implies that, conversely, it can have an immediate impact on human bodies" (xiii). In his more recent work, Gumbrecht connects this to the polysemic German term *Stimmung*—meaning mood, climate, or tuning and attunement—and elaborates that "'[r]eading for *Stimmung*' always means paying attention to the textual dimension of the forms that envelop us and our bodies as a physical reality" (2012: 5). He claims that exceptional "conditions of 'extreme temporality'" (2004: 58) potentially give rise to intense and pre-reflective encounters with a pure presence that "exclusively appeal to the senses" (vx). Presence, Gumbrecht insists, testifies to complexities of works of literature beyond the reach of Western metaphysics.

His daring epistemological quest against the metaphysical stance toward literary texts is tied to the rejection of what Gumbrecht calls the "institutionally uncontested central position in the humanities of interpretation" (21). According to him, the differentiation between subject and object resulted in the elevation of hermeneutic methods as the only legitimate analytical practice. Strangely resonating with the critique of what Best and Marcus call surface reading, Gumbrecht defines interpretation as a form of producing knowledge that considers materiality of secondary importance or an obstacle to be overcome in the search for deeper insights: "To interpret the world means to go beyond its material surface or to penetrate that surface in order to identify a meaning (i.e. something spiritual) that is supposed to lie behind or beneath it" (25). He believes that the sole emphasis on (the construction of) meaning ultimately results in "the loss of (belief in) a world-reference" (46). Consequently, in Gumbrecht's thinking, meaning forms the antithesis of presence—the two concepts are regarded as diametrically opposed and mutually exclusive.[1]

Stressing this notion of incommensurability, Gumbrecht conceives of their relationship as one of "an oscillation between presence effects and meaning effects" (107), implying a dynamic tension of a constant back and forth. It is at this point that a critique of his thinking can be launched, for the metaphor of an oscillation between two poles betrays his indebtedness to a form of thinking he supposedly wishes to overcome. No matter how irregular and rapid the movement between these effects may be imagined, this rendering cannot belie the fact that the dynamics remain controlled by and contained within the schematic binarism of a Cartesian coordinate system that identifies meaning and presence as two static poles on either end of its spectrum. This way, Gumbrecht's strategy of introducing presence in addition to interpretation mirrors the Romantic impulse of establishing sensuality next to reason as equally significant (cf. 52). However, leaving the dichotomy itself unquestioned, he implicitly reproduces the subject/object split underlying the division of reason and sensuality, as Romantic thinkers before him did. Gumbrecht's efforts remain distinctly metaphysical in nature. Ultimately, he falls short of his own ambitions to circumvent Cartesianism.

In fact, this covert binary reasoning engenders and revives problems that Gumbrecht's declared archenemies—cultural studies and (feminist) deconstruction—have been criticizing over the past 50 years. Reminiscent of Harold Bloom's notorious polemic against "the School of Resentment" (7), Gumbrecht's dismissal of these approaches goes hand in hand with a symptomatic disregard concerning their core issues of gender, race, and class.

Firstly, drawing attention to the significance of corporeality as something supposedly radically new exposes Gumbrecht's reluctance to consider existing work in Gender Studies. Judith Butler's *Bodies that Matter* appears as a side note but does not shape his thinking of presence any further. Gumbrecht thus runs the risk of reaffirming a Western phallogocentric attitude which implicitly (re-)stylizes a male heterosexual body as the active subject regarding the passive woman, as the following passage shows: "I want my students to live or at least to imagine that moment of admiration (and perhaps also of the despair of an aging man) that gets a hold of me when I see the beautiful body of a young woman standing next to me" (97). Gumbrecht's fantasy of a pure presence free from any semiotic taint entails fetishizing the female body and again strips corporeality of its epistemological potential by turning it into an object ready for the male gaze of aesthetic contemplation. Although Gumbrecht critiques the scrutiny of interpretation, he does not realize this penetrating quality in his own subjectivist stare (cf. Lorde 58f.); a lustful stare which does not constitute a mutual spatial sensual encounter but only a one-sided distant gaze of abusive objectification.[2]

Secondly, also his treatment of (foreign) cultures is indicative of the latent Cartesianism guiding Gumbrecht's work. He suggests that "the one strategy" to adequately conceptualize matters of presence lies in "the recourse to pre- or nonmetaphysical cultures and discourses of the past" (78). To illustrate this, he takes recourse to sociologist Max Weber's trope of the *Idealtyp* and distinguishes between presence and meaning cultures. Gumbrechts lists the pre-Socratics and medieval culture as discourses more on the presence side of the spectrum. Modern culture, on the other hand, is seen as mostly meaning oriented. One may wonder, though, what kind of modern culture Gumbrecht is imagining. It is certainly not the pluralistic society of the contemporary United States. A glimpse at his other references shows that he adheres to a strictly Eurocentric perspective. Devoid of a sense for otherness, this view implies that there either are no more "presence-cultures" today or that such cultures, if they exist, are to be considered anachronistic curiosities and not part of modern societies. Both options are highly contestable as—to name just two examples—Native and African American cultures, indeed, have always valued spatial sensual modes of relating to the world; and contrary to what Gumbrecht's typology suggests, this does not render these cultures less rational or modern, but only attests to the validity of what Mignolo has called the subalternization of non-European knowledges.

Lastly, Gumbrecht's defense of the remoteness of academia's ivory tower, whose distanced position supposedly allows for "the possibility of thinking what cannot be thought in our everyday worlds" (127), underlines that his envisioned epistemological reconfigurations of Western thought are less radical than he claims. This stance is immediately tied up with his notion of presence. Although defined as bodily in nature, Gumbrecht insists that it relates to "feelings of intensity that we cannot find in the historically and culturally specific everyday worlds that we inhabit" (99). By affirming the validity of academic insularity, he fundamentally contradicts his initial assertion of wishing to reinstate a more grounded relationship to the things of the world and, yet again, re-inscribes the subject/object paradigm on another level. His (willed) ignorance of what is happening outside the confines of the scholarly ivory tower throws a shadow of hypocrisy over Gumbrecht's efforts and bespeaks an epistemological superiority complex. As a matter of fact, from this angle his work takes on an esoteric character. His epiphanies of pristine presence seem restricted to a priestly class or cast of academic acolytes.[3]

Playing off presence against meaning in Gumbrecht's binary fashion results in the return to some of the central pitfalls of Western thinking and underlines the importance of deconstructive and cultural studies approaches when it comes to the conceptualization of presence. It is necessary to emphasize the importance of the dimension of the haptic, embodiment, and sensual perception—also in the context of literature—but simply opposing corporeality to hermeneutics keeps the Cartesian paradigm intact. Gumbrecht's attempt of legitimizing his longing for pure presence only works if pitted against a rather narrow Eurocentric view of interpretation. As Stefan Hajduk has pointed out, Gumbrecht ignores that the radical challenge an acknowledgment of presence and *Stimmung* in literary texts poses is to think the possibility of reforming the meaning of meaning as something not exclusively metaphysical (2012: 143f.). The challenge lies in thinking the ambiguity of "sense" as (meta-)physical and conceiving of presence and meaning as inextricably interwoven.[4]

Gumbrecht's work serves as stepping stone for this argument and its take on Heidegger's thought as a source of inspiration for a more nuanced perspective on the relationship between meaning and presence. Heidegger's work on art, in particular, can be integrated into the discussion concerning the other presences and reading other-wise by way of a creative ab-use. Gumbrecht develops the notion of oscillation by failing to grasp the scope of the dynamics between what Heidegger in his essay "The Origin of the Work of Art" respectively refers to as "world" and "earth."

Heidegger describes world as self-opening openness and earth as self-secluding shelter upon which the world rests (cf. 2011: 111).[5] Gumbrecht wishes to read this dyad in analogy to his distinction between presence and meaning. Colored by the one-sided contention that materiality and substance form an opposition to semiotics and hermeneutics, he holds that earth refers to "things appearing in their primordial material qualities" (74) and "seen independently of their cultural situations"; world, on the other hand, signifies discursive "configurations of things in the context of specific cultural situations" (76).[6] Gumbrecht acknowledges that both are, indeed, inseparable, but he understands this inseparability as an agonistic being-together of opponents in divergence (cf. ibid.). In one passage of "The Origin of the Work of Art" Heidegger himself does, in fact, render this struggle as a "rift," albeit a rather curious one, for he defines it as follows: "Strife is not a rift [*Riss*], as a mere cleft is ripped open; rather, *it is the intimacy with which opponents belong to each other*. This rift carries the opponents into the provenance of their unity by virtue of their common ground. . . . This rift does not let the opponents break apart; *it brings what opposes measure and boundary into its common outline*" (121; my emphases). Considering that what the English translation here casts as "opponents" reads "die Gegenwendigen" (51) in the original German, literally meaning "the counterturning ones," Heidegger's illustration of the rift takes on a different character. Paradoxically, it does not emphasize a diverging movement. Quite to the contrary, it portrays a dynamic of pushing up against or even into each other, which cannot be neatly broken apart. Instead of a movement between two poles, Heidegger thinks world and earth as thoroughly entangled (cf. Barison 154, Kern 169, Walker 101). Gumbrecht's metaphor of an oscillation could be compared to a boxing match where the contenders try to land hits and evade getting hit in diverging moves. Heidegger's notion of counterturning, in contrast, evokes a playful wrestling match where the combatants are doubly bound and constantly engaged in an intimate embrace where the space of the one is always already under occupation by the other and vice versa. It follows that if one reads the interrelationship between meaning and presence as analogous to that of world and earth, then meaning and presence cannot be neatly separated either: rather, as *counterturning*, the one always involves and at the same time withdraws from the other.

This form of inseparability also affects the relationship between interpretation and what Gumbrecht calls the reading for *Stimmung*. Only through misreading the mutual entanglement of world and earth as a dynamic of divergence can he require mood sensitive reading as the physical dimension of a (literary) text that relates to feeling and the senses beyond semiotic representation and is consequently to be practiced in addition to hermeneutics (cf. 2012: 5f.). Heidegger's understanding of interpretation, however, differs significantly from Gumbrecht's notion of a mere "identification and/or attribution of meaning" (2004: 1). Based on dynamic entwining of world and earth, interpretation in Heidegger's thought always entails and even requires *Stimmung*: there is no effect of the material that is not also meaningful, just as there is no meaning that is not also affecting. In other words, there is always the circular movement of *counterturning*. Instead of violently breaking this motion apart into easily distinguishable poles of a binary opposition and then fixing these in place as a stalemate between asemiotic presence and semiotic meaning, Heidegger's hermeneutics retains a released openness for this ever-turning wheel: "Thus we are compelled to follow the circle. This is neither a makeshift nor a defect. To enter upon this path is the strength of thought, to continue on it is the feast of thought" (2011: 90). For Heidegger, there is never the separation of interpretation and reading for *Stimmung*, but always already the ludic round dance of the hermeneutic circle between world and earth.

Although world and earth are thoroughly and reciprocally entangled, this does not mean that they dissolve into the static synthesis of a systemic harmony on a higher level. Although never entirely disconnected from it, as *counterturning*, earth constantly wrests itself from the grasp of world and remains ever-withdrawing from its ordering principles. The hermeneutic roundabout does not mend, but mirrors and takes place in the strife of world and earth as a rift. Heidegger plays on different shades of meaning contained in the German word *Grundriss*, implying "basic design, an outline sketch" (121) as well as a fundamental fissure. He thinks interpretation as involving the order of meaning and its *presencing* excess, or, in short, as requiring the dynamic simultaneity of the ordinary and the extraordinary. The rift constitutes a liminal space between world and earth—always connected to both and neither. Moving within this tearing circle, hermeneutics means residing somewhere in-between without completely entering into either territory and entails the idea of border gnosis or thinking *from* dichotomies. Forming an (extra-)ordinary space of ever-coinciding meaning and presence, Heidegger's rift can be conceived of, through creative ab-use and with the help of Mignolo, as a "dichotomous locus of enunciation"; a place located at an "intersection between incommensurable (from the perspective of modernity) forms of knowledge" (2000: 85), namely within a (meta-)physical borderland where sensuality and rationality uneasily commingle.

Border gnosis between world and earth encompasses far-reaching implications concerning the hegemony of Western reasoning which Gumbrecht does not follow through. Heidegger's critique of occidental metaphysics' structures is mirrored in Mignolo's call for epistemological disobedience

and, specifically, the urge to "delink from territorial and imperial epistemology grounded on theological (Renaissance) and egological (Enlightenment)
politics of knowledge" (2011: n.pag.). The two thinkers—differently and
yet akin—emphasize the necessity of developing a willingness to question
the legitimacy of established disciplinary frameworks in their predominant
forms by drawing attention to subalternized modes of knowing without
digesting them within systemic closure. By translating the playful motion of
counterturning into the metaphor of oscillation, on the other hand, Gumbrecht re-integrates spatial sensuality into the very Cartesian grid he supposedly seeks to do away with. A neat conceptual distinction of presence and
meaning as two incommensurate amplitudinal opposites only works within
a calculative Western form of thinking that annexes both into the territory
of its philosophical system by harnessing them in the fields of aesthetics and
logic as academic disciplines. Consequently, Gumbrecht's proclamation that
"a reflection on presence would show how hopeless it was for the humanities to try and justify their existence by pointing to some 'social function'
or 'political yield'" (2004: 133) takes on a rather hypocritical character. It
contains the veiled political agenda of bolstering a crumbling Western academic hegemony and securing the privileged position of white male scholars
that depends on this professed superiority. Through rejecting deconstruction
and Cultural Studies, Gumbrecht signals a reluctance to acknowledge that,
to conceptualize spatial sensuality as a way to *circum*vent the Cartesian
subject/object split, one also has to dismantle the phallically symbolic ivory
tower it erected.[7]

Heidegger's notion of *counterturning* between world and earth as border gnosis neither allows for an objectifying aesthetic stance, nor for an
exclusion of non-Eurocentric perspectives or the restriction of presence to
a handful of esoteric initiates. Gumbrecht's haughty declaration of corporeality's epistemological significance from a(n again) merely masculine
Eurocentric perspective is tantamount to reproducing a phallocentric matrix that, granted, elevates the sensual to the same level, but elevates it as
something that ultimately does not challenge the validity of established
notions of reason, which can, therefore, stay (in-)different toward the sensual. As *counterturning*, sensuality and rationality are ever-codependently
intertwined in circular motion. Moreover, related to the broader subjectivist
ramifications of his work, also Gumbrecht's assertion that his "objective
is to follow configurations of atmosphere and mood in order to encounter otherness in intense and intimate ways" (2012: 12f.) creates the strong
impression of an appropriating exoticism. Instead, the movement of *counterturning* initiates a process of unsettlement where the other *presences* in
withdrawal, thus underscores its claims and concerns, and asserts that a

form of radical otherness is always already at work within the self. Eventually, when Gumbrecht holds that reading for *Stimmung* "means discovering sources of energy in artifacts and giving oneself over to them affectively and bodily—yielding to them and gesturing toward them" (18)—then he has in mind the removed phenomena of allegedly unmotivated aesthetic pleasure. *Counterturning* hermeneutics, in contrast, refers to communal everyday modes of being-in-the-world, forgotten (or subalterinized) by the Western *ratio*, that harbor a specific political potential. While thinking presence and meaning as oscillation risks a recourse to previous mistakes, thinking them as *counterturning* opens up the occidental epistemological horizon to new opportunities.

All this is not to relativize the importance of reclaiming more spatial sensual modes of relating to the world, but to think them more radically still. In line with this chapter's argument, Alexis Shotwell points out that the sensual may not be simply opposed to what is rational in the fashion of Romanticism, for if one "synchronizes reason with passion, each of those categories hardens into conventional hierarchies of knowledge"; instead, she suggests, one should "look for an account of sensuousness that would assert a synchronicity without thereby positing irreducible distinctions and separability" (63). The next section works toward such an account by revisiting the term *Stimmung* through Heidegger's understanding of attunement in relation to Shotwell's concept of sensuous knowledge.

Attunement and Sense-Sensitivity

Stimmung is, by far, not a novel term, but has been inherently interwoven with the attempt of recuperating the validity of the sensual and the subsequent rise of aesthetics as a philosophical discipline in the Western tradition since the 1750s. While reflections on mood had meanwhile largely lost in significance—particularly during the second half of the twentieth century—scholars have more recently rediscovered their promising epistemological potentials (cf. Hajduk 2011: 89).[8] Gumbrecht's reading for *Stimmung* also constitutes an example of this revitalization. However, his specific take again remains deeply Eurocentric and results in the reproduction of old problems. Ironically, the covert subjectivism characterizing Gumbrecht's work—also apparent in his insistence on "aesthetic immediacy" (2012: 12) and an "intensified aesthetic fascination" where "matters of sense and meaning are secondary" (20)—is what had earlier caused the rejection of mood-based analyses in literary studies. Like notions of *Stimmung* based on Hegel's aesthetics in the late nineteenth century, Gumbrecht's thought promotes the individualization of mood and (subjectivist) aesthetic experiences. Instead of challenging these metaphysical tendencies, he implicitly reaffirms them, again subsumes the senses under the *ratio*'s systemic limitations, and re-perpetuates the pitfalls of the occidental tradition.

In contrast, Heidegger's critique of occidental aesthetics paves the way for productively incorporating a sense of *Stimmung* as attunement into the project of reading other-wise. In the essay "The Origin of the Work of Art," he assails the metaphysical subjectivism intrinsic to modern Western conceptualizations of art: "Almost from the time when specialized thinking about art and the artist began, this thought was called aesthetic. Aesthetics takes the work of art as an object, the object of *aisthēsis*, of sensuous apprehension in the wide sense. Today we call this apprehension lived experience. . . . Everything is an experience. Yet perhaps lived experience is the element in which art dies" (2011: 133). Heidegger argues that establishing sensuous perception (or lived experience) next to a conceptual experience of the world, as Gumbrecht would have it (cf. 2004: 39), replicates the subject/object logic insofar it conceives of a sensual form of approaching the world in analogy to the instrumentalist modalities of *rati*onal thought. This view, for him, results in the decontextualization of art as ready-to-hand objects for an allegedly immediate and engrossed aesthetic experience beyond the everyday that effectively strips artworks of their transformative force (cf. Young 9f.). From this perspective, even Gumbrecht's terminology remains a(nother) symptomatic indicator of a metaphysical worldview despite its claims to the contrary. For Heidegger, such a "triumph of the aesthetic view of art" is again synonymous with "the imperialism of reason" (Young 14) that subjects the world to its systemic grid.[9]

Nonetheless, this critical stance toward the aesthetic must not be mistaken for a complete rejection of sensual perception and corporeality. Heidegger shares with Gumbrecht—and Mignolo, for that matter—the urge to work toward a dehierarchization of philosophy and art or, of sensuality and rationality; but, rather than having Western reason again dictate the conditions of this relational renegotiation and consequently positioning the two in adversarial equality, as aestheticians since Alexander Gottlieb Baumgarten have been all too prone to do, Heidegger opts for a more radical mode of thinking that insists on an entangled reciprocity (cf. Bass 86). He claims that it is neither possible nor desirable to simply venture beyond aesthetics, as also Iain Thomson points out: Heidegger's understanding of art does not constitute an "anti-aesthetics" in the form of a "merely oppositional movement [which] remains trapped in the logic of what it opposes" (41). Overcoming the Cartesian axiomatic cannot be achieved through an inversion that replaces the illusion of a pure supra-sensual meaning with the fantasy of an untainted sensual presence, for this strategy remains complicit with the workings of a Hegelian strand of metaphysics, as Heidegger attests in critical distancing from Nietzsche (cf. 2009: 74ff.). True to his ludic notion of *counterturning*, Heidegger argues that an effective challenge requires a motion of "Verwindung" (ibid. 75)—literally a twisting or distorting. Thomson aptly summarizes this position as follows: "*the best way to get beyond aesthetic experience is to transcend it from within*" (56). Recovering the subalternized epistemological capacity of sensuality within the *ratio* calls for the creative twist of ab-use.

Stylizing Heidegger's philosophy of art into a "post-aesthetics," as scholars nowadays tend to do, is misleading, for this label obfuscates the—admittedly, implicit—centrality of sensual corporeality in his thought. "And while Heidegger notoriously says very little about sexuality," as Alan Bass attests, "he is a thinker of the body" and "says that we *are* as body" (83). This is important to keep in mind, for, Mignolo holds, "the suppression of sensing and the body" has always been the crucial scheme within the modern/colonial world system that first enabled a "theo- and ego-politics of knowledge to claim universality" (2011b: n.pag.). Although several contemporary scholars, such as Krzysztof Ziarek, continue to build their reflections regarding the transformative potential of art on Heidegger's thought and come to innovative conclusions, the tendency to proceed through a "postaesthetic manner" (Ziarek 2004: 7) to "rethink art's force beyond the boundaries of aesthetics" (3) appears thoroughly problematic. On the one hand, as pointed out above, formulations such as these create the impression of having fallen prey to a metaphysical cause-and-effect logic which Heidegger tries to avoid through *Verwindung*; and, on the other hand, this project effaces the significance of the body within *Dasein* and being-in-the-world. As such, Ziarek, too, remains largely Eurocentric in his outlook. However, in reference to Heidegger, Waldenfels highlights that, particularly in intercultural comparison, this elision of sensuality and the corporeal within the occidental tradition attests to the still prevailing phallocentric bias (cf. 2010: 318, 325). To situate Heidegger's thought in a transnational context, it is, hence, doubly significant to stress the relevance of corporeality as well as sensual perception in his work; it is important to insist on the insight that the system of "*aesthetics* will have to be reworked at the level of bodies" (Nancy 2008: 115), and from within, instead of trying to leave it behind.

Heidegger's work offers a useful hint in this direction. He writes that the *Verwindung* of metaphysics must coincide with the becoming-other of thinking which he calls "Besinnung" and further defines as "[t]he courage to turn the truth of one's own presuppositions and the scope of one's own aims into what is the most questionable" (2003: 75).[10] The German word *Sinn*—like its English counterpart "sense"—can indicate *both* meaning *and* the physical senses. Megan Altman writes that, through this striking equiv-ocality, *Besinnung* functions "as a mode of receptivity to changing mani-festations of meaning" (230) which is not restricted to the rules of reason but maintains a "non-discursive" (231) quality; reminiscent of Waldenfels's pathos and response, it retains an openness "for human being to 'receive' and 'respond'—to co-respond" (235)—instead of subjecting the world under-neath the projections of the *ratio*. Nevertheless, when the English translation usually renders the term *Besinnung* simply as "mindfulness," it one-sidedly unwinds the ambivalent doubleness of sense contained in this coinage, an-nuls its radical character, and reintegrates it into Cartesian logic. Literally, though, *Besinnung* expresses the supplementation of meaning with the physical senses, which can be indicated by adding a dash that signifies the entangling tension of sense between cognition and sensuality: *Be-Sinnung* can be related to what Shotwell calls "the realm of sensuous knowledge" (57) that is "not reducible to rational or logical form," but—just as the al-tered thinking Heidegger envisions—"communicates truths through taking us from our constraint," namely through the "contradiction and subversion of dominant consciousness" (54). Further explicating this *Be-Sinnung* as sensuous knowledge helps specify the fundamental role of sensual percep-tion and corporeality in Heidegger's philosophy.

The notion of *Stimmung* as attunement substantially differs from Gum-brecht's concept. In "The Origin of the Work of Art," Heidegger writes: "Per-haps, however, what we call feeling or mood, here and in similar instances, is more reasonable [*vernünftiger*]—that is, more intelligently perceptive [*vernehmender*]—because open to Being than all that reason which, having meanwhile become *ratio*, was misinterpreted as being rational" (2011: 95). When he describes mood as more intelligently perceptive and simultaneously emphasizes that reason within occidental thought always means *ratio*nality, he is not inverting the hierarchical dichotomy between sensuality and rationality; he rather provides another allusion to an ir*ratio*nal thinking where feeling and reason do not form a binary opposition, but are always already entan-gled (cf. Han 35; Ferreira 147). The responsive openness Heidegger evokes here is related to the understanding of hermeneutics as the *counterturning* border gnosis between world and earth. Mood in the form of attunement designates "the *whole range of disclosive affectivity*" (Storolow 8): it is *nei-ther* rational, nor sensual, *and* yet *both* at once. Heidegger further clarifies this connection by explaining that "[p]*hilosophy in each case happens in a fundamental attunement* [*Grundstimmung*; literally: ground mood]. Con-ceptual philosophical comprehension is grounded in our being gripped, and this is grounded in a fundamental attunement" (1995: 7). He once again (re-)states that the grasp of world is founded on a coinciding being-gripped by earth that withdraws from conceptual recognition but, nonetheless, affects by way of sense as attuned mood. Sensuality and corporeality, within Heidegger's work, (un-)contain the otherness of an irreducible telluric force via which *Stimmung* or feeling *figures* beyond individualist subjectivism as disrupting pathos (cf. Waldenfels 2010: 13f., 325; Barison 152).[11] Therefore, while he does not simply form a reverse binary hierarchy, the notion of attunement certainly draws attention to the subalternized potential of the senses: it expresses the call for *Be-Sinnung*; or, in the words of psychoanalyst Robert Stolorow, "without explicitly naming the lived body, Heidegger has placed it, along with affectivity, at the heart of Dasein's disclosedness" (9).

Corresponding to the existential concept of *Dasein*, mood constitutes a radical renegotiation of the epistemological role of localized substantial spatiality. Hubert L. Dreyfus elaborates that attuned "affectedness implies a disclosive submission to the world" (173) which, contrary to the logic of the Cartesian paradigm, acknowledges that human existence is not external toward this (life-)world, but always already part of it as an embodied "way of being-in-the-world" (172). The correlation of affect and space becomes even clearer when Heidegger synonymously refers to attunement as *Befindlichkeit*. With this term—meaning both a person's emotional state and (taken literally) also "how-one-finds-oneself-ness"—he describes, in one word, a location in space, or situatedness, that is directly linked to sensuality as well as feeling. Heidegger, thereby, outlines an emotionally atmospheric situation between pathos and response (cf. Ferreira 141f.; Waldenfels 2010: 323). He can be said to describe what Ursula Heise has called a "'sense of place'" (13)—but again with a decisive twist. Heidegger does not shed the ambivalent (meta-)physical tension of *sense* between meaning and sensation, although he accentuates the latter. With *Befindlichkeit*, he points toward the necessity of considering the affectation through a *sense* of place. The implications of this aspect are of central importance to the further course of this chapter's line of argument and will be clarified throughout the following pages.

To do so, one first needs to render more explicit the connection between attunement and sensuous knowledge. The *tertium comparationis* of this connection is Friedrich Schiller's conception of the play drive. There, two forms of creative ab-use overlap. On the one hand, Heidegger relates this aporetic aesthetic dynamic—Schiller himself describes it as a mediating free mood between thinking and feeling—to his more radical understanding of fundamental attunement as *Befindlichkeit* where rationality and sensuality are inherently intertwined (cf. Miroković 102f.). On the other, Shotwell, analogously, builds on the same imbrication of feeling and thinking within the playful aesthetic condition to put a stress on "the embodied situation *we find ourselves in* which situates us in time and matter" (59; my emphasis) and that is, consequently, inseparably co-constitutive of human existence, although it has been gendered into passivity within the Western tradition. Both thinkers follow the same ab-usive course of going beyond Schiller by insisting on the mutual entanglement of the rational and the sensual contained in the doubleness of *sense*. Heidegger's call for *be-sinnt* attunement resonates with Shotwell's search "for an account of sensuousness that would assert a synchronicity without thereby positing irreducible distinctions and separability" (63). In their respective ways, both Heidegger's existential *Befindlichkeit* and Shotwell's sensuous knowledge point toward a sidelined epistemological potential through propagating an ab-used notion of aesthetics beyond the logic of Cartesianism.

Attunement and sensuous knowledge involve an attempt of freeing sensual perception from the individualist-subjectivist limitations it has attained within the *ratio* to, then, recast sensuality as an innately grounded and communal affair. With existential *Befindlichkeit* Heidegger never refers to a merely private mental or emotional condition: "The world of Dasein is a *with-world*. Being-in is *being-with* others" (Dreyfus 149). Moreover, through its relation to the concealing force of earth, attunement (literally) incorporates a *sense* of otherness into the illusion of a homogeneous self. Heidegger's mood, Waldenfels elaborates, always unfolds as a corporeal and situated being-with others that entails the possibility of (reciprocal) affectation between pathos and response, in which the earthen vessel of the body draws attention to a need for renegotiating the static boundaries of self and other (cf. 2000: 275, 284f.). In the broader context, Waldenfels adds the following important clarification: "The sense of self also is part of this material corporeality, which belongs to us without us ever being able to fully appropriate it. The otherness [Fremdheit] of one's own body renders us susceptible to the otherness [Fremdheit] of the other [des Anderen]. We are only addressable, touchable, affectable insofar as we are never entirely with ourselves" (2010: 326).[12] Shotwell's description of sensuous knowledge, too, is in agreement with this observation. For her, sensuality constitutes "an expression of relationality [that] situates one in relation to others" (68) and, as such, "marks a material social relation" that opens up the potential for "non-alienated species-being" (69), namely in the form of a "non-reductive bodily experience" (125). Attunement and sensuous knowledge similarly oust the distanced and isolated mode of aesthetic contemplation to make room for an everyday spatial social embodiment of "aesthetic engagement" (Magrini 510). While Heidegger's *Verwindung* of the *ratio* supplements reason with existential attunement, Shotwell's critique induces a non-masculinist and non-racialist excess of sensuous knowledge that harbors a (socio-politically) transformative potential regarding encounters with otherness.

Reading Heidegger with Shotwell, therefore, serves as a fundamental stepping-stone toward the integration of attuned *Stimmung* as a *sense* of place into reading other-wise. The two thinkers conceptualize aesthetics beyond the static limitations of the subject/object paradigm by regarding the body as residing within the dynamic (meta-)physical doubleness of *sense*. What Shotwell renders as a non-binary synchronicity and what Heidegger describes as the movement of *counterturning* is geared toward the deconstruction of stable boundaries between mind and body through thinking the corporeal as the always already communal and transformative "taking-place of sense" (Nancy 2008: 119). Waldenfels expresses the resulting role of corporeality as follows: "Therefore, the body [*Leib*] functions not only as the 'transfer point' between mind and nature, between ownness and otherness, but also as a point of entanglement where the various threads of aesthesis, kinesis, and poiesis run together" (2010: 11).[13] In a next step, picking up on the body's in-between-ness and working as an intersection of different potentialities, attuned sensuous knowledge can, consequently, be further aligned with Mignolo's transnational concept of border thinking and de-colonial aesthetics as sense-sensitivity.

Marking a point of entanglement, situated corporeality is related to the *counterturning* border gnosis between world and earth and specifies the aspect of spatiality inherent within this dynamic motion. In *Corpus*, Jean-Luc Nancy writes that "[b]*odies don't take place in discourse or in matter*. They don't inhabit 'mind' or 'body.' They take place at the limit, *qua limit*: limit—external border, the fracture and intersection of anything foreign in a continuum of sense, a continuum of matter" (17). As such, *counterturning* bodies are always already bordering entities. They conserve the potential of a *sense* of sensual perception not bound by the subject/object split's world by doubly binding mind and body as attuned to and grounded upon earth: "it makes no sense to talk about body and thought apart from each other, as if each could somehow subsist on its own," Nancy continues, "they are only their touching each other, the touch of their breaking down, and into, each other" (37). It is within this reciprocal wrestling embrace, that rationality and sensuality together form what Mignolo calls dichotomous performative loci of enunciation instead of promoting "the universal ground of the [occidental] 'human' mind" (2000: 190) which regards all other entities as *res extensae*. The touching body of border gnosis enacts the taking place of *sense* where the other always already *presences* from within.

Mignolo's promotion of a de-colonial aesthetics, connoting "practices that challenge and subvert the hegemony of modern/colonial aestheSis" (2013: n.pag.), is connected to the call for a becoming-other of Western knowledge that also relates to Heidegger's *Verwindung* and Shotwell's ab-usive criticism. This becomes particularly apparent in Mignolo's bemoaning of a Eurocentric subjectivist "transmogrification of 'art' as skill into 'art' as norm, as good taste and beauty" which "enabled the disdain and the rejection of other forms of aesthetic practices, or, more precisely, other forms of aestheSis, of sensing and perceiving" (ibid.); a dismissal that, as does Gumbrecht's work, robs the aesthetic of any epistemological potential beyond a removed and individual experience. In the previously quoted passage from "The Origin of the Work of Art," Heidegger establishes a similar connection: regarding the hermeneutic circle, he writes that "to continue on it is the feast of thought" and eventually adds, "assuming that thinking is a craft" (2011: 90). For him, thinking, as an attuned mode of being-in-the-world (with others), takes on the character of art as a skillful and *poiētic* "*bringing forth* that causes beings in the first place to come forward and be present in assuming an outward aspect" (119; my emphasis) and implies communality. Similarly — bridging her own Marxian approach with Heidegger's ontological stance — Shotwell, too, develops her notion of "sensuous knowledge as craft" (148) that harbors a politically transformative momentum. With her explicit focus on the corporeal and mirroring Heidegger's terminology, she envisions a "form of understanding *bodied forth* through aesthetic experience" (49; my emphasis) that "subverts our perception and understanding of reality as it appears to us" (53). In their respective revision of sensual modes of perception, the three thinkers delineate an epistemological potential that allows for combining the political kinetics of Shotwell's sensuous knowledge, with the ontological poetics of Heidegger's *Stimmung*, as well as the decolonial aesthetics of Mignolo's sense-sensitivity; an ab-usive combination that ultimately results in what Shotwell herself refers to as a "knowing otherwise" (61).

From the angle of creative sabotage, which builds on the interconnection of these concepts, Heidegger's metaphysical critique attains a less resigning character and even alludes to forgotten opportunities. According to the philosopher, art, through the subjection of artworks to the framework of occidental aesthetics, "becomes marginal within the lives of those who choose to take it up. And it becomes marginal to the life of the culture as a whole" (12), as Julian Young explains. The project of reading other-wise does not take this position of marginality as cause for resignation, but turns it into an enabling gesture. It does not regard the *ratio*'s attempt of taming aesthetics via integration into its philosophical system as resulting in the entire eradication of the ir*rati*onal withdrawal of the sensuous that will always haunt the *cogito*. Reading other-wise ab-uses the subordination under the logic of Western reason, and the subsequent displacement and repression to the epistemological margin, by insisting on the *presencing* of a subversive and decentralizing potential within those cultures that are, at times, too much concerned with their own centrality. In line with Mignolo's notion of decolonization, reading other-wise holds that, hidden away within the occidental philosophical straightjacket, there resides the radically other "possibility of [sense-sensitized] re-existence through the everyday aesthetic practices and the senses" (2013a: n.pag.) from the boundaries of the *ratio*'s epistemological hegemony; a disavowed sensuously attuned knowledge that designates a *sense* of place in the form of an always already bordering locus of enunciation between world and earth; in short, a form of knowledge that constantly undermines the systemic discursive global designs of *ratio*nal metaphysics.

Dwelling and Literature

Regarding the overall argument of this chapter, two important questions have yet been left unaddressed: firstly, how does this *sense* of place fit into the broader perspective of a transnational approach? To make clear that the emphasis on place does not run counter to Transnational American Studies' professed goal of leaving behind parochialism, it is important, once more, to recall this book's initial thesis concerning the hegemonic status of the *ratio* and its dismissal of alternative epistemological horizons. Through (sense-)sensitivity for the voice from *el otro lao* one can avoid complicity with the reach of neoliberal globalization and infuse a *sense* of planet—that is, a global mode of thinking beyond the limitations of systematicity—into current transnational endeavors. Secondly, how does this form of sensuous attunement, with its strong focus on corporeality, relate to works of literature? In this context, also, it is necessary to keep in mind the noninstrumentalist notion of language underlying this project and already partially developed in other chapters;[14] otherwise one runs the risk of falling prey to similar objectifying tendencies as those characterizing Gumbrecht's reading for *Stimmung*. By considering the subversive force of figural excess in its concomitance with discursivity's logic, it becomes possible to illustrate how the (politically) transformative potential of sensuous knowledge pertains to the reading of literary texts, too. Responding to these questions will pave the way for engaging with Ondaatje's *Anil's Ghost*.

Another later text by Heidegger provides a significant hint toward answering these two questions and even exposes them as thoroughly interwoven. Borrowing a line from the German poet Friedrich Hölderlin, the philosopher entitled one of his essays ". . . Poetically Man Dwells . . ."; and the three terms contained in this title will function as the roadmap for what follows. Although "man"—which, it should be noted, reads "human" in the original German and does not include the gender bias of the English translation—at first glance might seem disconnected from the discussion above, Heidegger's particular notion thereof can help guard the argument against premature accusations of provincial nostalgia and stasis supposedly contained in the idea of dwelling. Since it also helps to pick up again on the connection to Bhabha, "man" is going to form the point of departure. A second step will, then, outline "dwelling" as a dynamic concept suitable to explain how attunement relates to both *sense* of place and planet. While turning to the "poetic" aspect last may initially appear as a deferral of the issue of language, this third step is going to illustrate how the preceding steps (within the *counterturning* hermeneutic circle) have always already resided in the very midst of this very question.[15]

In his *Introduction to Metaphysics*, Heidegger arrives at his specific concept of the human first by way of an analysis of Parmenides and, then, especially his widely discussed interpretation of the choral ode within Sophocles's tragedy *Antigone* whose first two lines (in English) read: "Many are the wonders, none / is more wonderful than what is man" (174). Heidegger famously translates the Greek *deinōn* (δεινόν)—which David Grene here renders "wonder"—as "das Unheimliche," meaning "the uncanny" or, more literally, "the unhomely." Within contemporary Anglophone literary studies, this German term is usually connected to Sigmund Freud's 1919 essay with the same title. There, Freud retraces the etymology of the word "heimlich"—that can mean both "secretive" and "homely"—to show that "unheimlich" does not simply form its antonym. He rather concludes that "*heimlich* is a word the meaning of which develops in the direction of ambivalence, until it finally coincides with its opposite, *unheimlich*. *Unheimlich* is in some way or other a sub-species of *heimlich*" (226). Heidegger's understanding of the unhomely bears strong resemblances to Freud's insistence on its semantic ambivalence, as also Derrida has repeatedly stressed (cf. 1987: 191; 2006: 218f.). Nonetheless, in his reading of *Antigone*, Heidegger apparently moves into another direction when he writes: "The Greek word deinon has that uncanny ambiguity with which the saying of the Greeks traverses [*durchmißt*] the opposed [*gegenwendigen*; in this part cast as "*counterturning*"] confrontations [*Aus-einander-setzungen*] of Being" (2000: 159). Put differently, he first distinguishes between two always already coinciding meanings of the uncanny or unhomely. The connection to the project at hand becomes clearer when he sees this doubleness of *sense* as inherently connected to the respective status of what he calls earth.

On the one hand, Heidegger relates the *deinōn* to *technē* (τέχνη), meaning "craft" (and, as such, also art) to point out the first modality of humans' stance toward their surroundings. In the choral ode, "man" is described as the one "who wears away / the Earth, oldest of Gods" and whose "contrivances /

make him master of beasts of the field and those that move in the mountains" (174). In using technical skills, humans have learned to model their surroundings and to shape their existence on earth—or to construct a world—according to the conditions of their environment. In this sense of *deinōn*, "man" is the "one who needs to use violence—and does not just have violence at his disposal but is violence-doing" (Heidegger 2000: 160). Humans appear as uncanny insofar they intervene into the concealment of earth but, as long as it remains in the motion of *counterturning*, Heidegger does not judge this attitude as negative *per se*. Nevertheless, he identifies it as the impetus of what would later render possible *rati*onal metaphysics, where technical skillfulness results in the misled "presumption and arrogance that we are not actually of this earth" (Davis 179) and have the power to subject it as a ready-to-hand object. This becomes particularly evident in the subjugation of other cultures under the hegemonic rule of what Mignolo has called the modern/colonial world system with its projection of Western knowledge to global designs (cf. 2000: 17). Through the sole focus on *technē* as "the violence-doing of knowing" (Heidegger 2000: 176), without any *sense* of place, the grasp of occidental reason's world assumes that it can control earth and, because of this domination, is at home in it. Heidegger, in contrast, reverses this *rati*onal logic. He holds that humans' militant misuse of *unheimlich* technical skills results in existential homelessness.[16]

On the other hand, however, Heidegger links *deinōn* to *dikē* (δίκη), usually translated as "justice" but here implying more than a merely judicative or moral concept, namely the "overwhelming sway" (159) of earth's concealment that always runs counter to its technical modification. In Sophocles's tragedy, "man" has to yield to this telluric force, at the latest, when faced with mortality: "He has a way against everything, / and he faces nothing that is to come / without contrivance. / Only against death / can he call on no means of escape" (174). This is nothing else than a reformulation of humans' irreducible connection to earth's withdrawal from world as a fact of finite corporeal existence often described within Western mythologies; but Heidegger derives from this the second meaning of "man's" unhomeliness which can be explicated by focusing, once more, on the body. As attuned sensuous bodies bound to the ungraspable force of earth, humans never exist as stable subjects, but remain in an (extra-)ordinary relation of "excess" (Shotwell 148) toward the ordering principles of their technically constructed world; a bond which permanently discloses them as "radically other-than-[themselves]" (136). This way, the withdrawal that characterizes embodied selves at the same time uncovers "man's" belonging to earth as that which ever-transgresses the localized confines of world but first provides the locales or places for constructing such a world. Regarding human beings as always already under the impact of *dikē* and its earthen excess, "Heidegger exposes the groundlessness of the security or what he might term the 'tranquilized self-assurance' (*beruhigter Vertrautheit*) [this is a quotation from *Sein und Zeit*] of being-at-home-in-the-world" (O'Donoghue 129). Residing within the *unheimlich* overwhelming sway of earth, mortally corporeal "man" is never entirely at home within the designs of world but remains foreign: "The unhomely does not allow us to be at home" (Heidegger 2000: 161).

However, these individual analyses of the different layers of *unheimlich* in Heidegger's thought only constitute a preliminary step. This becomes obvious in the following remark: "The deinotaton of the deinon, the uncanniest of the uncanny [*das Unheimlichste des Unheimlichen*], lies in the oppositional [*gegenwendigen*, that is *counterturning*] relation of dike and techne" (173). The English translation here, again, is misleading, as Heidegger reads both terms as inseparably enmeshed in a reciprocal relationship and so mutually constitutive. The technical modification of earth, according to the projections of world, through which humanity seeks to establish a home for itself, coincides with earth's uncanny overwhelming sway, which ever-annuls the sense of complete being-homely, and continuously testifies to humans' unhomeliness on earth and in themselves (cf. O'Donoghue 153f.; Davis 180). In other words: a sense of unhomeliness remains involved in the home, just as a sense of homeliness remains involved in the unhomely. Contouring Freud's *sense* of the uncanny, Heidegger's interpretation of *Antigone*'s first *stasimon*, ultimately defines "man's" existence—*counterturning* between homely and unhomely—as (un-)homely.[17]

Bearing this in mind—to ob-viate prejudiced verdicts of nostalgia—the argument can now move on to the concept of dwelling and its relevance in the context of reading other-wise. In "Building, Dwelling, Thinking," Heidegger writes: "To be a human being means to be on the earth as a mortal. It means to dwell" (2011: 245). What, however, does this imply? At the risk of redundancy, responding properly to this question requires an ab-usive—and at first glance rather—circumstantial or, better, *circumventional* exposition.

In short, for Heidegger, dwelling is the term designating the mode of human existence as re-siding within *counterturning* (un-)homeliness just described. It is important, though, not to mistake this for what he calls homelessness. The latter is the result of Western metaphysics' one-sided focus on the technical modification of earth, in which earth's force is—in a first step—disavowed to treat earth as nothing more than a material object to be mastered. Never being able to entirely free itself from earth's concealing force, as that which first enables a world's construction, the *ratio*—in a second step—then displaces this earthen force onto itself, claiming it for *technē* instead, and, thereby, creates the notion of static homeliness and its worldwide(ning) extension. The absolution or quasi apotheosis of technical metaphysics results in the global designs of the modern/colonial world system's most recent manifestation, namely global neoliberalism. Spivak writes: "The globe is on our computers. It is the logo of the World Bank. No one lives there; and we think that we can aim to control globality" (2012: 338). This militant treatment of earth, also for Heidegger, equals existential homelessness.

In contrast, he describes dwelling as technically "sparing" (2011: 246) earth by remaining care-fully exposed to its overwhelming sway.[18] "This 'sparing'," Ziarek writes, "comes to outline the new style of thinking ... which Heidegger calls *Besinnung*" (2013: 142) and constitutes a characteristic of a sensuously attuned existence with a *sense* of place; a mode of being always situated within the *counterturning* dynamics of world *and* earth.[19] Heidegger does not identify this as a lack but as something that is decidedly "*positive* and takes place when we leave something beforehand in its own essence [*Wesen*]" (2011: 246) not attempting to subdue and dominate it. This is not to say that dwelling merely results in isolated rural existence, for, grounded on earthen concealment, human beings are always already likewise embedded within broader existential spatiality (cf. Gorgone 129). Ab-using Heise's second term, this means that, precisely since earth grants a *sense* of place, which is one of ungraspable withdrawal into the unhomely, it paradoxically—and simultaneously—opens the radical possibility (appropriated by the *ratio* and twisted into exploitation) for a *sense* of planet beyond said Cartesian objectification.[20] Here is Spivak once more: "The planet is in the species of alterity, belonging to another system; and yet we inhabit it, indeed we are it" (2012: 338). In other words, outlining "a position that has this particular (non)relationship to the global" (ibid.), dwelling means to exist sensuously attuned within the (un-)homely simultaneity of place and planet.[21]

When Spivak here writes of "alterity," she does not mean discursive constructivism but rather a radical otherness to which dwelling is always related. In "The Origin of the Work of Art," Heidegger anticipates Bhabha's assertion that "[t]he unhomely moment creeps up on you stealthily as your own shadow" (13) when he designates "the silent call of the earth" (2011: 101) as that other which "once struck man as strange and caused him to think and to wonder" (94). Instead of appropriation, this implies the responsive attitude toward otherness familiar from Waldenfels. Robert Mugerauer renders this quality within Heidegger's dwelling explicit by defining it as a being "open to the excess of the given over our finite reception, which amounts to a call for our response" (90). Guzzoni suggests that this altered relationship toward spatiality coincides with a different—responsive—mode of engaging with other human beings as also grounded on and exhibiting earth's sway (cf. 2009: 121) that reveals a "mysterious belonging-together of own proper self and otherness" (130), as Sandro Gorgone phrases it.[22] Through the call of earthen otherness, the self *senses* an earthed-ness within upon which it rests but can never fully grasp, negating any clear separation of self and other. It turns out that the earthen otherness of the other is that upon which the self as well rests. There is always something else inside. Consequently, the other *figures* not as merely other—that is, completely withdrawn—but as another self that, through its very withdrawal from a self's fixating grasp—but through its still affecting difference or pathos— voices its own claims and concerns and, as such, denies a self's attitude of indifference toward an other: just as the self is always other to itself, the other also always appears as an-other self. With Waldenfels it is possible to characterize dwelling as happening "*a limine* as between-world" (1997: 66)[23]—namely within the (un-)homely entanglement of self and other.

In this context, also Heidegger evokes the notion of a "between" (2001: 218) which helps to further ab-usively connect his ideas to border thinking. The first links between the motion of *counterturning* and Mignolo's work have already been established above. Therefore, it comes as no surprise when Ben Vedder explicitly states that "dwelling is a kind of being at home within borders" (746). Likewise, Mignolo evokes such a connection when he describes border gnosis as "dwelling in the borders" (2000: xv). By now it has become clear that "within borders" or "in the borders" is neither meant to suggest a completely static place nor a total lack thereof. Contrary to the solely technical occupation of space, dwelling retains an ever-dynamic character, as also Guzzoni emphasizes (cf. 2009: 122), without shedding its *sense* of place. Seemingly contradictory to *ratio*nal logic, the (un-)homely "between" needs to be thought within the co-constitution of stasis and dynamics inherent within the *counterturning* of world and earth. Put differently, (un-)homeliness circumscribes what Mignolo calls dichotomous loci of enunciation. Formulating a similar paradox, he writes that these are "grounded on the movable grounds of border gnosis" (2000: 163). In fact, it is possible to understand the relationship between grounded and movable grounds as paraphrasing the concurrence of world's uncanny technical knowing and earth's overwhelming sway. This agonistic synchronicity marks an active performative process where ground (counter)turns into unground and grounded (counter)turns into grounding. Mignolo succinctly summarizes this as follows: in adherence to subalternized knowledge(s), (un-)homely "loci of enunciation are not given but enacted" (115).

Translating these concepts into more Heideggerian terminology, Mugerauer states that "mortals are guests within the fragility of locality" which—contrary to fixating territorial metaphysics—calls for repeated and continuous embodied (re-)enactments, namely through "acting with local knowledge" (93). As a consequence, rather than taking the unhomely homeliness of dwelling to be strictly utopian or anti-locative—as J.P. Riquelme does in his comparison of Heidegger and Bhabha (cf. 553)—interpreting it as a form of border gnosis casts the (un-)homely double bind of world and earth as bringing forth "a complex home, without guarantees" (Shotwell 151), on ever newly performed and movable (a-)*topoi*.

Heidegger's term for this kind of enactment is the German verb "bauen"—"to build." In asserting that "to build is really to dwell" (2011: 244), he indicates that "building" is not to be understood exclusively in the instrumentalist sense of erecting static structures (although this also belongs to *bauen*). *Bauen* forms a released creative "*posture* toward things and others" (Dungey 240) which "accepts fully the contingency and conditionality of whatever there is" (Edwards 1997: 191), namely by "cooperating with the earth" and "*letting things be*" (176) instead of subjecting them totally to the grasp of world. In acknowledging an irreducible connection to the force of earth, building defies the *ratio*'s militant epistemology and, instead, literally exhibits epistemological humility as stemming from the Latin root *humus* (meaning earth or soil). Building names the responsive modality of corporeal mortal dwelling as a technically sparing form of relating to things and human beings with a *sense* of place and planet. In contrast to binary Cartesian logic, the sensuously attuned *bauen* works within a *counterturning* "happening of presencing-absencing" (Dungey 245). While *technē* signifies a one-sided mode of world-disclosure, building *figures* as an (en-)*active* mode of bringing forth between concealment and unconcealment which Heidegger derives from the Greek *poiēsis* (ποίησις). As such, *bauen*, to him, is essentially *Dichtung* or, in other words, in the form of building, dwelling is inherently poetic.

At this point, the argument can explicate the link between sensuous attunement and the language of literary works. Rather than taking literary texts only as a particular form of discourse, Heidegger understands it from his notion of *Dichtung*. Contrary to what the English rendition may falsely suggest, this does not mean that he considers all art as poetry in the sense of lyric poetry (cf. Hermann 50). Although he often writes about poems, Heidegger makes clear that *Dichtung* is by far not restricted to this but—as derived from *poiēsis*—constitutes the modality of art in general. For this book's project it is particularly important to note that *Dichtung*, too, encompasses works of prose: "Pure prose is never 'prosaic.' It is as poetic [*dichterisch*] and hence as rare as poetry [*Poesie*]" (2001: 205). All this suggests that Heidegger does not adhere to established typologies of literature. In fact, that is precisely the point. He regards such categorization as a result of the metaphysical treatment of language. Timothy Clark explains that, for Heidegger, "[l]anguage is not just a system of signs whose code supposedly resides 'in' the minds of its users"; it forms an existential "environment, [namely] one which opens and maintains the shared horizon within which understanding is possible" (73). When the German philosopher writes that "[p]oetic creation [*dichten*], which lets us dwell, is a kind of building" (2001: 213) and that "[p]oetry [*Dichtung*] is what first brings man onto the earth, making him belong to it, and thus brings him into dwelling" (216), he does not indicate the mere construction of texts through an instrumentalist fashion. Heidegger designates the "care-ful tending of and attending to things" (59), as Joseph Fell writes, that "complies with, or defers to—and so lets things lie forth in their own configuration or conformation, that is, in their own proper, fitting, or appropriate place" (43). Therefore, this kind of bringing forth enunciates "a sensual coming-to-appearance" (Guzzoni 2009: 149)[24] in the unfolding locale of the (literary) work of art which ousts the metaphysical separation of sensuality and rationality and the sole focus on discursive signification by considering the excess of sensuous attunement (cf. Sonderegger 95). In the *counterturning* of world and earth, Heidegger thinks poetic language as entangled between the sensual and the rational.[25]

From this angle, it becomes possible to think literary texts and the corporeal character of Shotwell's sensuous knowledge as not mutually exclusive or, more precisely and radically still, it becomes impossible to think them as separate. This point requires further clarification. Linking corporeality and literature, indeed, appears *fundamentally* implausible when the epistemological position from which this link is attested remains within a subject/object logic that (tacitly) begins its reasoning from the separation of body and mind. However, from loci of enunciation (en-)actively opened up by the border gnosis between world and earth, such a static binary foundation is denied. *Dichtung*—as "*non-foundational thinking*" (Clark 2002: 53)—is (un-)grounded. Here, the position which distinguishes between embodiment and signification is, strictly speaking, impossible. Instead—resonating with Shotwell's Marxian approach to sensuous knowledge—*Dichtung* entails "a transformation of thought from the ground up, from its non-ground (*Abgrund*) held open by the poietic momentum of language" (Ziarek 2013: 144) which brings forth entirely different understandings of discourse and corporeality: a body, accordingly, cannot be regarded as a mere substance or a piece of matter, just as literary discourse cannot be regarded as pure signification; both always already coincide in dynamic fashion. As mentioned above, "[b]*odies don't take place in discourse or in matter*. They don't inhabit 'mind' or 'body.' They take place at the limit, *qua limit*" (2008: 17), Nancy explicates, and "they *are* only their touching each other, the touch of their breaking down, and into, each other" (37). As *poiēsis*, literature constitutes an attuned form of knowing that in-volves a certain bodily dimension.[26]

Lyotard's notion of the figural sheds light on this aspect of Heidegger's *Dichtung*. In contrast to the discursive systematicity of instrumentalist linguistic conceptions of language, poetic discourse's opening of an existential space cannot be thought from a scientifically calculable and objective notion of spatiality as that of Cartesian mathematics (cf. Mitchell 13). In *Discourse, Figure*, Lyotard explicates that language rather unfolds, or discloses, "a thick space where the game of concealing/revealing can be played out" (74) by the simultaneous workings of figurality and discursivity. The hints toward Heidegger's jargon contained in this assertion become even more explicit in a paragraph later in the book where Lyotard specifically draws attention to the aspect of corporeality in language's active spacing. Since the passage also ties together several strands of this chapter's argument, it will be quoted in full:

> This action [of spacing] places the elements of discourse in perspective, ordering them in a deep expanse where they play the role no longer of carriers of signification, but of thing-signs that *show* us one face while withholding the others, and that we will need to *circumvent* in order to understand. This suggests that the poet (the everyday speaker when she or he invents expressions, turns of phrases, metaphors) introduces into discourse properties that derive from the sensory. To which this new suggestion must be added: *not only does this discourse become opaque, difficult to fathom, perilous like a world, but it acts upon our bodies*! The key property of arbitrariness, which radically distinguishes language from all sign-systems, is precisely what the figure subverts in discourse. *Through the figure words begin to induce in our bodies* (as would colors) *such and such a hint of attitude, posture, or rhythm*: yet further proof that discursive space is dealt with as plastic space, and words as sensory things. (2011: 283; my emphases)[27]

What the figure induces here when Lyotard speaks of rhythm, posture, and attitude is nothing less than what Heidegger himself calls the *counterturning* of world and earth that, through sensuous attunement, renders possible a different mode of relating to phenomena and human beings. In other words, as earthen excess, "the figural is exactly that which comes as *Unheimlich* into language" (Ionescu 2014: 49); it brings forth within discourse "imaginations as perceptible embeddedness of otherness [*des Fremden*]" (Guzzoni 2009: 125)[28] which—the withdrawal from discourse's fixation (not)withstanding—*presence* through bodily affectation. In *grazing* the figure, "[w]e are touching on a certain interruption of sense, and this interruption of sense has to do with the body, it is body. And it's no accident that the body has to do with sense, in the other sense of sense, sense in the sense of sensing, in the sense of touching" (Nancy 2008: 125). Through this doubleness of *sense*, *Dichtung* circumscribes a (meta-)physical locality amidst worldly discourse and earthen figure.[29]

In his "Letter on Humanism," Heidegger has formally designated this locality with one (in)famous expression: "Language is the house of Being. In its home man dwells" (2011: 147). Like the individual concepts it is connected to—home and dwelling—the idea of a house has been criticized as problematically nostalgic. In one such criticism, Dieter Thomä identifies two, by now already familiar, major issues of this notion: stasis and interiority. Firstly, although acknowledging an element of dynamics in Heidegger's thinking of language throughout his *oeuvre*, Thomä holds that the aspect of motion stands in stark contrast to the static construct of the house: "Language, within Heidegger's philosophy, is something *stationary*" (311).[30] Instead of pursuing the insight that the house's stasis should not to be seen as blindly opposed to movement, Thomä concludes: "It remains unclear inhowfar motion is to be thought within the pre-history or genesis of the 'House of Being'" (312).[31] Secondly, and similarly, he critiques the house's enclosing nature. Even though Thomä realizes Heidegger's negotiation of the inside, the outside, and openness, he still writes that the house's diagnosed interiority entails "specific ordering of the things that are in the house (for instance through the assignment to floors and rooms)" (314)[32] or results in a new categorical grid. Responding to Thomä's criticism can serve to pre-*limin*arily conclude the discussion of poetic dwelling regarding its relevance in the context of reading other-wise.

The first point of critique can easily be refuted because the language-house of Being simply is not brought forth as static structure according to an occidental cause-and-effect logic that Thomä's question concerning its genesis implies. He correctly notes that Heidegger thinks the spacing of the house as encompassing a "Bezirk" (313)—usually translated as "precinct" in English. However, literally, *Bezirk* says more than that; it contains the word "circle." That Heidegger takes this meaning into account becomes evident in his description of the Greek temple in "The Origin of the Work of Art." There, he thinks the temple from its Latin root *templum*—which in German can also be translated as *Bezirk*—as "temple-work" (2011: 107):

an instance of the playful strife between world and earth and ever within the motion of *counterturning* and never just static. Heidegger, then, adds: "The same holds for the linguistic work [*Sprachwerk*]" (ibid.). One could say that as *Bezirk*, the house *figures* as on*going Ent-Stehung* (literally un-standing, but usually translated as genesis), that further underscores the understanding of "dwelling as a mode of wandering" (Guzzoni 2009: 122)[33] instead of fixed categorical stability. The precinct of language continuously (r-)evolves as hermeneutic circling (*Kreisgang*) of world and earth, in which human beings always already dwell within dynamic circumvention.[34]

The rejection of Thomä's critique regarding the house's supposedly interiorizing impetus is directly tied to this notion of *Bezirk*. Heidegger explicates that "[m]an does not dwell in that he merely establishes his stay on the earth beneath the sky, by raising growing things and simultaneously raising buildings. Man is capable of such building only *if he already builds in the sense of the poetic taking of measure*" (2001: 225; my emphasis). This form of measuring is not a method of calculative reason that attempts to map out a technically fixed categorical territory. Heidegger makes clear that poetically "'[f]ixed' means outlined, admitted into the boundary (*peras*), brought into the outline" (2011: 137). As such, poetic measuring—sensuously attuned—designates the *Grundriss* between world and earth: a rift or, as Lyotard puts it, a "tear, integral to language" (2011: 8), that—by way of its tearing strife—outlines a liminal (extra-)ordinary space where discursive meaning and figural presence are inextricably entangled. Thus (dis-)entangling, Heidegger's house defies simple inside/outside logic and never appears "as anterior or posterior, exterior or interior to the signifying order—but at the limit" (Nancy 2008: 25); always responding to the figural pathos of earth that disrupts the discursive grasp of world (and vice versa), the house is always "*touching* upon *sense*" (17). The *Bezirk* circumscribes dichotomous loci of enunciation neither inside nor outside but both at the same time.

Sensuously attuned to earthen figurality and irreducible to solely instrumentalist conceptualizations of language, Heidegger's house of Being poetically [*dichterisch*] unfolds a "[d]iscourse that is *somehow beyond control*" (Bhabha 18). It outlines a locale that requires continual (re-)enactment and so forever remains an "'unhomely' house" (ibid.). (A-)*topos*—which is to say, emplaced and simultaneously exceeding this emplacement (cf. Waldenfels 2001: 445)—in the *counterturning* border gnosis of world and earth, this *Bezirk* (per)forms a *sense* of place and planet; and it is in this way that Heidegger's notion of dynamic (border) dwelling becomes important for the project at hand. Through the (meta-)physical doubleness of *sense*, it ab-usively relates to what Spivak calls "planetary *poiesis*" (2012: 346). Contrary to the global designs of a modern/colonial world system, human beings, therein, *figure* as "planetary accidents rather than global agents" whereby "alterity remains underived from [them]" (339). *Grazing* literature as *Dichtung* has the potential to bring forth an "indefinite radical alterity of the other space of a planet to deflect the rational imperative of capitalist globalization" (348) and is relevant for further unfolding the operationalization of reading other-wise.

[6]

COUNTERTURNING THE LIFE-WHEEL

HERE, WITHIN THE LIMINAL space between the two main chapters of this part, it is helpful to recall Bhabha's quotation of Heidegger at the beginning of *The Location of Culture* which served as this part's point of the departure: "A boundary is not that at which something stops but, as the Greeks recognized, the boundary is that from which something *begins its essential unfolding* [or *presencing* in Bhabha's rendition]" (Heidegger 2011: 250); remembering this passage serves to indicate that the subsequent analysis is not simply supposed to appear as a linear step into another territory, namely that of literary texts. The boundary, or border, is also a space of reciprocal touch. What *presences* unfolds from this touch. In this *sense*, throughout the following interpretation, Heidegger's thought is going to touch upon Ondaatje's novel *Anil's Ghost* and vice versa. Read in sensuous dialogue with the narrative's postcolonial context, the significance of the philosopher's (ab-used) concepts of attunement and dwelling for current transnational endeavors will become clear. As such, this border space between the (first and second chapter) moves along with the circular hermeneutic motion of its line of argument; a motion—as it will turn out—which also characterizes *Anil's Ghost* and is already evoked in the Ceylonese miners' folk song functioning as the novel's epigraph. The circle happily keeps on *counterturning*: "*Blessed be the chain attached to the life wheel . . .*" (Ondaatje 3).

Struggles

Anil's Ghost unfolds an epistemological struggle around two of the main characters that is highly reminiscent of Heidegger's striving relationship between world and earth, and has been similarly (mis)interpreted. The narrative is set in the context of the civil war raging in Sri Lanka from the mid-1980s to the early 1990s and (r-)evolves around a United Nations human rights investigation seeking evidence for politically motivated cases of murder committed by the ruling regime against its opponents.[1] More specifically, it follows the Ceylon-born but Western-educated forensic scientist Anil Tissera—who has only recently returned to her native country—and her colleague assigned by the government, the archaeologist Sarath Diyasena, in their soon joint endeavor of uncovering the circumstances behind the recent burial of a skeleton hidden among ancient human remains. In this scenario, several scholars have established a clear distinction between the two protagonists as representatives of fundamentally incompatible epistemological systems; while Anil—due to her occidental academic training—is engaging in "an enlightenment project," Sarath remains "steeped in the religious philosophy of his country" (103), writes John Bolland. The former is interested in universal and empirically verifiable and fixable truth, whereas the latter is concerned with the elusive singularity of local particularities (cf. Babock 61, 69; Spinks 218). Correspondingly, Margaret Scanlan asserts that "[w]here Anil looks for permanent truths in chemical traces that survive in bones, Sarath insists that truth is inseparable from life" (307). Implicitly reading the two perspectives as mutually exclusive, these commentators suggest that, in Ondaatje's novel, "'truth' is divided among cultural lines" (Ratti 135): it oscillates between Anil's and Sarath's respective approach.

There is no denying that, indeed, plenty of evidence can be found to support this impression of incompatibility regarding the protagonists' respective epistemological attitudes. Anil's academic education in the US and the UK certainly shapes her mode of relating to the things of the world and her own identity. Her Western(ized) scientific rigor demands that she "interpret Sri Lanka with a long-distance gaze" (Ondaatje 11). Anil, at first, relies entirely on the analytic arsenal of occidental reason and its violent objectifying tendencies. Enlisted in this militant epistemology, she regards her mission of identifying the skeleton, nicknamed Sailor, as requiring her "to break things apart to know where someone came from" (259) and then realigning the pieces according to the rules of the *ratio*'s categorical grid. Trained in the binary logic of Cartesianism with its separation of *res cogitans* and *res extensae*, or mind and matter, Anil is convinced that her abstract methodology is universally applicable and that material phenomena are devoid of meaning until subjected to the analytical grasp of science (cf. Bolland 107). This becomes particularly evident in a passage where she examines Sailor "under sulphur light, summarizing the facts of his death so far, the permanent truths, same for Colombo as for Troy" (Ondaatje 64); a highly-effective source of light whose cold full-spectrum radiance symbolizes Anil's decontextualizing neo-enlightenment tendencies. Her insistence on empirical evidence turns out to be complicit with an imperial form of knowing. Within the broader global designs of Anil's *ratio*nal(ized) world-view, "scientific knowledge as a form of hierarchical knowing is aligned with the powers of the West, and a power that is epistemologically sanctioned to discount local postcolonial knowledges" (Burrows 167). Instead of engaging with local insights, Anil initially only gathers evidence to retreat back into the objective space of the laboratory which she calls her home (cf. Ondaatje 67). Through a "removal from the thickness of location" (136), as Manav Ratti puts it, and her subscription to the superiority complex of Western reason, she herself exercises an epistemic form of violence. Hence, "without actively causing suffering, Anil nonetheless participates in the objectification of the corporeal by assuming that the scientific tools at her disposal enable her to access and explain the painful experiences of many others" (Marinkova 81). In short, her distanced scientific approach digests local epistemological horizons within the dis-locating systemic world of the *ratio*.

Throughout the narrative, Sarath's perspective on knowledge in multiple instances appears in stark and direct contrast to Anil's. He critiques her abstractions and detachedness, accusing her of "talk[ing] like a visiting journalist" (Ondaatje 27) in whose investigations the "truth [is] broken down into suitable pieces and used by foreign presses" catering to Western audiences in "[a] flippant gesture towards Asia" (156). Sarath—on the contrary—perceives every phenomenon as irreducibly embedded in a particular context or place. Consequently, he wishes to take Anil to the sacred Buddhist site at Bandalawera where the skeleton had been found so she can come to "understand the archaeological surround of a fact" (44). This, however, calls for more than her impulse to "break up the ground and brush it away" (33) in an empirical fashion. It necessitates the development of a different kind of epistemological sensitivity. Well-versed in and deeply impacted by Sri Lankan folklore, architecture, as well as poetry, Sarath himself has entered into a "dark trade with the earth" (29); a mode of engaging with things and entities beyond mere instrumentalist objectification. Unlike his colleague, he "regards knowledge as more tactile and earthy, but also as ambiguous" (Kertzer 120)—an ambiguity that he thinks needs to be maintained. From Sarath's subalternized position, *ratio*nal scientific "clarity is not necessarily truth" (Ondaatje 259) all by itself and the mystery around Sailor's death, accordingly, not to be solved within the boundaries of the horizon of occidental knowledge alone.

These epistemological differences between the two protagonists are important to the further analysis of the unfolding narrative. However, holding on to the idea of their mutual exclusivity, some scholars bring forth a reductive and somewhat simplistic account of the text which remains indebted to a colonialist logic of cultural difference. By "bringing into play different and incompatible modes of knowledge," Lamia Tayeb, for instance, asserts, "the narrative pits Western empiricism against Eastern mysticism" (237). With these fixed ascriptions of a "scientific mode" and a mode of "mystical correspondence or artistic re-creation" (ibid.) as definitive characteristics of two cultures, she seems to suggest that the text equates Western with "empirical" and Eastern with "mystical" within a polarizing and essentializing gesture that mirrors Gumbrecht's questionable typecast dichotomy between meaning and presence cultures. If this idea of two incompatibly distinct epistemological systems, in fact, (in)formed the novel, then it would again be operating along the lines of the Orientalist binary opposition between East and West, or mystics and rationalists, as the title of Bolland's essay suggests (cf. 102). Tayeb's interpretation also moves into this direction. She reads the fact that, in order to reconstruct the skeleton's face, Anil and Sarath seek help from the artist Ananda—who is supposed to reproduce the face through sculpting—as an implication that a mystical form of "artistic imagination . . . is brought to the fore as the only way to beset the myriad questions" (238) raised by the supposedly political motivations behind Sailor's murder.[2] According to this rendering, Ondaatje's text constitutes a counter-discourse which simply inverts a Eurocentric perspective in favor of an Eastern one. Like Gumbrecht's notion of oscillation, such an interpretation remains fundamentally indebted to a metaphysical conceptualization of knowledge that leaves the static binary logic of separating East and West, rationality and sensuality, or presence and meaning, itself unchallenged.

The novel's literary work does more, though, than just warming up, once more, the contrast of an allegedly Western with an Eastern point of view. The epistemological struggle surrounding the two main characters presents "a much more fraught relationship" (Kertzer 125) than the polar binarism of the Gumbrechtian oscillation laid out above. Although Anil as well as Sarath exhibit differing tendencies regarding their understanding of truth and knowledge, they do not stand in for ossified or unchanging perspectives; both repeatedly deviate from these attributed stances. Their pairing is, therefore, not to be seen as one of stagnant opposition. The interaction is better described as a correlation of non-preferential reciprocity and strained entanglement in which the two protagonists are always already mutually implicated. To explicate how this interwoven liaison *figures* throughout the narrative another look at the characters of Sarath and Anil will prove helpful— this time with a focus on aspects running counter to and subverting their apparently inflexible epistemological convictions.

Throughout the novel the conflict concerning concepts of knowledge time and again turns out as not only taking place between the two protagonists but, further complicating the matter, also within them. Although Sarath often entertains a different attitude toward truth, he is not simply cast as an irrational Eastern religious mystic. Like Anil, he is a professional scientist who "believed in truth as a principle" and "would have given his life for the truth if the truth were of any use" (Ondaatje 157). As such, Sarath assists her and even defends her methodology. When introducing her to his former teacher, the hermit Palipana, he appreciates his colleague's capabilities: "We can identify an architect by his habit of building winter and summer palaces. . . . She can cut a cross-section of bone with a fine saw and determine the skeleton's exact age at death that way" (95). His local knowledge is far from irrational. In contrast to Anil, it enables him to remain reasonable when confronted with the cruelties and desperation caused by the civil war. When Ananda slits his throat in a fit of drunken stupor, it is Anil—in her disconnected, indifferent, Western(ized) ignorance—who attempts to provide a metaphysical explanation and seriously believes the artist is engaging in a necromantic ritual, while Sarath—despite his ascribed tendency toward (religious) mysticism and folk-artistry—explicates matter-of-factly: "No. He's just one of those who try to kill themselves because they lost people" (196). In a similar fashion, close to the end of the narrative, Sarath again makes use of his local insights when Anil naïvely gives away information about their investigation to the government, who promptly confiscates the skeleton (cf. 270f.). Through an act of shrewd subterfuge, by which Anil thinks he betrayed her, Sarath manages to return the skeleton to Anil and, thereby, ensures the possibility of her safely carrying on her research concerning the true circumstances surrounding Sailor's death after her return to the US or the UK, an exploit—in keeping with his word—that costs him his life. Contrary to what the attestations of incompatibility regarding their differing epistemologies suggest, Sarath's local perspective is not detrimental to Anil's empirical cause. As her fellow scientist, he contributes to their common investigative project.

That Anil does not also represent one side in an occidental logic of stable binaries becomes particularly evident in the tale surrounding her name. Despite her family's objections, she changed her given name—which remains unknown—into her brother's middle name because "[e]verything about the name pleased her, its slim, stripped-down quality, its feminine air, even though it was considered a male name" (68). This is an important indicator of the protagonist's function in the narrative. Victoria Cook writes that "[i]n acquiring her name Anil ruptures the boundary between 'Self' and 'Other'" (9) and, in extension, also between masculinity and femininity, as well as rationality and sensuality. The passage introducing her—temporally preceding the events of the plot—depicts the protagonist as moved by the pain of a grieving widow sitting in a mass grave mourning her dead family (cf. Ondaatje 6). Prior to the onset of the main strand of the story, where, after her return to Ceylon, the repressed or "buried senses from childhood [become] alive in her" (15), Anil appears as guided by perceptual modes beyond the limits of occidental reason: "In the West she'd read, *The dawn comes up like thunder*, and she knew she was the only one in the classroom to recognize the phrase physically" (9). The narrative draws attention to "a gut feeling" (Brusasco 142) or affective dimensions within her relationship toward her surroundings which "continually undercut Anil's faith in rationality" (Kertzer 124). The same affective-ness, deviating from her rational inclinations, again appears shortly thereafter in the examination of a recently deceased, where Anil is momentarily unsettled because she "translated the time of death into personal time" and feels that "[i]t was still someone" (Ondaatje 13). Normally, she would carelessly treat a dead body as nothing but a lifeless object to analyze and joke around with (cf. 19). However, exposed to "physical proximity," the hegemony of her Western(ized) scientific approach temporarily breaks down within her, which allows for a more sensuous discernment: "Anil's methods both challenge and are challenged by the national and local particularities she encounters" (Babcock 74). In short, the epistemological struggle within her, too, serves as a foil to renegotiate several of the *ratio*'s central dichotomies.

In fact, Anil's sensuousness surfaces repeatedly throughout the plot not as juxtaposed, but as directly interspersed with her more rational inclinations. At college, she attended classes on Greek tragedies next to her regular forensic curriculum and the narrative portrays her as ever-open for the recitation of poetry or the solace she finds in reading novels (cf. Ondaatje 11, 34, 54). This interest in literary works goes beyond the obligations of general education and fundamentally shapes her being-in-the-world. As evident in a scene setting in with her musings over the comfort she finds in books, two modes of knowing collide within Anil. Her praise of literature "so thick with human nature" (54) seamlessly turns toward science's levelling taxonomical methodology that breaks down "bodies into representatives of race and age and place" (55). Here, a complicating tension between the sensuous and the rational is outlined which also *figures* in her love for the laboratory. To Anil, the lab constitutes a utopian space where "time would be forgotten" and any sensuous bodily dimension—like hunger, thirst, and sex—categorically expelled; nevertheless, her keen sense for the aesthetic, such as a "slight rake" or "earnest tilt forward" while sitting in her chair, the arrangement of "bottles that held beet-coloured liquids" (67) around her, as well as the soothing noise of her colleagues, in the same stroke contradicts this initial assertion of non-sensuousness. It attests to a disavowed but lingering presence of the sensuous that impacts her perception. Lastly, in a third related passage later in the novel where Anil interrupts her work and begins to dance to a musical tune, the aesthetic dimension appears even more prominently: the narration describes her as "waking every muscle in herself, blindfolding every rule she lives by, giving every mental skill she has to the movement of her body" (181). In the character of Anil, just as within that of Sarath, the novel portrays the logic of reason as consistently challenged by the (bodily) motion of the sensuous and vice versa.

Due to what can be described as their internal epistemological heterogeneity, it turns out that the two protagonists' perspectives are not mutually exclusive. Victoria Burrows even goes so far as to state that "[t]heir knowledges are commensurate" (172). However, she seems to reproduce the strict dichotomy East and West, too, when she writes that, "despite the power imbalances between the Western-authorized Anil and Sarath's role as a local archaeologist, Sarath acts as Anil's subaltern foil, and his constant questioning of her motives and methods occasionally destabilizes Anil enough to encourage her to rethink some of her long-held assumptions" (ibid.). Again, while this is certainly partially correct—and below the argument will return to the specific change Anil undergoes in more detail—it has been shown that the novel does not devalue Western reason to celebrate subalternized positions in an uncritical manner. Instead of erecting a new hierarchy, it unhinges the construction of binary stasis altogether to embrace both within a process of reciprocal supplementation: Anil's position does not (only) discredit Sarath's; Sarath's position does not (only) discredit Anil's. Faced with their respective otherness the very own-ness of their perspectives is persistently being challenged. The struggle brought forth by the narration neither constitutes a polarizing oscillation, nor a "dialectical relationship" (Spinks 219) promising the relief of Hegelian sublation, but something else besides. Rather than as amplitudinal wavering, its motion *figures* as entangling circulation. Rather than as merging synthesis, its junction *figures* as intertwining collapse. The struggle is ever-revolving; the conflict is never resolved: it is neither oscillating, nor sublated, but constantly *counterturning*.

This ludic motion of *counterturning* is also fundamentally tied to the novel's structure. Several scholars point out that Ondaatje's text—on one hand—works according to the logic of a (forensic) detective story, driven by the human rights investigation in search of Sailor's identity and to unearth the exact circumstances of his death (cf. Kertzer 117ff.; Ratti 133; Hillger 209). In this scenario, Anil plays the leading role and functions as "another Cartesian observer" (Kertzer 119), unerringly working toward attaining teleological truth. However, another observation shared by many interpreters is that, simultaneously, the novel integrates what is usually termed "postmodern" elements into the plot. Similar to Ondaatje's previous literary works, *Anil's Ghost* is filled with a-chronological schisms, moments of intertextuality, changing narrative perspectives, as well as other forms of textual disunification (cf. Brusasco 146; Bolland 104). The text collapses two seemingly contradictory narrative modes, namely a linear and teleological scientific quest for the truth and the coetaneous breakdown of this (grand) narrative in frequent temporal ruptures. "As the detective structure advances steadily toward a promised resolution that never comes," Jon Kertzer holds, "it is interrupted by digressions"—such as "abrupt flashbacks" (127)—and, this way, the novel "both imposes and renounces order" (128). Thereby, the narrative's structural principles further contribute to the development of the unfolding epistemological struggle between Anil and Sarath.

In fact, *Anil's Ghost*'s textual structure itself needs to be thought from (within) this *counterturning* conflict. The a-chronological elements within the text indeed subvert notions of Western teleology; but they also serve to bring forth the central epistemological attitudes in the narrative as always already entangled. On the one hand, the frequent flashbacks to Anil's past serve to draw attention to other modes of knowing residing within her, as implied above in the discussion of the paragraph which introduces her and several other instances in the novel. At the same time, the temporal cuts serve to show that also in the plot's present, where Anil certainly undergoes a certain development, she never entirely sheds her Western(ized) perspective. The other already quoted passage where Anil explains that she needs to break things apart to understand them, for instance, is not clearly temporally located and only introduced as "[a] rainy-night conversation at the *walawwa*" (Ondaatje 259). Despite its being situated toward the end of the text, after Anil has already been influenced concerning her relationship to the world through her interaction with local particularities, with this scene, the narrative again returns—or, better, *counterturns*—to her preformed scientific inclinations. However, in this struggling motion, these tendencies take on a different character. Her rationality appears as one co-constitutive form of knowing inseparable from a more sensuous one within a reciprocal embrace which entails the dehierarchization of rationality and sensuality. Renouncing the Cartesian split, *Anil's Ghost* shows that "cognition and affect are not juxtaposed but conjoined" (Marinkova 19). The novel offers no solution in either possible direction. The different epistemological strands in the text surface (dis)continuously in an ever-interweaving strive.

This means that stopping at the attestation of the breakdown of an occidental *grand récit* betrays a remaining-stuck within the very metaphysical logic one seeks to critique through a one-sided focus on negation. Tayeb, too, correctly asserts that *Anil's Ghost* "unsettles the received form and matter of narrativity as a way of challenging centered and hegemonic structures of knowledge" (232); but she also adds the important emphasis that its literary gestures are "not only exposing the discursive fractures and quibbles of imperial hegemony but also conceiving alternative narrative forms and methodologies" (241). This indicates that—by way of the negating submersion of occidental reason's sole predominance into the collapse of the rational and sensual—the text also affirms and opens (to) new epistemological potentialities, which only *figure* in their withdrawal from the *ratio*'s fixating grasp and systemic closure. Or, as Hilde Staels puts it in psychoanalytical manner: "*Anil's Ghost* disrupts the rules of 'normal' communicative discourse and gives expression to the Other within the self" (978). In short, dis-closing Western reason, the narrative harbors the potential for a knowing/reading other-wise in which the other *presences* and it is for this reason that it constitutes a "transnational narrative that goes beyond established patterns" (Brusasco 152).[3]

To wrap up this section, it can be noted that the epistemological struggle characterizing Ondaatje's novel mirrors Heidegger's relationship between world and earth also concerning the defiance of literature's status as restricted solely to representation. Through what Mrinalini Chakravorty calls a "volatile aesthetics" (544)—an aesthetics that deeply links the (e-)motional conflict between Anil and Sarath on the level of content to the narrative's a-chronological structural as well as formal specificities— *Anil's Ghost* draws attention to a certain literary performativity: instead of an oscillation between meaning and presence, or a dialectical sublation of thesis and antithesis, its (en-)active figural dynamics casts "the poetic text as a happening all at once, backwards and forwards" (Clark 2002: 114) in what can aptly be de-scribed as a "*counterturning* configuring" of differing forms of unconcealment. The narrative suggests that also in the reading of literature "conceptual and physical knowings can never be disentangled" (Shotwell 137); or, in yet other words, through its poetic workings, the novel intimates that more than *ratio*nal (re-)cognition is needed to perceive the narrative's unfolding.

Within the a-chronologically (dis-)located rainy-night conversation between the two protagonists, the archaeologist holds against the forensic scientist's Western(ized) dissecting analytical stance that truth does not reside in empirical facts alone: "It's in character and nuance and mood." (259).

Senses

Anil undergoes a certain epistemological change throughout the course of the text. This process cannot constitute a linear development of shedding one point of view in favor of another one. In fact, instead of a teleological de-velopment, it is better described as a cyclical en-velopment of different forms of knowing always already residing within her. More precisely, the modification pertains to Anil's strict "mind-body polarization" (Staels 981); for, although she is open to both science and aesthetics, her habitualized Cartesianism requires her to keep the two neatly separated. From this angle, Anil dismisses Sarath's first attempt of drawing her attention to the surroundings of a fact, or, to the qualities of character, nuance, and mood, as an "abrupt switch to something aesthetic" (Ondaatje 52)—a switch her scientific paradigm does not allow for. However, through the continued interaction with Sarath, as well as two other major characters, Anil is encouraged to partially "convert her obsession for straight-line truth into an oblique, circular, approach" (Brusasco 144) where the truth (r-)evolves in the (meta-)physical doubleness of *sense*. Entering into the playful motion of this peculiar circle, Anil goes through a de-constructive process of attunement, or *Be-Sinnung*, that *at the same time* runs counter to her teleological quest of the human rights investigation.

The first decisive moment regarding this sense-sensitizing occurs in Anil's encounter with Sarath's former teacher, Palipana, in the so-called "Grove of Ascetics" (Ondaatje 77). In the character of Palipana, Anil is, again, faced with a radically different conceptualization of truth. His methodology stands in stark contrast to hers: although Sri Lanka's most distinguished archaeologist (once), he has always preferred "the pragmatic awareness of locally inherited skills" (82) over archival academic knowledge; an epistemological stance that eventually disgraces him entirely within his own discipline and forces him to seek recluse in a forest monastery. Due to his reliance on local knowledges not fulfilling the empirical standards of established archaeology, he is labelled a mere fraud and his work dismissed as fiction. From his unconventional position, though, "he began to see as truth things that could only be guessed at. In no way did this *feel* to him like forgery or falsification . . . The point was not that he would ever be proved wrong in his theories, but that he could not prove he was right. Still, the patterns that emerged for Palipana had begun to coalesce. They linked hands . . . And so the unprovable truth *emerged*" (83; my emphases). For Palipana, truth can never be simply forced forth, merely pro-positionally determined, and empirically fixed: it actively "de-termines, *be-stimmt*" (Vattimo 293). Like Sarath, Palipana believes that truth unfolds through the engagement with local particularities. Through its affective quality, it resists being subjected under the hegemony of cognition (cf. Marinkova 14). As such, Palipana's concept of truth reaches beyond the *ratio*nal epistemological horizon in which Anil has been trained to remain distanced, and—in extension—indifferent and insensitive toward her *object* of inquiry (cf. Burrows 168; Haar 170). He emphasizes that truth defies such violently possessive empiricism: "We have never had the truth. Not even with your work on bones" (Ondaatje 102).[4] Consequently, as Chakravorty puts it, "Palipana's presence serves as a counterincentive to the human rights narrative Anil seeks to valorize" (546). According to the hermit, Sri Lanka's (postcolonial) situation calls for a "step to another reality" (81), namely through less distanced and more sensuous forms of knowing with a *sense* of place.

In this scenario, the necessity of attunement is underscored through Palipana's blindness. The epistemological shift represented by his departure from academia and its methodology, and the subsequent recourse to local knowledges in the forest monastery, is mirrored in his slowly losing his eyesight. This serves to further "expose the violence of optical incursions and the inaccessibility of experience to transparent forms of representation" (Marinkova 18). Through his sightlessness, "Palipana too was now governed only by the elements" (Ondaatje 84). However, this loss of eyesight functions according to the ambivalent logic of the *pharmakon* and has also granted him a heightened sensibility for his surroundings: sensory deprivation confirms his insistence on local particularities and further remedies the epistemological reductions resulting from a "desire to see and know the world through the limited and narrow lens of scientific investigation" (Magrini 503); a desire that only leads into a different form of *sense*lessness. Via his "potent sightlessness" (Ondaatje 97)—silently acknowledged by Anil—Palipana has come to perceive all phenomena as part of "a *corpus* imbued with the specificity of real lives rather than the abstractedness of grand ideas, a *corpus* defined by its opacity and resistance to the scopic consumption of optical representation" (Marinkova 83; my emphases). It is not coincidental that Anil's vision, due to a tropical disease she picks up shortly before she and Sarath visit the forest monastery, is temporarily clouded, too, and she can see the world around her only as "out-of-focus" (Ondaatje 59). The episode of her sickness already anticipates the impulse she receives from Palipana regarding the reconstruction of the skeleton's face. Through the encounter between Anil and the hermit, the novel moves from the epistemological distance of a Western(ized) "ocularcentrism" (Marinkova 2) to a form of sightlessness to stress the significance of attuned modes of sensuous knowing.

At this point, the narrative introduces a theme of continued importance for the further course of the text as it coincides with "Anil's [partial] conversion from visitor, voyeur, and witness of violence to intimate participant" (Chakravorty 550): the dimension of haptics and bodily gestures. Unlike her own scanning gaze, the blind Palipana greets the forensic scientist in the following manner: "He reached out and held her forearm, touching the skin, feeling the muscle underneath; she sensed he was interpreting her shape and size from this fragment of her body" (Ondaatje 85). Through the already mentioned interaction and conversation concerning the character of truth with the hermit, it becomes clear that Anil does not take his behavior as merely a consequence of his condition. Rather, beginning to realize that the singularities of life cannot simply be translated into the systemic taxonomical grid of abstract universals—but simultaneously also still unremittingly skeptical—Anil is imbued by Palipana's way of approaching phenomena with a renewed awareness for the sensuous that has an impact on her habitualized *rational* visionary mode (cf. Spinks 219). This becomes apparent in a passage where she cleanses herself at a well: "She repeated *the mantra of gestures* again and again. When she had finished she unwrapped her wet cloth and stood naked in the wind and the last of the sunlight, then put on the dry sarong" (Ondaatje 90; my emphasis). According to Staels's reading, too, "[t]his language of physical and vocal gestures is associated with the reawakening of affects" (985) or, more precisely, the reciprocal and mutually supplementing (re-)entanglement of affects with the protagonist's scientific inclinations. As evident within the plot's ensuing unfolding, the novel here already begins to imply that a rising haptic sensibility in Anil's epistemological stance also brings about a form of voluntary "cognitive vulnerability, which enables a more ethical encounter with otherness" (Marinkova 11). Through Palipana, Anil begins to realize that uncovering the circumstances surrounding Sailor's death requires the inclusion of sensuous attunement instead of exclusive *rational* dissociation.

In the forest monastery, Anil renegotiates the supposedly fixed boundaries of the following opposition: "The reality of life versus a concept" (Ondaatje 95). Accepting the relative blindness of her Western(ized) gaze—increased due to lack of proper equipment—she starts to acknowledge the validity of sensuous knowledge. Although not shedding her scientific methodology completely (but also no longer apotheosizing it), Anil's adopted Cartesian binarism between *res cogitans* and *res extensae* opens up to *give way* to a sense-sensitized understanding of the "emergence of truth" as *taking place* within a borderland of "the interplay of disclosure and concealment" (Guignon 106). The stay with Palipana prepares a processual shift in Anil's mode of engaging with the world.

This shifting continues in a second pivotal encounter within the text's epistemological roundabout where the relevance of sensuous knowledge is further underscored; an encounter that (r-)evolves around Anil's collaboration with "Ananda, the eye-painter turned drunk gem-pit worker turned head-restorer" (Ondaatje 168). Initially, frustrated with the artist's drinking habits and the seeming lack of means to communicate with him, Anil, again, exhibits an attitude of occidental superiority, and considers the "project as Sarath's folly" (ibid.). However, in this passage, too, Ondaatje's novel (counter)turns from what, at first, appears to be a situation of binary mutual exclusion into one of entangled co-constitution: via Ananda's character, the text renews its insistence on the potential of "*aesthetic* experience as constituting a link between the subject and 'the world'", namely through "performing rituals of re-creation" (Hillger 216). It is again haptics that brings about the change toward reciprocity. Especially through the focus on the poetic process of sculpting, the novel reinforces the significance of attunement and the modifications of truth-concepts this entails. Rather than the *ratio*nal notion of a fixating categorical grip on things, here the sensuous knowing of touch expresses, as Kertzer writes, "how we fumble with the cumbersome foreignness of things even as we caress them into human shape through work and art. The sheer physicality of the world is at once within our reach and beyond our grasp" (118). It requires a mode of bringing forth which responds to the affective pathos of local particularities beyond a subjection to the objectifying impetus of Western reason (cf. Herrmann 45f.). Therefore, Anil further learns to value the help of local knowledge as a supplement to her own methodology.

Like the encounter with Palipana in the secluded forest monastery, this (a-)logic of supplementation unfolds at a particular place, namely a room with a somewhat mystical quality in the house which Sarath and Anil choose as their base camp: "Now the whisper of Anil's foot was beside him. Then her quiet voice. '*What's that?*' They'd entered a room off the courtyard, where someone had charcoaled two Sinhala words in giant script on the walls. MAKAMKRUKA. And on the wall opposite, MADANARAGA. '*What's that? Are those names?*' 'No.' He reached up so his hand could touch the brown lettering" (165). More specifically, the renegotiation of Anil's mind/body split is designated by the two Sinhala words on the walls. Sarath explains that *makamkruka* means "churner" or "agitator," implying "[s]omeone who perhaps sees things more truly by turning everything upside down"; whereas *madanaraga* is a "word you find in ancient romances" and signifies "'with the speed of love,' sexual arousal" (ibid.). Scanlan, too, in her interpretation of the text, appears to disrupt her aforementioned tendency to dichotomize the epistemological strands of the novel, when she writes that *makamkruka* refers to both Ananda's art and Anil's forensic scrutiny at once. However, she does not develop this thought any further. Shortly thereafter, she repeats her prior leaning when she ascribes the word *madanaraga* solely to Sarath and his brother, the doctor Gamini (cf. 315). Scanlan's insightful claim of simultaneity can be decisively bolstered, though, when reading the second term instead as also pertaining to the relationship of Anil and Ananda. Or, more precisely, when one takes *madanaraga* as the very possibility of their epistemological stances' simultaneity.[5] This becomes evident when reading the sexual implications of *madanaraga* in relation to what Shotwell—drawing on the work of Audre Lorde—calls "the erotic"; a mode of knowing which "names a rejuvenating memory and experience" and "carries a sense of working in concert with others" (141). In this *sense*, the erotic quality of *mandanaragas* implies a relational dynamic of affecting pathos and creative response in "non-appropriative encounters between self and other, signification and reality, body and discourse" (Marinkova 5). The following passage illustrates how such a notion of *mandanaraga* commences to en-velop the characters of Anil and Ananda:

> Now Ananda picked up the skeleton and carried it in his arms. She was in no way appalled by what he was doing. There had been hours when, locked in her investigations and too focussed [*sic*] by hours of intricacy, she too would need to reach forward and lift Sailor into her arms, to remind herself he was like her. Not just evidence, but someone with charms and flaws, part of a family, a member of a village . . . Ananda held Sailor and walked slowly with him and placed him back on the table, and it was then he saw Anil. She nodded imperceptibly to show there was no anger in her. Slowly rose and walked to him. (Ondaatje 170)

In this moment of observing Ananda *care*fully *hand*ling Sailor, Anil sheds her objectifying gaze by recognizing therein her own repressed sensuousness as always already inextricably bound with her scientific approach. Her polarization of mind and body collapses, making room for a more corporeally attuned, because less *rati*onal, mode of knowing; a form of "erotic knowledge" (Lorde 56) which contains the possibility to "share the power of each other's feelings" (58) in moments of non-exploitative reciprocity. *Makamkruka*'s agitation applies to both Ananda's art and Anil's science at the same time only in its irreducible entanglement with *mandanaraga*'s sensuous erotic knowledge. Lodged within this reciprocity, *makamkruka*'s turning around of things does not indicate a one-sided reversal, but an instance of the motion of *counterturning*.

Reading *mandanaraga* with Shotwell and Lorde as a form of the erotic does not seem far-fetched when pursuing the relationship between Ananda and Anil a bit further. Impressed by his sensuous handling of Sailor and respectful treatment of her tools, Anil eventually comes to recognize within Ananda "[a] mind of science" (Ondaatje 170)—albeit different from hers—and wishes to share her insights with him, wants to explain her theories to him, and, likewise, learn from his approach of engaging with his surroundings, watching the locals' behavior, and observing their facial features and postures (cf. 166). Through this entangling epistemological collapse, Anil steps out—to(ward) some ex-tend—of the systemic closure of her *ration-al(ized)* worldview. She, thereby, enters "a condition of exteriority, of open-ing, and passivity or vulnerability" in which she is "exposed and not just posed" (Nancy 2013: 58) or pro-positing. Ultimately, this opening results in "a pact" (Ondaatje 171) between artist and scientist; a pact sealed with the haptic supplementation of touches exchanged in a scenario where the com-munication by way of a shared spoken language is impossible. Eventually, "Anil put[s] out her hand and touche[s] his [Ananda's] forearm" (171) to ac-knowledge his perspective.[6] Shortly thereafter, upon realizing that Ananda's face-sculpting creates an-other form of truth than the reconstructed fixed identity of Sailor, Anil becomes (even) more attuned to the realities of war around her and begins to cry. In this situation, Ananda reciprocates her touch in a moment that underscores the potential of erotic sensuous knowledge:

> He moved two steps forward and with his thumb creased away the pain around her eye along with her tears' wetness. It was the softest touch on her face. . . . Ananda's hand on her shoulder to quiet her while the other hand came up to her face, kneaded the skin of that imploded tension of weeping as if hers too was a face being sculpted . . . This was tenderness she was receiving. Then his other hand on her other shoulder, the other thumb under her right eye. Her sobbing had stopped. (187)

In this seeming lack of articulated discourse's muteness, as Staels writes, "[t]he hand's healing *gesture* as it reaches out for the other is part of the signifying process" (987; my emphasis). The sensuous *deixis* of hands points toward and *ex-presses* from within this silence that which remains unsaid be-tween Anil and Ananda. At the ex-posing opening of significatory discourse's systemic closure, otherness *presences* within reciprocal haptic affectation. There, science touches upon art, just as art touches upon science: while the *makamkruka* Ananda works "into the uncertainty that lay ahead" (Ondaatje 171), the *makamkruka* Anil works toward empirical clarity. Through *man-danaraga* both now coincide in a struggling alliance, changing both the meanings of science and of art: these no longer indicate a mutual exclusivity, but rather an irreducible co-responding.

The encounters with Palipana and Ananda both unlock, or ex-pose, from the basement of Anil's systemic *ratio*nality previously repressed forms of sen-suousness. This ongoing process of sense-sensitizing, or *Be-Sinnung*, lastingly affects Anil and does not eradicate, but supplement her propositional knowl-edge (cf. 202). It is through another touch, and considering local factors, that she finally discovers Sailor's former occupation. This constitutes an important step in the search for his true identity (cf. 178f.). In other words, throughout these episodes, the (e-)motional disruption of static discursive closure (en-)actively enables a kinetic en-veloping (com-)motion of different modes of unconcealment; and, as such, it harbors the potential for genuine (political epistemological) change (cf. Nancy 2008: 135; Shotwell 25). Via the interaction of Anil, Palipana, and Ananda, the text suggests that calculative empirical methodology alone is insufficient to come to terms with the complexities of Sri Lanka's postcolonial situation: it requires *counterturning* in the movement of attuned sensuousness and rationality.

This process of sense-sensitizing is also transported in the formal aspects of *Anil's Ghost*. In fact, the narrative's *counterturning* interweaves the levels of the text and the reader. By drawing attention to possibilities of not merely reading the novel as discourse, but grazing its figurality, the work(ing) of art in*corporates* its readers into the *poetic* performance of re-creating Sailor's identity and face. The narrative itself affects and, as such, "must involve the body, *shall* involve it, almost immediately" (Nancy 2008: 51). In its meaning of "to touch lightly in a fleeting manner," grazing always carries this corporeal dimension with it. The narrative ex-tends and continues its critique of Western ocularcentrism by suggesting that "the reading act can be 'hapticized' into a multisensory, embodied, and emplaced engagement with a book" (Marinkova 10). Grazing, consequently, turns out as a holistic mode of text-engagement that does not strictly distinguish between the sensory and the sensuous: through the bodily doubleness of *sense*, the "gaze touches" and "the page itself is a touching" (Nancy 2008: 51). Pre*figuring* the (non-)ending of the narrative, the artwork's performative enactment of gazing and grazing collapses optics and haptics into the erotic knowing of g(r)azing: "instead of scanning the outline", as Milena Marinkova explains, this "haptic vision reads in depth, penetrates the surface and rejoices in texture and grain" (8). Showing how *Anil's Ghost* stimulates such a hapticized mode of reading leads to the last section of this analysis.

A first instance of the novel's formal performance resides in the seemingly minor detail of frequently omitted page numbers (an element which can be found in every edition of the novel). Of all the scholars dealing with Ondaatje's work, only Geetha Ganapathy-Doré takes this feature into account: "Some of the novel's pages are not numbered, interrupting the linearity of the reading time and perhaps imitating the human weakness to forget. The meticulous reader is obliged to go back and find out the page number" (par. 8). Her observation is certainly correct that this irregular pagination constitutes another element of disruption concerning the novel's partially teleological detective story; it transposes this potential into the reading process itself. Nonetheless, instead of emphasizing the shortcomings of forgetfulness, focusing further on Ganapathy-Doré's notion of meticulousness proves helpful in the context of g(r)azing: the lack of page numbers can also be *seen* as resulting in "tectonic slippages of evidential truth" (Marinkova 86); namely of a form of truth forced forth through a mode of reading that functions according to the objectifying principles of calculative thought. Heidegger describes this kind of truth as follows: "by the use of something known—measuring rods and their number—something unknown is stepped off and thus made known, and so is confined within a quantity and order which can always be determined at a glance" (2001: 222). *Anil's Ghost*, however, defies this sort of static, pre-calculated containment. The meticulous determining glance only perceives a disturbing lack. The text, thereby, enacts what Heidegger describes as a specifically poetic mode of measurement "which does not consist in a clutching or any other kind of grasping, but rather in a letting come of what has been dealt out" (2001: 222). Put differently, this kind of measuring does not enclose: with the seeming lack constituted by elided numbers, the text's measure circumscribes a potential for something un-containable to emerge through an affective *presencing*. Responding to such an incalculable pathos requires more than a distanced glance. It requires readers to participate in a bodying forth through attuned haptic engagement.

Another stylistic element which, in connection to irregular pagination patterns, encourages the hapitcization of the reading process is the numerous italicized passages interspersed throughout the narrative. The novel begins with such a section. It is the already cited scene of Anil's interaction with the mourning woman during one of her forensic investigations, another affecting encounter beyond *ratio*nal scientific rigor. In a similar manner, the subsequent passages that appear in italics designate the horrors of Sri Lanka's (postcolonial) civil war situation by outlining experiences of "painfully inexplicable death with intermittent stories of violence" (Burrows 170). In other words, accounts into which the story around Sailor, as just one instance of those inexplicable deaths, fits as well. Furthermore, these renderings of cruelty, at the same time, often point toward the local particularities of the settings in which they take place, as is the case in the passage recounting the story of Ananda's deceased wife Sirissa:

> At five-thirty in the morning, Sirissa wakes and bathes herself at the well behind the house she is living in. She dresses, eats some fruit, and leaves for the school. It is the same twenty-five-minute walk she is familiar with. She knows she will turn lazily after passing the boys on the bridge. There will be the familiar birds, Brahimny kites, perhaps a flycatcher. The road narrows. A hundred yards ahead of her is the bridge. Lagoon on the left. Salt river on the right. This morning there are no fishermen and it is an empty road. She is the first to walk it, being a servant at the school. Six-thirty AM. Nobody to whirl

for, her gesture that shows she knows she is equal to them. She is about ten yards from the bridge when she sees the heads of the two students on stakes, on either side of the bridge, facing each other. (174)

Victoria Burrows draws attention to the fact that "this brief history of a traumatic end to a life is prefaced by a three-page sketch of intimate, grounded, lived knowledge that is focalized through Sirissa" (171). Therefore, it is no coincidence that most of the italicized sections are also unmarked by page numbers. These stories of death and local knowledge fall out of and disrupt the *ratio*'s categorical grid. Instead, they rather (per-)form what Chakravorty befittingly calls "[e]ncrypted stories of loss [that] *circulate recursively* within the narrative" (548; my emphasis). As italicized and unnumbered, they correspond to Palipana's notion of "interlinear texts," that is, of "hidden stories, intentionally lost, that altered the perspective and knowledge of earlier times" (Ondaatje 105). The stories bring forth a different kind of truth that is unprovable within the systemic horizon of Western methodology; a truth that cannot be written in the form of a straight, calculated, and linear teleology, but which Palipana "still wrote in cursive script, racing the truth out of himself" (84). *Videlicet*, it requires an-other type of reading that enters into the narrative's (re-)*cursive* circulation by way of engaging in sensuous g(r)azing.

With the help of missing page numbers and sections in italics, *Anil's Ghost* provides visual-haptic stimuli for this attuned engagement, emphasizing the "mutual imbrications of the affective, cognitive, and sensory-motor" (Marinkova 14). These aspects contribute to the novel's *counterturning* structural con*figuring*. Through the disruption of calculative reason in the poetic measurement of elided pagination and the integration of (re-)*cursive* traumatic passages, the reader h/erself is incorporated into a poetic process of reconstructive (re-)creation that en-velops both Ananda's non-linear sculpting as well as Anil's teleological forensics. By *counter-turning* the pages of the book, the reader (co-creatively) participates in a textual-haptic performance which brings forth an-other kind of truth that *presences*—beyond the limitations of discursive closure—from within the sensuous depths of figurality (cf. Scanlan 302; Kertzer 128; Magrini 514). Just like the clearing of Palipana's forest monastery, or the house where Ananda, Anil, and Sarath set up camp, the narrative's *counterturning* con*figuring* circumscribes a poetic *Bezirk*: a dichotomous locus of enunciation between discourse and figure, or between art and science, "at the threshold between the imaginary and the real" (Babcock 78). Partaking in the co-(re-)creative (r-)evolving of truth as happening through attuned engagement with the narrative "make[s] our perceptions of reality, as of ourselves, contingent on our imaginary capacity to be in in the place of others" (Chakravorty 555)—always already. Ulti-mately, from within this hermeneutic *Bezirk*'s "creative splicing of the tex-tual, visual, and tactile" (Marinkova 12), as well as self and other, the novel *poetically* unfolds the *human* rights investigation concerning the circum-stances of Sailor's death.

Places

"'The problem up here is not the Tamil problem, it is the human prob-lem'" (Ondaatje 245)—explains the doctor Lakdasa, a colleague of Sar-ath's brother Gamini, shifting the focus back to the text's broader scope and drawing attention to the fact that the human rights investigation remains its overarching theme. The question, therefore, arises of how to accommodate what is normally considered a matter of universal ethics with the novel's emphasis on the significance of attunement to local particularities. Hannah Arendt's work offers a first hint toward a possible explanation. In the first volume of *The Life of the Mind*, she points out that the Greek word *ēthos* (ἔθος) originally "is derived from habitat, like our 'habits'" (5); it is tied to an en-gagement with one's immediate surroundings. The link to the question at hand becomes more apparent when Shotwell writes that taking seriously the validity of the sensuous "implies changing our habitus, what feels natural to us" (145). Read in the light of Arendt's elucidation, one can say that what Shotwell has in mind is a profound epistemological modification with a decidedly "ethical" component that affects the very notion of being human; a notion which in the first chapter of this part has been outlined with the help of Heidegger's concept of dwelling. Picking up on this, and further building on the novel's negotiation of epistemological struggles, as well as its en-velopement of the senses, the following section will probe the specific political dimension of *Anil's Ghost* with its criticism of occidental concep-tualizations of human rights—all regarding the relevance of its critique for current transnational approaches in literary studies.

In fact, a critical look at Cook's reading of the novel's transnational character through the lens of dwelling provides a suitable point of entry into this discussion. In her essay on *Anil's Ghost*, she argues that the text traces the de-velopment of the protagonist from an alienation with respect to her parental culture, via her subsequent adoption of a foreign culture, eventually, to her return to the homeland where she, then, "substitut[es] the outmoded idea of a fixed cultural identity with the emerging concept of one that is truly transnational" (11); a new identity "which incorporates, encom-passes and contains various fragments in one unified being" (7). What Cook omits entirely, however, is that the change Anil undergoes never attains such closure. As the text's *counterturning* structure makes clear, Anil neither ever altogether sheds her adopted Western(ized) conviction, nor does she drop her native cultural heritage. Not taking this into account results in a problematic simplification regarding the text's transnational potential. Cook holds that Anil's multicultural background positions her as "outside of the accepted order that is required for belonging to a single nationality" (12). However, this is not exactly what is at stake in the narrative. Anil, indeed, never identifies herself as part of a single nation, but what she repeatedly identifies herself with is the abstract entity of the West and its anonymity (cf. Ondaatje 26, 36, 72). Therefore, while she does not subscribe to one national identity, she does espouse the unifying epistemology behind the logic of the nation-state. Put differently, it is not primarily a particular national language she takes on: instead, she works "alongside the language of science" (145) that first maps out and delimits these territories and subjects all entities to its technical empirical skills. All this implies that Anil remains part of a systemic order on another level; a dimension Cook largely ignores. Her argument appears stuck in the static confines of Western epistemological hegemony she critiques: although Cook insists on a crumbling of stable concepts of identity, the teleological framework of substitution, containment, and unification into which she integrates this breakdown simultaneously reintroduces the notion of stability. The linear progression toward a fashionable new human identity that she praises is precisely the *ratio*nal tendency which the narrative problematizes in the epistemological en-velopement Anil undergoes. As the previous section has shown, the text implies that, unless supposed to turn into a new manifestation of violent occidental imperialism, the *ratio*'s technical uncanniness alone must not dictate the terms of transnationalism.

Anil's Ghost unfolds a mode of the transnational that does not offer idealized models of multicultural identities which, upon closer inspection, turn out to be global extensions of Western ordering principles in disguise. The narrative exceeds this type of thinking through its continued insistence on sensuous attunement. However, from a Eurocentric point of view this focus on local particularities is sometimes perceived as nothing more than a problematic nostalgia or, even worse, the revival of essentialist claims connected to notions of earth or soil. Joseph R. Slaughter, though, clarifies that "Ondaatje's novel is profoundly antinationalist"; it discards any "ethnonationalist claims of predetermined group filiation based on mythicized primordial cultural coherence and distinction" (195). Nevertheless, where the narrative enacts "a withdrawal from the conventional terrain of politics", as Slaughter continues, "Western reviewers of the novel have tended to insist upon its nationalist engagements, ironically by invoking an ultimately ethnocentric image of a supranational court of world opinion in which *Anil's Ghost* speaks to an imaginary community of cosmopolitan readers without borders" (ibid.). By affirming the overwhelming earthen sway of a *sense* of place—underscored through untranslated terms linked to ex-positions of Ceylonese daily life (cf. Scanlan 303)—the text unmasks the insufficiency of this remnant of Enlightenment thought.

The attunement to local particularity within *Anil's Ghost* is not a matter of territorial sovereignty; it marks a responsive relationship to one's surroundings that potentially results in a *sense* of planet beyond the global designs of a Western *ratio*nality which subjects the earth to its systemic ordering principles from the dis-located vantage point of an ivory tower. In contrast to this homogenizing digestion of otherness in the modern/colonial world system's alimentary tract, attuned haptic sensuousness, within the narrative constitutes, an "immersive knowing" (Shotwell 70) with a released attitude of openness for that which withdraws from a categorizing grip. The text does not promote a totalizing cosmopolitan transnationalism that—in line with a militant occidental epistemology—turns the globe into one large utopian home-state without borders and with all of humanity as its citizenry. Rather, Ondaatje's novel evokes the possibility of a planetary situation of dwelling in (extra-)ordinary (un-)homeliness that is connected to a "responsive aesthetico-political approach" which "exposes the ambivalences of hegemonic power" (Marinkova 21). The text acknowledges "difference *within* and *without*, without appropriating it into sameness" (7). And in this scenario the text, then, specifically "employs the character of Anil as a site through which to enact differing notions of the human, almost always cultured along the east/west divide" (Ratti 134). Deconstructing this binary within its poetic *Bezirk*, the narrative suggests that the problem of humanity is never just something universal; it is also always already particular. The novel points toward the necessity of a transnationalism which thinks the politics of human rights and identity from within the border gnosis of *sense* of place and planet.

Nonetheless, Ondaatje has often been criticized for this responsive aesthetic approach. As the accusations go, his later work is characterized by apolitical irresponsibility steeped in exoticism and lacking social commitment (cf. Kertzer 131). Ondaatje supposedly indulges in "postmodern" aestheticization of (postcolonial) trauma and violence. In his scathing review, Tom LeClair finds *Anil's Ghost* guilty of all this, too. Bemoaning the text's apparently missing political dimension, he writes that Ondaatje's attitude falls under the same critique that Sarath utters intradiegetically regarding those disconnected journalists catering to Western audiences, who objectify victims, eschew political analyses, and leave as fast as they arrived (cf. LeClair n.pag). LeClair identifies the novel's aestheticism as the root of this deficient politics: "Anil distrusts Sarath for his retreat into the 'aesthetic.' Ondaatje should distrust himself. Now I don't trust his collage method. It's a way to avoid banal, 'old coin' cause and effect, the logic by which human rights are denied or defended" (n.pag.). It needs to be conceded, as Marinkova remarks, that aestheticization—if conceived only in a *ratio*nal framework—risks "'translating' extreme pain and suffering into palatable cultural products or trite historical truisms" (15). But she also points out that *Anil's Ghost* is not reducible to the occidental aesthetic tradition. The novel's (en-)active sensuous potential does not "encourage personal identification or subjective ownership by the reader/viewer, but their openness to otherness" (15). Avoiding linearity in the circumscription of a scenario where every conflicting party is partaking in atrocious acts and side-taking futile, the novel suggests that judging the Sri Lankan *situation* from a removed position, which assumes moral superiority, merely reproduces the war's violent *sense*lessness on a political epistemological level: "no more high horses" (Ondaatje 133), says Gamini, when dealing with crises, as his brother Sarath adds, where "we all have blood on our clothes" (48). The critique of the narrative's specific aesthetic modality for its reputed lack of a political dimension, however, is uttered from precisely the elevated *ratio*nal perspective that the text debunks and deems insufficient.[7]

How exactly does politics *figure* within *Anil's Ghost*? Annick Hillger attempts to respond to this question by interpreting the narrative in relation to Sophocles's *Antigone*. In her analysis, she focuses on the image of the mourning woman as a leitmotif of the text that mirrors the Greek tragedy's heroine (cf. 205): "[l]ike ancient Antigone, Anil insists on preserving the memory of the dead" (206), Hillger observes. Then, via a slightly incomprehensible move, and in contradistinction to Hegel's interpretation of *Antigone*, Hillger argues that Anil is part of a tradition of women in grief who subvert occidental notions of (historical) progress (cf. 205). Although this aspect of subversion constitutes an important insight, its persuasiveness suffers due to Hillger's silence regarding a fundamental difference between Anil and Antigone, namely their respective relationship to the established *polis*: Antigone, on the one hand, challenges the phallocentric city–state's authority in disobeying its ruler, her uncle Creon, and moving beyond the confines of the *polis* to bury her brother Polyneices. Anil, in contrast, at first, largely works in the logic of the *polis*, albeit in a globally extended modern version, through her technical scientific worldview, and does not even regard such a challenge as necessary. While Antigone realizes that justice cannot solely be determined on the grounds of the *polis*, Anil believes that it can only be determined there. Only by way of sense-sensitization to the importance of sensuous excess does she question the exclusive hegemony of her

Western(ized) epistemological systematicity. She realizes that this potential has been relegated to the margins of the *polis*—where also Antigone has to go—as it poses a challenge to a closed-off *ratio*nal Eurocentric world-order (cf. Lorde 53f.). Within its *counterturning* con*figuring*, the narrative, conse- quently, pursues the potential of a sensuous politics. Building on Hillger's notion of subversion, it can be stated that insofar politics is taken as tied to the confines of the *polis*'s phallic teleological system which, in a Hegelian manner, expulses sensuous knowledge as inferior and anachronistic, *Anil's Ghost* poetic performance contrastingly unfolds (a-)political space.

(A-)political, in this case, is not to be taken in the sense of LeClair's—and Shotwell's (cf. 155)—understanding of the "apolitical," but rather in rela- tion to radical otherness. In an interview with Petra Gehring and Matthias Fischer, Waldenfels—also referring to *Antigone*—explains that the Greek *alpha privativum* does not imply a straightforward negation. "Apolitical" does not mean "unpolitical"; it refers to a de*via*ting excess: "The a-political, hence, designates that *within* politics itself there resides something which withdraws from political scales and measures" (2001: 444f.).[8] Just as (a-)*topos* does not indicate complete dis-location, but always remains tied to a place, the (a-)political also retains a link to the political order which it exceeds as a de*via*tion from within. In fact, when Waldenfels explains that, to avoid the danger of (global totalitarian) systemic political closure, it is necessary to bear in mind the location from where one thinks, then he resonates strongly with Mignolo and his insistence on loci of enunciation. Waldenfels, thereby, provides a significant hint concerning the interconnectedness of (a-)*topos* and (a-)politics as concepts of border thinking that becomes more evident in the following remark: "I am, therefore, never completely bound to the po- litical order with body and soul. *This* would be the boundary: the political that does not lock itself within itself without, thus, being negated from the outside" (2001: 445).[9] *Anil's Ghost* further underscores this connectedness as the de*via*ting excess, in the novel, *figures* within the (e-)motional sensuous attunement with a *sense* of place. Circumscribing it as irreducibly entan- gled with reason, the text unfolds sensuousness as an-other epistemological mode that harbors (a-)political force; namely "to pursue genuine change within our world, rather than merely settling for a shift of characters in the same weary drama" (Lorde 69) of exclusive *ratio*nal predominance.

The novel renders this hegemony of occidental political reason as result- ing in an attitude characterized by dissociation, dislocation, and abstraction. Anil remembers one of her former US teachers express the opinion that in human rights investigation "[o]*ne village can speak for many villages. One victim can speak for many victims*" (Ondaatje 176). This reductive, synec- dochic logic is critiqued, again, when the novel evokes the image of the Very

Large Array radio astronomy observatory in New Mexico—where Anil visits her friend Leaf—to suggest that the telescopic gaze of Western epistemology turns human beings, irrespective of their cultural backgrounds, into minor characters from the subplot of its grand narrative of universal justice (cf. Ondaatje 256). In this way, particular experience is abstracted into objectified particularity which can be "grabbed and collected as evidence" in order then to be "copied and sent abroad to strangers in Geneva" (42), who judge individual cases from a safe distance. Human rights efforts dominated by occidental reason are, consequently, rendered to be complicit with "the common sense and hermeneutic assumptions of an international community constituted elsewhere *that attempts to impose its international will from on high*, without regard for dialogue with the people it seeks to assist" (Slaughter 196; my emphasis). Contesting this assumption of superiority, Gamini describes what the West considers a benevolent humanitarian discourse as yet another manifestation of "*careless* power" (Ondaatje 119; my emphasis) that *sense*lessly subsumes everything and every-body under the categorical grid of technical scientific systematicity. More specifically, *Anil's Ghost* illustrates that Western "human rights and humanitarian assumptions are cultivated in an international order that is based on the Westphalian culture of national sovereignty" which, contrary to its professed goals, "ultimately reinforce[s] the logic of the nation-statism that fuels the war" (Slaugther 196) raging on Ceylon. From this angle, the invocation of universal human rights appears as a perfidious re-activation of a militant, colonialist epistemological impetus.[10]

The narrative exposes the insistence on the universal equality of all human beings exclusively from the perspective of a *rati*onal political order as inherently contradictory. As indicated above, this exclusivity entails the elevation of said order to a (higher) position which is (supposedly) capable of uttering such an insistence; an elevation over that which it wishes to declare universally equal. Such equality could only be convincingly declared from the level ground of a common humanity that is intrinsically heterogeneous and cannot be defined from one single political epistemological vantage point. Waldenfels, however, is correct when he writes "we do not simply stand on the ground of some common polity or cosmopolitically on the ground of some realm of humanity" (2001: 444f.).[11] Human beings never stand on but make up and are always already immersed in this ground. This immersion constitutes the very possibility for conceiving of the reality of human universality. Nevertheless, it also renders human experience as always emplaced, local, and particular. As such, being immersed in this ground is, simultaneously, what keeps the full attainment of universality out of reach, or ever in withdrawal from a totalizing fixating grip. Hence,

Anil's Ghost does not simply reject notions of the universal. Its emphasis on the significance of a *sense* of place outlines a mode of engagement where human universality—belonging to all humans and all humans belonging to it—*figures* in continuously (re-)repeated negotiations through *counter-turning* motion with singular *situations* of particular human lives. Unlike the hierarchizing abstractions of systemic politics, the text stresses singular "affective signatures" as "deliberate transnational gestures" to "reenvision human subjectivity on the basis of a politics of collective human sentience that goes beyond the individuated forms of human sovereignty allowed by legal, juridical orders" (Chakravorty 543) such as the nation-state. Through the sense-sensitization with regard to an un-resolvable (extra-)ordinariness of human-ness, the narrative enacts a kind of transnationalism that coincides with a dynamic conceptualization of human rights beyond global designs, but with a *sense* of planet.

It has become clear that the prominent aesthetic dimension in *Anil's Ghost* neither serves to avoid questions of politics, nor to turn human suffering into a pleasurable commodity—the opposite is the case. As a form of sense-sensitizing to modes of engaging phenomena beyond the subject/object paradigm, aesthetics is of utmost importance to the human rights issues in the text. Instead of the *polis*'s *ratio*nal closure, "[t]he aestheticization and literarization of the letter of the law allows for a form of witnessing . . . that challenges the limits of the law's abstract univocality. That witnessing is not simply, in Ondaatje's *literary* case, specular detachment, or detached legal formulation, but rather a kind of participation" (Ratti 123f.). Through this participatory potential, the novel unfolds its sensuous politics in which universal human rights always remain tied to a *sense* of place beyond the confines of the *polis*. It is thus that within *Anil's Ghost* "the space of the aesthetic becomes inextricable from the space of the ethical" (Ratti 132)—again in the original Greek meaning of "habitat" explained by Arendt: instead of a commodification of violence, the text's specific form of aestheticizing the politics of human rights encourages readers, as Shotwell puts it, to "dwell in sensuous experience" (148)—responsive to affecting pathos—precisely to circumvent the "estrangement produced by capital and its kind of objectification" (69). Rather than re-presenting a case of remote political moralism, *Anil's Ghost* (en-)actively makes a case for reading other-wise via an attuned corporeal contiguity which exceeds a-pathetic moralistic discourse (cf. Babcock 80; Marinkova 17). All this confirms that criticism condemning the text's aesthetics as entailing a lack of political engagement stems from hegemonic notions of the aesthetic as harnessed within the straightjacket of *ratio*nality and misses that what the novel negotiates via its aesthetics is the very terms of such engagement.

Within the performance of the narrative's *counterturning* con*figuring* of *sense* of place and planet, the text's literary poetic gestures negotiate the local and the global, the particular and the universal, as well as the sensuous and the rational as inherently interrelated (cf. Spinks 243; Ratti 132); gestures that, circumscribing a "polyphonous space" (Ratti 122), evoke (a-)political critique with a possibility to conceive of human rights beyond abstract and univocal systematicity. Instead of rendering the strife for transnational human rights as another Western-dictated utopian vision emerging at the same time as other (failed) grand narratives crumble (cf. Moyn 122), *Anil's Ghost* outlines what Shotwell calls "a utopia that is precisely not a 'no place'" (150). Or, in the terms of this part, the text unfolds a dynamic (a-)topical *Bezirk* in which place and planet reciprocally supplement each other through the doubleness of *sense*. By way of the sensuous haptic experience of *counter-turning* the pages of the book, "*Anil's Ghost* takes us toward fathoming the problem of collective death as an ethical bind that moves beyond our conception of ourselves as individuated, nation-bound subjects governed exclusively by reason," suggesting that "we cannot fully separate ourselves (even if we live in the West) from deaths in the postcolony" (Chakravorty 555): within the *Bezirk*, the affectations of (un-)homeliness prevail. These circular (e-)motions throughout the text in-volve readers coconstitutively into a poetic performance beyond cognitive contemplation, turning them into an (en-)active part of the human rights investigation around which the narrative (r-)evolves: "These hermeneutic circles *incorporate* their participants as *coactors* in a common story through the *collective act of reading* common texts and through the *shared interpretive modes that emerge from that reading*, settling not only the means by which meaning is to be given to the text but, more importantly, establishing the *tacit terms* of enfranchisement and the discursive lines of the group's binding force" (Slaughter 192; my emphases). The text's emphasis on sensuous bodily knowledge as a mode of performative partaking and being-with-others *figures* as a re-grounding of human-ness within (un-)homely border dwelling with a *sense* of place and planet to reintroduce (subalternized) forms of reading other-wise. Stressing the significance of local knowledges, the narrative describes particularity and universality as always already entangled; a fraught epistemological entanglement wherein human rights appear—in Mignolo's terms—as a "pluriversal rather than universal" (2011a: 23) matter: ultimately, *Anil's Ghost* unfolds a transnational *situation* that does not promote another Western grand narrative of a universal *u-topos*, but which rather circumscribes a pluriversal (a-)*topos* where the other *presences*.[12]

❖

Anil's Ghost concludes with two shorter chapters respectively entitled "The Life Wheel" (267) and, ultimately, "Distance" (297). Anil, in the end, leaves Ceylon once more to return to the West. Several scholars have read this in relation to a passage where Gamini describes leaving the area of conflict behind as typical occidental behavior: "'American movies, English books — remember how they all end?' Gamini asked that night. 'The American of the Englishman gets on a plane and leaves. That's it. The camera leaves with him. . . . He's going home. So the war, to all purposes, is over. That's enough reality for the West. It's probably the history of the last two hundred years of Western political writing. Go home. Write a book. Hit the circuit'" (Ondaatje 285f.). Chakravorty, for example, states that despite its criticism of Western politics and epistemology, the text "returns us once more to a world-dividing difference "(552). However, does the distance evoked at the end of the narrative really only reproduce this Western attitude and, thereby, annul the stimulation of sense-sensitivity? Or is distance, here, in some way connected to this kind of sensitivity? What kind of circuit does the book *Anil's Ghost* hit? After all, one needs to keep in mind that it is not simply Anil's decision to leave — although she certainly does not have any wish to stay after her having been humiliated by the government and deeming all her research lost (cf. Ondaatje 282). It is Sarath who sends her back to the West — including what he could save of their work — so she can continue their investigation: "You will have to re-create them. You can buy new equipment in Europe. You can replace nearly everything. It's just you who has to be safe" (ibid.). Consequently, it seems rather simplistic to close by asserting the novel's complicity with a Western market logic, although the text itself certainly does not deny this possibility. It leaves room for interpretation; which might precisely be the point, for the real question then becomes: what are the modalities of this interpretation going to be?

The last scene within the novel provides a hint toward a possible answer. The passage focuses on Ananda's ceremonious re-creation of a destroyed Buddha-statue's face and — similar to the scene of Anil's departure — has sometimes been *one-sidedly* interpreted, namely as the nostalgic restoration of (Buddhist) notions of unification or "the re-assertion of life itself" (Ganapathy-Doré par. 14). However, the re-creation is not characterized by unblemished wholeness, but bears the scars of violent demolition. The narrative (dis-)closes with a paradox, as Marlene Goldman observes: "The novel thus registers a shift from the unifying and protecting image of the thread of the *pirit* ceremony to the image of quilting, a form of stitching that likewise unifies and yet, at the same time, acknowledges separation and difference" (36). This paradox points toward an-other *sense* of distance. When Ananda, eventually, paints the eyes of another new and unblemished statue of the

Buddha that will only perceive "the figure of the world" and "only from a great distance" (307), his own vision nonetheless, from halfway up the ladder to the statue, is one residing between world and earth; that is, within a paradox of simultaneous unification and separation (cf. 306); a liminal vision that, unlike the objectifying telescopic stare of the West, remains sensuously attuned: "And now with human sight he was seeing all the fibres of natural history around him," rendering him capable to concretely "witness" and "feel" and "smell" as well as hear the "noise" of "[t]he great churning of weather above the earth" (307)—and not only observe an abstract world.

Which kind of distance is it going to be? The straightforward distance which has both Anil and Ananda hit the circuit of (in-)different cultural discourses' respective closure, namely Western objectivity and Buddhist harmony? Or is it rather the paradoxical liminal distance which remains involved in the *counterturning* hermeneutic circle of world and earth? If read together as forming one more *figural* gesture of the narrative's poetic performance, the titles of the last two chapters suggest the latter. As Heidegger writes, in sensuous attunement, "[e]ven when we relate ourselves to those things that are not in our immediate reach, we are staying with the things themselves. We do not represent distant things merely in our mind . . . so that only mental representations of distant things run through our minds and heads as substitutes for the things" (2011: 251). In sensuous attunement, a collective human sentience, touching upon and binding one to the realities of the postcolonial world through its connectedness to earth, *"persists through [durchsteht]* the distance to that locale" (ibid.); even if—to once again invoke Nancy—"[t]his touch is infinitely indirect, deferred—machines, vehicles, photocopies, eyes, still other hands are all interposed— . . . it continues as a slight, resistant, fine texture, the infinitesimal dust of a contact, everywhere interrupted and pursued" (2008: 51). Ultimately, the narrative leaves it open whether one choses to return to a world dividing systemic closure, or whether one wishes to de*via*te by walking along the *figural* lines of the *counterturning* border gnosis between *sense* of place and planet.

PART FOUR

PRECARIOUS IN-DIVIDUALITY AND THE OTHER: NEGOTIATING SIMULATION AND PRESENCE WITH JEAN BAUDRILLARD AND RICHARD POWERS'S *PLOWING THE DARK*

At their best, some media representations of suffering at a distance compel us to give up our more narrow communitarian ties and to respond, sometimes in spite of ourselves, sometimes even against our will, to a perceived injustice. Such presentations can bring the fate of others near or make it seem very far away, and yet, the kinds of ethical demands that emerge through the media in these times depend on this reversibility of proximity and distance.
—Judith Butler, *Notes Toward a Performative Theory of Assembly*

THROUGH DEALING WITH LITERARY texts revolving around Indigenous ceremonies, shamanistic rituals, as well as Buddhist asceticism in their art-work, this book shows how what Mignolo would describe as non-Western—subalternized—modes of knowledge pose a challenge to the occidental fantasy of *ratio*-systemic closure, even from within its aesthetic system. However, is this challenge from the inside restricted to prior inclusions of different epis-temological horizons into the digestive tract of the epistemic violence which characterizes occidental thinking? Or is there a potential for resistance even within what is usually referred to as the Western tradition of thought? This part assumes that this potential exists, and it traces this question in the part of modern (computer) technology.

However, turning from the previous part's discussion of sensuous knowl-edge via an ab-usive treatment of Heidegger to issues of technology may appear as somewhat of a risk. Is not Heidegger precisely the problematically nostalgic philosopher who, as Fredric Jameson puts it, "continues to enter-tain a phantasmatic relationship with some organic precapitalist peasant landscape and village society" (34)? How does the turn to technology in what follows relate to this accusation? And, more problematically still, does this accusation maybe, in retrospect, question the validity of the previous analyses?

A brief, and again playfully ab-usive, excursus on Heidegger's notion of technology will pave the way for this part's actual concern of uncovering a subversive epistemological potential in the so-called Western tradition of thought. Due to his bucolic, agrarian terminology and his connectedness to his birth place, as well as the pastoral idyll of the eerie Black Forest surrounding it, Heidegger may appear as a rural philosopher whose thinking's relevance ceases in an increasingly technological world.[1] The German philosopher's thought does, indeed, in many instances, justify such an assumption. In line with his apparent rural posturing, his work apparently demonizes all things modern, and especially modern technology. The United States (and Russia), as the main perpetrator(s) of the increasing technologization of the world, seem(s) to function as the scapegoat for Heidegger's polemic. The following passage from his *Introduction to Metaphysics* illustrates this:

> In America and Russia, then, this all [modern technology's influence] intensified until it turned into the measureless so-on-and-so-forth of the ever-identical and the indifferent, until finally this quantitative temper became a quality of its own. By now in those countries the predominance of a cross-section of the indifferent is no longer something inconsequential and merely barren but is the onslaught of that which aggressively destroys all rank and all that is world spiritual, and portrays these as a lie. This is the onslaught of what we call the demonic [in the sense of the destructively evil]. (48f.)

For Heidegger, the United States represents the putting into operation of a techno-logical mode of relating to the things of the world which levels all things into identical indifference and robs otherness of its sting. Modern technology coincides with the impetus of calculative reasoning. This is based on the impetus to regard everything within the objectifying confines of geometric-mathematical thought where everything appears as an accumulation of material objects to be mastered (cf. Henry xiiif.). Contrary to older forms, such as the windmill and traditional agriculture that, as Heidegger argues, functioned within a quasi-symbiotic relationship with the surrounding nature, modern technology subjects the things of the world to its controlling grasp. That is, it results in a violent mode of world-appropriation which stands in contrast to the released revealing of sensuous attunement that was outlined in the last part. In *The Question Concerning Technology*, he writes: "the revealing that holds sway throughout modern technology does not unfold into a bringing-forth in the sense of poiēsis. The revealing that rules in modern technology is a challenging [*Herausfordern*]" (6). That is, instead of the *Hervorbringen*, or bringing-forth, of *poiēsis*, *Herausfordern* literally denotes the "forcing-forth" that is characteristic of *technē* in its modern guise.

Heidegger uses a specific term to describe the unconcealment produced by this form of relating to the world, namely "standing reserve [*Bestand*]" (8). It serves to express an absolute availability which deprives objects of any sort of opposing agency — as the German *Gegen-stand* indicates — it might possess. This does not only apply to the inanimate, but also to animals and, to a certain extent, human beings, who, with the onset of modernity, find themselves subjected to modern technology's forcing-forth. It is in this relationship toward the world and its accompanying mode of disclosure that Heidegger finds modern technology at work. He calls this *Gestell* — meaning en-framing, positioning, arrangement, etc. — and explains it as follows: "Enframing means the gathering together of that setting-upon which sets upon man, i.e., challenges him forth, to reveal the real, in the mode of ordering, as standing-reserve. Enframing means that way of revealing which holds sway in the essence [this is, *Wesen*] of modern technology and which is itself nothing technological" (10). If this quotation aptly describes Heidegger's attitude toward modern technology, it also shows that, upon closer inspection, it is not technology per se which he critiques, but rather the epistemological stance to which it is connected in modern Western thought. As Dreyfus points out, it is the specific "technological understanding of being" which Heidegger repeatedly criticizes, "rather than the destruction caused by specific technologies" (2006: 370) that would then result in a demonization of technics as such. Heidegger is not concerned with the technical in itself, but with the mode of unconcealment that undergirds modern technology. The term *Gestell* neither constitutes a technophobic backlash of a nostalgic rural thinker, nor a condemnation of the natural sciences via a blatant irrationalism, but an insightful analysis of the historical development of a destructive epistemic megalomania, where all too often crude technological mastery has turned into the only plausible conceptualization of truth (cf. D. Hart 2008: 231). Therefore, far more than just an abstraction of the technical aspects of contemporary machinery, the *Wesen* of modern technology as *Gestell* presents itself as nothing less than an entire technology of thought guiding Western humanity's understanding of (human) being(s).

In what appears, perhaps, as a rather surprising twist, however, Heidegger also insists that the *Gestell* as forcing-forth remains irreducibly related to *poiēsis* as bringing-forth, and, thereby, always already harbors a potential for change. That is, the *poiētic* mode of disclosure remains present, albeit buried or, more specifically *ver-stellt*, in the *Gestell*'s *en-framework*. Paradoxically, what appears as the most destructive effacement of difference and levelling of radical otherness, as Heidegger has it, contains the potential for a turning (*Kehre*) toward a more released and sensuous mode of relating to the world. Somewhat cryptically, he claims that

[i]t is precisely in Enframing, which threatens to sweep man away into ordering as the supposed single way of revealing, and so thrusts man into the
danger of the surrender of his free essence—it is precisely in this extreme danger that the innermost indestructible belongingness of man within granting
[releasement] may come to light, provided that we, for our part, begin to pay
heed to the coming to presence of technology. Thus the coming to presence of
technology harbors in itself what we least suspect, the possible arising of the
saving power. (17)

It is by way of this description of the *en-framework* of modern technology as
related to both *technē* and *poiēsis* that Heidegger's thought forms a point of
departure for this part. In what follows, this curious simultaneity of *technē*
and *poiēsis* is going to be further negotiated, albeit not with Heidegger himself, but with the thinking of Jean Baudrillard and Richard Powers's novel
Plowing the Dark, both of which go beyond Heidegger in the scope of their
discussion of the potential of modern technology.

With Baudrillard's thought, this part picks up on this book's claims regarding the subversive character of what is called "poststructuralist" or
"postmodern" thought. Providing a critical extension of Heidegger's work,
Baudrillard's notion of simulation informs the following discussion of modern technology in relation to the question of the other to show how even the
Western tradition of thought cannot rid itself of a radical otherness that is
always already at work (from) within the *ratio*'s horizon of systemic closure.
With ab-usive help of Judith Butler's more recent work, and taking recourse
to Bernhard Stiegler's ideas, this part is ultimately going to tie this back to
the notion of aesthetics as a sense-sensitized mode of relating to phenomena;
a form of relationality that Powers's novel expresses in its per-formative
art-work.

Chapter seven will, firstly, relate what Baudrillard, regarding his understanding of simulation, has termed a loss of reference to what Stiegler calls a
loss of (social) participation. Extending Heidegger's notion of the *Gestell*, it
will be shown how modern technology can be regarded as a form of Mignolo's
modern/colonial world system. However, not remaining with a bleak picture of (demonized) technology, the argument is going to arrive shortly at a
different conceptualization of human beings' relation to technology via the
concept of technogenesis as developed by Stiegler (and as refined by Katherine Hayles). Ultimately, this section will point toward an-other potential of
simulation for encounters with (*presencing*) radical otherness.

Secondly, again echoing Heidegger, the line of argumentation will be developed by relating Baudrillard's critique of the screens of integral reality to
Butler's analysis of frames. The chapter will point out how the two thinkers

conceive of screens and frames, respectively, as harboring the potential both for epistemological levelling and rupturing. Building on the previously developed notion of technogenesis, the argument will renegotiate the relationship between *technē* and *poiēsis* to develop an ab-usive concept of *technopoiēsis* that allows for conceiving of aesthetics other-wise.

Thirdly, the concepts will be related to Baudrillard's critique of the banality of Western individualized life in contrast to Butler's notion of precariousness as a certain form of relational pluriversality. I will show how the connection of Baudrillard and Butler can prove fruitful to avoid pitfalls in both philosopher's work: Baudrillard's critique of individualism (related to the ideas of Waldenfels) serves to contour Butler's precariousness with regard to relationality. She writes that the notion of the precarious marks "an insurrection at the level of ontology, a critical opening up of the questions, What is real? Whose lives are real? How might reality be remade?" (2006: 33). Her conception (in relation to the *figural*), in turn, can serve to alleviate an apparent nihilism of Baudrillard's analyses of simulation and hyperreality. Taken together, this section is going to further unfold what is at stake if the radically other(s) are to be perceived as acting entities rather than mere constructs.

Chapter eight will, then, illustrate how Powers's novel *Plowing the Dark* engages with the issues raised in the previous chapter. Eventually, it is going to show how literary simulation potentially outlines an interstitial space where the other *presences*. First, the chapter will analyze how the novel's first plotline deals with matters of technology, simulation, and virtual reality, and the problematical epistemological assumptions underlying these concepts. It will trace how the text discusses notions of epistemic violence concerning the levelling of all forms of otherness (as suggested by Baudrillard). This first section will conclude with pointing out how the novel ties the conceptualization of (Western notions of) the imagination and the resulting possibility of the reader's relating to fictional characters via a third-person narrative perspective to this form of epistemic violence (as mirroring the non-relationships between the characters in the novel's *diegesis*).

The second section is going to analyze how the second plotline deals with matters of in-dividuality as a form of relationality revealed in a space and/or situation of precariousness. It will explain how the text outlines an irreducible and necessary connection to radical otherness and relates this to matters of literary art and the imagination between *technē* and *poiēsis*. Mirroring the first section (just as the second plotline of the novel mirrors the first), this second section is going to conclude with an analysis of the effect/affect of the second-person narrative perspective in one of the novel's plotlines concerning the reader's encounters with the other(s).

The third section is, finally, going to analyze — on a more abstract level — how Powers's novel interweaves the two plotlines in the manner of what Baudrillard has referred to as the potential for reversibility. It will show how the text itself per-forms (by way of simulation) an interstitial space where the other potentially *presences* and how it, thereby, also outlines the possibility for conceiving of simulation other-wise in relation to the concept of *technopoiēsis*.

TRANS-FIGURING TECHNOLOGY

IN *SYMBOLIC EXCHANGE AND DEATH*, Jean Baudrillard writes that "[t]he arbitrariness of the sign begins when, instead of bonding two persons in an inescapable reciprocity, the signifier starts to refer to a disenchanted universe of the signified, the common denominator of the real world, towards which no-one any longer has the least obligation" (1993a: 50). This notion of an inescapable reciprocal relationality renders Baudrillard's thought pertinent to this study. Perhaps surprisingly so, his work provides the pathway for a renewed discussion of "postmodern" or "poststructuralist" thought, and its potential beyond notions of infinite deferral. If it is correct, as Robert Eaglestone asserts, that "[p]ostmodernism begins when the mainstream of western thought encounters otherness and does not—or tries not to—consume it but instead respond to it, using the only language it can, its own 'Greek' language" (189), then Baudrillard can help better understand the paradoxical fact that the so-called "postmodern condition" has not even started (yet), and, at the same time, has always already pre-*figured* in Western thinking from its very earliest manifestations. The following sections are now first going to unfold how Baudrillard's ideas on simulation and beyond ultimately *reverts* into an acknowledgment of an irreducible radical otherness's pathos, in *ratio*nal thought's systemic confines, that calls for a response beyond a hopeless calculative reasoning.

Simulation: The World between Hyperreality and Hyperindustriality

"Jean Baudrillard's theory of the three orders [of] simulacra as addressed in *Simulations and Simulacra* (1981) is well documented, well read and well, done" (n.pag.)—declares Alex Wade and labels Baudrillard's thought as outdated, irrelevant, or even both. While it is certainly true that the conceptions of simulation have been discussed extensively and in various contexts, the scope of his radical ideas has rarely been acknowledged or taken seriously. For if one does take it seriously, these concepts "by their very nature demand an assessment of their potential impact on the whole of [Western] epistemology" (Weinbrot n.pag.). This epistemological dimension is precisely where the relevance of Baudrillard's work for this study becomes apparent. Instead of reading the well-known three orders—as well as the fourth one he added in his later thought—as a reductive and/or "strictly phasal and subsumptive" summary over the history of modern Western reason, taking another look reveals how the theory of simulation, in fact, provides "a more ambiguous 'hypothetical trajectory'" (Genosko 44); a trajectory which not only alters the character of the four simulacral orders, but also the thinker's work in general. From this angle, Baudrillard's philosophy can be seen as not merely relishing in a "postmodern" relativism of "a semiological Baudrillardean world where signs refer to other signs" (Eid 149) that, consequently, merely erects a "prison house of the sign" (ibid. 150), and that is devoid of constructive critique (cf. Torkian n.pag.). From this angle, it rather points toward another potential altogether, namely toward "Baudrillard [as] the thinker on otherness" (Akinwumi n.pag). With this in mind (*qua* the work of Bernard Stiegler), the four orders will now briefly be discussed anew.

The four orders of simulacra, in general, describe the process of the signs' liberation from the feudal insistence on the possibility of stable reference. Baudrillard describes this "emancipation of the sign" (1993a: 7)—always tied to certain technological developments—however, as a highly problematic process whose modern liberating impetus is ultimately geared toward the attainment of epistemological sovereignty, as a re-vision of the first two orders shows. While the first order works according to a logic of imitation and counterfeit, the second order is based on a principle of identical (industrialized) (re)production (cf. Baudrillard 1994: 121 and Blask 26f.)—effecting a "homology between the sign and the commodity" (Genosko xviii). Therefore, the two orders differ in form; but, as Baudrillard asserts, even the level of the counterfeit, although "not yet on relations and structures . . . is already aiming at control of a pacified society, cast in a synthetic substance which evades death, an indestructible artifact that will guarantee eternal power," and outlines a fixating epistemological quest: "a project which aims at political and mental hegemony, the phantasy of a closed mental substance" (1993a: 53). He suggests that the signs' liberation does not effectively challenge, but only invert Western thought's notions of "a universal substance and a universal combinatory of substances" (ibid. 52). The structure which allowed for the illusion of fixed reference in the first place, consequently, guides the emancipatory goals of the modern *ratio*; or, as Victoria Grace explains, "the very axiological and semiological codification that prefigures the possibility of a hierarchical form of representation and social practice" (35) remains unchallenged: "this critique simply shifts the code from one of equivalence to one of polyvalence and leaves the fundamental structure intact" (9).[1] For Baudrillard the emancipatory semiological venture of escaping the straightjacket of fixed reference only masks a deeper wish for a full appropriation of (epistemic) power, founded upon the utopian fantasy of "total liberty—no duties, disaffection and general disenchantment" (1993a: 7). The process of simulation erodes stable referential representation, and with it established notions of the real, but, at the same time, retains or even expands the underlying epistemological framework—a framework where ever more abstract models allow for meaning to be subsumed under codified systemic notions of signification (cf. Levin 167). Baudrillard argues that what appears as the signs' emancipation effectively installs "the principle of operativity" (1993a: 54) where the fluid proliferation of signification entails a reduction to the now "only law: indifference" (ibid. 34). For him, "loss of reference" (ibid. 10) goes hand in hand with "the disenchantment of the world and its abandonment to the violence of interpretation and of history" (1994: 160); a form of violence that installs Western epistemology as the supreme ruler over the things of the world.

The identification of different levels of simulacra is dependent upon modifications concerning the techno-infrastructural possibilities—themselves, of course, in part stemming from the epistemological urge aiming for increased control, mastery, and intelligibility (cf. Pawlett 75)—for realizing Cartesian supremacy of the *cogito* over all *res extensae*. That is, the same violent impetus remains the undergirding principle also in Baudrillard's renderings of the third and fourth orders of simulacra. They simply describe the latest technological state—most prominently linked to computer technologies—of this epistemological stance. Baudrillard describes the third order as being "characterized by a *precession of the model*" (1994: 16), and the complete "liquidation of all referentials" (2) that brings forth (or forces forth) what he has famously termed the hyperreal. This precession is nothing but the always already presupposed validity of applying the unfolding Western epistemological framework. In the order of simulation, such an application is made possible and realized by the increasing dominance of calculative reasoning: "Baudrillard suggests that hyperreality is produced algorithmically . . . like the virtual reality of computer code, that is to say, detached from notions of mimesis and representation and implicated, for example, in the world of mathematical formulae" (Lane 84).[2] Put differently, Baudrillard outlines an installment of a crude—or cruel—Cartesianism which opts for "a state of pure operational intelligence, and, thus, of radical disillusioning of thought" (2008: 19) that coincides with a repeated disavowal of the world's uncontrollability.[3] This disavowal is made possible by an apotheosis of man through the (tacit) assumption of the very divine position outside the world that structured the supposedly surmounted feudal referential system (cf. 2003: 7). Baudrillard sees in the increased virtualization of the real not the eradication of the reality principle, but rather its fullest realization. Simulation, despite—or precisely through—the emancipation of signification from fixed reference, constitutes yet another manifestation of a Hegelian insistence on the possibility of pure, pristine presence (cf. Phillips 2009: 164; Weiss n.pag.). It constitutes "an absolute idealism" (Baudrillard 2013: 33) that envisions "the immediate total presence of a thing to itself"—with the consequence that "reality is henceforth the privilege of that which is identical with itself" (23). The goal of this enterprise is the suffocation of (the things of) the world, as Chris Turner aptly formulates it, in an "asphyxiating immediacy" (6). That is, the goal is the disavowal and/or eradication (or rather an eradication through disavowal) of anything that resists said epistemic control: "in the digital or, more generally, the computer-generated image there is no longer any negative, no longer anything 'deferred'" (ibid. 75). With the fourth order, virtual reality gives way to its radical techno-logical fulfillment in what Baudrillard terms "Integral Reality" (2013: 21) or "[t]he perfect crime," namely "an unconditional realization of the world by the actualization of all data, the transformation of all acts and all events into pure information: in short, the final solution, the resolution of the world ahead of time by the cloning of reality and the extermination of the real by its double" (2008: 27). Ultimately, Baudrillard's critical analysis unmasks the process of significatory liberation, and the ensuing loss of reference, as a prerequisite for an elevation of modern Western reason to a quasi-transcendental position outside the world that, simultaneously, disavows this position through (re)constructing a controllable immanent world stripped of all that resists epistemic manageability.

What is often sidelined or ignored in discussions of Baudrillard's theory of the precession of simulacra, and the epistemological apparatus from which it stems, is its fundamentally societal emphasis: "simulacra do not consist only of the play of sings, they involve social relations and a social power" (1993a: 52). At the core of his thought lies a profound criticism of simulation's drastic impact on Western cultures, particularly regarding human interaction. For Baudrillard, the onset of integral reality—subject to indifference—coincides with "a principle of dissociation" that brings about "the end of the social" (2005: 154) and entails a development of "[r]adical disaffection" (1993a: 74). He argues that the signs' liberation is tied to "a fierce strategy of neutralization" (ibid. 35). Due to its "transfiguring [of the] loss of representation into a vertige of pure presence" (2001: 142), this erad-icates all cultural and societal heterogeneity, again, by a violent integration into its superimposed epistemological framework. Thereby, this strategy ef-fects the utter implosion of the social in a devouring and homogenizing systematicity that manifests itself in "the operationalization of all social and individual life" (1994: 48).[4] This is to say nothing less than that the precession of simulacra—with its striving for epistemological sovereignty shrewdly veiled as emancipating impulse—is always already geared toward the eradication of possibly alternative modes of relating to the (things of the) world; modes which cannot be contained within the horizon of occidental reason (cf. Gane 42). From this perspective, the specifically epistemological potential of Baudrillard's ideas pertain to the Cartesian *ratio*'s regulation of human interaction and a possible radical critique thereof; a dimension in his thought that, at this point, can be further elucidated with the help of Stiegler's philosophy.

It is by way of Stiegler that the intimate link between indifference and disaffection in Baudrillard's thought can be shown. The hyperreal correlates to Stiegler's hyperindustrial epoch (as reads the subtitle of the first volume of his series *Symbolic Misery*); a correlation that stems from both thinkers' reliance on Marx to develop a critique of capitalism's (exchange) logic. Ac-cording to Baudrillard, notions of capital—sidelining or erasing the concept of use value—form the basis of the occidental loss of reference and the assumption of manipulation's omnipotence in technologies to which it gives rise (cf. 1994: 22). In this context, Stiegler observes that the workers' alien-ation from the products of their labor via industrialization is only one side of the coin. At the same time, the increasing technologicalization of Western societies results in "the generalized loss of participation, or the evisceration and enervation (in the sense of weakening) of sensing bodies, which is also the desocialization of souls" (2015: 78). The reduction of epistemology to a commodifying level of calculative reasoning does not only alienate from the *products* of labor, but from the very *skills* necessary to produce. As such, it coincides with a form of "*proletarization* which is to be found here as the loss of *living-knowledge*" (ibid. 74)—it is this situation that Stiegler refers to as hyperindustriality. What, for Baudrillard, marks the process of hyperrealization, constitutes, for Stiegler (in line with Mignolo's notion of a lost sense-sensitivity), "the obsolescence of the culture of the senses" (2015: 78), which ensues in a veritable "deficit of sensibility" (40). Both go hand in hand. In the Stieglerian reading, too, the prevailing condition of apathetic disaffection and social implosion which characterize Western societies at large are the consequence of a consumptive techno-epistemological frame-work that structures every mode of engaging with the (prefabricated) world (cf. Howells and Moore 2; Beardsworth 213). Stiegler expresses this as follows: "The necessity of a *functional reduction of singularities* has led to the submission of almost every human experience to aesthetic and affective—as well as cognitive and informational—control" (2014: 82f.). This means, the logic of consumption (of sensibility) mirrors the logic of indifferent integration of (alternative modes of relating to) forms of difference. But Stiegler insists that, "other than mathematics, all thought is aesthetic, and always, at the origin of a concept you will find an affect" (2014: 82). Affirming this book's main argument, he argues that what is necessary is a revaluation of the aesthetic dimensions of knowing; "aesthetics here in its widest sense, where *aisthēsis* means sensory perception, and where the question of aesthetics is, therefore, that of feeling and sensibility in general" (ibid. 1): read from the angle of hyperindustriality, Baudrilard's epistemological critique of hyperreality turns into "the question of the *sensibility of the other*" and pertains to the possibility of "the relation to the other in a feeling-together or *sym-pathy*" (Stiegler 2014: 1). Baudrillard's (indifferent) loss of reference correlates to Stiegler's (disaffected) loss of participation. Both point toward the necessity of relating to the world other-wise.

The affinity between Baudrillard's and Stiegler's thoughts becomes even more apparent when taking a closer look at the latter's notion of symbolic misery. He defines it as an instrumentalization of the aesthetic for economic purposes that coincides with the "destruction of the experience of the sensible which is then substituted by aesthetic conditioning" (2015: 173); an industrial form of conditioning which culminates in a *katastrophē* of the sensible (as the subtitle to the second volume of *Symbolic Misery* reads). Strongly resonating with Baudrillard's argument, Stiegler asserts that this is caused by an attempt of harnessing aesthetics in a closed epistemological system, whose function it is to erase, or disavow through devouring, any possibility for the incalculability of singularity to emerge. All entities (and beings) of the world are levelled by way of hyper-synchronic technological transformation (cf. Crowley 126f.). He describes: "capitalism began to wage an aesthetic war against difference, against the difference between what exists and what consists, where the experience of singularity opens up the difference of works . . . —since singularity is essentially what cannot be calculated, anticipated, or controlled, what in its structure resists massification" (Stiegler 2015: 173). Therefore, for Stiegler, the objective of this industrialized "machinic systematization" (2015: 12) of aesthetics (in the sense of *aisthēsis*), is also the full attainment of epistemological sovereignty. Affirming Baudrillard's remark on social power, he describes this systematization as tantamount to the establishment of a mechanism capable of *"controlling the conscious and unconscious rhythms of bodies and souls"*

(2014: 2). As such, Western cultures' symbolic misery is not restricted to semiotic processes of signification, but always connected to "a libidinal and affective misery" through which "individuals are stripped of their ability to form aesthetic attachments" (5). This is to say that the *ratio*'s insistence on pristine presence particularizes and levels all humans as closed-off monads devoid of social or relational potential and, thereby, evokes an existential condition that Stiegler sees epitomized in the mythic creature of the Cyclops in Homer's *Odyssey*: "A Cyclops has only one eye: he has no perspective, no stereoscopic vision and for him everything is flattened: he has *neither depth of field, nor depth of time*. This Cyclops who sees *Nobody* is the figure of our ill-being" (2014: 20).

Taken together, Baudrillard's and Stiegler's philosophies shed light on the decidedly techno-epistemological bent of the modern/colonial word system's mono-logic discursive constellation. Hyper-industrial-reality "spreads to all latitudes and countries *qua* the disappearance of the referent [which coincides with the reduction of sensibility] and the triumph of globalization" (S. Hart n.pag.). What Stiegler—referencing Heidegger—delineates as a "project of *mathesis universalis*," which opts for "the domination of nature by technics" (2014: 47), Baudrillard simply refers to as "[t]he imperialism of reason" (1994: 137; cf. also Pasco n.pag.). In fact, both thinkers identify and challenge the colonizing impetus of the modern Western tradition;[5] a challenge that resonates strongly with Mignolo's epistemological critique of the modern/colonial world system. Stiegler picks up on the criticism of the subalternization of deviating knowledges and describes hyperindustrialization as "a process of colonization based on the *alienation of the spirits [esprits] of the colonized by the imposition of Western intellectual technology*" (ibid. 57).[6] Baudrillard, throughout his entire *oeuvre*, has repeatedly offered his critiques of the occidental monoculture of the mind when he detects in simulation an urge "to colonize and tame all wild spaces" (2003: 98) and, as a consequence, a "turn to an objective world, shorn of all hinterworlds" (2013: 29), that gives rise to "whitewashed social relations, whitewashed bodies, whitewashed memory—in short, to a complete aseptic whiteness" (1993b: 50). Through the stereoscopic lens of combining Baudrillard and Stiegler, the subalternization of knowledges, and the establishment of a violent monoculture of the mind turn out as the product of the coinciding losses of reference and participation through hyper-industrial realization.

This hyper-industrial realization of the occidental epistemological framework outlines, for both thinkers, the complete *ratio*-nal domination of the world—and, as such, the "global culmination [*achèvement*] of the West" (Stiegler 2014: 89)—where the disavowal of negativity, singularity, and incalculability is shorthand for the foreclosing of any possibility for

encountering otherness in its very otherness. Western symbolic misery—
with its eradication of sense-sensitivity—entails an indifferent and disaffected assimilation of the other(s) to the status of forms of difference that
remain entirely legible within the *ratio*'s epistemological horizon. Otherness
is, thereby, effectively domesticated through its integration into a systemic
One for which each other is only ever another other of the Same (cf. Nordin
n.pag.; Gane 18). For Baudrillard, the precession of simulacra is, at the bottom, always already geared toward "the aesthetic mastery of the world by
the subject" (2005: 123), which first allows for this preclusion of the other.
The dream of pure pristine presence, in fact, constitutes "a kind of epilepsy
of presence, epilepsy of identity" (2008: 55); a dream where distance from
oneself is dissolved within the self-identical, and radical otherness denied.
Baudrillard forcefully elaborates: "With the Virtual, we enter not only upon
the era of the liquidation of the Real and the Referential, but that of the
extermination of the Other. It is the equivalent of an ethnic cleansing which
would not just affect particular populations but unrelentingly pursue all
forms of otherness" (ibid. 109). This shows that Baudrillard's critique of
simulation, albeit on the surface a theory of the loss of reality, constitutes a
profound challenge of the techno-epistemological reduction of radical otherness that forms the core impetus of the Western tradition of thought.

However, even if the conceptualization of simulacral orders is not merely
restricted to theorizing a gradual loss of reference and entails a far deeper
critique of the *ratio*, it remains unclear how Baudrillard's trajectory must
not be read as another one-sided demonization of technology. How does
his analysis open toward more ambiguous potentials? Though maybe not
apparent at first sight, Baudrillard and Stiegler do not merely seek to perpetuate technophobia. It would be reductive to label Baudrillard's ideas a
"nightmarish vision of technological hyperalienation" (Coulter-Smith 100)
where "science and technology will eventually obliterate nature, leaving
only a cold and empty Cartesian virtuality" (98). Baudrillard's thought does
not operate within the oppositional paradigm of *res cogitans* and *res extensae*; or, in extension, between nature and culture. Influenced by Gilbert
Simondon, he sees human being(s) as equiprimordial with technics. That is,
Baudrillard's analysis is not a negating indictment that gives rise to despair,
but, first of all, an ethnological diagnosis to be grappled with (cf. Levin
169; Blask 40; Weiss n.pag.). In his work, the complete installment of integral reality has not yet occurred. He even claims that "[f]ortunately, all this
is literally impossible" (2008: 36). This does not mean, however, that the
underlying techno-epistemological system and its dire implications are not
to be taken seriously. Stiegler explains how to deal with this framework: "It

is certainly not a matter of condemning the industrial and technological fate of humanity. Rather, it is a case of reinventing this fate" (2014: 4).

Like Baudrillard, Stiegler's ideas have been shaped by Simondon as well as the non-anthropocentric conception of technology's history developed by André Leroi-Gourhan (cf. Johnson 35). From this angle—beginning in his series entitled *Technics and Time*—Stiegler develops an alternative account of the interrelation between human beings and technics; an interrelation beyond the erroneous metaphysical binary of anthropocentrism and technocentrism that conceives of the human in opposition to the technical (cf. 1998: 95). He grounds this effort on Simondon's insight that "[i]f there is such a thing as the alienation of humanity (or of culture) by technics, it is caused not by the machine but by the misunderstanding of its nature and essence" (Simondon in Stiegler 1998: 66). Extending Baudrillard's ethnological analysis with a broader evolutionary dimension, Stiegler develops the concept of "technogenesis" (1998: 26) to underscore his argument. More precisely, he develops a perspective on evolution that stresses the relevance of epigenetic factors—that is, mutations stimulated by environmental changes—to emphasize that human being(s) and technics have always already been mutually determining, emerging, and dependent (cf. Johnson 39). Or, as Hayles succinctly puts it: "technical beings and living beings are involved in continuous reciprocal causation in which both groups change together in coordinated and indeed synergistic ways" (104). Their separation, for Stiegler, is a metaphysical fallacy of the West. The division of technics and the human is the *ratio*'s strategy to disavow consciousness's decidedly technical character. The *res cogitans* requires insisting on its absolution from all technical material *res extensae*.[7] In the first volume of *Technics and Time*, Stiegler clarifies technogenesis's epigenetic character:

> matter organized technomorphologically is not passive; the tendency does not simply derive from an organizing force—the human—it does not belong to a forming intention that would precede the frequentation of matter, and it does not come under the sway of some willful mastery: the tendency operates, down through time, by selecting forms in a relation of the human living being to the matter it organizes and by which it organizes itself, where none of the terms of the relation hold the secret for the other. (1998: 49)

That is, the separation of the human from technics stems from occidental thought's quest for epistemological sovereignty. In instrumentalizing technics, Western reason integrates its epistemic potential as ready-to-hand into the *ratio* and, subsequently, transfers it onto a notion of an Ideal(ist) human consciousness: "the reduction of *techne* to pure calculation—the aim of this metaphysics being to *control all affect*" (2014: 97). With the introduction of technogenesis, in contrast, Stiegler poses a radical challenge to this epistemological framework.

From a technogenetic perspective, the supposedly dystopic flavor of both Stiegler's and Baudrillard's work potentially takes on a decidedly different character; it fundamentally alters the catastrophic implications of both hyperreality and hyperindustriality that both invoke. From the assumption of an irreducible co-evolutionary entanglement of humans and technics Stiegler argues: "the struggle for a new organization of the sensible does not have the deindustrialization of aesthetics as its objective, but a new thinking of industry, starting from the experience of the sensible" (2015: 119). If the human is always already technical—albeit not in the instrumentalizing version of the Western *ratio*—then critical thought must remind humanity of its primordial technicity. This is connected, for Stiegler, to a revision of the Cartesian paradigm's dissociation of subject and object (cf. ibid. 60). Paradoxically, it is the *katastrophē* of the sensible itself which may bring about the possibility of such reminiscence. Stiegler explains that this catastrophe does not have to be regarded as apocalyptic only, but can also constitute the turning-point toward something new (cf. ibid. 174). That is, the hyperindustrial condition itself harbors the possibility for a subversive potential to arise (from) within the Western techno-epistemological framework. But it remains unclear how this is to be conceived. Here, Baudrillard's take on the catastrophic regarding an increasing hyperrealization provides an important hint: "one must realize that 'catastrophe' has this 'catastrophic' meaning of end and annihilation only in relation to a linear vision of accumulation, of productive finality, imposed on us by the system. Etymologically, the term itself only signifies *the curvature, the winding down to the bottom of a cycle* that leads to what one could call the 'horizon of the event'" (1994: 83; my emphasis). What Baudrillard describes as the catastrophic is nothing less than an-other way of referring to the irruption of the figural at the curvature of the occidental epistemological horizon which can bring forth the winding down toward the irreducible cycle *as cycle* of the epigenetic link between humanity and technics. The *katastrophē* circumscribes the deeply pharmacological quality of technics: it is that dangerous supplement which—restraining but not restrained by ontological and epistemological frameworks—first enables control and at the same time ever-results in the loss of said control; that dangerous supplement due to which any critique of technics (and its hyperreal and hyperindustrial consequences) must be aware that said critique is always already made possible by the continued development of what it critiques (cf. Beistegui 186; Barker 264; Crowley 130). It is this supplementary character of technics with its catastrophic potential that unfolds the full scope of ambiguity in Baudrillard's (and Stiegler's) thought and points beyond a simplistic demonization of modern technology.

The *katastrophē* of the sensible, as a *pharmakon*, discloses the possibility of a new form of sense-sensitization, an-other form of feeling. Already in *Technics and Time*, Stiegler insists on "the need for a thinking radically other than that predominant since the beginning of the West" (1998: 23). A similar urge has been at the heart of Baudrillard's work from his earliest publications. He repeatedly shows that the ideological category of the real is a Western phenomenon. Hence, Stiegler calls for a different mode of thinking, which he describes as "the perspective of a *total organological revolution*—a double epochal redoubling of machinic noetic sensibility" (2014: 57); a revolution that "constitutes a limit to the process of Western individuation—and, in this respect, the end of the West" (ibid. 56). He aims at an-other thinking of aesthetics in the horizon opened up by technogenesis that, then, may trigger, once again, a process of constructing sym-pathy that specifically characterizes human aesthetics: a sym-pathy that "transforms the world in view of building a new communal sensibility, forming the *inquiring 'us'* of an aesthetic community to come" (ibid. 3).[8] This sensibility breaks with the split of mind and body, defying its hegemony over (modes of relating to) the world (cf. Baldwin n.pag.). Such a reading of a new sensibility differs radically from other interpretations of hyper-industrial reality, which bemoan the replacement of pristine "Presence with a pseudo-presence, a doppelgänger, a specter" (Mendoza n.pag.), or which detect a problematic "technological re-reading of Freud that flattens out the vagaries of human affect and human conscience" (Beardsworth 222). As will be elaborated in the following, both Baudrillard and Stiegler argue that, "seeping through the interstices" (Baudrillard 2008: 44), there ever-remains the potential for other presences to arise (from) within the techno-epistemological framework.

(De-)Framing: The Aesthetic between Technē and Poiēsis

Before pursuing this line of argument further, it is necessary to examine more closely Baudrillard's attitude toward art, aesthetics, and the senses. Is it at all possible to read his work in relation to a renewed sense-sensitization through a catastrophic turning of the sensible? For Baudrillard, the third and fourth orders are characterized by the selective display of the screen: "The virtual space of the global is the space of the screen and the network, of immanence and the digital, of a dimensionless space-time" (2003: 92), or "that non-place, that pre-eminent empty space of representation that is the screen" (2013: 32). The screen, here, functions as the central framework of world engagement in an increasingly integral reality. It constitutes the frame of (non-)reference which guides all forms of sensual/sensory perception. Through the continuing profusion of screens and images, Baudrillard asserts, "[t]he whole paradigm of the sensory has changed. The tactility here is not the organic sense of touch: it implies merely an epidermal contiguity of eye and image, the collapse of the aesthetic distance involved in looking" (1993b: 61; cf. also 2005: 114). This means that the screen forms the prime manifestation of the techno-epistemological framework that reduces the world to the operations of calculative reasoning (cf. Hegarty 59). Everything perceptible must be screenable, or, maybe more precisely, vice versa: only what is screenable counts as perceptible, too. Consequently, Baudrillard describes the operationality of the screen as follows: "the screen works much like a mirror, for the screen itself as locus of the interface is the prime concern. An interactive screen transforms the process of relating into a process of commutation between One and the Same. The secret of the interface is that the Other here is virtually the Same: otherness is surreptitiously conjured away by the machine" (1993b: 60). The screen, here, is the mechanism which puts into operation what Stiegler's refers to as processes of aesthetic and affective control: "Within integral reality, the brain itself becomes a screen, and all of our senses are made aesthetic" (Bishop and Phillips 149). Always geared toward reproducing or readjusting the techno-epistemological framework via repeated procedures of inclusion and exclusion, the screen brings about the levelling of radical otherness. As related to the operations of the screen, aesthetics and sensory perception, in Baudrillard's work, appear as entirely immersed within the shallows of integral reality.

Baudrillard anticipates Stiegler's argument concerning the conditioning of the senses. With his reading of the screen's functioning, he suggests that art and aesthetics, in hyper-industrial reality, are determined by the systemic operations of calculative reasoning. In *The Conspiracy of Art*, Baudrillard even writes of "a corruption of art by science, or at least by the spirit of objectivity" (2005: 52). This is not to say that he mourns the loss of true and pure art, or an aura free from the workings of technological reproducibility. His critique, again, pertains to the epistemological implications of the aesthetic in the orders of simulation. "Art was turned into something pretentious with the will to transcend the world, to give an exceptional, sublime form to things", Baudrillard argues, and adds that, consequently, "[a]rt has become an argument for mental prowess" (2005: 64). Art and, in extension, also aesthetic sensibility, has become complicit with "the epistemology of scientific rationalism" (Pawlett 114).[9] They are entirely in the service of the Western reality principle insofar as they, based on the apotheosis of human beings' *ratio*-technological excellence, merely serve to reproduce the controllable—that is, calculable—immanence of integral reality.

By heightened abstraction and the omnipresence of the screen, aesthetic sensibility, is voided of difference, and, henceforth, contributes to the proliferation of ever more homogeneous hyper-industrial reality (cf. Baudrillard 2005: 89f.). In fact, in line with Stiegler's ideas, also Baudrillard's perspective asserts that this situation effectively "attenuates the social space for affect" (Levin 185). From this angle, sense-sensitization seems highly unlikely.

The impression is confirmed when Baudrillard describes aesthetics not only as subject to but even one of the main mechanisms for subsuming the world under the occidental techno-epistemological framework. He sees cultural imperialism not initially as manifestation of an extrapolation of capitalist economic principles. It derives, rather, from particular ways of seeing, that is, sensory/sensual modes of perception, upon which these principles depend: "It is often said that the West's great undertaking is the commercialization of the whole world, the hitching of the fate of everything to the fate of the commodity. That great undertaking will turn out rather to have been the aestheticization of the whole world—its cosmopolitan spectacularization, its transformation into images, its semiological organization" (1993b: 17). The commodification of the (things of) the world is first made possible by the *ratio*'s specific aesthetic parameters; parameters that, writes Baudrillard, through a constant informational *screening* of every phenomenon, unfold "a general aestheticization of everyday life, giving way to a pure circulation of images, *a transaesthetics of banality*" (1993b: 12f.; my emphasis; cf. also ibid. 171f.). The transaesthetic, for Baudrillard, as a result of the dissolution of art and sensory/sensual perception in integral reality, marks not a disappearance, but rather an omnipresence of the aesthetic within all spheres of life and sociality; an omnipresence that coincides with a loss of art's privileged status and subversive potentiality (cf. Lotringer 11). The transaesthetic saturation of life equals the unilateral conditioning of perceptual modes according to the centralized and centralizing focus of Western metaphysics which puts everything, literally, on an objectifying display and, thereby, turns the world into "a giant museum" (Baudrillard 2005: 80).[10] Transaesthetics, does away with aesthetics as informed by established rules of judgment or pleasure. It "brings aesthetics in the traditional sense to an end" (ibid. 52; cf. also 1993b: 15) and replaces it with the calculative logic of the screen.

However, Baudrillard always insists on ambiguous potentialities and his analysis of the transaesthetic, thus, needs to be read with his notion of catastrophe, too. For some commentators of Baudrillard's work, such as Garen Torikian, who aims to disentangle art from hyperreality, this undecidability is unbearable (cf. Torikian n.pag.). But they miss Baudrillard's central argument. He does not at all wish for "a form of ontologizing simulation that betrays, perhaps, nothing so much as a desire for the real, a nostalgia of loss" (Huyssen 8). From his anthropological angle, he even celebrates the hyperreal dissolution of traditional art and aesthetics. Baudrillard asserts that "[w]e are almost lucky to live at a time when aesthetic value . . . is foundering" (2005: 61). In fact, in almost Benjaminian fashion, he regards the increasing aestheticization of the world not only as a severe threat, but through its erosion of established aesthetic categories—and almost in contradiction to some of his previous statements—also as a democratizing potential for change available to the public (cf. Toffoletti 65). This can be seen when one reads the subversive potential of art not simply regarding a negation of the processes of hyper-industrial reality, but rather as the possibility of creatively ab-using these very processes. Just as he does not merely condemn or demonize technology and simulation, Baudrillard does not one-sidedly criticize the technological perfusion of the aesthetic.[11] It is misleading to blame the supposedly solely pessimistic take on the imbrications of aesthetics and technology, as Graham Coulter-Smith does, on a form of Marxist humanism oscillating between alienation and reification in Baudrillard's thinking that seemingly contradicts his more "poststructuralist" insistences on ambiguity (cf. Coulter-Smith 92, 94). Baudrillard's anthropological perspective, founded upon Simondon and Leroi-Gourhan (and again resonating with Stiegler), is—quite to the contrary—precisely what maintains this ambiguity; an ambiguity which is not merely related to simulation, art, and the aesthetic, but the entire techno-epistemological framework, and, consequently, to the notion of the human itself. As John Phillips asserts, "Baudrillard's arguments are attempts to make a difference to how we think about the frameworks that govern our thoughts and actions" (166). At this point, the ongoing relevance of Baudrillard's thought in general and the significance of his contributions concerning current issues of scholarship, also within (transnational) American Studies, can be even rendered more plausible.

This significance can be seen when linking the ideas brought forth so far, finally, to the thought of Butler, and particularly her notion of the frame as developed mostly in *Frames of War*. A first similarity to Baudrillard's concept of the screen can be glimpsed when Butler describes frames as the "implicit schemes of conceptualization [which] operate quite powerfully to orchestrate what we can admit as reality" (2010: xxf.). In fact, Baudrillard—referring to Heidegger's *Gestell*—writes of a "technological 'enframing'" (2013: 106). Screen and frame both define the composition of reality, namely via (frequently tacit) processes of inclusion and exclusion. Butler emphasizes that this strategy is not always entirely successful, or rather that the very success of these processes simultaneously coincides with their (inevitable) failure: "When versions of reality are excluded or jettisoned to a domain of unreality, then specters are produced that haunt the ratified version of reality, animated and de-ratifying traces" (2010: xix). There remains an irreducible subversive potential (stemming from) within the frame: a potential that, outlining an-other similarity to Baudrillard, concerns the societal dimensions of framing, as well. Butler explains that frames serve to bolster and perpetuate social norms and their fulfillment. At the same time, they also—in ways to be clarified—solicit an-other potential that refuses these enforced regulations (cf. ibid. xix). As modes of conditioning human interactions, frames harbor the (catastrophic) potential for both reification and destabilization. In her *Notes Toward a Performative Theory of Assembly*, Butler links this ambiguous potentiality to a conceptualization of the human (and society) that bears strong affinities to Stiegler's insistence on technogenesis. She argues that the infrastructures of the media and technology—i.e. various modes of framing—have become part of how people are defined: they do not just play an assisting role but constitute the hegemonically contested fabric that renders this definition possible (cf. 2015a: 20). Hinting again toward ambiguity, she asserts that this "dependency of human and other creatures on infrastructural support *exposes a specific vulnerability* that we have when we are unsupported, when those infrastructural conditions start to decompose, or when we find ourselves radically unsupported in *conditions of precarity*" (ibid. 65; my emphases).

The question of how framing and vulnerability figure in this book's argument is closely linked to the role of the status of the senses in the occidental techno-epistemological framework. Reminiscent of Baudrillard and Stiegler, Butler argues that "to understand the operation of technology we have to consider how it works on the field of the senses" (2010: ix). She stresses the fundamental role of aesthetics in engaging the world—that is, within the constitution of reality, of what counts as real. In fact, Butler insists on an ever-irreducible entanglement of the rational and the sensual. For her, "[t]here is no thinking and judgment without the senses" (ibid. xvi). The Western tradition, however, according to Butler, harnesses—and disavows—aesthetics to ensure the absolute hegemony of its socio-normative (en-)framework; or, in terms of this chapter, through "establishing and disposing the sensuous parameters of reality itself—including what can be seen and what can be heard" (2010: xi)—the *ratio* ensures the epistemological sovereignty of the *res cogitans* over the things of the world. Consequently, if Butler's notion of the frame is related to Baudrillard's concept of the screen, then her thought further underscores the decidedly aesthetic character of occidental reason's techno-epistemological impetus and bolsters Stiegler's claim that "the control through affects in control societies" (2014: 91)—or, more precisely, their framing—constitutes a particularly powerful normative mechanism.

Butler's thinking confirms that framing, or screening, hyper-industrial reality via the straightjacketing of the sensible ultimately serves to erase more sense-sensitized modes of affective knowing.

Beyond that, Butler outlines a possible way of conceiving of the potential for an-other aesthetics (as *aisthēsis*) to arise from inside the *ratio*nal framework—unlike Baudrillard or Stiegler, who both remain somewhat elusive on the specificities of what they call the catastrophic ambiguity of the sensible within hyper-industrial reality and a possibility for "aesthetic experience [to be] able to fight aesthetic conditioning on its own terrain" (Stiegler 2014: 83). Butler uses the term "apprehension" to unfold a sensible/sensory form of thinking other-wise; she describes it as "a mode of knowing that is not yet recognition or may remain irreducible to recognition" (2010: 6). This mode of knowing is related to the aforementioned disintegration of frames that always already coincides with processes of normative framing: it is a kind of perception that resides "at the limits of established norms for thinking, embodiment, and even personhood" (2015a: 38); at the limit where the frame is permeable. What causes this permeability? Butler draws on the thought of Derrida to argue that the techno-epistemological (re)production of (en-)framing norms is determined by the condition of iterability. As has been shown already in the discussion of Taylor's work with Walters's novel, the specific repetitive character of iterability, for Derrida, marks the possibility for singular events to occur even in systems of signification. Accordingly, Butler argues that "the norm is repeated, and in this sense is constantly 'breaking' with the contexts delimited as the 'conditions of production'" (2010: 168). She explains that this break merely constitutes multiple changes arising from the norm's iterable structuring, which underscores the continued relevance of "postructuralist" concepts of spectrality, *survivance*, and continuation (cf. ibid. 169).[12] These moments of (en-)active continual cannot be contained by the framework itself. They always keep frames, or screens, open for possibilities of figural irruptions that defy normative systemic closure. Therefore, apprehension can be described as a mode of thinking beyond rational (re-)cognition (that, nevertheless, always remains tied to it and even stems from within its system): a non- or para-conceptual form of knowledge that is tied to sensation and perception and does not rely of *ratio*nal re-cognition (cf. ibid 4f.). However, as has been shown in the preceding part, it is this very lack of conceptual precision that, through its openness for the possibility of knowing other-wise, is, in a certain *sense*, more precise than the (en-)framework of Western calculative reasoning. When Butler writes of an irreducible modality of "sensate understanding" (ibid. 100) at the limits of the frame, she describes nothing less than what Mignolo would term a sense-sensitized mode of border gnosis and what Shotwell calls sensuous knowledge.

It is also via the concept of Derridean iterability that Butler clarifies what she means by the vulnerability of life; a vulnerability that further clarifies the notion of a *katastrophē* of the sensible, namely by enriching it with a particular existential(ist) element that, in turn, is again tied to a specific potential of the aesthetic. She explains that, at the breaking points of frames, "we are exposed to what it means to be at the limits of recognizability: this situation can be, depending on the circumstance, both terrible and exhilarating. To exist at such a limit means that the very viability of one's life is called into question, what we might call the social ontological conditions of one's persistence. It also means that we can be at the threshold of developing the terms that allow us to live" (2015a: 40). It might seem surprising that Butler identifies poetry as one of the possible locales where life's viability is questioned and the framework (momentarily) breaking. In her readings of poems written by tortured prisoners in Guantánamo and elsewhere, Butler emphasizes the inscription of corporeality within these texts, and—hinting toward the iterable—writes: "In these poems, the body is also what lives on, breathes, tries to carve its breath into stone" (2010: 61). By insisting on what she calls a form of "bodily signifying" (2015b: 15), Butler argues that it is due to the body or, more specifically, due to the discursive irreducibility of the corporeal, that life, in a certain sense, remains uncontainable within normative frameworks (cf. ibid. 4).[13] For her, poetry is a possible (liminal) site for the (figural) excess of life to surface, since, as part of this strange institution called literature, it functions in an established discursive system that sanctions its own repeated artistic questioning; a mode of questioning made possible by the necessary iterability of the system itself. In other words, Butler reads poetry along the Heideggerian lines traced in the previous part as containing the potential for *poiēsis*: a mode of creative production—or bringing forth—beyond (and yet always within) the (en-)framework. She describes a moment where epistemic (and physical) violence turns into what Baudrillard calls "virulence:" a moment where an-other potential irrupts from the inside: "a virulence that ravages the entire system, and against which the system is defenceless [sic] precisely because its very integrity paradoxically engenders this alteration" (1993b: 70). Butler argues that *poiēsis* (as a sense-sensitized mode of relating to the world), possesses a potential to remind one of one's own irreducible corporeal exposure to others; an exposure through which one remains possibly subject to injury even within hyper-industrial reality (cf. 2010: 61). It is precisely in this condition of vulnerability that the frame disintegrates, that "the experience of the other in the same" (Stiegler 2015: 146) is rendered possible, and that the system is opened toward a form of "presence [that] is not yet contained within the framework" (Mendoza n.pag.). Stressing the body's vulnerability in its inextricability with discursive systematicity, Butler supplements and inter-links Baudrillard and Stiegler's ideas. It unfolds a way of conceiving of the *poiētic* potential of the aesthetic as a modality for thinking other-wise even (from) within the hyperindustrial/hyperreal modern/colonial world system's techno-epistemological framework.

Before returning to Butler's understanding of bodily vulnerability in more detail in the next section, at this point, the significance of the inherent am-biguity of catastrophic sensuality will be developed a bit further. Reading Baudrillard's work in light of Stiegler's technogenesis as well as Butler's frames pave the way for revaluing the potential of the virtual (or simulation) or, more specifically, for conceiving of the virtual *as* a potential. A longer passage from Marie-Laure Ryan's *Narrative as Virtual Reality* 2 proves helpful:

> Etymology tells us that virtual comes from the Latin *virtus* (strength, manliness, virtue), which gave to scholastic Latin the philosophical concept of *virtus* as force or power. (This sense survives today in the expression "by virtue of.") In scholastic Latin, *virtualis* designates the potential, "what is in the power [*virtus*] of the force." The classic example of virtuality derived from Aristotle's distinc-tion between potential and actual existence (*in potential* vs. *in actu*) is the pres-ence of the oak in the acorn. In scholastic philosophy, "actual" and "virtual" exist in a dialectical relation rather than one of radical opposition: the virtual is not that which is deprived of existence but that which possesses the potential, or force, of developing into actual existence. Later uses of the term, begin-ning in the eighteenth and nineteenth centuries, turn this dialectical relation to actual into a binary opposition to real: the virtual becomes the fictive and the nonexistent. (18)

The interconnections between Baudrillard, Stiegler, and Butler offer a *theo-retical (de-)framework* in which it becomes possible to move beyond a static dichotomy and, instead, maintain the productive entanglement of virtuality and actuality. Perceived from the perspective of a technogenetic relation be-tween corporeality and technics, the virtual must no longer be viewed as merely erasing bodily experience and sensuality altogether, but can rather be seen as enabling "new kinds of embodied experiences" (Hayles 98).[14] Put differently, instead of taming the virtual (as potential) by reading it as entirely subject to the confines of *ratio*nal systematicity, one should focus on its potentially excessive force which it executes *in relation* to the system as a form of dis-closure, *videlicet*, as a form of *poiēsis*. That is also why Ryan can draw on the metaphor of the "Möbius strip" to describe "creativity as a two-way process involving both a phase of actualization and a phase of virtual-ization" (27); a two-way process which, never divisible into a one-plus-one logic, mirrors the relationship of discourse and figure.[15] When Ryan writes that "language exercises a virtualizing power" (28), then this means that in discourse there always remains a *presencing* of the figural (and vice versa). The technogenetic link of the human (in its irreducible corporeality) and the technical extends this particular mode of relationality also regarding conceiving of the dynamic interplay of *technē* (as mode of framing), and *poiēsis* (as an-other mode of revealing).

"At the peak of our technological performance, the irresistible impression remains that something eludes us", Baudrillard writes and explains that the ambiguity of technics results in an ironic situation: "in effect, it is not we who are winning out over the world, but the world which is winning out over us" (2008: 73). The subtle destabilization of the (en-)framework through its iterabile perpetuation of an "unbridled virutality" (2000: 52) results in what Baudrillard terms "an inexorable reversibility" (76). It is precisely this reversibility that harbors the potential for an-other form of thinking. Keeping in mind Ryan's reference to the etymological roots of "virtual," it becomes clear why Baudrillard homonymously describes the dynamics of reversibility as the possibility, inherent in the system itself, of a "poetic turnabout" (2001: 8). According to him, this turnabout should not give rise to lamentations about the disappearance of the real in the hyperreal but rather praise for the potential of an irreducible eventful singularity to occur (cf. ibid. 158).[16] Moving along the same lines as Butler's argument, Baudrillard suggests that the *ratio*'s harnessing of *technē*—and, with it, the senses— cannot quench the figural force always already tied to it. Its increasing instrumentalization, in paradoxical fashion, once more brings to the fore the irreducible imbrication of technics with the *poiētic*. Consequently, Baudrillard outlines "an art of simulation" that is also characterized by a decidedly "ironic quality" (2005: 109); a kind of simulation which offers the possibility of a "poetic resolution of the world" (2000: 68). This, for him just as for Ryan, is related to the irreducible singularity of poetic language itself (cf. 69). Strongly reminiscent of Lyotard's description of figurality's elusive motions, Baudrillard goes on to explain that "[i]n the anagrammaticality of poetic language, the words seem to have come from elsewhere, to have covered their tracks, and yet to have been there forever" (2013: 167). This "elsewhere" can be read as an irruptive effect of the figural toward which the *ratio*'s techno-logical system, in its de-framing reversibility, cannot help but remain open. The *virtual* generation of an integrally real systemic closure dis-closes a recalibrated *sense* for that which ever-withdraws from epistemic fixation and, through(out) technology, always *presences* other-wise.[17]

What has already been implied in the first section of this part can now be explicated. Due to this poetic reversibility, it is possible to *think simulation other-wise*, namely in the sense of a border gnosis between *technē* and *poiē-sis*. According to Baudrillard, critical thinking in hyper-industrial reality can no longer be geared toward the achievement of utmost clarity but must creatively sabotage—or ab-use—the *ratio*'s framework by insisting on the potential of the poetic turnabout. He repeatedly calls for a radically para-doxical mode of thinking, neither positive nor negative, that maintains a *sense* for the strange or uncanny in the system and which cannot be reduced to the ordering principles and rules of calculative reasoning (cf. 2000: 68; 2003: 96; 2005: 81; 2013: 101).[18] In this context, Baudrillard again hints toward figurality: "Radical thought does not decipher. It anathematizes and anagrammatizes concepts and ideas, *just as poetic language does with words*. And in its *reversible progression*, it accounts for the fundamental illusion of meaning while at the same time accounting for meaning" (2005: 175; my emphases). That is, this type of thought moves along the margins or limits of the Western techno-logical framework and outlines a dynamic positionality—a positionality "that slips across ontological and epistemo-logical limits and boundaries" (Barker 264) and that, as Baudrillard him-self puts it, "remain[s] at the limit, in a borderline state really" (2005: 82). Richard Lane describes this philosophy as a "limit-writing" (95) and Sally Hart writes of "Baudrillard's 'liminal' thinking" (n.pag.). Liminal as it at-tempts to think *both* from the confines of *ratio*-systemic screening *and* its irreducible figural-aesthetic irruptions. As such, this kind of thought, too, again relates to Butler and her notion of an apprehension at the edges or margins of the process of framing (cf. 2010: xxx). Ultimately, both derived from Stiegler's technogenesis and complemented with Butler's framework, Baudrillard's poetic turnabout can be said to sketch out a sense-sensitized mode of relating to (the things of) the world which can aptly be referred to as *technopoiēsis*.

Via the notion of poetic reversibility, Baudrillard's philosophy destabi-lizes the central parameters of the *ratio*-epistemological (en-)framework by breaking down its distinction between fact and fiction. In fact, *technopoiēsis* is constituted precisely by a refutation of the binary opposition between reality and fiction. Baudrillard's thought, as "postmodern" form of border gnosis neither empirically refutes simulation nor regards it as purely fictional but, seemingly paradoxical, does both at the same time. Mocking the apoth-eosis of the human through the appropriation of technology and the sub-sequent impetus for (re-)creating the world, Baudrillard opts for an "ironic transfiguration" (2008: 98) of the Western tradition itself. In his ironic read-ing, the "artifice is in no way concerned with what *generates*, merely with what *alters*, reality. Artifice is the power of illusion" (1993b: 58)—an idea he again shares with Stiegler who, insisting on the relationality of fiction and reality as inextricable composition, promotes a renewed "belief in the *truth* of art as fiction, belief in a truth that can only be given *as* fiction" (2015: 94). Consequently, replete with performative contradictions, Baudrillard's work (r)evolves around a fictionalization of theory and a theorization of fiction, namely by way of increasingly poetic—that is, virtualized—language; all qualities which grant his work a highly playful and literary quality (cf. Lane 135f.). Or, as Samuel Strehle succinctly summarizes, for Baudrillard, "thinking is a *performative act*" (n.pag.).[19] Thinking simulation *other-wise* in the *sense* of *technopoiēsis* circumscribes a trans-*figured* form of theory drawn from within the *ratio* itself.

Precariousness: The Social between Banality and Simplicity

Before unfolding the notion of *technopoiēsis* in dialogue with Richard Powers's *Plowing the Dark*, it is necessary to return to the question of social interactions. How does *technopoiēsis* relate to the issue of the social? As has been shown, Baudrillard's thought is tied to a critique of the dis-affecting consequences of hyperrealization on the self and others. Insofar as he conceives sociality as inextricably bound to occidental techno-epistemology, he views the problematic liberating impetus of the signs as guiding the emancipation of the self, too: the apotheosis of *res cogitans* over against all *res extensae* results in the Idea of individualism or, more precisely, "it generates the fantasy of being a self-subsistent agent, an abstract individuality beyond all relations" (Williams 174). For Baudrillard, the Enlightenment concept of individuality constitutes an abstraction and the discourses of liberation function as processes of interiorizing a notion of subjectivity that stems from the Cartesian split of subject and object (cf. Grace 18f.). That means that the liberation of the self is perceived as another manifestation of the same impetus for epistemological sovereignty which structures the *ratio*'s conceptualization of signification; an impetus that transfers the longing for pristine presence also onto the self as modern individual, and, consequently, culminates in an effective homogenizing and levelling of otherness. In fact, for Baudrillard, it is precisely this levelling which functions as the catalyst of the occidental techno-epistemological engine: "It all comes from the impossibility of conceiving of the Other—friend or enemy—in its radical otherness, in its irreconcilable foreignness. A refusal rooted in the total identification with oneself around moral values and technical power" (2003: 62).[20] This attempt of eradicating otherness and of establishing Ideal selfhood as individual is what breeds dis-affecting dissociation.

According to Baudrillard, the urge for the liberation and emancipation of the self as an individual turns out as a mere ruse for creating a society of total control where all forms of radical otherness are subsumed under the Western *ratio*'s techno-logic. "Despairing of confronting otherness . . . , we invent the easiest solution: freedom" (2013: 37), he asserts; a freedom, however, that is founded upon the impetus for epistemological sovereignty, and, coinciding with it, on a crude notion of *ego se absolvit*—a (self-)absolution of an Ideal, independent Self (with regard to each *other* and from the rest of the world). As complicit with this process of framing, Baudrillard—strongly reminiscent of Irigaray's thought—characterizes the status of the "liberated individual" as follows: "We can't exactly even speak of individuals any longer. Individuation was part of the golden age of the subject-object dynamics. Since he has become truly indivisible, and has thus achieved his perfect—that is to say, delirious, self-referential—form, we cannot speak of the individual any longer, but only of the Selfsame and the hypostasis of the Selfsame" (2008: 126).[21] Modern individualism, as described by Baudrillard, forces forth a situation in which human (non-)relations are guided primarily by an insistence on a primacy of the self which—however fragmentary or internally different it may be thought—mirrors the epistemological framework from whence it originates by conceiving of itself as a closed and controllable system; the result being an a-social attitude of "every-One for h/er-Self." The individual's total self-determination equals the total denial of radical otherness; or as Baudrillard himself writes: "The dream of identity ends in indifference" (2013: 49) that, consequently, just as the now only law of emancipated signification, becomes the only law— and, thereby, negates any possibility—of human interaction. Sociality, as such, is (dis-)affected by "a disturbing relational *disfigurement*" (Akinwumi n.pag.; my emphasis). Disavowing the potential for encountering radical otherness, as Stiegler elaborates, the self transforms (itself) into "a *figure of the individual that finds itself disfigured*" (2014: 48). Baudrillard formulates it most drastically when he writes that, due to the *ratio*'s Self-apotheosis as *res cogitans* geared toward ridding itself of all uncontrollable otherness, the techno-epistemological framework effectively turns society into a "hell of the Same" (1993b: 140).

Here, the argument can slowly pick up on the thread left off above and return to Butler's notion of bodily vulnerability that is also tied to a criticism of modern (rugged) individualism. More precisely, her critique aims at "an ontology of individualism that fails to recognize that life . . . implies a social ontology which calls that form of individualism into question" (2010: 19). Again, several overlaps with Baudrillard's thought are apparent. Just as for Baudrillard, for Butler, this specific ontology culminates in a "foreclosure of alterity [in the sense of otherness]" (2006: 41). As Baudrillard, who— in terms of hyperrealization—describes modern individuals as "virtual monads" (2001: 65), Butler argues that the self within the occidental frame-work becomes "enclosed, monadic, and individual" (2015a: 149). And just as Baudrillard critiques Self-appropriation and the striving for Ideal iden-tification (cf. 2001: 61, 70), Butler draws attention to the "insufficiency of identitarian ontologies" (2015a: 68). Furthermore, both Baudrillard and Butler agree that a central hallmark of modern individualism is its sidelining of the (epistemological and existential) significance of the body. Modern in-dividualism is built on "a technological purification of bodies" (1993b: 67), Baudrillard holds. Butler's more elaborate position, here, functions as a vital supplement. For her, it is the body that poses the most fundamental chal-lenge to the *rational cogito*. Even if disavowed, the *cogito* is always already, and ever-remains, bound to embodiment. Western techno-logic is character-ized by the continued attempt to master what it perceives as its corporeal constraints to ensure (existential or epistemological) security. However, But-ler argues that the bodily dimension can never be entirely overcome. The sting of the body remains that "implies mortality, vulnerability, agency: the skin and the flesh expose us to the gaze of others, but also to touch, and to violence, and bodies put us at risk of becoming the agency and instrument of all these as well" (Butler 2006: 26).[22] As irreducible medium persistently (re-)introducing into the framework the potentials for lack of control, in-jury, affect, and inevitable death, the body represents—or rather *presences* as—everything that Western techno-logic seeks to overcome. The body is the limit of the modern individual's Self-determination.

In Butler's work, bodily vulnerability and radical otherness are equipri-mordially related. Reminiscent of Nancy, she argues that being embodied, or being as body, human beings are ever-plunged into a precarious existential condition that circumscribes an irreducible relationality with otherness: "Pre-cariousness implies living socially, that is, the fact that one's life is always in some sense *in the hands of the other*. It implies *exposure* both to those we know and to those we do not know; a *dependency* on people we know, or barely know, or know not at all" (2010: 14; my emphases). What Baudril-lard and Stiegler respectively call societal dis-affection, through Butler's lens appears as a result of the *ratio*'s techno-epistemological disavowal of human *ek-sistence* as bodies via simulating a completely immanent integral reality; a totalizing form of immanence in which *ex-posed relational existence* is re-placed by an *im-posed monadic individuality*. For Butler, precariousness out-lines a form of being-in-the-world with others as corporeal entities wherein each (human) being is always already affected by an incalculable *presencing* of others (as other bodies); or, as she herself formulates it: "That the body invariably comes up against the outside world is a sign of the general pre-dicament of unwilled proximity to others and to circumstances beyond one's control" (2010: 34) that subjects one to "a vulnerability to a sudden address from elsewhere that we cannot preempt" (2006: 29).[23] It is this unforeseeable *pathos* of otherness that the Western framework seeks to (Self-)contain within its notion of pristine presence. Occidental reasoning transforms a dynamic *presencing* of the other into a fixed and closed-off Idea. This means that this transformation of presence constitutes nothing other than an attempt to extinguish said ex-posed corporeal dependency on others and, consequently, the possibility for conceiving of presence as a form of dynamic *presencing* at all. Western thought, in fact, can be said to "flee from [a] presence, which is too horrible to contemplate" (Levin 164), as it can never be entirely contained within its Self-drawn epistemological boundaries. The framework of the *ratio* functions as *a violent form of knowing which seeks to erase human beings' precarious existential condition in relationality with others* as well as any awareness of this condition.

According to Butler, preserving, or retrieving, an awareness for precariousness requires an epistemological shift. In contradistinction to an identarian ontology, she envisions a "new bodily ontology, one that implies the rethinking of precariousness, vulnerability, injurability, interdependency, exposure, bodily persistence, desire, work and the claims of language on social belonging" (2); an ontology that, as such, is always already a fundamentally "social ontology" (3). Its point of departure is existence as co-implicated in an interdependent embodied condition—and, thereby, as being-in-the-world—of all human being(s), or, of every-body.[24] For Butler, the body is formed socially via perspectives it cannot occupy (i.e. one cannot hear one's own voice, somebody else sees one's face, etc.), which indicates that, as embodied, one is in a certain sense dispossessed, always already elsewhere, and exceeding oneself (cf. 2015a: 97). That is—in terms of Waldenfels—the self as body is never entirely at home within itself. Being body, the self is never completely closed-off, but always dis-closed toward the affect—or *pathos*—of the radically other; or, even more explicitly along the lines of Waldenfels: "In this way, the body is less an entity than a relation" (Butler 2016: 19). And this is exactly why Butler's shift toward a bodily ontology is linked to a rethinking of aesthetics. She holds that "[t]o encounter the precariousness of another life, *the senses have to be operative*, which means that a struggle must be waged against those forces that seek to regulate affect in differential ways" (2010: 52; my emphasis). The bodily ontology that keeps a *sense* for the precarious as conceived by Butler is tied to a sense-sensitization of knowledge beyond the limitations of *ratio*nal (re-)cognition.

This leads to a profound question: how does precariousness *figure* within cultures striving toward the full simulation of an integral reality? Or, in other words: if Baudrillard is correct that such cultures are heading toward "the fall into banality" (2013: 19), and marked by "the idiotic certainty and inexorable banality of numbers" (1993b: 46) that has the other(s) dissolve within a Selfsame—then, how is it possible to relate Butler's understanding of precariousness as irreducible existential relationality with the other to "the banality, the superficiality and the brashness of a zero-sum signification society" (S. Hart n.pag.)? Once more, the answer resides within the concept of reversibility. When Baudrillard outlines integral reality as the completion of full simulation and the replacement of the world with its Self-created double and "theorises this as the collapse of a culture into the banal illusion of the world, [where] the brilliant cultures of destiny and predestination collapse into their residues—*banal chance and chaos*" (Gane 22; my emphasis), then, as has been shown above, he alludes to a potential beyond the *ratio*nal framework. Via interlinking reversibility with precariousness, Baudrillard's somewhat cryptic description of "a subtle interplay involving death and the Other into the bland eternity of the Same" (1993b: 130) begins to make *sense* (in an-other way). And it is here that one can begin to spell out the relationship between *technopoiēsis* and the social.

This relationship unfolds within the dynamics of systematicity's inherent iterability. When Baudrillard writes that "[e]very system that approaches perfect operativity simultaneously approaches its downfall" (1993a: 4), this is because the very operativity necessary to reproduce systematic closure itself tacitly relies upon a process that is never part of said closure. Simulation is characterized by the utmost degree of significatory liberation. However, the endless reproduction of emancipated signs that is supposed to generate the totally controllable immanence of integral reality itself is based on a performative action. The very iterability of the sign necessary to uphold the simulacral system is responsible for the paradoxical fact that "[t]he closer one gets to the perfection of the simulacrum . . . the more evident it becomes . . . how everything escapes representation, escapes its own double and its resemblance" (1994: 107). Simply put: the greater the extent of framing or screening, the greater the potential for de-framing or de-simulation. How this relates to the social aspect of *technopoiēsis* becomes clearer when he clarifies elsewhere that "any act [of signification], even an exact one, is preceded by a trembling, *a haziness of gesture*, and it always retains something of it" (2013: 77; my emphasis). Taken together, these passages underscore that Baudrillard's insistence on something that escapes significatory representation and on a negation of systemic closure does not only result in "poststructuralist" and/or "postmodern" relativism. By drawing attention to an irreducible deictic potential always already involved in the process of signification, he outlines a possibility for thinking an-other form of "positivity." That is, a positivity related to the irruption of the figural. Again, simply put: if the system of simulation's reproduction is generated with a necessary reliance on iterability, and if this reliance necessarily increases in the strive toward integral reality, then the potential for repeated irruptions of figurality is augmented as well. The system's iterability installs at/as its core the dynamics of the figural.

The performative workings of the figural, through their sensory/sensual dimensions, are what links *technopoiēsis* to Butler's bodily ontology, and, with their renewed focus on sense-sensitization, toward precariousness. Via the iterability involved in constituting the system's systematicity, a certain form of bodily or corporeal potential remains irreducibly tied to the organization of frame and screen. Therefore, in line with Butler's notion of apprehension, Baudrillard can assert that "[a]n image . . . *affects* us directly, below the level of representation: at the level of intuition, of *perception*" (2013: 71; my emphases)—*despite his repeated insistence on the banality of images*; *or, maybe even due to this banality*. Ever since the choral ode in Sophocles's *Antigone*, occidental thinking concerning technics has struggled with one major banality that does not quite let itself be subsumed underneath a technological framework: "the banality of the anomaly of death" (1994: 113)— *every-body dies*. Mortality, although constantly disavowed by human technology's force, remains and attests to a *presencing* of a "more powerful force that resides *everywhere and in each of us*" (S. Hart n.pag.); a dynamic force that holds every-body in relationality. Technogenetically linked to the (things of the) world, *human innermost being is ever-irreducibly figural-excessively ex-posed*. For Baudrillard, this is related to a "potential change and becoming" which resides in every-body and that opens onto "an inspired form freed from the straightjacket of our individual being" (2013: 166). And, for Butler, this dynamics is linked to the grievability of life, or the possibility for grief to occur at all, particularly when regarding the pain of others, even—or precisely—in the transaesthetic proliferations of screens and frames (such as representations of violence done to prisoners at Abu Ghraib or Guantánamo): "Perhaps we can say that grief contains the possibility of apprehending a mode of dispossession that is fundamental to who I am" (2006: 28).[25] The techno-representational make-up cannot contain a *poiētic* potential for singular irruptions of the figural to arise (from) inside the frame. As such, it always harbors a possibility for a renewed awareness for precariousness. Though hidden away in the confines of the *ratio* through a harnessing of aesthetics, *technē* remains bound to *poiēsis*. Corporeally exposed (or ex-posing) modes of apprehending *other*-wise cannot be cancelled entirely by calculative reasoning.

As implied above, the irreducible potential for the apprehension of precariousness is connected to human beings' technogenetic con-figuration.

Thought as always already technical(ly with)in nature, human being is ever-dependent on a form of living knowledge which remains ever-bound to the corporeal and situates human being in the world with others. With Butler, one can describe this as a particular "function of openness, that is, of being open to a world that is not fully known or predictable" (2015a: 149). With recourse to the thinking of Emmanuel Levinas, she regards this openness as a form of sensibility toward the world and its phenomena; a sensibility that holds open a mode of "responsiveness that precedes the ego" (ibid. 102) as conceived in the Cartesian hierarchy. Instead, it unfolds "a form of responsiveness that implies a dispossession of the ego-logical" (ibid.). Elsewhere, she clarifies that this kind of "self-dispossession" entails "a move away from self-preservation as the basis or, indeed, the aim of ethics" (2015b: 89). In other words, although the Western techno-logy of the Self with(in) its epistemological framework seeks to disavow corporeality as that which ties the *cogito* to the world as (just) an-other of its "things," it never manages to do so due to an ambiguity of the technical on which the *rati*onal system is built: what Butler calls precariousness is nothing else but the ambiguous technogenetic condition which always already links human being(s) to the other(s): *techno-genesis always already breeds techno-poiēsis*. This ambiguity is what allows for the disavowal of the corporeal. But it is, at the same time, that which allows for a sensual/sensory re-vision, or apprehension, of said disavowal. It is thus that *technopoiēsis* relates to the social and its possible *reconfiguring*. The ever-remaining *technopoiētic* potential inherent within human being's technogenetic evolution is what harbors the possibility for becoming aware of every-body's always already precarious *ek-sistential* condition through which all beings ever-reside in a relationality with others that does not allow for a monadic Self-closure; a sense-sensitized mode of being together in a mutual dynamic of pathos and response. The banality of life within the integral reality of simulation includes the possibility for its reversion into the apprehension of life's simplicity: life, then, unfolds itself as simply precarious.

Techno-epistemology's difficult or complicated processes of existential emancipation or liberation eventually culminate in a simple in-sight of their ineffaceably precarious prerequisites. For Butler, this constitutes a chance for social modification: "This consideration of the differential distribution of precariousness and grievability constitutes an alternative to those models of multiculturalism that presuppose the nation-state as the exclusive frame of reference, and pluralism as an adequate way of thinking about heterogeneous social subjects" (2010: 31). This means that the *technopoiētic* apprehension of precariousness as the simple—albeit for the *ratio* without a doubt disquieting—condition of being(s), also from, or precisely from, inside virtuality, opens onto an *ek-sistential* dis-position where the other *presences*.

Precariousness, as such, also constitutes another supplement of this book's broader project. In connection to Baudrillard's "postmodern" thinking, Butler's "poststructuralist" argument serves to clarify further how the *ratio*'s greatest efforts notwithstanding, there always remains a potential for thinking *other*-wise that stems from inside the occidental order itself. In almost Waldenfelsian terminology, Butler herself writes: "It is about a mode of response that follows upon having been addressed, a comportment toward the Other only after the Other has made a demand upon me, accused me of a failing, or asked me to assume a responsibility" (2006: 129). Everybody is always already bordering on the world and its entities and subject to an irreducible vulnerability as well as "a primary helplessness and need . . . to which any society must attend" (2006: 32). From this kind of powerlessness, no-body is exempt. Precariousness is never instrumentalizable. Butler elaborates: "it [*i.e.* precariousness] testifies to an ontological interrelation that is prior to any calculation. *Precariousness is not the effect of a certain strategy*, but the generalized condition for any strategy whatsoever. A certain apprehension of equality thus follows from this invariably shared condition, one that is most difficult to hold fast in thought" (2010: 181; my emphasis). Precariousness—in a certain *sense*—circumscribes a new form of universalism (or pluriversalism) and essentialism, as described in the chapter that unfolds a dialogue between Irigaray's thought and Cha's *Dictée*.[26] Precariousness outlines "a generalized condition whose very generality can be denied only be [*sic*] denying precariousness itself" (ibid. 22) and that, consequently, can never be merely one-sidedly (strategically) appropriated or determined. This way, Butler's understanding of the precarious alludes to what Baudrillard calls "an eternal irreducibility whose ineradicable presence is easier to sense than to analyse" (1993b: 159). The sheer simplicity of this irreducibility through which life remains ever saturated with radical otherness is what has Baudrillard write, in almost resigning manner, that "[t]here is no solution to Foreignness. It is eternal—and radical. It is not a matter of wanting it to be that way. It simply *is* so" (ibid.). This specific *sense* of simplicity guides the last stage of this section's argument.

The apprehension of precariousness provides a modality for thinking the social beyond the confines of the modern individual, which can be related to the (b)ordering principles of the project at hand. As implied throughout this chapter, Butler's understanding of the precarious bears striking similarities to Mignolo's critique of occidental modernity. In fact, her insistence on human beings' *ek-sistential* interdependence can even be read as a "Western" form of border gnosis which moves beyond Mignolo's own epistemological prejudices: "But if we are social beings and our survival depends upon a recognition of interdependency (which may not depend on the perception of likeness), then *it is not as an isolated and bounded being that I survive, but as one whose boundary exposes me to others in ways that are voluntary and involuntary* (sometimes at once), an expose that is the condition of sociality and survival alike" (Butler 2010: 54; my emphasis). In contrast to Mignolo's occasional claim that subalternized modes of knowledge can only be found "outside" the modern/colonial world system, Butler effectively argues that the dis-closure of border gnosis—albeit disavowed—always already conditions being also "inside" the so-called West, and ever-undermines the *ratio*'s general monadic conception of being. Consequently, particularly when read with Stiegler's concept of technogenesis, the apprehension of precariousness can be perceived as a *technopoiētic* border gnosis that exposes modern individualism as a Western Self-deception. Stiegler, too, explains that the process of individuation in which one partakes is not entirely one's own but always shared with a group which one addresses, and to which one belongs due to this addressing (cf. 2014: 46). For Stiegler, Baudrillard, and Butler, this address and participation is connected to a process of catastrophic sense-sensitization. As operating "at the margin of what appears or as riddling its surface" (Butler 2010: xxx), Butler's apprehension outlines a mode of sensory/sensual perception at the curve of the *ratio*nal centralizing framework. Contrary to the techno-logical freedom forced forth via the Idealist liberation of the sign with its focus on pristine Self-presence, precariousness insists upon a (Baudrillardian) paradox: "The exercise of freedom is something that does not come from you or from me, but from what is between us, from the bond we make at the moment in which we exercise freedom together, a bond without which there is no freedom at all" (2015: 52). In terms of the broader argument of this book, the freedom which an apprehension of the precarious unfolds, always (r)evolves within the irreducible dynamic border gnosis of pathos and response.

Precariousness exceeds the limitations of representational signification. However, it does so not by merely annulling the semiotic system altogether, but rather through creatively (ab-)using it against itself. Once again, it is the urge of "going beyond," and the utopic prospect of being able to achieve this transcending move completely, that resulted in the techno-epistemological system.[27] Butler clarifies that "[f]or representation to convey the human, then, representation must not only fail, but it must *show* its failure. There is something unrepresentable that we nevertheless seek to represent, and that paradox must be retained in the representation we give" (2006: 144). In other words, it is the paradox of an irreducible entanglement of discourse and figure that must be retained. Only within the breaking of the framework can the irruption of radical figural otherness take place. Apprehension out-lines a reading *other*-wise and not a mere epistemological counter-discourse. As such, it does not collapse into an oppositional logic that seeks to do away with all frameworks. Or, as Stiegler puts it: epistemological modifica-tion cannot occur "unless bodies and works, apparatuses and organizations, are brought together in new ways, unless a new process of individuation is invented" (2015: 110). With its emphasis on a being-bound to the other, Butler's thinking on precariousness allows for attempting precisely such an invention.

The apprehension of the precarious simplicity of (human) being(s) unfolds—in connection with Baudrillard's reversibility and Stiegler's tech-nogenesis—that the actual scandal that the *ratio* seeks to disavow is not the otherness of the other, but the other's very sameness in precariousness; a sameness that cannot be fully grasped or fixed, but that *figures* as an un-canny *presencing*.[28] Butler writes: that "[t]o kill the other is to deny my life, not just mine alone, but that sense of my life which is, from the start, and invariably, social life" (2010: xxvi). Within precariousness, the other, conse-quently, *figures* as an-other sameness which is never restricted to a proper Self and its notions of ownness. As Baudrillard explains, the *ratio*'s disa-vowal of otherness ex-poses a deep-seated existential angst of precarious dependence: "But if I am inseparable from the other . . . , then all destinies are linked, and no one can claim to have his own life or his own thought" (2001: 110). Within precariousness, the other *figures* as a *sense* of radical otherness (from) inside the self. It is this form of sameness that circumscribes a being-bound in separation that occidental epistemology has attempted to overcome, particularly by installing the Cartesian split between subject and object. The fear of otherness "consists solely in the insight that the 'I' needs the other in order to survive, that the 'I' is invariably relational, that it comes into being not only through a sustaining, but through the formation of a capacity to sustain an address to another" (Butler 2010: 176). Insisting on this sameness in precariousness, however, is not at all to say that otherness is effectively levelled once again—quite to the contrary. It is this ungraspa-ble notion of the same that simultaneously lets the other be the other in its otherness without reducing it to a negative foil that can be measured against a proper self. For Butler, an apprehension of precariousness opens onto a fundamental ethical question anew: "how to treat the Other well when the Other is never fully other [but still radically other], when one's own sepa-rateness is a function of one's dependency on the Other, when the difference between the Other and myself is, from the start, equivocal" (2015b: 160).[29]

This question cannot be answered with a clear-cut solution, but calls for residing within the tension of a sense-sensitized insight: the scandal is that the individual is *always already in-difference* through precariousness; the scandal is that the individual is *always already in-dependence* with radical otherness; the scandal is that the individual is *always already in-dividuality* with the other. It is as such that a *banality of integral sameness* possibly *reverts* into a *simplicity of precarious sameness*.

THE VIEW FROM NOW HERE

HERE, WE TURN, OR *REVERT*, to the analysis of Richard Powers's novel *Plowing the Dark*. What Gerry Coulter writes of Baudrillard's thought applies just as well to Powers's prose: "His writing is one of the delightful examples of the way in which theory and literature begin to communicate with such affection in the late 20th century" (n.pag.). Both the philosopher and the writer—who has a background in computer programming (cf. Dewey 5)—do not simply insist on a binary opposition between *technē* and *poiēsis*. Where Baudrillard engages in an ambivalent kind of "theory fiction" or a "poetic way of thinking" (Coulter n.pag.), Powers "refuses to situate fiction in an easy position *in addition or in contrast to science*" (Latour 273), and rather insists on "the *joint* inventions of literature and science" (ibid. 278). Powers's work has been described as located "at the crossroads of literature and the sciences" (Ickstadt 2012: 24), or as "breaking down the (partly imaginary, partly institutional) barriers to the sciences" (Sielke 242). In other words, his works of literature bear strong *technopoiētic* tendencies. Powers explains:

> The novel I'm after functions as a kind of bastard hybrid, like consciousness itself, generating new terrain by passing 'realism' and 'metafiction' through *relational processes*, inviting identification at one gauge while complicating it at others, refracting the private through the public, story through form, forcing the reading self into *constant reciprocal renegotiations* by always insisting that *no level of human existence means anything without all the others.* (2008: 308; my emphases)

This strong emphasis on relationality and reciprocity also characterizes *Plowing the Dark*: the two plotlines of Powers's narrative not only reflect the ever-inextricable entanglement of *technē* and *poiēsis*, but also an ever-ineffaceable *presencing* of radical otherness (from) inside systemic closure.

As a "contrapuntal narrative" (Dewey 136), the textual performance, alludes to the interstitial neighborhood of theory and fiction where the two plotlines themselves retroactively turn out as having been always already irreducibly entangled. They outline a con*figuring* that also applies to the two chapters of this part.

(En-)Framing and (In-)Difference

The first plotline of *Plowing the Dark* outlines the epistemological implications of Western hyper-industrial-reality via the story of a group of scientists and researchers working for a start-up called the Realization Lab (RL); a branch of the multinational computer corporation *TeraSys* engaged in constructing a "*Computer-Assisted Virtual Environ*," or short: "*the Cavern*" (9). In the text, the Cavern functions as an allegorical rendering of the workings of the Western techno-logical framework. Dogmatically adhering to the principles of a rigid scientism—that is, "a special form of idealism" which "puts one type of human understanding in charge of the universe and what can be said about it" (Nagel 9)—the RL's goal is nothing less than a full putting into operation of what Baudrillard calls integral reality.[1] In fact, through its location on a mountain (cf. Powers 2000: 25), the Cavern resembles a modern monastery, albeit secular, where "shaggy dungeon creatures" withdraw into a "subterranean wonderland" (ibid.) to develop "*the escape valve for surviving the pressure of culture*" (129), as coder Jackdaw Acquerelli puts it in the narrative.[2] For the software engineers, virtual reality (VR) constitutes "the heaven of last imagination" whose room promises "[t]he paradise of detachment. The room of no consequence in the least. Of making no difference in the known world" (145). In other words, the Cavern aims to simulate what Thomas Nagel describes as *The View from Nowhere*: a form of zero point epistemology which is based on an entirely "impersonal standpoint [that] produces in me a sense of complete detachment" (61); a view, Nagel elaborates, that allows for the appropriation of a quasi-divine objectivity in the spirit of Descartes, who also "tried to recapture knowledge by imagining his relation to the world from the point of view of God" (130). For the programmers of the RL, virtual reality enables the techno-logical realization of the sovereignty of human agency over the world and its entities. For them, this effort marks "civilization's crowning capstone" (Powers 2000: 29). However, their techno-scientific impetus can also be regarded as "revived and reconfigured form of idolatry" (Pasco n.pag.) and/or as a "desire for ultimate transcendence" (Huyssen 16). Appropriating a perspective formerly ascribed to some divine entity, the Cavern's coders are "acting *sub specie aeternitatis*" (Nagel 130) to enter into a "*war with the rest of creation*" (Powers 2000: 263), or, more precisely, to deny and replace the world entirely in their own image. By way of virtual reality, the Cavern turns life into a huge sandbox game where everything is ready-to-hand (cf. ibid. 110). In constructing such a virtual framework, so the programmers' dream goes, human agency is going to be able to constantly act as if in God-mode.

Promising the possibility of immersion in the high definition of integral reality, the RL seeks to realize epistemological sovereignty through a Cartesian certainty where the world appears fully as will and imagination: "a world built from scratch and for which we will be accountable to no one" (Baudrillard 2013: 25). In the narrative, the coders seek to realize nothing less than a nostalgic inversion of the idea of the world's creation: a technologic inversion of the myth of *Genesis* (cf. also Kley 2009: 439).[3] As Charles Harris writes, in the Cavern, the "neo-Platonic apotheosis" (251) of the mind's capabilities is fueled by what can be called "Technoromanticism:" the uncritical celebration of VR as "promising a transparent, unmediated perception of reality" (252). The realms of virtuality, so the staff of the RL prophecies in the novel, will bring with them the utter erasure of the boundaries between sign and referent. The poet-turned-programmer Stevie Spiegel announces: "*With software, the thing and its description are one and the same*" (Powers 2000: 307). According to Spiegel, human language attains the power of divine creation through its functioning as a computer code. His colleague Ronan O'Reilly expands this vision even further. He hopes that the power to alter the configuration of space-time, ultimately, is going to culminate in the ability to "*determine the future*" (ibid. 193). Spiegel elaborates: "*It's the grail we've been after since the first campfire recital. The defeat of time and space*" (ibid. 159). *Plowing the Dark* outlines the Cavern as a space for the putting-into-operation of the impetus of an "ungodly, omnipotent technique" (285); an epistemic order that, through the perfection of virtuality, aims to install a "Cartesian maelstrom" (38) where everything and every-body is plunged "[i]nto pure conception" (267). Immersed in the systematicity of the virtual, the world is subsumed underneath the control of the supreme reign of the apotheosized *ratio*.

The Cavern's technical appropriation of a quasi-divine agency represents a striving toward the full realization of the Cartesian paradigm. This realization does not only entail a blurring of the boundaries between representation and reality (cf. Kley 2009: 437), but also—and maybe at first glance paradoxically—of subject and object. The retreat into the virtual that the Cavern epitomizes in the narrative, operates via "a collapsing of the subject-object polarity and its spatial coordinates, such that the internal and the external, the proximal and the distal, become inextricably intertwined, as in a Moebius strip" (Levin 172). However, this collapse is a problematic one, for it is founded upon the mathematization of the world at the hands of the supreme *ratio*nality.[4] Virtualization augments the position of the human subject exponentially and, thereby, allows for "an ego experience of effort-less thought expansion in an infinite field of spatial coordinates free of ob-stacles" (ibid. 176). This is evident when Adie Klarpol's excitement for the possibilities of the virtual turns into "a proof-perfect knockoff of St. There-sa's ecstasy" (Powers 2000: 63); not the ecstasy brought about by humble supplication, but rather by a vision of human creative power. In a conversa-tion on the epistemological stakes of the RL's project, O'Reilly asserts that "[t]*he world is a numbers racket, all the way down*" (ibid. 83). He regards it as potentially calculable and, as such, entirely malleable. Within the novel, the Cavern's elevation of the human subject culminates in the reductive ob-jectification of all (other) being(s) that aims "to supplant physical space with total representation" (Harris 269). As the narrative's title suggests, in virtual reality, epistemological humility gives way to the urge to "plow through the unpromising stuff of the earth as if brusquely cutting through a stubborn obstacle; facticity is to be defeated" (Dewey 135) through calculative rea-soning. All objectified worldly entities are to be devoured in the high defini-tion of virtuality. In the first plotline of the novel, the complete realization of crude Cartesianism is, paradoxically achieved via a crumbling of the sub-ject/object split within virtual reality, that, in turn, is achieved via the total objectification of the world and the total apotheosis of the human mind. Both coincide. But, upon closer inspection, this collapse turns out as a one-sided levelling of everything, and every-body, which/who resists calculation. The scientism of the RL dis-solves the problem of incalculability by a simple cancelling underneath Ockham's razor.[5]

Plowing the Dark outlines the Computer-Assisted Virtual Environ, with its erasure of the incalculable, as a space where epistemic agency is fully unfolded. In the Cavern, as the coder Sue Loque remarks, "*[W]hat's done can always be undone*" (Powers 2000: 39). She, thereby, utters the phrase which summarizes the underlying motivation for the entire endeavor of virtualiza-tion: the liberation, or emancipation, from the constraints and limitations which determine human being-in-the-world. In other words, within the nar-rative, the ultimate goal of the retreat into the virtual is the overcoming of precariousness. In the simulation of complete controllability, the precari-ousness of human existence is effectively undone. The RL's integral real-ity seeks to re-create life without its dangers. According to the rules of the Cavern, "[a] simulated object had to bend or droop or bruise or any of several dozen verbs that real things did when bumped up against in the grotto that the Cavern stood for" (Powers 2000: 60). However, it is to do all that without the possibility to inflict actual injuries or wounds itself.

The material-immaterial composition does not grant room for a precarious bodily exposition of its users; quite to the contrary. Immersion within virtuality is supposed to provide "the final escape from brute matter: the room that would replace the one where existence lay bound" (62). For the RL-staff, entering the calculated and en-coded space of the Cavern constitutes "[m]ankind's next migration" (75): the exodus from the precarious *eksistence* into "a place wide enough to house human restlessness" (125). The Cavern's ultra-digital transcendence promises a sanitized immanence where precariousness is effaced by way of a *ratio*-computational detachment.

This effacement of precariousness emerges as the wish for a radical redefinition of human being(s). The striving for transcendence betrays the primordial longing for escaping from or side-stepping the limitations of corporeality (cf. Kley 2009: 431; Levin 176). The team of programmers is convinced that their efforts "would overhaul the terms of human existence" (Powers 2000: 300). As Spiegel explains to Klarpol, calculative thought enhanced by computer technology "*redefines what it means to be human. All those old dead-end ontological undergrad conundrums? They've now become questions of engineering*" (160). However, at closer inspection, this desired remodeling of humanity turns out as nothing less than the climax of a levelling patriarchal logocentrism. In his own analysis of the text, Bradley Smith writes that the yearning for an "erasure of the body symbolizes a desire of masculinist culture to *erase the difference associated with the body*" (Smith 105).[6] The Cavern's VR, which simulates the gestural activities and all actions that "real" objects execute (cf. Lane 35), expands physicality and sensory perception by purging them of their precarious sensuousness. It factors out the body to construct a perspective from where it becomes possible to view the world from a standpoint of objectivity without having to shed the aesthetic altogether (cf. Ryan 1). The programmers' aim to overcome matter, in the text, expresses that "the soul simply wanted better accommodations. Something more like itself than that dying animal" (Powers 2000: 268). As such, the novel exposes the virtualization of the body in virtual reality as constituting nothing less than the Hegelian dream of a pristine presence as Idea in a digitalized (dis)guise.

Also within Powers's narrative, this epistemic longing for pure presence coincides with the levelling market logic of the modern/colonial world system. Eventually, the Cavern's VR-project is geared toward producing "*more of the same*" (ibid. 143). In the virtual reality chamber, there is (to be) no room for an otherness which resists the *ratio*'s grasp. Everything needs to be able to be consumed in/by a violent Western epistemological horizon. Virtuality functions as the modality of "[t]he colonization of the universe by human calculative thought" (Pasco n.pag.), which elevates the logic of the

Conquest to its utmost level. In the first plotline, it is the Sri-Lankan-born scientist Rajan Rajasundaran who, in an argument with the RL's director, Jonathan Freese, succinctly comments on the Cavern's colonialist marketization of the world: "*Must you Americans oversell everything?* Rajasundaran asked. Freese liked the aggressive ones. *Oversell? You can't oversell this. We're engineering the end of human existence as we know it*"; to which Rajasundaran curtly replies: "*Not as I know it, White Man*" (Powers 2000: 270). Another conversation afterwards between Rajan and his fellow coder Ari Kaladjian, continues this line of argumentation: "Kaladjian gave a victimized shrug. *Progress is destruction with a compass*"; whereupon "Raj's nod accelerated a couple of hertz. *It does make one wonder what the finish line looks like*" (275). The novel's allusions to possible finish line scenarios of this kind of virtualization are bleak. Freese encountered the technologies of virtual reality during his time in the military, where he witnessed the potential of simulation first hand. As Loque explains to Klarpol, "[t]*he Air Force was building simulators a decade before you were born. Before digital*"; Klarpol's astonished confusion prompts Loque to elaborate: "*Everybody wants make-believe. It's the most powerful leverage over non-make-believe you can get*" (296f.). The Cavern's VR, supposedly a sanitary space free of precariousness, operates on a crudely colonizing impetus; an impetus which, through the violent consumption within its systemic digestive tract, renders precarious everything, and every-body, which/who deviates or differs to ensure Western political epistemological sovereignty.

The increasing production of and consumption into the same, with its co-inciding effacement of otherness, reflects and further propagates a monadic individualism that obstructs relationality. The epistemological elevation of the subject over the object constitutes a radical "movement into the self" (Dewey 132) that strives toward the realization of a detached Ideal Self. In the novel, the software engineers of the RL have mostly given up on the intricacies of human relationality. Ironically, to install their dream of a new humanity within the Cavern, they have to flee from their own personal, social, and political problematics of their lives before virtuality (cf. Pock 133). The Irishman O'Reilly, for instance, has already turned the perfection of the Cavern into a life quest and removed himself from all personal relations. Completely immersed within the project of virtualization, "[h]e took the vow of cultural poverty gladly, throwing over his Neanderthal country without a backward glance. Even the vow of silence—the forfeiture of intelligent conversation—cost him little, in the light of the potential payoff" (Powers 2000: 80). He cannot fathom how his girlfriend, Maura, does not support this retreat into the virtual. In love and feeling abandoned, she writes him a letter in which she asks him to come back, but he does not comprehend how she can ask such a thing: "*The Cavern is the race's next step. The consolida-tion. Nothing comparable has ever existed, except in our imaginations. And Maura wants me to walk away from it. How long has history been working at this device? Centuries. Millennia*" (197). O'Reilly's character represents the broader stance of what is at stake here. For him, the completion of vir-tuality has become a quasi-existential task that compromises relationality.

Others even fear relations altogether. The developer Acquerelli, who spent his childhood playing sandbox games, takes an escapist leap and plunges himself into the supposedly safety of vr as a parallel universe (cf. Kley 2009: 435). Spider Lim does not know "how to interact with such things" as human beings (cf. Powers 2000: 64), and for Michael Vulgamott, the problem is "*humanity at large. A persistent source of stress to* [him]" (137). Klarpol, too, the artist who only joined the virtual chamber orchestra after having been hired by her friend, Spiegel, has long ago detached herself from (more inti-mate) relations. Disillusioned concerning the possibility "to fix all that had been wrong with civilization since the very beginning" (207), after having lived together with Spiegel and their friend, Ted Zimmerman, during college, and after a failed marriage to the latter that resulted out of this situation, Klarpol secludes herself. Spiegel, thus, once asks her: "*Don't you miss . . . surprising behavior? Something not reducible to axioms. A being as big and complicated as you are*"; but to her as well, drawn into the vortex of virtu-ality, self-imposed singleness is "*better than any other configuration* [she] *can imagine*" (226). The staff of the Realization Lab, despite their shared goal, constitutes a collective where "everything that each of them saw, he saw alone" (236). Therefore, Philipp Löffler argues that the characters in the narrative "all individually hang on to the fantasy that the creative powers of their minds will eventually help them overcome or control the predicaments of their life worlds" (106f.). However, the first plotline of *Plowing the Dark*, does not promote monadic individualism; quite to the contrary. The text rather exposes how "cybertechnologies merely amplify the I" (Dewey 144) and, thereby, potentially pull the screen over an "emptying loneliness" and "valiant search for connection" (5) underlying this condition. In the novel, virtualization into a one-plus-one-plus-one-logic of sameness entails a social breakdown into closed-off individuals.

In its function as an allegory of the Western techno-logical framework, the first plotline of Powers's narrative unfolds the Cavern's striving for episte-mological sovereignty, and the reduction of the significance of corporeality it is connected to, as resulting in the vision of disconnected, detached, (human) being(s). More precisely, according to the text, the constant (re-)production of the same and ongoing movement into the Self forces forth a world where everything, and every-body, is not only detached, but completely out of touch. The programmers and scientists of the RL are characterized by "the inability to abide much direct human contact without flinching" (Powers 2000: 26): Acquerelli, self-confident only when immersed within VR, is afraid of all non-virtual encounters and touching (cf. 173, 262), Lim even forgets to breathe when working on the computer (cf. 58), and Karl Ebesen is "ready to flee at anything that resembled intimacy" (94). For the RL's developers, existence becomes bearable only as "domesticated into mathematics" (116). This also confirms Antje Kley's observation that *Plowing the Dark* describes simulation as a coping mechanism with existential angst (cf. 451). The touch of the body constantly reminds the *ratio*nal *cogito* of its inseparable connection to a precariousness being-in-the-world, which, consequently, needs to be effaced through its reconfiguration in virtuality, as a longer passage from the novel further underscores:

> But reality had never been large enough, because the body had never been large enough for the thing it hosted. Where else but in the imagination could such a kludge live? The engineers carried on speculating. Human appetite would not stop short of the fully deformable universe. The walk-in hologram was right around the corner. Full-body force-feedback devices would extend illusion to the crucial sense of touch. Electronic skin promised pleasures deeper than the real thing. Full six-direction telepresence would follow shortly thereafter, linking the mind to remote robotic agents anywhere in space, lifting human senses off the face of the planet. (Powers 2000: 337)

Through the detaching digitalization of the senses, the body's potential to touch is stripped of its precarious exposition to the world's incalculable precariousness. Only after an integration into the logic of the same is one allowed to relate to the things of the world. But in this way detached, the touch is de-touched. Filtered through the virtual, everybody becomes nobody, and, paradoxically, touches without touching or being touched. The novel, therefore, describes what Baudrillard calls "a body immanent to itself, deprived of otherness, of contextualization, of transcendence; a body abandoned to the implosive metabolic vagaries of cerebral and endocrine flows; a sensory body, but not a sensitive one, because it is connected up internally only" (1993b: 138). Under the aegis of the *ratio*, corporeality no longer constitutes an *ek-sistential* condition of being exposed to others. It is subsumed under subjectivity's systemic monadic closure.[7] The coders of the RL seek to create a space where "nothing bleeds. Nothing rots. Nothing breaks. There is pain here, but there is no suffering. Things do grow, but never past their prime" (Powers 2000: 144). The narrative, however, unfolds how this is achieved only by paying a high price. Virtualization yields the potential for "the elimination of direct human interdependence" (Harris

261). In *Plowing the Dark*, epistemological sovereignty over existence's precariousness culminates in the violence of relational indifference.

The novel does not only represent this systemically infused malfunction of relationality on the diegetic level, but performs it by way of its form, particularly through the narrative perspective of the first plotline. Its realist third-person narration mirrors the objective stance of the view from nowhere shared among the scientists and programmers of the RL on the story-level. As Christoph Reinfandt argues, the heterodiegetic narrator's retrospective distance and its neutral view enable the drawing near to the characters' own perspectives, whereby a sense of closeness is created (cf. 361). The detachedness of third-person narration puts the reader in the position where one can relate to the characters and their specific issues. Concerning Cartesian scientism, Thomas Nagel writes: "[b]ecause a centerless view of the world is one on which different persons can converge, there is a close connection between objectivity and intersubjectivity" (63). *Plowing the Dark*'s first plotline integrates this into its textual enactment. Exactly like the observational vantage point of the view from nowhere, impersonal narrative distance allows for the reader's immersed proximity in the diegesis of the novel. The reader is free to plunge h/erself into the safe and controlled proximity held in check by the framework of fiction to empathize with the characters. The narrative, however, problematizes these realist conventions. By at first apparently adhering to these conventions, the text seeks to draw attention to the lack of relationality involved within this scenario. (En-)actively drawing attention to the distancing character of the third-person narrative perspective, the novel has the reader and the characters within the text "bond yet remain stubbornly isolated" (Dewey 136). It shows, as Butler writes in a different context, how such an immersed proximity in narrative distance serves to "evacuate my situation in an effort to secure the distance that allows me to entertain ethical feeling and even feel myself to be ethical" (2015a: 104). When enclosed in the novel's narrative simulation, this ethical stance remains decidedly detached and its affective potential is effaced. That is, throughout the process of reading the first plotline, analogous to the Cavern's developers on the diegetic level, the reader and the characters share a common story, but still form a disconnected community of closed-off monads. *Plowing the Dark*'s textual performance effectively interweaves the diegetic and the extradiegetic levels of the novel to expose the dangers of detached relational indifference.

One character's perspective, however, differs significantly from the rest of the RL-staff's objectifying gaze. It is through the eyes of the artist Klarpol that the first plotline further pursues its critique of a levelling view from nowhere and invites the reader to see other-wise. Unlike most of the other

employees working on the Cavern, the artist Klarpol is, although later
drawn into simulation's mesmerizing potential, at first, an outsider with
regard to computer technologies. She entertains "a general hatred for all
things that the cabled world hoped to become" (Powers 2000: 17). After
having been convinced by Spiegel to join the team, her character functions
as a designator for the need to relate to the world beyond the crude Western scientism the RL entertains. Spiegel, himself formerly a poet, and his
colleagues themselves realize that the success of their project depends on another perspective: "*We're all coders and chrome monkeys. A bunch of logic
monsters, trying to make walk-in, graphical worlds. We need someone who
can see*" (9). Their objectivizing view blinds them to the particularities of the
world. Klarpol's expertise as an artist, on the other hand—acquired "from a
lifetime of looking"—enables her to perceive "[t]he heft and feel of a thing,
its list of nicks and bruises, the deed of its actions and of all the actions upon
it" (37); that is, all the precarious relationality characteristic of being-in-the-
world that her colleagues' detached view always already effaces. Without
her specific perspective, the Cavern's VR would constitute nothing but a pix-
elated planarity devoid of worldly liveliness or depth (cf. 58). As Joseph Dewey
explains, "Adie brings to that project the traditional understanding of the
aesthetic enterprise as a strategy for overcoming the haunting loneliness of
the isolated self" (133). Unlike her new co-workers—such as Acquerelli,
who strictly "refused eye *contact*" (Powers 2000: 27; my emphasis)—Klarpol
"started to make eye *contact*" (23; my emphasis). Again, on a more abstract
level, this is to say that the first plotline, with its distanced third-person narration, installs in its story an aesthetic perceptual angle which poses a challenge to the logic of that very narrative perspective itself. Dewey succinctly
draws attention to this ironic juxtaposition of Klarpol's perception and the
virtualized perspective of the Cavern that is mirrored in the detached view
of the narrator: "Adie helps the team fashion convincing playscapes where
the intricate mathematics of software create surface, depth, nuance, sound,
even collision, and where the goggled participants are de facto disengaged
from the immediate, enveloped by an ever-expanding and terribly convincing simulation" (134). Through Klarpol's eyes, the text indicates a shift of
the narrative perspective which arises (from) within the distanced third-
person narration itself. The novel introduces already in its first plotline, a
figural-aesthetic potential that enables a critical (re-)vision of simulation,
which is further unfolded as the narrative performance proceeds.

The third-person narration of the first plotline, which mirrors the scientific view of the RL-staff, consequently, exposes itself as deficient in the
face of life's irreducible complexity. It illustrates that attempting to elevate
subjectivity to the status of objective sovereignty culminates in the detached

contemplation of human being(s) that Nagel describes as "objective blindness" (7) and elaborates:

> An objective standpoint is created by leaving a more subjective, individual, or even just human perspective behind; but there are things about the world and life and ourselves that cannot be adequately understood from a maximally objective standpoint, however much it extends our understanding beyond the point from which we started. A great deal is essentially connected to a particular point of view, or type of point of view, and the attempt to give a complete account of the world in objective terms detached from these perspectives inevitably leads to false reductions or to outright denial that certain patently real phenomena exist at all. (ibid.)

While the project of the Cavern is founded on the impulse to leave a merely subjective view behind in favor of scientific objectivity, the virtual environment ultimately remains dependent on this very angle. In analogy, the first plotline's distanced narrative perspective enables relating to the story's characters, but it remains bound to a detached objectivism that has "objects begin to vanish in pure visibility" (Pasco n.pag.), and alleviates more affective potentials. While, in full acceptance of the framework of simulation, "[m]any of the novel's characters prefer representational forms to—or confuse them with—the physical world" (Harris 260), Klarpol, "from the beginning, resists a world of total representation" (255). She sees other-wise. While the Cavern's VR focuses on "foveal concentration" and tries to exploit the fact that "[o]nly the smallest fraction of the eye actually saw with any degree of resolution—say 5 percent of the full field of vision, with the rest shading off into soft focus" (Powers 2000: 115)—so as to save processing power, Adie realizes that the vision at this blurred curvature, in fact, harbors essential in-sights. Instead of simply subscribing to the logic of perspective that, according to Kaladjian, enabled the West to believe that *the whole globe was up for grabs* (373) as it became entirely transparent, Klarpol realizes that it *"depends on what you mean by 'see'"* (179). Through her eyes, the narrative shows how the distanced centralizing perspective of the West often entails an "objective nihilism" (Nagel 146) that levels existence's radical otherness. Put differently, through a textual performative self-contradiction via the character of Klarpol, *Plowing the Dark*'s narrative perspective in the first plotline offers a critique of a Western culture of distanced seeing; a culture of detached perception where vision has been stripped of its affective potential of touch (cf. Lane 97; Reinfandt 367). With the help of Klarpol, the novel opens the *figural* potential for an-other mode of seeing that maintains the sensuous potentials of the sensory. As Heinz Ickstadt writes in a slightly different context, it "translates the act of seeing into an act of participation and thus also, at least by implication, a call for action" (2012: 29). Ultimately, the first plotline relates the distanced view of the characters of the diegetic level to its detached third-person perspective to expose how the reader potentially subscribes to a logic that seems to offer full access to human being(s) by through narrative simulation. Gradually revealed by way of an interplay with the text's second plotline, to which this analysis is now going to turn, *Plowing the Dark*, thereby, urges its reader to read other-wise.

(De-)Framing In-Dividuality

Next to the hyperreal scenario of the novel's first plotline, *Plowing the Dark* juxtaposes a second narrative strand that unfolds the story of Taimur Martin. Urged on by "the need to escape" (Powers 2000: 20), the American teacher travels to Beirut to flee from his (inter)personal problems with his girlfriend, Gwen Devins, but ends up being taken hostage by a never fully identified group of political radicals. The novel presents Martin, at first, as "[j]ust one more naïve Westerner" (100) indulging in an exoticizing and simplifying idealization of the other: "In your sleep, you already speak fluent Arabic" (21), he muses upon arrival. Whitewashing a situation of civil war and ongoing violent conflict, for him, Lebanon is merely a (completely exchangeable) place far, far away where he can forget his issues and start anew: "It's better than you imagined. All white and marine and accepting. A recovering place. A good place to recover" (22). One day, however, this escapist vision breaks down in an instance and Martin is captured. At this point, he realizes his "willed ignorance" and "stupid refusal to have learned any more than the basics of the war you so blithely waltzed into" (101). According to the narrative, it is due to the "fatal stupidity" (49) of his Western escapism that Martin ends up shackled and blindfolded in the closed-off space of a windowless prison cell.[8]

In this dark room, at the mercy of his captors, Martin is (pain)fully exposed to the precarious life of an embodied human being. He finds himself immersed in a situation of high precariousness that seems to stand in a stark contrast to the sanitized virtual environment of the Cavern. Deprived of almost every vital necessity, "Taimur discovers the quintessential role of his body in defining his existence" (Pock 125). In the confines of his soon defiled cell, devoid of sanitary facilities, he starts to feel less than human (cf. Powers 2000: 70), considers himself "fetid, sticky, lower than an insect, a dung beetle" (152), and eventually begins to socialize with the cockroaches around him (cf. 186). In addition, he must endure the violent mistreatments at the hands of his captors. Martin is repeatedly ridiculed, insulted, and injured:

"They haul you to your feet and slam you down again. A knee swings up, smashing your genitals against the back of your pelvis. One spongy testicle smears against this vise of bone. The wave of red shoots up through your spinal column and comes out through the seams of your skull" (327). Dis-located far beyond the amenities of Western wealth and plunged into the precarious darkness of a cavernous cell, his body—the length of his hair and beard—becomes the sole measure of his life, "the sole vestige of growth in a growthless place" (294). While the immersion in the VR of the Cavern represents a fantasy of total control, Martin's immersion in the precarious reality of his cage invokes a vision of total loss of calculative agency. Instead, "the body imposes a principle of humility and a sense of the necessary limit of human action" (Butler 2015a: 47). That is, in the second plotline, precar-iousness prevails seemingly over *ratio*nal reasoning.

By way of Martin's story, the text begins to unfold a fundamental irony. It is precisely his naïve Western attitude concerning the controllability of the world which leads him directly into "the imperfect, often brutal real world" (Dewey 142). His romanticized occidental version of the Lebanon— "[t]he thing [he] half wished away, half sought out" only due to this very Idealization—begins to reveal itself other-wise in precariousness. Martin comes to see that "[j]ust behind the *ivory* facing, just beneath the *glinting* amethyst [of Western nostalgia], the world is still shelling itself down to rub-ble" (Powers 2000: 43; my emphases). Throughout Martin's confinement, the narrative, thereby, dis-closes, and affirms, an existential insight that But-ler poses in the form of a question: "Could the experience of a dislocation of First World safety not condition the insight into the radically inequitable ways that corporeal vulnerability is distributed globally?" (2006: 30).

Martin's involvement in the broader scheme of (the) things (of the world) begins to dawn on him. In the midst of precariousness, that is, in circum-stances where "civilization's ground rules disperse into the mists of fantasy" (Powers 2000: 47), his idealizing perspective slowly starts to morph into a spectral *revenance* of things past; a vision strongly reminiscent of Walter Benjamin's dialectic at standstill which brings into alignment his Western experience with his present situation in captivity: "Your single life replays all existence, the way your fetus quoted the fish it came from. All innocence, all mistakes, from your first frightened grunts to your late-night adult con-fusion, are yours again. All your moments condemn you to line them up and relive them, one by one. Your Enlightenment, your Dark Age, your puddled afternoons of Hundred Years' War. All times collapse into now, in the mind forced to a standstill" (384). Through this moment of Martin's realization, with its allusions to occidental (intellectual) history, the novel prepares a twist concerning the seeming contrast between the first and second plotline.

As nostalgia turns into nightmare—and civilization into barbarity—the central irony of Martin's naivety alludes to a more intricate entanglement.

The entanglement of the two plotlines *figures* in the juxtaposition of the space of the Cavern and Martin's cell. As already indicated above, the Cavern and the cell appear to form two entirely different environments. While an immersion in the former harbors the potential for total calculative control of reality, immersion in the latter's hermetic sealing entails a complete loss of any grasp on reality (cf. Kley 432): an apparent opposition. Nonetheless, the similarities between the two spaces are already alluded to in the novel's first renderings of Martin's cage: "You come to in a white room. Even this feeblest of lights overwhelms you. When your eyes adjust, you make out where you are. Nothing to make out. A squalid plaster box. The room is maybe ten feet wide and twelve feet long" (73). Just as the Cavern, Martin's cage, in a certain sense, constitutes a "placeless place" (Powers 2000: 344): the one a virtual reality chamber that can simulate any place; the other a torture chamber whose location is unknown to its blindfolded inmate. As such, both outline empty white rectangular rooms where existential scenarios begin to unfold. In the novel, Cavern and cage coalesce as two existential spaces.

A room, as Elaine Scarry writes in *The Body in Pain*, is "the simplest form of shelter, [and] expresses the most benign potential of human life" (38). It implies an enlargement of a body's shell and the simultaneous transgression of the body in this very enlargement since a room can (supposedly) exist independently of the bodies it shelters. This transgression is indicative of "the human impulse to project himself out into space beyond the boundaries of the body in acts of making, either physical or verbal, that once multiplied, collected, and shared are called civilization" (39). Scarry elaborates that "[i]t is, though, back in the inward and enclosing space of the single room and its domestic content that the outward unfolding . . . of civilization originates" (ibid.). The Cavern, in the novel, can be seen as the utmost extension of this outward impetus. Via simulation, the RL's room appears to achieve the ultimate transcendence of the body. It constitutes a space that replaces and contains everything, and every-body, which/who was formerly regarded as part of the world outside, in the confines of its virtual reality. For the RL's coders, this is civilization's crowning accomplishment. However, Scarry importantly adds that "[e]very act of civilization is an act of transcending the body in a way consonant with the body's needs," wherefore, "even . . . when most exhilaratingly defiant of the body, civilization always has embedded within it a profound allegiance to the body" (57). A body's needs play no role in the Cavern. It rather opts for the effacement of corporeal dependence in virtual reality. Therefore, according to this reasoning, the chamber *figures* as an extremely violent space; a space that, in a paradoxical fashion, mirrors the physical violence of Martin's cell; a space — to remain with Scarry's diction — that appears as "uncivilized," or, more precisely, *de-civilizing*.

Powers's narrative does not merely oppose (Middle) Eastern barbarism to Western civilization but shows how occidental epistemic violence is mirrored in the physical violence of Martin's captivity. His exposure to bodily pain in the prison cell reflects and simultaneously twists the Cavern's logic of Idealist logocentrism. Scarry explains that a torture chamber distorts the existential dimension of a room. It usually "accommodates and thereby eliminates from human attention the human body" (39): instead of giving shelter, the torture chamber houses an eradication of shelter, including that of the body itself. This also holds true for Martin's confinement. In the cell, his existence is stripped down to the precarious (un-)ground of his embodied being.

The room turns from a civilizational construct into an "agent of pain" (40). Within this space, the systemic referentiality of Western conceptions of language gives way to the de-signification of painful yelling and wailing. Describing the relationship between corporeal agony and the workings of language, Scarry explains that "physical pain — unlike any other state of consciousness — has no referential content. It is not *of* or *for* anything. It is precisely because it takes no object that it, more than any other phenomenon, resists objectification in language" (5). Hence — in counterintuitive fashion — Martin's cell mirrors the functioning of the Cavern's virtuality. Pain is here rendered as similar to the techno-logical emancipation of the sign from fixed reference. Just as signification's gradual liberation in *rati*onal thought is ultimately geared toward the attainment of pure or pristine presence as Idea, "the most crucial fact about pain is its *presentness*" (9). Consequently, while the Cavern one-sidedly resolves the subject/object paradigm in the direction of the supreme *rati*onal Subject, Martin's cell one-sidedly ties it back in the direction of a bodily Object. In both cases, however, the violent epistemo-logic is the same. Both inflicting pain and calculative reasoning devour the (things of the) world into the digestive tract of a violent mode of relating to (human) being(s). In other words, in the novel, pain's irreducibility to a static system of signification exposes the violent impetus underlying the quest for supremacy by way of total virtualization: the narrative juxtaposes the Cavern's liberation of the sign in VR within the first plotline and Martin's violent confinement in the precarious, de-signified reality of his cell within the second plotline.[9] Thereby, *Plowing the Dark* unfolds how the supposedly sanitizing calculative reasoning of Western epistemology constitutes a violent encroachment into the things of the world that is tantamount to the isolating infliction of physical pain.

The narrative, however, does not cease its twisting of logocentrism with this alignment of epistemic and physical violence. Outlining Martin's bodily abuses as a mirror of a brutal Western epistemology starts to turn into an ab-use strategy for drawing attention to the *ratio*'s irreducible entanglement with aesthetic corporeality that bears an inherently relational dimension. In the isolation of his cage, through touching its walls and "feeling its way along the smooth-bore corridors into open defiles of feeling," Martin regains a long-forgotten form of sense-sensitivity: "[a]mazement, here in the pitch-black passages, is a tactile thing" (Powers 2000: 326). This modality of approaching the things of the world stands in stark contrast to the individualist escapism that led him into his prison cell: "The whole reason you came to this country in the first place was to escape human connection" (187). Martin's spatial temporal confinement brings forth his drastic dependence on sociality. He starts to understand that without others, he himself is nothing either, and that such concepts as liberation and identity have meaning only within relationality (cf. Kley 468f.). In confirmation of Scarry's attestation that "[i]n the isolation of pain, even the most uncompromising advocate of individualism might suddenly prefer a realm populated by companions" (11), Martin recognizes his existential need for the other(s). Emphasizing the bodily quality of Martin's situation, the narrative renders this as follows: "isolation warps you into someone you don't recognize. *You feel the thing in all its nakedness*: a need so great that you'd stupidly tried to shed it"; that is, his isolated state initiates "[Martin's] trueing, [his] delight, [his] sanity, [his] only health. Others" (Powers 2000: 187; my emphasis). Robbed of the discursive framework that allowed for the nostalgic fantasies of Self-fulfillment of his modern individualism, Martin experiences what Butler describes as "vulnerability that we have when we are unsupported, when those infrastructural conditions start to decompose, or when we find ourselves radically unsupported in conditions of precarity" (2015a: 65). He realizes that the conflict with his girlfriend, Gwen, from which he fled, was due to his incapability of responding to her otherness as well as his impetus to "[c]*ontrol the whole exchange*" (Powers 2000: 245). Through his individualist ego-centrism, "[he became] her oppression, her tyranny, and whatever else she may have turned [him] into no longer matters. [He] always thought she pushed away, when, in fact, she only stood still against [his] pulling" (390). That is, almost fully deprived of human interaction, "something as seemingly mundane as the ability to have a relationship" (Pock 130) attains a completely new quality which goes beyond an egotistic wish-fulfillment:

"[t]he easy reciprocity that you once thought could underscore all exchanges between people who cared for each other" (Powers 2000: 249). Confronted with a precarious condition of being reduced to nothing but an embodied human being, Martin's individualist escapism faces the relational existential necessity of being with others.

As such, being shackled within the confines of his cell triggers in Martin an-other form of escapist longing that further reveals the connection between the violent techno-logic of the Cavern and that of the cage in Beirut. As Charles Harris observes, "[t]he first VR, Taimur's narrative makes clear, is the mind" (266). Contrary to Scarry's account of the torture chamber, Martin's imprisonment does not culminate in the complete destruction of his language and imagination. Instead, Martin's mind, in his isolated state, becomes the only pathway for a (temporary) relief from his situation: he "start[s] to perform superhuman feats of synthetic memory. Desperate feats, deranged, like the reflex acts of mothers lifting two-ton beams off their pinned infants" (Powers 2000: 249). The narrative, here, unfolds the processes of the mind as a vital existential performance. It renders the mind as a coping mechanism which creates the sense of distance from the things of the world that is necessary to be able to deal with existential threats; a distance, however, that is geared toward the other and not toward individualist Self-seclusion. The novel does not withhold this more problematic potential of the mind in isolation. Still mirroring the techno-logic of the Cavern, where bodies are levelled or tamed completely, Martin's mind, in fast motion, replays the process of significatory liberation as resulting in a form of self-imprisonment: "Where the body is chained, the brain travels. In captivity, every inference is the freest flight. Nothing stops your associations or keeps them accountable. Your thoughts run through maniacal stunts, like radio-controlled drones at an air show. They blast through the countless embassies that offer limited asylum. Unchecked, your mind's maneuvers twist back on themselves in all directions, a nest of million twigs that knits its own prison in the static air" (185). The narrative outlines a fundamental ambivalence regarding the functioning of the mind whose resolution depends on the direction of the sense of distance it creates. While the RL's Cavern seeks to realize distance from the (things of the) world via virtualized Self-distancing, his confinement stimulates within Martin the need for a distancing from the Self that frees him toward the other(s). The text picks up, once again, on Butler's insight: "Could the experience of a dislocation of First World safety not condition the insight into the radically inequitable ways that corporeal vulnerability is distributed globally? To foreclose that vulnerability, to banish it, to make ourselves secure at the expense of every other human consideration is to eradicate one of the most important resources from which we must take our bearings and find our way" (2006: 30). *Plowing the Dark*, however, does not one-sidedly solve the problem of the mind, but rather unfolds its ambivalent potential further in showing how Martin's individualist techno-logical escapism can turn into a form of escapism from the Self which is geared toward relationality. The text unfolds how, in precariousness, the mind does not opt for an effacement of all phenomena and their otherness via integration into the *ratio*, but potentially functions decidedly other-wise.

Martin hopes to realize this other form of escapism through immersion in books. *Plowing the Dark* outlines "an important connection between imagination and the sensual" (Szadziewicz 94) that twists and bends the techno-logic of calculative reasoning even further. Dewey also holds that, in his confinement, "Taimur taps an unsuspected need for the aesthetic" (138). However, when he argues that Martin, thereby, "relinquishes the con-siderable tyranny of time and slips into the self-sustaining dimension of an interior world entirely shaped by the only energy not diminished by such an ordeal [of confinement]: his imagination" (137), this is slightly misleading. For Martin, aesthetics remains tied to the radical experience of isolation and embodied existence. Aesthetics retains/regains a sense-sensitizing potential. As sensory/sensual mode of perception, for Martin, the aesthetic performs other-wise. His repeated begging for something to read indicates not the wish for an interiorizing aesthetic experience as defined by the rules of taste and/or judgement, but a longing for otherness, as the following somewhat longer passage from the narrative reveals:

> "What is it that you need from these books? What can you learn from them?" . . . "I . . . *I can learn from them how not to be me.* For an hour. For a day. You are crushing me, Muhammad. I need someplace to go. I need some-thing to think about. *Somebody else*, somewhere else." "Go here," he com-mands you, touching your sternum. "Think about what is inside you." "I can only think about that . . . for so long." "We have a saying. Everything in life is imagination. But in fact it is reality. Whoever knows this will need nothing else." "*I need . . . someone to talk to. I need . . . to hear someone else thinking.*" (Powers 2000: 292; my emphases)

It is precisely the potential for a retreat into the interior, which Martin, counterintuitively, seeks to escape via reading. His imagination is not geared toward the Self, but toward the other: books *act* as a means for becoming other-wise. At first glance, Martin's longing for otherness certainly appears to mirror the nostalgic escapism that also underlies the techno-logic culmi-nating in the Cavern's VR, since, for Martin, a book also constitutes a "cun-ning made world" (Powers 2000: 253). The novel unfolds writing as one more form of technics (or *technē*, as described in the previous part); albeit a form of technics that need not necessarily shed embodied sense-sensitivity's relational character, but *act*-ually harbors a potential for uncovering this sensuous dimension even from inside systemic techno-logic.[10] Therefore, Dewey is correct that, in the text, "the imagination is a potent *connecting* force that is at once intensely private and splendidly communal" (2; my emphasis). In Martin's precarious situation, the art—technics, *technē*—of written texts (and the reading thereof) dis-closes an aesthetic, that is, sensual/sensory, dimension, which "supports difference" by circumscribing "conjunctions of the disjoined *I* and *we*" (Stiegler 2015: 165). In *Plowing the Dark*, this relational aesthetic dimension is represented by the Qur'an, which the novel describes as "[a] volume to be read no end of times. *Words that can take you out of yourself.* A book for those who believe in the unseen. The *world-changer*. The Reading" (Powers 2000: 296; my emphases). Through immersion within the writings of the Qur'an, Martin remains ex-posed to otherness instead of isolating himself deeper into the confines of his cage. This book, for Martin, dis-closes an-other world that opens onto the encounter with radical otherness. Through the immersion in his situation of high precariousness (dislocated from all occidental amenities), Martin gradually begins to learn how to read other-wise.[11]

In contrast to the third-person narration of the first plotline, the text unfolds Martin's story via a second-person perspective; an un-narrating, descriptive, narrative perspective (cf. Reinfandt 362) that plays with the reader's mode of relating to the text and (en-)actively s(t)imulates a potential for reading other-wise. As a product of Western modernity, the genre of the novel can be said to promote individualist escapism by way of an immersive experience of reading.[12] The first plotline of Powers's *Plowing the Dark* outlines this experience, through its use of third-person narration, as based on a mode of representation which enables calculative distance; a form of distance that is similar to the one Martin also seeks, at first, to flee from the obstruction of his Western context (cf. Kley 453). The text's second plotline, however, through its use of a second-person perspective, as well as its repeated renderings of bodily pain, alludes to language's ability to express (the) things (of the world) as un-confined by the rules of significatory representation. Scarry may argue that physical pain resists language's objectifying impulse; but this is not to say that language and pain are ever separated altogether. Pain's inexpressibility within a systemic horizon of signification does not challenge language's ability of expressing pain *per se*, but alludes to its potential to designate other-wise. This also pertains to Martin's situation and his repeated request for something to read. In the novel, the happening of pain in the cell, in conjunction with the process of sense-sensitization that Martin undergoes throughout his ordeal—albeit resisting objectification in language through an integration into a referential system—emphasizes that mind and body, language and corporeal gestures, are always already irreducibly entangled (cf. also Scarry 48f.). Through its twisting of Western logocentrism toward the *significance* of embodiment, the novel reminds the *ratio*nal *cogito* of its aesthetic corporeality, and its entanglement within the relationality of all phenomena. The text ab-uses a second-person narration to en-acitvely in-*volve* the reader in the twisting of the *ratio* (back) toward a relational encounter with radical otherness.

To say that Powers's novel ab-uses the second-person perspective toward an in-*volving* relationality is to claim that *Plowing the Dark*'s second plot-line figurally en-acts a form of pathos, which calls for a certain response of the reader. Through the juxtaposition of the detached third-person narra-tion in the first plotline and the second-person perspective of Martin's story, as Ickstadt writes, in reference to John Harris, "Powers' work forces us to reconsider the meaning of 'realism' in terms of a quasi-mimetic, map-like, correlation between a textual and an analogous, yet different, extra-textual reality—a 'simulacrum of mimesis' (thus Harris) that allows, on the one hand, a self-referential emphasis of language and design . . . , and, on the other, an interaction between world and text via the participation of the reader" (2012: 26). While the third-person narration of the first plotline always remains at a distance, the second-person perspective of the second plotline constantly, and directly, addresses the reader in a way that pulls the reader into the ex-istential situation of Taimur's captivity. Harris and Dewey also have pointed out that this textual strategy reduces distance and has the reader take part in Martin's isolated state: while Harris writes of "the reader's vicarious iden-tification with Taimur's agonizing incarceration" (264), Dewey argues that "the reader 'shares' the difficult isolation of the lonely Taimur" (140). How-ever, as a figural pathos, the second-person perspective per-forms more. As the novel in-*volves* the reader in the situation, it does not have h/er *identify* with Martin's suffering as such but brings forth an existential relationality beyond the confines of representation; that is, a mode of relationality ir-reducible to an identification between one monadic Self and another. The reader shares, and/or participates, in Martin's situation in such a way that the novel s(t)imulates an existential being-bound to the other(s); albeit not as yet more individuals but in the always already precarious *in-dividual* (that is, indivisible) togetherness of all being(s).

It is this (en-)active relational in-dividuality in precariousness, in-voked by the second-person narration, that calls for a response of the reader. As Johanna Heil succinctly explains, "[t]he 'you' becomes the crucial narrative device to bridge the gap between a neutral and detached narrative mode and one that winds itself around the reader's awareness" (2012: 154). She then goes on to argue that the "use of 'you' has to be understood as a signal of defamiliarization" (164). However, for Heil, this defamiliarization results in the relative (or, maybe better: relational) indifference of a "generic 'you'" (157), whereby the novel does indeed address the reader, but that does not entail an identification with Martin's torment. She sums up that "[t]he you-perspective thus generates a vantage point for interpreting the existential void of Taimur's captivity. He refuses to acknowledge that the 'you' he is talking about is identical with himself, which the pronoun 'I' would linguistically denote" (161). While her insistence on the defamiliarizing potential of the second-person perspective is helpful to outline how the novel does not opt for a monadic identification with Martin, it seems slightly misleading to argue that the narrator's appellative use of the pronoun "you" only serves as a means of Martin's defamiliarization from his own existential situation as outlined by the novel (cf. 158). Bearing in mind Martin's realization concerning his need for others, the ab-use of second-person narration certainly entails a moment of defamiliarization; but a mode of defamiliarization that does not function as a mechanism of existential disavowal, but that rather outlines the self's residing within a relational in-dividuality first brought forth in the precarious circumstances of Martin's confinement.

As such, the second-person perspective harbors the figural potential for the becoming other-wise of the reader h/erself as well. Powers's texts are often "appellative, pragmatic: They are meant to affect the reader" (Ickstadt 2012: 29). This applies to *Plowing the Dark*, too. As the novel's second plotline draws the reader into the existential situation of precariousness that it outlines, it does so to relativize—or, better, *relationalize*—the distanced immersion of the first plotline. In reference to Levinas, also Kley insists that the narrative operationalizes a form of speculative—or *poiētic*—saying, irreducible to propositional statements, with a certain defamiliarizing potential that may enable an intimate encounter with things beyond their mere linguistic framing (cf. Kley 458f.); *videlicet* a (de-)framing form of (written) saying which, simultaneously, via its being irreducible to propositionality—that is, irreducible to the Cartesian subject/object split—(en-)actively s(t)imulates the becoming other-wise of the reading process as well. The text calls for a mode of relating to its performance beyond calculative thought; an embodied mode of reading that remains open for the pathos of the other(s). The novel figurally en-acts what Butler describes as follows: "When any of us are affected by the suffering of others, it is not only that we put ourselves in their place or that they usurp our own place; perhaps it is the moment in which *a certain chiasmic link comes to the fore* and I become somehow implicated in lives that are clearly not the same as my own" (2015a: 120; my emphasis). Through its twisting of occidental calculative reasoning toward an embodied encounter with the other(s), the text invites the reader to reflect upon the physical epistemic violence stemming from the *ratio*. The novel figurally evokes a response similar to the one which overcomes Martin's guards upon realizing the pain they inflicted: "A change comes over your remaining guards, a horrified respect, the best measure of how gruesome the Technicolor highlights of your new face must be. They serve as your ghostly shaving mirror, these men whose cause must now look upon its own lustrous effect" (Powers 2000: 183).[13] Putting the reader face-to-face with the other(s) in precarious in-dividuality, *Plowing the Dark*, invites h/er, by way of this ex-posing immersion, to read decidedly other-wise.

Technopoiēsis *and Reversibility*

The outlined interplay between the novel's two plotlines hints at a deeper connectedness of the narrative strands that not only characterizes the make-up of Powers's text, but points toward an irreducible entanglement of representation and *presencing*, of mind and matter, of discourse and figure. From the beginning, this connectedness becomes apparent through various short passages describing specific room settings: "*This room is never anything o'clock*" (Powers 2000: 3), the passage setting the scene of the entire text opaquely reads. This section is followed, throughout the novel, by a "Crayon Room" (18.), a "Jungle Room" (67), the "room of economics" (85), "imagination's room" (144), the "room life lends you to sleep in" (170), a "Therapy Room" (228), a warm room (cf. 239), the "room of holy wisdom" (342), a dark room (cf. 390), the "room of the Cave" (400), and a room that disintegrates into open space (cf. 407). All these — read in context, or, more precisely, *as con-text* — gradually unfold the relational character of the text. While Heil reads the passages as forming a third plotline that, although in many ways mirroring the rooms simulated in the RL within the first plotline, is discretely independent from the two other narrative strands (cf. 2012: 146), it appears more appropriate to read these (apparent) sections as a kind of ligament that is neither part of the first, nor of the second plotline, but simultaneously part of both; that is, to read them as moments or spaces of liaison which, as Mark Taylor puts it, have the, at first glance, distinct strands of the text "become intertwined in a way that suggests that these seemingly opposite worlds share more than it appears" (98).[14] The resemblance to the rooms generated in the RL's virtual reality chamber does not merely refer to either one of the text's plotlines, but de-scribes, on a somewhat more abstract level, the potentials of simulation in general that enable and entangle both strands. As such, these passages indicate that *Plowing the Dark*'s narrative strands form more than just "two separate and oppositional, yet metaphorically related plot lines" (Ickstadt 2012: 31), and a lot more than "two separate plot lines which only briefly intersect at the very end" (Pock 122). Like the chemical links connecting the two irreducible strands of the double helix, as Reinfandt argues, the interactive room passages—both employing the same second-person perspective as the plotline revolving around Martin and, at the same time, documenting the developments of VR of the first plotline—outline an interrelation of the plotlines which is, granted, only revealed toward the end of the novel (cf. 363). However, this revelation is retroactive in nature, for this interrelatedness always already, albeit at first implicitly, characterizes the text from the start. The narrative unfolds an epistemological in-between (cf. Heil 2012: 144), which, as will be explained in more detail throughout what follows, unfolds the potential of a fundamental reversibility by way of which simulation *figures* beyond calculative reasoning.

There are several instances on the diegetic level somewhat randomly scattered throughout course of the narrative that confirm this insistence on the plotlines' specifically relational character. Firstly, it is not only the room passages which are held in the second-person perspective. The first indicator of overlap is the rendering of Acquerelli's childhood obsession with text-based sandbox games in the first plotline. These games' descriptive rhetoric, with its textual illustrations, such as "You are standing at the end of a road before a small brick building" or "Around you is a forest. A Small stream flows out of the building and down a gully" (Powers 2000: 102), directly mirrors the second plotline's as well as the room passages' appellative and/or immersive narrative impetus. The situation of Klarpol and Spiegel's friend, Zimmerman, outlines another instance of interrelation in the text. His confinement due to his suffering from multiple sclerosis to a wheelchair in a hospital room reflects Martin's scenario in Beirut. Both are, in a certain sense, confined to a "room [that] is never anything o'clock" (3). Just as for Martin, also for Zimmerman in his corporeal ordeal, the mind becomes the only functioning existential coping-mechanism: "[t]*rying to remember gives him something to do all day*" (320). Spiegel's vision upon visiting Zimmerman of the "*cedars of Lebanon*" (313) adds to this interconnection and foreshadows the further development of the entanglement of the novel's plotlines. Lastly, the room of the Cave provides the most profound indicator of relationality in the text. The passage outlines this space as a "continuous chasm" in which the "chambers all connect" (400) eventually.[15] The room evokes not only images of Plato's cave-parable concerning the nature of reason, but also of the caves at Lascaux with their primeval wall paintings as revolving around the central question concerning the relationship of mind and matter; the question that still occupies the programmers of the RL, as explicit references to cave painting attest (cf. 10f. and 40f.).[16] This *passage* (literally a pathway of sorts), as textual ligament, transports the question beyond the narrative's *diegesis* and outlines how it characterizes the text itself as a whole. What is true for the cave room applies to the textual space of the novel as well: "The room of the cave is something more than allegory. But the room of the cave is something less than real. Its wall shadows ripple with an undercurrent of substance, more than representation, but not yet stuff" (400). In other words, the text's contrapuntal polyphony (cf. Dewey 11), its "hybrid conceptual substructure" (Löffler 92), or "cavernous puzzle of aesthetics" (Szadziewicz 90), coalesces in the primordial question of representation's potentials between rationality and sensuality. In fact, with the room passages as textual ligaments, the novel outlines the irreducible double bind of reason and the senses that modern Western thought has been trying to disavow by installing the epistemological horizon of *ratio*nal systematicity.

The interrelatedness of the plotlines becomes fully apparent toward the end of the novel as Klarpol decides to simulate the Hagia Sophia in the Cavern. In the text, the palimpsestic space of the virtualized former Byzantine church—which later also provides the setting for the text's climax—outlines "*the place where civilization wavered*", as Spiegel asserts, and "*where West almost traveled East. Or should that be the other way around?*" (Powers 2000: 340), as Klarpol replies. The Hagia Sophia, here, functions as a space where the supremacy of Western reason with its civilizational ideals is being challenged. One of the room passages, namely the one which presents the room of holy wisdom (a direct translation of Hagia Sophia), picks up on this conversation in the first plotline and renders the space of the room as "*neither of the East nor the West . . .*" (344)—but both at the same time, one would like to add. Unlike what Benny Pock suggests, *Plowing the Dark*, therefore, does not represent a clash of cultures between East and West (cf. 126). Powers's novel, once again, does not trade in such crude binaries. In fact, as Kley observes, beyond the questioning of an East-West divide, the Hagia Sophia project of the RL in the first plotline reveals reciprocal links, not only between architecture and computer technology, but also between several established occidental dichotomies: past and present, human and medium, sensuality and rationality (cf. 2009: 462f.). In other words—and important to keep in mind throughout what follows—the Hagia Sophia, in the entire narrative, *figures* as an interstitial space of double binds where the limitations of calculative reasoning alone do not apply. Circumscribing a dichotomous locus between East and West, the (virtual) room of the Hagia Sophia outlines a space for becoming other-wise.

As an interstitial textual space, the room of the virtualized Hagia Sophia does not remain restricted to the level of the narrative's *diegesis*. As the

prime room that reveals the novel's plotlines' chiasmic intertwinement—
that is, as a textual space where the detached narrative perspective and the
affective second-person perspective commingle—the realms of fiction and
the reader also become entangled. As Katherine Szadziewicz explains, "[l]ike
the Cavern, the novel is itself a technology of representation that transforms the
user in its reflexivity" (112); as such, the text *both describes and simulates
an experience of virtual reality*" (91; my emphasis). *Plowing the Dark*, as a
whole, forms another (extended) room passage that interrelates not only its
narrative strands but transcends its diegetic boundaries and reaches into the
extradiegetic life-world of the reader. Put differently, the narrative circumscribes a space between simulation and reality; and as such a dichotomous
space, the novel draws attention to the "nature" of *virtual* reality. Just as
Acquerelli realizes in the first plotline, the Cavern, as a space of virtuality,
harbors nothing less than "pure potential" (Powers 2000: 112). The ambiguity of the virtual ever-hovers "between *We can do anything* and *What have
we done?*" (198). The narrative plunges the reader into this ambiguous potential; and via this plunging, the novel has the reader exposed to Klarpol's
insight: "*It messes us up*, Adie decided. *It really screws us over, representation*" (298). Through its inherent interstitiality, the novel's representation
messes with the reader as it screws over h/er very sense of representation and
simulation. With its insistence on a double bind of detachment and affection,
Plowing the Dark per-forms and outlines a "necessary reversibility of proximity and distance" (Butler 2015a: 103). De-scribing (textual) simulation by
way of entangling cognition and sentiment, Powers's text itself *figures* as an
interstitial existential space where the other *presences*.

To understand the text's coalescence of imaginative distance and affective
proximity in its simulated textual space, some more elaboration is in order.
How does the text *figure* as such a space? As Ryan writes in reference to
Lévy, "the virtual as potential represents not only the mode of being of the
literary text but the ontological status of all forms of textuality" (32). To her,
the text's potential is not restricted merely to stimulating different interpretations. It is linked to its irreducible materiality that first enables their cre-
ation(s) (cf. 33). How does this relate to Powers's narrative? This question
can be approached by reading it as what Hayles terms a "technotext"; that
is, a text which "embodies in its material instantiation the complex temporalities that also constitute the major themes of its narrations" and which
"can be seen as a device for evoking responses at all levels of engagement
and, through reflexive feedback loops that connect affect to conceptualization, bring them into metacognitive awareness" (106). In *Plowing the Dark*,
these feedback loops can be seen as arising from the interstitial space(s)
between the plotlines. The novel unfolds its narrative space in accordance

with Ryan's elaboration on textuality's virtual potential. She explains that a "textual universe cannot be a homogeneous Cartesian space with stable reference points but a self-transforming expanse riddled with invisible black holes through which we are unknowingly [but not unfeelingly] sucked into parallel worlds" (92). Again, in the text, such holes become manifest in the random irruptions of overlap of the novel's narrative strands on the diegetic level, as well as more explicit moments of entanglement in the room passages. It is through these loops and holes that the narrative per-forms (as) a cave-like con-*figuring* of mind and matter.

The textual simulation, as such, breaks with notions of static narrative closure. Just as the virtual reality in the Cavern is subjected to "new shocks to the invented landscape, shocks requiring perpetual invention to smooth them over" (Powers 2000: 256), the *figural* space of Powers's novel remains in motion throughout the entire reading process. What, at first, appears as controllable simulated imaginative space, warps into the circumscription of precarious reality as the reader is, retroactively, subjected to and/or immersed in the text's ex-posing relationality. Just as "[l]atency kill[s] the sense of presence" (259) in the Cavern, disrupting the sanitized vision of virtual reality, the novel itself repeatedly breaks with its realist representational mode of a mimetic textual world. However, in this latency of pristine presence an-other potential reveals itself: a potential for an unforeseeable *presencing*. Taylor draws on the notion of the fractal, also employed by Baudrillard, to describe a dynamism of singular textual events that are determinable only in retrospect (cf. Wade n.pag.). Taylor argues that, in the novel's *figural* performance, "imagination reveals a concealment that can never be decoded. This opening keeps everything in play" (2013: 107). In Powers's technotext, virtuality prevails, albeit not as self-sufficient, closed-off system, but as ever-dynamic and ambiguous potentiality.

Insisting on the virtual as ambiguous potentiality, *Plowing the Dark* exposes how both technoromanticism and technophobia constitute one-sided reductions of technics' complexity. The novel remains within the tension of "*Yeki bood. Yeki nabood*" (Powers 2000: 146) — it was so, and it was not so. This sense of ambiguity threatens the systemic impetus of calculative reasoning, just as it undermines the radical demonization of all things technological. It shows how, as Nagel puts it, "[t]he transcendent impulse [as reflected in the text's portrayal of the proliferation of virtual reality] is both a creative and a destructive force" (4), wherefore "[t]he extension of power and the growth of insecurity go hand in hand" (67). The text echoes *Antigone*'s choral ode and its insight that technics sometimes brings forth good and sometimes evil. In fact, Powers's novel can be said to express the ever-irreducible connection between *technē* and *poiēsis* discussed in the previous chapter. It transposes the counterturning motion of the in-separable forces into the con-text of computer technology. As an interstitial space where "art and science conspire" (Powers 2000: 64), the text relates simulation and the creation of virtual reality not only to technology's vi-olent mode of world-appropriation, but, at the same time, to the released openness of *poiētic* creation. *Plowing the Dark* outlines what Harris calls a "poetry-cybertechnology continuum" (259). That is, it does not relinquish simulation to the violent epistemology of calculative reasoning which, in the first plotline, is complicit with the apparatus of military violence (cf. Powers 2000: 396). Instead, the narrative, with its insistence on virtuality as poten-tial, points toward the *poiētic* dimension of simulation that stems from in-side the disruptive interstices of virtual reality's framework. Throughout the course of its polyphonic narrative, *Plowing the Dark* reveals what Baudril-lard refers to as simulation's inherent reversibility.

Plowing the Dark, thereby, opens the possibility of conceiving of simu-lation other-wise. Instead of merely employing it as a systemic mechanism of absolute screening or (en-)framing, an ironic twist, or creative sabotage, brings forth "technology's potential benefit" (Harris 278), namely by ren-dering simulation as a form of *technopoiēsis* which opens onto encounters with the radically other. In this sense, what Harris describes as the text's "critique from 'inside' representationalism" (265) can be read as repeated irruptions of the *figural* from inside and through textual simulation. *Plow-ing the Dark* circumscribes a *technopoiētic* narrative space that does not exclusively operate inside the horizon of representational signification. Its questioning of representation and reference does not propagate the com-plete separation of the sign from the things of the world as a liberating impe-tus. It rather shows how signification always necessarily remains tied to and is first enabled by the *res extensae* in their irreducible materiality and how this entanglement harbors an-other form of liberation that is not restricted to the calculative logic of the *ratio*. The text draws attention to a world-composing form of "representation" beyond mere mimesis which still does not buy into the Cartesian separation between mind and matter (cf. Kley 2009: 443 and 452). Instead, within its (en-)active composition, *technē* and *poiēsis*, cognition and sensation, as well as technics and body commingle. Residing within a technogenetic tension of detachment and affection, the narrative defies both anthropo- and technocentric accounts of simulation and outlines what Kley refers to as the hopeful possibility for a re-formed and re-forming view of what counts as real (cf. 2009: 467). In other words, in *Plowing the Dark*, simulation's reversibility per-forms a "metafictional turning to a primary realm of creativity (to the possible *within* the real)" (Ickstadt 2012: 40): a turning toward *figurality* (from) inside discourse's systematicity. It is by way of this altered and altering re-vision of the figural relation between simulation and reality that the text, ultimately, opens onto encounters with radical otherness.

Plowing the Dark's de-framing entanglement repeatedly reveals that, also within virtual reality, figural irruptions of "*something that will break out of the frame*" (Powers 2000: 277) potentially arise, as Klarpol puts it in the first plotline. These irruptions are always already at work in the simulated environment. As explained in the first section of this analysis, Klarpol is the one who first sees other-wise. Her engagement with virtuality differs significantly from the other members of the RL. When Acquerelli introduces her to the simulations of the Cavern, Klarpol reacts excitedly: immersed in the virtual, "[s]he forgot herself. Or she remembered. Dancing inside her dance, she could not say which. She embarked on a spiritual aerobics" (Powers 2000: 168). This passage marks a first indicator of the novel's climax and ties the de-framing of the modern individual to the *technopoiētic* experience of simulation. In this section, Klarpol's body is not levelled by calculative reasoning, but actively shapes the virtual environment: "Her body *was* the sound and light" (ibid.) and her movements cause motion within the simulated space. Read again through its relation of cognitive distance and corporeal proximity, *Plowing the Dark*, as Pock writes, illustrates that "[n]arrative patterns . . . occupy a position in between the virtual and the physical, i.e. they both shape and are based on bodily experience" (120f.). The novel, once again, through its narrative performance, interweaves Klarpol's experience on the diegetic level with the extradiegetic reality of the reader, as its simulation suggests that also the reading process itself is always irreducibly constituted by corporeal gestures. Pock, therefore, elaborates that "*Plowing the Dark* . . . traces points of intersection between things and signs, moments when the mental representation of a novel crosses over into 'the real' and causes concrete effects in the physical world or is itself the effect of a physical, embodied process" (120), whereby the novel "dismantles the myth of hermeneutic understanding which dictates that the transfer of meaning through signs is independent of persons, bodies, ad material carriers" (124). Through its de-framing simulation, Powers's narrative, at the same time, s(t)imulates a form of reading other-wise.

It is at the end of the text, in the virtual Hagia Sophia, that the narrative's inherent *figural* potential is revealed as Martin and Klarpol inexplicably find themselves in the same existential space. While deleting all she has added to the development of the Cavern upon becoming aware of its ties with the military, Klarpol makes a startling discovery in the virtual room of the church: "deep beneath her, where there should have been stillness, something moved," namely "a man, staring up at her fall, his face an awed

bitmap no artist could have animated" (Powers 2000: 399). After this peculiar incident, she tells Spiegel: *"There's . . . something in there. Something
that wants out. Something we didn't make"* (404). In the simulation, there
is something that resists the calculative grasp. This de-framing encounter in
the first plotline is matched by a passage in the second strand where, suddenly, Martin perceives something beyond his confinement:

> Then you heard it, above your head: a noise that passed all understanding. You
> looked up at the sound, and saw the thing that would save you. A hundred
> feet above, in the awful dome, an angel dropped out of the air. An angel whose
> face filled not with good news but with all the horror of her coming impact.
> A creature dropping from out of the sky, its bewilderment outstripping your
> own. That angel terror lay beyond decoding. It left you no choice but to live
> long enough to learn what it needed from you. (414)

This moment constitutes the most radical break with *Plowing the Dark*'s
otherwise supposedly realist representational mode. It "disrupts the neat
order of representation" (Heil 2016: 131): within the simulation, the other
presences. Here, at the latest, it becomes explicit that the two plotlines are
not disconnectedly isolated from one another. In the narrative, simulation
remains linked to precariousness, and individuals irreducibly tied to being-
with-others. Harris describes this textual incidence as "[t]he epistemic shift
at the end of *Plowing the Dark*—a culmination of several less intrusive
perturbations scattered throughout the novel to this point [that have already
been discussed above]—[that] resonates on multiple levels, the epistemological, the political, and, of course, the aesthetic" (274): a shift that occurs as the novel's simulation *reverts* from calculative distance to precarious
proximity, or from discourse to figure, by way of "[s]omething like *a poetic
transference of the situation, or a poetic situation of transference*" (Baudrillard 2001: 112).[17] Not restricted by the rules of modern techno-logic, in
this *figural* situation of being faced with a radical otherness, epistemology
happens beyond *ratio*nal control, aesthetics operates beyond objectification,
and politics moves beyond individualism.

Within the virtual Hagia Sophia of the text, the other *presences* as both
Klarpol and Martin see other-wise, albeit initially from different angles.
While Martin looks up at a divine figure, Klarpol looks down on a helpless
figure. Clearly marked by her position in the Hagia Sophia's dome, Klarpol
occupies "[t]he God's-eye view: in the simulation, but not of it" (Powers
2000: 399); that is, the apotheosized view from nowhere of modern Western *ratio*nality. Through Klarpol's eyes, however, this view *reverts* into an
entirely different perspective. The apparent hierarchy between Martin's and
Klarpol's positions dissolves in the moment of encounter. While, at first, it

is Martin, in his epiphanic vision, who believes he is seeing what will save him, he shortly becomes the one who must figure out the apparent need of an undecodable terror (cf. 414). Klarpol's supposedly superior perspective, through her bewilderment, turns into a frightened vision which requires help. Consequently, both Martin's limited view and Klarpol's detached view collapse in the *hic et nunc* of the face of the other. In other words, as their perspectives shift from their own situation toward the pathos of the re-spective other in a "nonegocentric respect for the particular" (Nagel 222), the distancing view from *nowhere* turns into a shared relational view from *now here*.[18] Subject to "the excessive nature of time and alterity that always exceeds our timing (and taming)" (S. Hart n.pag.), simulation, in the narra-tive brings forth something it cannot contain within its calculative systemic boundaries: "Taimur and Adie, isolates, have met, defying the conventional logic of time and space" (Dewey 147) in the existential space of the virtual Hagia Sophia. Speaking with Butler, the text has the two characters realize that "prior to any calculation, we are already constituted through ties that bind and unbind in specific and consequential ways" (2010: 182). The view from now here, irrupting (from) inside the interstices of simulation—"on the critical edge of the recognizable and . . . in the limelight of the dominant media" (2015a: 59)—outlines a planetary entanglement in "shared precar-iousness" (2010: 182). As Klarpol's and Martin's re-spective views *revert*, and as they meet face-to-face across time and space, *Plowing the Dark* per-formatively reveals what Butler further describes as follows: "it is only when we understand that what happens there also happens here, and that 'here' is already an elsewhere, and necessarily so, that we stand a chance of grasping the difficult and shifting global connections in ways that let us know the transport and the constraint of what we might still call ethics" (2015a: 122). Through this epistemic shift of the view from *nowhere* to *now here* the text circumscribes an existential textual space where epistemology, aesthetics, and politics function decidedly other-wise to bring forth a relationality in precariousness that ever-transcends systemic closure.

Tied to the text's interstitiality, this relationality is also not restricted to the diegetic dimension of the narrative. Said disruption of simulation rather indicates a *figural* openness of the narrative through which the reader is always already implicated, and implemented, in the textual realm. *Plowing the Dark figures* as a "room of shared experience" (Powers 2000: 407), which in-volves characters and readers alike, to bring forth a space from where "no one walks out the way he [*sic*] came" (410): a space of becoming other-wise. As elaborated above, via interrelating the Cavern's simulated space with Martin's cage, the text not only weaves together two levels in the narrative itself—namely a fiction in fiction and an existential crisis situation in the fictional reality—but "obscures the line separating the real and the virtual" (Taylor 2013: 84) also beyond the diegetic level. Just as the Cavern in the *diegesis*, *Plowing the Dark*, as a textual simulation, harbors the irreducible potential for an encounter with radical otherness. The process of reading the novel turns from an individual escape in sanitized fictionality into a being-thrown into precarious relationality; or, as Dewey holds: "within the aesthetic enterprise the reader comes to understand that every individual is part nevertheless of a vast, intricately, patterned whole" (149). Just as Klarpol and Martin start to realize their shared precariousness, the textual performance ex-poses the reader to the face of the other through a *figural trompe l'oeil* where "you simply reach the edge of a story" and "you see where things lead" in order to, then, "step through the broken symbols, into something brighter" (Powers 2000: 401), as the passage circumscribing the room of the Cave tellingly renders it. Looking through Martin and Klarpol's eyes, the reader, too, potentially begins to see, or read, other-wise. The *figural* re-vision at the interstices of the novel's narrative strands "allows the act of reading to become a change of consciousness" (Ickstadt 2012: 40); a shift whose "healing power consists in replacing compulsive and self-deluding fictions of coherence with more flexible ones in which the mind in all its fiction-making fragility is seen as part of a larger natural order that connects all living creatures" (38). Through its per-formative *figural* agency, the novel has both its characters and readers implicated in a vision of mutual responsibility instead of propagating crude individualist notions of independence (cf. Kley 465; Reinfandt 365); a responsibility that, faced with radical otherness's pathos, ex-poses an existential in-dependence, and, thereby, s(t)imulates in the reader *a response-ability beyond* ratio*nal re-cognition.*

Throughout *Plowing the Dark* precarious in-dependence prevails. The novel's sustained meditation on the capabilities of imagination dis-closes the *ratio*'s fantasy of an apotheosized supreme Self as a problematic self-delusion and, instead, ends with a vision of being-with-others, or even being-toward-the-other: human creativity is not exploited as a means of Self-realization, but rather serves as a s(t)imulator of relationality. Or, as the text eventually puts it with Spiegel's realization: "*Nothing I can make . . . makes much sense. Without someone to make it for*" (Powers 2000: 406). However, Powers's novel also shows that handing over the calculative control of the *ratio*nal view from *nowhere* to a possibility of a precarious vision from *now here*, as Nagel explains it, "would require an immediacy of feeling and attention to what is present that doesn't blend well with the complex, forward-looking pursuits of [what supposedly constitutes] a civilized creature" (223). The novel, nevertheless, asks for nothing less than a reconsideration of the reductionist scientific mode of relating to the (things of the) world as well as the understanding of civilization it entails. That is, as art-work, the novel's *poiētic* performance is not geared toward, or even bolstered by, the attainment of epistemological sovereignty. As Sally Hart argues in a different context, the text (en-)actively poses "a question of challenging the productivist ontology with the unpredictable, the irrecuperable, the radical other which shines in all its glorious alterity [i.e. otherness]—even if only for a moment" (n.pag.). Through an other-wise (in-)explicable *figural* act, *Plowing the Dark reverts* the RL's religious zeal, and, by way of its interstitial character, "performs something of a narrative miracle" (Szadziewicz 108) to bring forth an ungraspable precarious sameness where, always already, the other *presences*. Powers's novel shows that *ratio*nal re-cognition always remains irreducibly tied to the radical dis-closure of otherness which pries open (from within) the systemic confines of calculative reasoning.

With the miraculous scene toward the end of the text that challenges the confines of mimetic realism, *Plowing the Dark* emphasizes what Butler in *Frames of War* describes as the incapability of the frame to contain what it seeks to delimit: that which makes the inside of the frame possible is always something that simultaneously exceeds the frame and that does not fit in with established conceptions of things (cf. 9). Ultimately, Powers's novel unfolds how the Western techno-logical *en-framework* can never reach the *ratio*-systemic closure it claims to operate on. There always remains something which resists the calculative grasp characterizing a Western society that, as Baudrillard puts it, "is entirely dedicated to neutralizing otherness, to destroying the other as a natural point of reference in a vast flood of aseptic communication and interaction, of illusory exchange and contact" (139). The text ex-poses the danger of a "triumphant globalization [that sweeps] away all differences and all values, bringing into being an entirely in-different culture (or lack of it)" (2003: 91), to an existential precariousness, irreducible to an indifferent and non-differentiating techno-logic systematicity. Instead of promoting the indifferent vision of the RL, *Plowing the Dark* insists on being-in-difference, and is "[e]xpanding the interpersonal to a global scale" (Harris 274). The novel shows that even (from) within neoliberal globalization, there remains a potential for planetary entanglements beyond the horizon of a violent Western epistemology to unconceal themselves.

This also means that neither Powers's novel nor Baudrillard's philosophy hold that modern (Western) technology is to be demonized altogether. They rather trace out how the tension between *technē* and *poiēsis* is always at

work, even within the virtual environments of simulation's integral reality. "*Plowing the Dark* participates in the ongoing postmodernist critique
of representational thinking" (Harris 250) and insists on language's inherent *figurality*. If "the ultimate concern of *Plowing the Dark* is to encourage
readers to think beyond the conceptual confines of representational premises, such as mimesis, truthfulness, or objectivity" (Löffler 108), the text does
what "poststructuralist" or "postmodern" thought has been trying all along,
namely not to integrate the (things of the) world into the Self-sufficient digestive tract of the *ratio*, and, instead, hold open a path for encounters that
do not rob radical otherness of its sting. To conclude with the words of Butler, the novel outlines—further resonating with Baudrillard's thought—that

> If I am to lead a good life, it will be a life lived with others, a life that is no life
> without those others; I will not lose this *I* that I am; whoever I am will be trans-
> formed by my connections with others, since my dependency on another, and
> my dependability, are necessary in order to live and to live well. (2015a: 218)

(IN-)CONCLUSION: AN APOPHATIC (RE-)TURN

But because the necessities of action often oblige us to make a decision before we
have had the leisure to examine things so carefully, it must be admitted that the life
of man is very often subject to error in particular cases; and we must, in conclusion,
recognize the infirmity and weakness of our nature.
— René Descartes, *Meditations*

(Re-)Turn

At the beginning of this project, you were assured that what can be called
reading other-wise does not constitute a systematic framework for a coming
to (fixed) terms with otherness. At this point, (re-)turning to this assertion
and recalling Julia Kristeva's far-reaching question that has served as one of
the guiding im-pulses of the previous meditations is in order. She explains
that "[t]he foreigner [as other], as it has often been noted, can only be defined in negative fashion," and then asks: "Negative with respect to what?"
(1991: 95). She implies that the prevalent negative renderings of otherness
in the (hegemonic) Western tradition stem from a discursive foil, or backdrop, against which otherness is defined; be this racial, social, political, religious, or a combination of such categories. It is the very epistemological
urge to define the other that requires such discursive framing. Talk of the
negativity or opacity of otherness takes as its point of departure one's being
bound to discursive systematicity; a systematicity that is an extension of the
rational cogito, that is, of a proper self. This book, however, has shown that
this point of departure is neither absolute nor necessary and that it is, in *fact*,
possible to read in response to an insoluble pathos of radical otherness; that
it is possible to read decidedly other-wise.

You might wonder what this entails regarding Kristeva's question. What
happens when one reads it other-wise? It brings forth an apophatic (re-)turn
vis-à-vis a negating systematicity: an ab-usively playful negation of a negating impetus. This book is *not* an attempt to define the other(s) in the context of transnational perspectives in American Studies. Instead, it has shown
how radical otherness always already exceeds such contexts from within.

This means that the readings in this book do *not* just trace the discursive construction or representation of otherness, but de-scribe how the other (en-)actively *presences* in event-like singularity. Presence is *not* to be conceived as the traditional notion of a static, logocentric Idea. Both plural and verbal, it designates a dynamic *presencing* that repeatedly reveals itself in its withdrawing from discursive fixity. This is also to say that with its stress on the aesthetic, this study does *not* erect just another (en-)framework for judging the other according to established systemic categories of taste; as modes of sensory/sensual perception, aesthetics operationalizes a sense-sensitized knowing that ever-supplements *ratio*nal (re-)cognition. The chapters do *not* read literature as constituting another closed-off archive of discursive representation: as that strange system allowing for *poiētic* transformations to emerge from inside the systematicity that constitutes its system, literature dis-closes an existential space for a *figural presencing* of radical otherness. If you expected conclusive findings, this (re-)turn is maybe going to strike you as disappointing. Engaging with radical otherness, without robbing it of its sting, does not grant such simple satisfaction and remains happily inconclusive.

(De-)Tour

Donald Pease writes that "[t]ransnational initiatives can refer to efforts to expand the exercise of power or to impede it; they can describe the reach of multinational formations; they can also inaugurate memberships in a global civil society" (2011: 5). This study introduced you to these promising as well as problematic potentials of transnationalism. To avoid repeating the pitfalls of exceptionalism and turning the paradigm into another, expanded version of Manifest Destiny, the book calls for an epistemological re-con-*figuring*. With Walter Mignolo's border gnosis functioning as a critical interface that offers "a decolonial perspective seeking to avoid and overcome methodological nationalism and epistemic Occidentalism" (Roth 252), as you have read at the beginning, this project wishes to unfold a way for de-limiting American Studies' epistemological framework. Taking as its point of departure the critiques regarding the so-called "transnational turn" in the field, this book sets out to circumvent a hegemony of Western reasoning. (R)evolving around Gayatri Spivak's concept of creative sabotage, or ab-use, Bernhard Waldenfels's notion of radical otherness, and Jean-François Lyotard's figural, the parts, therefore, initiate specific critical dialogues, and urge you to enter these dialogues: they initiate dia-logues between works of critical thinking and works of literary writing to contribute to a dehierarchization of the relationship of philosophy and literature where it becomes possible to conceive not only of a critical writing, but also of a form of *poiētic* literary thinking; a critical mode of *relating* to phenomena that remains responsive to the pathos of otherness (en-)actively voicing particular claims and concerns: you were solicited to read other-wise.

Building on said de-limitation, *regarding* matters of presence, this book emphasizes the potentials of aesthetics. In an attempt of a "re-definition of the aesthetic" (Ickstadt 2016: 14)—beyond its ideological harnessing—as an important dimension of cultural analysis, it draws on the Greek *sense* of *aísthēsis* as (possibly everyday) sensual/sensory modes of perception which ever-coincide with and supplement processes of *rational* (re-)cognition. Highlighting this irreducible entanglement, radical otherness reveals itself to you as a form of *presencing*. As such, otherness does not merely signify a presence of absence; it does not only appear as a gap (which it certainly does when pitted against cognition) (cf. Lösch and Paul 2016: 332): in the embrace of subject and object, mind and body, rationality and sensuality, otherness *figures* as dynamic *presencing*—non-graspable within the *ratio*, but affective (from) inside. This calls for a becoming-other of cognition/perception itself. Just as otherness is thought as always relational in this book, presence, here, is thought as always motional. As such, the *presencing* of radical otherness potentially stimulates and/or retrieves within you modes of sense-sensitization which undercut the occidental binary opposition of sense and sensibility.

The part "Ghosts in the Archive" takes its point of departure from an account of the role of (written) language during the so-called Conquest of the "New World" and its aftermath to in-volve you into a dia-logue between Anna Lee Walters's novel *Ghost Singer* and Diana Taylor's work; and, in particular, her distinction between the concepts of archive and repertoire. More precisely, the part outlines how the ephemeral performative workings of the repertoire *figure* also in literary works of art and how this necessitates a radical re-*vision* of Western conceptions of historicity and temporality. Re-negotiating the relationship between materiality and time, the part unfolds how the other *presences* even in the archive. As a live spectral repertoire, Walters's narrative harbors an (en-)active *sense* of what Gerald Vizenor calls *native* survivance; a potential that blurs the boundaries between life and death, mind and body, as well as archive and repertoire: unfolding a nexus of spectral recurrence, the text has past and present commingle and questions established concepts of archival fixity. Thereby, the part attempts to show you that Transnational American Studies must begin by coming to terms with an often-sidelined colonialist past whose effects can still be felt today; by coming to terms with the fact that, from an Indigenous perspective, what is today called the United States has always already been transnational.

"Being-Two with the Other" also develops the peculiar figural-performative workings of language, this time by enacting a dia-logue between Theresa Hak Kyung Cha's *Dictée* and the philosophy of Luce Irigaray. Elaborating on the corporeal dimensions of (literary) texts, the part outlines your relationality to the other with the help of Irigaray's concept of being-two; a relationality, countering the phallic rule of the one, where the radically other is always already irreducibly, indivisibly, and bodily entangled with the self. Renegotiating ideas of universalism and essentialism in Irigaray's work in the context of transnationalism, this part argues that Mignolo's concept of planetary conviviality as pluriversality should not be understood as mere multiplication of separable universalisms, but rather be read as an inherently relational embrace. Therefore, within the part's dia-logue, Cha's *Dictée figures* as a creative sabotage of phallogocentric reasoning that does not simply do away with the Western tradition of thought by installing yet another form of counter-discourse. Mimicking hegemonic colonial languages, the text's decolonial *écriture féminine* ab-usively plays with occidental notions of essentialism and universality to embrace you in the moist lips of its textual passage: deconstructing the relation between vision and touch, *Dictée*, per-forming an embodied shamanistic ritual, *figures* as a vaginal space — a corporeal dichotomous locus — where the other *presences* in being-two.

Taking its point of departure from the assertion that a transnational paradigm implicitly calls for an-other mode of being-in-the-world, "Poetic Dwelling in the Borders" unfolds an ab-usive dia-logue between Michael Ondaatje's *Anil's Ghost* and Martin Heidegger's problematic thought. Introducing you to a creative sabotage of Heidegger's terms in conjunction with the work of Alexis Shotwell, the part develops a form of attuned sensuous knowing that, unlike Gumbrecht's notion of oscillation, conceives of meaning and presence in the *counterturning* motion of world and earth. The transnational, thereby, does not *figure* as an ideal u-topic non-place, but rather as an a-topic dynamic being between place and planet. The art-work(ing) of *Anil's Ghost* mirrors this dynamic within its rendering of an epistemological struggle between so-called Western science and a supposedly Eastern folklore. Per-forming a sense-sensitizing process that stresses the relevance of the haptic, the novel deconstructs seemingly oppositional epistemologies and interweaves them in its poetic textual space. Urging you to read other-wise, namely by way of a haptic-sensuous g(r)azing, the part shows how Ondaatje's text undoes transnationalisms that are no more than disguised forms of Western expansionism, and outlines, instead, a form of border dwelling equally open to particularity and planetarity at the same time.

Extending this book's take on "poststructuralist" or "postmodern" thinking,

"Precarious In-Dividuality and the Other" negotiates the relationship of presence and simulation regarding a critique of modern forms of individualism through a dia-logue between Richard Powers's *Plowing the Dark* and the thought of Jean Baudrillard. Returning to the theory of simulacra in connection to the more recent work of Judith Butler and Bernard Stiegler, you are ex-posed to the decidedly social quality of Baudrillard's ideas. Tying Butler's concept of precariousness to the latter's notion of reversibility, the part ultimately de-scribes a mode of *technopoiētic* art-work-ing, which affectively alleviates seemingly demonizing critiques of (digital) technology without, however, failing to draw attention also to its potential dangers. The part unfolds this via its reading of Powers's text as an interstitial space of textual simulation where the other potentially *presences*. The novel challenges crudely Cartesian notions of objectivity and also critiques a violent epistemological impetus of high definition. It does so by interweaving this violent form of thought with an existential situation of high (corporeal) precariousness. Emphasizing this entanglement, the part in-volves you within a sense-sensitized in-dividual relationality with the other between the virtual and the actual: drawing, once more, on the notion of *technopoiēsis*, it conceives of a possibility to read the potential of (literary) simulation other-wise.

(Dis-)Close

In ritualistic fashion, throughout all chapters, this book re-*iterates* its central claims concerning the other presences: "each time in the same way and each time differently, one more time" (Derrida 1992: 67) — ever (a-)new. It invites you to join in its meditations; to heed the pact which it in-vokes; to continue reading other-wise. And this also goes for this project itself regarding the ways the in-dividual chapters resonate with one an-other: they do not constitute neatly separable, closed-off unities, but merely outline pre-liminary constellations in this book's kaleidoscopic con-*figuring*.

Challenging the neat teleology from original beginning to absolute ending, this project "begins" its analyses with a discussion of the potentials of language in the context of iterability, recurrence, and playful *native* simulation and *survivance* — the concepts that will have recurred within the chapter with which the analyses "end." The book itself *figures* as a spectral nexus. Challenging notions of the validity of statically fixed wholeness by moving from a Navajo healing ceremony to the creatively sabotaging mimicry of a Korean shamanistic ritual, this project alludes to its own dynamic interstitiality. The book itself *figures* as a fluid passage. Challenging concepts of the centralized, and centralizing, perspective of Western oculocentrism by flowing from the discussion of vision and touch via the speculum's concave mirror to the negotiation of an occidentalized forensic gaze in relation to an attuned hapticity, this project outlines a process of sense-senistization. The book itself *figures* as a g(r)azing experience. Challenging reductions of the globe to an expanded Western trans-nation-state by turning from the irreducible interrelation of particularity and planetarity to a recalibration of the relationship between presence and simulation, this project s(t)imulates the potential of poetic dwelling in the borders. The book itself *figures* as a *technopoiētic* virtuality chamber. Challenging the neat teleology from original beginning to absolute ending, this project "ends" its analyses with a discussion of the potentials of language in the context of precariousness, reversibility, and a *poiētic* virtual encounter with the other—the concepts that will have recurred within the chapter with which the analyses "begin." The book itself *figures* as an interface where all chapters are always already resonating with *one an-other*.

This study operationalizes a relational mode of reading from the interstices, passages, precincts of place and planet, and *technopoiētic* spaces: (de-)touring in the spectral *revenance* of the past, a being-two between pathos and response, a *counterturning* of world and earth in sensuous attunement, and the irreducible reversibility of technological frameworks, it (dis-)closes with a call for an-other (re-)turn to the *presencing* of radical otherness. As such, the project does not constitute a closed-off whole, but *per-forms an open dia-logue between me and you.*

Introduction: (B)ordering Principles: Negotiating the Parameters

1. Throughout my book, the term "Western" (capitalized) refers to a hegemonic epistemological framework that provides the parameters of acceptable thinking within the so-called West. As will become apparent below, my usage of this term is related to what Latin Americanist Walter Mignolo describes as the "modern/colonial world system" (2000: 11)—an epistemological horizon geared toward the levelling of all deviating forms of knowledge. In what follows, this epistemological framework, and the term "Western" used to indicate it, will be thoroughly de-framed—that is, challenged—from various angles via engaging with forms of radical otherness.

2. This terminological way of going about things also picks up on Judith Butler's insistence that the use of specific terms within certain power regimes "does not entail that we ought never to make use of such terms, as if such terms could only and always reconsolidate the oppressive regimes of power by which they are spawned. On the contrary, precisely because such terms have been produced and constrained within such regimes, they ought to be repeated in directions that reverse and displace their originating aims" (2011: 83). I concur with Ann Laura Stoler who has recently insisted that critical thinking is not simply about dismissing problematical concepts, but that "thinking otherwise is to inhabit them differently" (9). In the terms of my project, this is to say that in the book at hand, the terms "presence," "otherness," "aesthetics," "transnational," and even "literature," undergo an ab-usive twist. I also retain some of these terms in order not to subscribe to certain trends in academia: instead of (quasi-teleologically) turning to the next new or fancy term, I would rather like to (re-)turn to certain (more or less) established terms and probe their still not yet unfolded potentialities.

3. Briefly stated, American exceptionalism can be defined as an ideological discourse promoting the belief in the unique and predestined status of the United States as well as its inherent cultural superiority in contrast to other nations. For a more in-depth definition that considers American exceptionalism's religious, political, and economic dimension, as well as an overview on the historical genesis of the concept, its impact, and exceptionalism's entanglement with the project of American Studies, see Heike Paul's *The Myths that Made America* (14ff.).

4. In the English translation of his *Phenomenology of the Alien*, Bernhard Waldenfels writes that "[w]e often speak of 'otherness' when we mean 'alienness.' In other Western languages that do not have the rich semantic field provided by the German word *fremd*, the question of alienness is usually treated as the *question of the Other* or as *la question de l'Autre*" (2006: 72). While the translators of *Phenomenology of the Alien*, in fact, choose to render the German *fremd* as "alien," I am deliberately going to use the term "other" throughout my book to retain a terminology more familiar to literary and cultural studies

scholars—although I still have in mind what Waldenfels means by "alienness." That this move is not entirely arbitrary becomes clear as Waldenfels himself, when speaking in English, uses the terms "alien" and "other" interchangeably—as also the title of his lecture "The Question of the Other" (2007) indicates. However, again, just like Waldenfels himself, I would like to emphasize that, in my own argument, "otherness" must not be understood in an exclusively constructivist sense; it designates a phenomenon that always (also) exceeds such a kind of framework.

5. My translation; the original German reads: "Das Fremde ist *mehr* und *anderes* als das, was sich 'repräsentieren' läßt, doch ist es, was es ist, *nicht ohne* all dies" (1999b: 149).

6. Concerning my drawing on "poststructuralist" and/or "postmodern" philosophy, I ask from the start for something that I can only begin to show and explicate as my arguments are unfolded throughout the following chapters: to read "poststructuralism" and "postmodernism" other-wise—that is, beyond their ossified American renditions, to uncover its potentialities as "'borderline' inquiries" (Hutcheon 11) that pry open notions of Western logocentrism from within, namely via "a rethinking and putting into question of the bases of our western modes of thinking" (ibid. 8). Instead of adding to a "nihilistic reduction of meaning to non-meaning, not to say nonsense," which for Eid "deconstruction has led to in its application" (36), I will insist on an irreducible doubleness of *sense* (namely through its relatability both to the aesthetic as well as to the semiotic); a dichotomous doubleness of sensuality and rationality in which meaning itself *figures* other-wise. As such, the project at hand does not attest, once more, the "'loss of meaning'" (38) but asks for rethinking the meaningness of meaning (more precisely, its being meaning, its (en-)active mean-ing).

7. My translation; the original German reads: "Je wichtiger Gewißheit und Sicherheit für das Bewußtsein werden, desto bedrohlicher erscheint auf der anderen Seite alles, was aus der sicheren Ordnung herausfällt und gleichwohl fordert, beachtet zu werden, was—als Fremdes—nicht auf das unerschütterliche Fundament der Gewißheit des 'cogito ergo sum' gegründet ist" (2012: 14).

8. My translation; the original German reads: "Es ist das *Eröffnende*; das Denken und seine Begriffe, die Zeichen und Symbole das Nachträgliche" (39).

9. Gumbrecht's qualification that one can only perceive presence in "conditions of 'extreme temporality'" (58) does not alleviate this problem. That I am not arguing against sensory/sensual approaches in general—quite to the contrary—will become clear. My critique is geared solely toward the appropriative assumption of the *absolute* accessibility of presence as substantial presence through sensuality.

10. Instead of a doing away with meaning altogether, or juxtaposing it with "meaningless" presence, taking the figural into account implies a fundamentally different sense of meaning, where presence, even though not according to the standards of Western reason, is decidedly meaningful. Timothy Clark succinctly summarizes this point when he writes that there is no "reduction *to* meaning, only a reduction *of* meaning" (1992: 125).

11. Throughout this book, I will employ the verb "to *figure*" (in italics) to indicate the workings of the figural.

12. Despite—or rather precisely due to—its character as an "anti-determinist, acausal force of eventhood, of inexplicability" (2005: 3), as Clark once again puts it, "the singularity at issue here is not just part of a merely negative claim about the literary's resistance to meaning" but rather "something positive" and "irreplaceable" (8).

13. Unfortunately, it is correct that the current state of Western aesthetic theory still betrays a certain obliviousness toward the question of the other: "it should be recognized," as Emory Elliott notes, "that a wide range of discussions of subjects related to aesthetics and culture are being carried on with little reference of subjects related to multiculturalism" and connected "issues of ethnic and racial difference" (8). A quick glance at several contemporary publications confirms this impression. None of the 62 entries in Berys Gaut and Dominic McIver Lopes's critical companion (*The Routledge Companion to Aesthetics*)—divided into sections dealing with the history, theory, and challenges (!) of aesthetics, as well as discussions of individual art forms—explicitly focuses on questions of otherness. The selection of the 55 texts in Steven Cahn and Aaron Meskin's supposedly comprehensive anthology (*Aesthetics: A Comprehensive Anthology*) exhibits a similar lack. It illustrates that the revision of the philosophical canon is (still) far behind. Recent publications, such as Sianne Ngai's *Our Aesthetic Categories*, with its introduction of the zany, cute, and interesting as new aesthetic modes, as well as Jacques Rancière's *Aisthesis*, with its critique of the regime of the arts, set out to rectify some of the wrongs Americanists accuse the field of aesthetics of and point in the right direction. But they ultimately also remain largely Eurocentric in scope and neglect the issue of cultural difference. As useful as all these publications may be, this short overview underscores Elliot's assertion. Therefore, a thorough critique of the field of aesthetics certainly continues to be justified and necessary.

14. My translation; the original German reads: "Fremdwerden der eigenen Erfahrung" setting in when "es nicht durch Rationalisierungen überdeckt wird" (2008: 42).

15. The compatibility of aesthetics with border thinking becomes even more apparent when—in reference to Mikhail Bakhtin's work—Thomas Claviez paraphrases Mignolo's notion of sense sensitivity as a "polyphonic 'openness' of the aesthetic" that "seems virtually predisposed to . . . represent the multi-voiced plurality of the innumerable local, ethnic, and gender groups that vie for a voice and recognition" (Claviez xix).

16. What Waldenfels means when he speaks of a becoming other of sensual perception is that when we are faced with radical otherness, and resist simple *rational* re-cognition, the other *makes itself felt* in the form of affective incursions (from) beyond aesthetic categorization that do not leave the senses unchanged (cf. 1999a: 126) or, to maintain his own voice: "Fremdheit macht sich auch im Bereich der Sinne geltend in Form von Abweichungen, Störungen, Beunruhigungen, von Gegenrhythmen, blinden Flecken, Echowirkungen, Heterophonien, Heterotopien und Gleichgewichtsstörungen, in all dem, was aus dem Rahmen fällt, den un seine autonome Ästhetik vorgibt" (ibid. 14f.). This also ties in with Luce Irigaray's call for a practical application of this insight when it comes to approaching otherness: "We have to open our ears to other meanings, other sounds, other accents and rhythms in speaking, other tones and pronunciations. We also have to open our eyes to other gestures, behaviors, but also other clothes and ways of investing the body. We have to accustom ourselves to other tastes, other fragrances or flavors, and even to other manners of meeting with: touching or not touching the other, greeting with a sound, a word or a gesture" (2002a: 111).

17. F.E. Sutcliffe elaborates on Descartes's attitude toward the senses as follows: "Descartes . . . had rejected the validity of the evidence of the senses: we cannot say of a material object that it has the property of heat or cold, for these are not clear and distinct ideas. The only clear idea one can have of objects is that they are extended in height, depth

and breadth, that is to say the idea of them which can be expressed mathematically" (18). That is, everything that does not fit into the systematic horizon of mathematics is regarded as deficient concerning the attainment of knowledge. This horizon can only be conceived within the *cogito*, as Sutcliffe further explains: "The Cogito is a first principle from which Descartes will now deduce all that follows. . . . Moreover, he knows himself only as a thinking being, he is therefore assured that the soul and the body are entirely distinct. Since he has been able to understand his own being and essence without yet knowing anything about the world outside him, it follows that his self—or soul—is completely independent of the outside world, mind is distinct from and superior to matter" (19).

18. I cannot possibly provide, here, a full-fledged analysis of the critical genealogy that challenges the dichotomy between rationality/sensitivity in the Western philosophical tradition. For a, as the author himself proclaims, "ruthlessly short," but nevertheless significantly more substantial overview of this genealogy than offered here, I would therefore like to refer the respective passage in Martin Seel's *Ästhetik des Erscheinens* (15ff.).

19. My translation; the original German reads: "Je dichter die Menschen . . . mit dem kategorialen Netz übersponnen haben, desto gründlicher haben sie das Staunen über jenes Andere sich abgewöhnt, mit steigender Vertrautheit ums Fremde sich betrogen" (191). The grammatical object of "übersponnen" in this sentence is not simply elided here, but also missing in the German original. This implies a play on words with the second possible meaning of the German verb "spinnen," namely as signifying something like "to be bonkers."

20. As Wolfgang Schoberth has shown: "Mit der ästhetischen Theorie Adornos kann die künstlerische Produktion als Versuch verstanden werden, die verdinglichten Weltdeutungen zu überwinden; die Rezeption von Kunst erscheint dann als die Erfahrung eines veränderten Umgangs mit Welt" (11). The project at hand extrapolates on this insight insofar as it outlines that literary works of art—their art-work—(en-)actively unfolds potentially everyday modes of perception and being-in-the-world beyond the elitist institutional apparatus of which literary texts are (necessarily and subversively) part: from within an aesthetic systematicity, art-works potentially serve as reminders of sidelined aesthetic modes of relating to (the things of) the world beyond crude objectification.

21. Throughout this book, the term "*rati*onal" serves to indicate a restrictive form of rationality in the confines of the *ratio*. That is, with the help of this term, I am not dismissing rationality altogether but only its Western appropriation.

22. Mignolo himself rejects geographical determinism and writes: "I am emphasizing that loci of enunciation are not given but enacted. I am not assuming that *only* people coming from such and such a place could do X. Let me insist that I am not casting the argument in deterministic terms but in the open realm of logical possibilities, of historical circumstances and personal sensibilities" (2000: 115).

23. Krzysztof Ziarek's book *The Force of Art* constitutes an example of this usage. The reason for adding the prefix "post-" is the assumption that "because aesthetics tries to describe artworks from the perspective of a subject confronting an external art object, the aesthetic approach begins always-already 'too late'" (Thomson 56), and that one needs "to move from a modern aesthetic experience of an art object to a genuinely postmodern encounter with a work of art, so that we can thereby learn from art how to transcend modernity from within" (63). While I certainly support this goal in itself, I believe that

this type of prefixation ultimately leads into the wrong direction and presents itself as counterproductive toward the initial radical quest.

24. Derrida himself explicitly corrects critics who misunderstand his famous dictum *il n'y a pas de hors-texte* as saying that everything is predetermined by a static and closed system of instrumentalized language when he writes: "The critique of logocentrism is above all else the search for the 'other' and the 'other of language'" (1984: 123).

25. This is not to say that the encounter with the other precedes consciousness, but only a form of consciousness dominated by the hierarchical ordering of the supreme *ratio*.

26. Klaus Lösch elaborates on this: "Im Vergleich zum pragmatischen Diskurs vermag der literarische Diskurs eher das kulturell Fremde bzw. die kulturelle Alterität anderer Gruppen auf nicht-aneignende Weise zu präsentieren. Während der pragmatische Diskurs der Herstellung von Konsistenz verpflichtet ist, gilt dies für fiktionale Literatur nur bedingt. Da literarische Sprache eine welterschaffende Funktion hat, ist ihr auch ein besonderes Moment des Spiels und des handlungsentlastenden Experiments zu eigen" (42). This also resembles, to some extent, Antje Kley's description of literature as transcultural contact zone, which is connected to a claim reminiscent of Waldenfels's logic of otherness between pathos and response. She explicates that "das Lesen von fiktionalen Texten als Fremdheitserfahrung, als ein *Sich-selbst-fremd-werden*, als *eine in Frage stellende Präsenzerfahrung* und Begegnung mit einem Anderen beschreibbar ist" (2013: 232; my emphases); a becoming other where the modalities of perception and, consequently, the conventions of understanding are being repeatedly challenged and transformed (cf. Clark 2005: 125). My project seeks to build on these insights and resituate them within a transnational context to further uncover and/or stress the relevance of literary writing's epistemological dimension, particularly concerning the question of the other.

27. Heather Love clarifies that "[i]n place of a depth hermeneutics, they [surface readers] offer descriptions of surfaces, operations, and interactions. In doing so, they suggest an alternate model of reading that does not depend on the ethical exemplarity of the interpreter or messenger" (375).

28. An alleviating factor should be pointed out. My study does not restrict itself to English or shun other languages altogether. Particularly immigrant writer Theresa Hak Kyung Cha's *Dictée* is, although mostly written in English, a thoroughly multilingual text. Next to English she integrates French, Latin, Greek, Japanese and Korean passages into her work. Walters, Ondaatje, and Powers, respectively, weave Navajo, Sinhalese, and Persian, as well as Arabic expressions into their texts.

29. Each chapter is going to focus more thoroughly on the ideas of one thinker in dialogue with one literary text. However, as the structure of the project makes clear, thereby, this book does not seek to solidify the eminent position of established great thinkers, but rather to deconstruct such a position—albeit without rejecting or disregarding the thought of such (more or less) canonical thinkers altogether—by always contextualizing and supplementing them with the work of other thinkers. It needs to be stressed, once more, that all chapters unfold (or enfold) by way of ab-use: that is, this book does not just celebrate great names; these names should rather be regarded as pre-liminary markers that will be relativized—or, more precisely—relationalized throughout the course of the book's performance. By teasing out untapped potentials from within the work of some very problematic figures by way of reading other-wise, the respective thinking is supposed to become effectively (and radically) other. In ab-use, Taylor does not just remain Taylor,

Irigaray not just Irigaray, Heidegger not Heidegger, and Baudrillard not Baudrillard. They always appear in the light of the literary text discussed, just as, vice versa, each literary text is read from a chiastic relationship with a specific thinker's work. Thereby, I pick up, once more, on Hutcheon's description of the "postmodern" as "an energizing rethinking of margins and edges, of what does not fit in the humanly constructed notion of center. Such interrogations of the impulse to sameness (or single otherness) and homogeneity. . . . This is not a rejection of the former values in favor of the latter; it is a rethinking of each in light of the others" (42). There is never just one but always (at least) two figures in each chapter.

Part One: Ghosts in the Archive: Negotiating Historicity and Survivance with Diana Taylor and Anna Lee Walters's Ghost Singer

1. For the sake of convenience and variation, and despite the problematical political implications, this chapter uses the collective terms "Native American" and "American Indian" (with and without the national qualifier), as well as "Indigenous population" synonymously. Furthermore, occasionally the terms "native" (non-capitalized) and "*indian*" (italicized and non-capitalized) appear through the analyses. These are Native scholar Gerald Vizenor's coinages and are used with their specific meaning in mind. Whenever possible, specific tribal affiliations replace the collective terminology as a gesture of appreciation regarding the rich variety of Indigenous American cultures.

Chapter 1: En-Active Textuality

1. Historian Gesine Krüger also confirms this active perpetuation of vanishing beyond the borders of the United States in a broader colonial context: "So ist es ein koloniales Paradox, dass die angeblich aussterbenden 'Ureinwohner' und 'Naturvölker' in vielfacher Hinsicht diskursiv und als soziale Gruppen erst im Zug ebenjenes Kolonisationsprozesses geschaffen worden sind, der auch für ihren Untergang sorgte, indem er ihnen jede Lebensgrundlage außerhalb des Kolonialstaates entzog und die Überlebenden der Kolonialkriege, der eingeschleppten Krankheiten und gewaltförmigen Landraubes zu Relikten aus der Urzeit erklärte, deren Schicksal es sein würde, in Reservaten konserviert oder innerhalb der Kolonialgesellschaft assimiliert zu werden" (480). The treatment of Native Americans at the hands of the European invaders *figures* as an instance of a larger Western political epistemological configuration of colonization of which the United States, too, is a part; a configuration that, as already mentioned, Walter Mignolo refers to as the modern/colonial world system.

2. A passage from Derrida's *Of Grammatology* sheds some light on Heidegger's critique of the relationship between what the German philosopher calls "being" and language: "Heidegger reminds us constantly that the sense of being is neither the word 'being' nor the concept of being. But as that sense is nothing outside of language and the language of words, it is tied to a particular word or to a particular system of language (concesso non dato), at least to the possibility of the word in general. And to the possibility of its irreducible simplicity . . . Does a modern linguistics, a science of signification breaking the unity of the word and breaking with its alleged irreducibility, still have anything to do with 'language?' Heidegger would probably doubt it" (21).

3. Concerning the continuance of performance in its documentation, Bamford mentions Marina Abramović's *Seven 'Easy' Pieces* (2005) and Vito Acconci's *Seedbed* (1972).

In both cases, Bamford argues, inexact forms of documentation, for instance in newspaper articles, did not simply fix the performances on paper and annul its ephemeral character; they rather extended them. He quotes Abramović herself, explaining that inexact forms of documentation brought forth a "total mystification" of her art and opened up "a huge space of projection and speculation" (30). According to Bamford, this space then constitutes "a realm that is conducive to the contingent" and "a lack of certainty reigns", where the destabilizing effect, which was the aim of many performances, can be continued" (ibid.). To him, this subversive potential alludes to the workings of the figural within discourse.

4. This aftermath, again, is shaped by Cartesian inflections. In fact, Cartesiansim, with its split of mind from body, provided the crucial philosophical extension for the ongoing — albeit in different guises — occidental Conquest's dominating impetus: "As mind, infinitely separated from a world which is matter, the role of man can only be that of dominating his surroundings, of becoming 'master and possessor of Nature'. However much Cartesian dualism of mind and matter has bedevilled [sic] philosophy, it opened the doors to the development of modern science" (Sutcliffe 21). The dominating impetus that had gained momentum with the so-called Conquest of the Americas was also to guide subsequent developments in Europe: "What characterizes the men of the generation of Descartes is above all the will to dominate, to control events, to eliminate chance and the irrational. This attitude is present in every field: the political, the military, the scientific" (ibid.). As Walters's *Ghost Singer* illustrates, this attitude is still largely — albeit, again, in different guises — prevalent throughout Western thinking.

5. Taylor certainly raises a valid point of criticism concerning notions of performance as solely discursive in nature without any possibility of (figural) excess. This chapter's argument (and this entire book) shares this critique but attempts to develop it in a different direction. The relation of discourse and performance as thought within the project of reading other-wise will be further elaborated, by way of Judith Butler, at the beginning of the next chapter.

6. Lyotard describes the relative stasis of the text, which nonetheless gives rise to the dynamics of figurality, as an "immobile mobility" (2011: 3) that "continually fall[s] into obilivion in the process of signification" (3). Again, Taylor's instrumentalist notion of writing — with its sole emphasis on communication and cognition — does not allow for this paradoxical poetic force that cannot be "read" but only seen. Only grazed the corpus of a written text reveals itself to be more than archival matter.

Chapter 2: Native American Revenance
1. Biologist Richard Dawkins's reaction to Indigenous claims and convictions concerning the repatriation of the so-called Kennewick Man, a supposedly 9,000-year-old skeleton found in Washington State in 1996, confirms that the attitude of Newsome and Evans is not restricted to the confines of Walters's novel, but an ongoing reality of a Western delusion. Robert Eaglestone describes how, in his book *Unweaving the Rainbow*, "Dawkins is extremely unsympathetic to these [American Indian] others, to these other beliefs that he sees as clearly wrong. Indeed, he finds them laughable. His scientism has comprehended the Native American beliefs [founded on oral traditions] as 'superstition' and as 'false beliefs' — the opposite to his 'science' and 'true belief' — and so he is no longer attending to them as others to his discourse, but only as terms within his discourse" (191).

2. Several laws preceded and paved the way for NAGPRA. The Antiquities Act of 1906 constitutes the first legal effort to control the looting of Native American graves, making it a crime to damage, destroy, or rearrange artifacts. Human remains, however, were exempt from this law. In 1935, the Historic Sites Act granted the Secretary of the Interior the power to control federal preservation; in 1960, the Reservoir Salvage Act established that the Secretary of the Interior must be informed prior to any construction work threatening to destroy significant archaeological sites. In the eyes of legislation, Native American burial sites did not possess such significance. Only in 1979 did the Archaeological Resources Protection Act rectify this situation by requiring prior notification to Native American tribes of possible dangers regarding burial sites or important cultural places on federal land. However, the act did not grant the Indigenous population any rights of repatriation of items found on this land (cf. Talbert 175ff.). Furthermore, these acts did not cover any items already in the possession of federal institutions such as the Smithsonian.

3. An entry from the diary of the anthropologist Ales Hridlicka, for decades chair and curator at the Smithsonian, confirms the indifference and immorality regarding the treatment of Native human remains and artifacts at the hands of Western science: "Open three older [graves]—in two the remains are too fresh yet, but from the third secure a good female Eskimo skeleton, which pack in a new heavy pail left there on occasion of the last funeral. Then back, farther out to avoid notice through swamps and over moss. . . . Reach home very wet and tired. Have to undress and, wrapped in blanket, dry clothes and underwear about the stove" (quoted in Pensley 46).

4. According to modes of approaching the (things of the) world shaped by Cartesianism, such phenomena are completely inconceivable as any cosmological implications, there, are devoured in the systemic horizon of the *cogito*; a mathematical epistemological horizon that constitutes a break with previous cosmological reasoning: "By excluding all forms, qualities and forces, and by reducing matter to its mathematical expression, Descartes, at the same time, ruins the very notion of the ancient cosmos. Henceforward, *the only spectacle which presents itself to the inquiring eye of man* is that of matter agitated by movements according to mathematical laws" (Sutcliffe 21; my emphasis). It does not come as a surprise that Native cosmologies, from this perspective, were just as inacceptable as, for instance, ancient or medieval cosmological conceptualizations of the world.

5. The avid reader of Derrida may want to diagnose a contradiction regarding the relationship between dates and haunting in *Specters of Marx* and the essays in *Sovereignties in Question*. In the former, the French philosopher writes that "haunting is historical, to be sure, but it is not dated, it is never docilely given a date in the chain of presents, day after day, according to the instituted order of a calendar" (3). However, Derrida here clearly means a(n) (purely) archival form of ascribing dates that serves to ensure the pastness of the past and not a poetic *dated*-ness harboring the *presencing* of the past as a future anterior which conflates repertoire and archive in the strange institution called "literature." The poetically inscribed date, residing between singularity and iterability, is never docile, but haunted and exceeds the calendar's institutionality.

6. Resonating with the argument at hand and extrapolating on the connection to US violence in Vietnam, in her essay "'Branches of the Same Tree': Chicano/a Vietnam Solidarity and the Making of Aztlán," Carmen Brosig traces phenomena of transnational solidarity between the liberation movements of the 1960s within the United States. She argues that the Chicano/a Movement and the struggles for liberation from US interference

and occupation in Vietnam are both "reactions against decades of suppression" which "revealed broader patterns of colonization that became manifest locally but at the same time fostered or produced counter-hegemonic positions, both local and global" (79). Brosig's essay is part of a larger research project on transnational solidarity in the 1960s between marginalized groups claiming independence from the United States from within and the oppressed Vietnamese population.

7. One might interject that museums have seen significant change since the publication of Walters's text. This is certainly correct. The most prominent example is the establishment of the Smithsonian's National Museum of the American Indian (NMAI). First planned in 1989 and eventually opened in 2004, it almost appears as a direct reaction to Walters's novel. The creation of the NMAI attests to a willingness to change museum practice regarding the representation of the tribes. For the first time, Native Americans themselves have designed and selected the contents of the displays in collaboration with the Smithsonian. Like *Ghost Singer*, the exhibits at the NMAI emphasize Native American voices and promote multiple tribal perspectives over a reductive and collectivist one. This marks a major shift in museology, although many institutions remain unaffected by these developments. Furthermore, the location of the museum on the National Mall in Washington, DC, in connection with the NMAI's silence concerning the consequences of colonization, once more harbors the danger of Termination through a celebratory integration of Indigenous perspectives into the national narrative of the United States. One can critically ask with Amy Lonetree whether these changes are sufficient: "Will the new museum challenge people to reflect on the atrocities committed against Native people and on those responsible for such actions? *The new museum needs to challenge the very core of American consciousness.* American identity is defined by what took place on the frontier and the supposed disappearance of the Indian is central not only to the idea of America but also to what it means to be an American" (2012: 106; my emphasis). Challenging American thinking in this way requires more than perspectival pluralism; it calls for a mode of vision that considers the ongoing presence of Native Americans as well as the specters of the colonial past.

Part Two: Being-Two with the Other: Negotiating Relationality and Mimicry with Luce Irigaray and Theresa Hak Kyung Cha's Dictée

1. The argument is going to return to Butler's thought, and particularly her notion of the intersubjective character of the body in the part "Precarious In-Dividuality and the Other."

2. Critical literature on Cha's text spells its title variously from *DICTEE* (as it appears on the cover of the book), to *Dictee* without an accent, to the proper French spelling *Dictée*. Unless the title appears in a quotation where it is spelled otherwise, this chapter will employ the usual French spelling.

Chapter 3: Dia-Logical Caress

1. The concept of a zero point epistemology is mirrored in the description of what Thomas Nagel has described as *The View from Nowhere*: rational objectivity's detached and distancing view. Zero point epistemology, in the guise of a view from nowhere, is discussed in more detail in the part entitled "Precarious In-Dividuality."

2. My translation; the original German reads: "Der konstruktivistische Logos, der

Code, das Programm, die kulturelle Regel sind *neutral* wie jeder traditionelle Logos. Der konstruktivistische Logos ist *geschlechtslos*" (Waldenfels 2000: 362).

3. My translation; the original German reads: "*Fremdheit des anderen Geschlechts*" (Waldenfels 2000: 359).

4. My translation; the original German reads: "Prozeß der Ein- und Ausgrenzung" (Waldenfels 1997a: 69).

5. As Ellen Rooney asserts in her foreword to the reissue of Naomi Schor's *Reading in Detail*, "The word 'invoke' activates the poetics of the vocative, of apostrophe, a mode of address that seeks, even requires response" (xviii).

Chapter 4: Moving the Spirit-Heart

1. The religious elements in *Dictée* are not only indicative of a colonialism that the text one-sidedly opposes, as Oh would have it (cf. 7); they draw attention to "the mythical sacrality of languages" (Kang 2002: 223) that is integrated into the textual ritual to emphasize *Dictée*'s "own powers of willful creation" (224). Stephens testifies to this syncretistic dimension when he identifies "a blending of Christianity (the rhythms of the Bible) and what appears to be an early dynastic form of Buddhist transcendence" (201), and Chambers attests that "[i]n religious senses, the Eucharist is not too far removed from the shamanic and Taoist Korean tradition" (132).

2. As Elaine Kim asserts, "the Western racist notion of the Asian and Asian American woman as a male-identified, passive, self-sacrificing Madame Butterfly is directly challenged in *Dictée*" (1994: 16), albeit in a very different manner than critics like Kim herself believe, as will be shown below.

3. This is also why critics have argued that "the text simultaneously breaks apart and binds together" (Park 231) or that it engages in "a double movement of attachment and detachment, retrieval and interment" (Cheng 1998: 120; 2001: 142).

4. Sakai elaborates: "more often than not, the critique of English-language imperialism has been conducted on the basis of a particularism premised on the identity of national language and national culture. In this particularism, it is taken to be a norm that each people should express itself in its own 'natural' language, and the world is construed as the configuration of particular languages" (19). Regarding a lost mother tongue, she argues that "the mother tongue was not yet one's natural national language: nature and the nation had yet to be communicated" and explicates that "the figure of the mother tongue as the natural national language was brought into being through a configuring schematism" (21).

5. Feminist theologian Grace Ji-Sun Kim explains: "*Han* is suffering when the social, political, and religious system is set up to oppress, dominate, and subjugate another or groups of people. *Han* becomes the opposite of grace. Grace is a free undeserved gift from God. *Han* is the undeserved pain, suffering, and turmoil that one endures due to systemic structures that oppress and harm individuals and communities" (2015: 39). Resonating with *Dictée*'s shamanistic invocation of subversive spectrality, Kim—starting from her very own life experience of *han* as a Korean immigrant to the US—sets out to unfold a Christian theology emphasizing the transformative potential of the Spirit: "The Spirit is the heart and soul of Christian theology. While we are living in a period of great division and conflict, God's Spirit can bring healing and hope. While we often make people who are different from us the Other [in the sense of a construct of alterity], the scriptural vision calls us not to ignore and neglect the Other, but rather to embrace the Other. It is the

power of the Spirit that opens our hearts to cross borders and embrace the Other" (4f.). Resonating with Cha's choir of transnational ghostly women, Kim further elaborates that "Spirit is ubiquitous. Spirit of life energy is an idea that we see throughout the world. Chinese call it Chi or Qi, Japanese call it Ki, Hindus call it Prana, and Greeks called it Pneuma. In all languages, Spirit is associated with breath, wind, or life-giving energy. We need to recover the transformative power of life energy, the font of divine love and justice" (5). In other words, and as *Dictée* does, instead of creating new counter-discourses, Kim outlines a relational Christian theology that, through "[r]ecognizing that Spirit is what connects us all," is going to "open doors for further dialogue, understanding, and acceptance" (ibid.) and releases "the erotic power that energizes the work of social justice for the vulnerable" (10): dia-logue instead of a mere inverted oppositional mono-logue that merely reads Christian theology as a colonial discourse of worldly power.

6. Chew clarifies that "[a]n examination of Sappho's fragments reveals that no such lines exist in the poet's extant writing. Cha has made them up; in doing so, she invokes Sappho's authority as archetypal woman poet" (63).

7. On the origins of this wall carving, Wong elaborates as follows: "The inscription, taken from the wall of a coal mine in Japan, is attributed to a Korean exile, one of thousands who were pressed into various kinds of labor by the Japanese early in [the last] century" (107).

8. Anglo-American discourses on identity politics mostly ignored such a take on the text or dismissed it as politically compromised. More recently, however, critics have begun to either implicitly allude or explicitly point out, once again, the affinity between *Dictée* and French feminism, particularly *l'éctriture feminine*, and the potential this might entail (cf. Lee 2006: 77; Eileraas 84; Frost 191).

9. Her own oppositional inclinations notwithstanding, Lowe nevertheless correctly asserts that "[i]n the United States, pluralism admits the existence of differences, yet requires conformity to a public culture that tends to subordinate alternative cultures (1994: 53).

10. Readers well-versed in Greek mythology will have realized that one of the muses has been replaced by another one. Critics have come up with various—more or less plausible—explanations for this gesture. McDaniel, for instance, explains this as follows: "Of the nine muses, one is altered by Cha: the Greek Muse 'Euterpe' is omitted, and Cha's refashioned muse, 'Elitere,' takes her place. This is a significant alteration because the etymology of 'Euterpe' means 'to please,' and this memoir does not attempt to please its readers through simplification. Instead, Cha constantly challenges her readers to rethink assumptions about gender, nation, language, and self-representation" (73). In a somewhat far-fetched reading, Chew suggests that "Elitere" alludes to Cha's first name and at the same time to Demeter: "This muse is linked to Cha herself: The first syllable of Cha's name *The*resa is echoed in 'Elit*ere*.' 'Theresa' is from the Greek for 'reaper'; reaping is an activity associated with the harvesting of grain and so with the Greek goddess Demeter" (64). Park, eventually, alludes to an epistemic move inherent in the replacement: "In converting lyric poetry into a muse, Cha turns this genre into one of the arts and sciences embodied by the muses" (Park 228).

11. Joyce questions whether *Dictée*, in fact, only alludes to Hesiod and writes: "despite the extensive scholarly attention to the connection between . . . *Dictée*'s invocation and that of the *Theogony*, critics have been focusing here on the wrong Greek epic. The use of the Muses does connect with the *Theogony*, but the invocation is actually a condensed version of that which begins Ennis Rees' 1961 translation of *The Odyssey*" (145).

12. It is highly questionable whether this passage is about "Koreanness" and it is even more questionable whether such a notion could, in fact, be reduced to Western conceptions of national identity. Also, the evocation of a relation to place or locality does not necessarily imply national identity as understood in Western rationality. If anything, *Dictée* establishes nationality other-wise, namely, in spectrality beyond Western spatio-temporal limitations, as "Phantomnation" (Cha 140).

13. Fusco writes that, in contrast to archival objectification, "employing the second person as a narrative strategy is a step toward an important recognition: that of the other's voice" (189) whose (en-)active pathos requires an appropriate response.

14. The imagery of dynamic fluidity continues throughout the part: it repeatedly evokes "the rain" (Cha 67, cf. also 71) and alludes to motion: "Pages and pages / in movement / line after / line" (Cha 69). Joyce asserts that *Dictée* "suggests that the flow of blood can overcome the materials designed to contain it, just as in Cha's writing the physicality of the body can seep through those forms designed to entrap it" (167). More-over, drawing attention to the *mater*-iality of the text, Park asserts that "[t]he diseuse is herself a boundary, and the blood that flows from her is textual: its inky quality defines and marks the surface it touches" (219) and concludes that "we can see Cha insisting on a physical intervention, a reminder of the body" (225).

15. McDaniel writes that, thereby, "Cha challenges the ways in which her audience perceives and understands the distinction between letters and images" (74).

16. The argument will focus more on the specific cinematographic qualities and references to film within *Dictée* in the last section of this analysis.

17. Several earlier interpreters are on the right track when they write, for instance, that "Cha will then make her text the site of re-creation and ideological resistance" (Kang 1994: 88) or that "the in-between is a personal dwelling place that makes survival possible" (Kim 1994: 21). But it is misleading to assert that "Cha creates and celebrates a kind of third space, an exile space that becomes a source of individual vision and power" (ibid.). This would, again, entail a remaining stuck within the hegemonic phallogocentric horizon. Nguyen explains this as follows: "While *Dictee* does offer a negative critique of ideology — in that sense offering a vision through the eyes of a bad subject—its own solution of a return to an innocent vision of the world does not correspond with the materialist, neo-Marxist approach" (Nguyen 156) which most critics of Cha's art-work entertain.

18. While Joyce first insists that "Cha asserts a physical bond between nation and individual, writing the body into the land and the land into the body" (163), he, eventually, seems to contradict himself when he asserts, toward the end of his analysis, that "Cha's epic . . . concludes with the creation of a community of women, rather than a nation" (196).

19. Park succinctly relates this back to *Dictée*'s cinematographic qualities: "Cha insists on a cinema freed from the demand of temporal progression, creating instead a textual and supremely malleable film on the page. The page is the divide between the world above and Hades, but it is also a surface on which blood and ink flow and images are projected. Cha imagines the screen as a surface that can bear life, an echo of the diseuse's labors in bringing forth the others she gives voice to. The cinema screen exemplifies the kind of transformation she wants to effect: before the movie starts, the screen is an opaque, ma-terial object, yet once the projection begins, it becomes a surface for living entities" (234).

20. Chambers also draws attention to the ambiguity of the void regarding the religious dimensions of the art-work: "We only see a void; but is this an imposed, colonizing void,

or is it a religious one that creates in the individual an openness to receiving strength? If this is the inability of the subaltern to speak, then Christ too, by St. Thérèse's comparisons, is silenced; if it is a refusal to work within the hegemonic context, then Christ too refuses, just as he did when put on trial before Herod (Luke 23:6–9)" (140). What Chambers can be read to imply here is that an-other rereading of *Dictée*'s religious dimensions within the luminous darkness of negative theology's apophatic voids could prove a fruitful endeavor for understanding the text's ab-usive mimesis and/or creative sabotage of Roman Catholic Christian liturgy and theology beyond an attestation of a total dismissal. Cha's *Dictée* can be read as an urge to read Christianity decidedly other-wise.

Part Three: Poetic Dwelling in the Borders: Negotiating Attunement and Sensuousness with Martin Heidegger and Michael Ondaatje's Anil's Ghost
 1. The gradual publication of Heidegger's ominously titled *Black Notebooks*—beginning in 2014 (in the original German)—has posed new and grave challenges concerning an easy apologetic separation of Heidegger's politics and philosophy; challenges whose magnitude cannot be fathomed yet in their entirety (cf. Trawny 119). However, Heidegger's involvement with National Socialism is by far greater than many would have wished it to be. As the *Black Notebooks* are being published, ever more abominably anti-Semitic tendencies in his thought have been revealed (cf. Fried 373f.). Nevertheless, the simple condemnation of Heidegger's work is maybe not a desirable option. Gregory Fried has sketched out a mode of thinking with and against Heidegger that resonates with the approach that guides this project's dealings with the controversial philosopher, and will, therefore, be quoted at length: "Wo stehen wir nun in unserer eigenen Konfrontation mit Heidegger: Feind oder Gegner? Es sollte niemanden . . . überraschen, dass ich die zweite Option bevorzuge. Ich glaube, dass Heideggers Denken *weder* notwendig *noch* zufällig zum Faschismus führt. Und deshalb müssen wir selber darüber nachdenken, wie es ihn dennoch auf den Weg brachte und wie wir aus seinen Texten und Fragen Aufklärung darüber erhalten, was für die Philosophie auf dem Spiel steht, damit wir uns diese Frage erneut auf unsere Art zu eigen machen können. Indem wir mit ihm denken, werden wir nicht notwendigerweise kontaminiert, denn die Seinsfrage selbst, sogar wie Heidegger sie stellt, ist nicht faschistisch" (380f.). Fried, then, further elaborates: "Heidegger als Feind zu behandeln würde den totalen Krieg gegen ihn bedeuten, Kampf bis aufs Messer: Es würde heißen, in Abrede zu stellen, dass irgendetwas philosophisch Relevantes aus dem Denken mit ihm und selbst gegen ihn erwachsen könnte, weil wir darauf bestehen müssten, dass Heideggers Denken nichts enthält, das nicht hoffnungslos vom Nazismus kontaminiert ist. Eine philosophisch produktive Begegnung könnte es dann mit ihm nicht geben. Die einzig verbleibende Aufgabe wäre, ihn zu entlarven und mit ihm abzuschließen" (381). Fried argues regarding a mere dismissal: "Dies hat zwei problematische Konsequenzen. Die eine führt zu bloß polemischen Verzerrungen von Heideggers Denken . . . Die wichtigere Konsequenz ist, dass sie uns der Möglichkeit beraubt, unserer eigenen historischen Situation durch die philosophische Auseinandersetzung mit einem Denker, der auch Nazi war, zu begegnen. Wir können die andauernde Bedrohung durch den Faschismus nicht aufhalten, indem wir Heidegger verbannen. Wir müssen das Wagnis, τόλμα, eingehen, ihm als *Philosophen* ins Auge zu sehen, denn das Problematische am Schicksal der westlichen Welt *im* Faschismus bleibt sowohl Teil unserer Geschichte als auch unsere Zukunft, wenn wir es nicht konsequent durchdenken" (ibid.).

2. In the German context, apparently more so than in English-speaking ones, many critics regard Heidegger's work as utterly compromised. Even more so after the publication of the first volumes of the *Black Notebooks*, which, as the German philosopher Marion Heinz writes, reveal "die intrinsische Verbindung Heideggers Philosophie mit Rassismus, Antisemitismus und Nationalsozialismus und entziehen damit der okkasionalistischen Deutung den Boden" (10). In his book *A Poetics of Homecoming*, Brendan O'Donoghue discusses other established critical positions in a context related to the argument of this chapter and can be referenced in lieu of an(other) extensive list of (often well-known) publications concerned with Heidegger's politics (cf. 114ff.).

3. My translation; the original German reads: "Oder wir können auf das Heideggersche Werk *als einen Weg achten*, einen Weg mit immer neuen vorwärtsweisenden wie rückerinnernden Denkerfahrungen, von seiner frühen Auseinandersetzung mit den Philosophen des beginnenden vorigen Jahrhunderts, über die Auseinandersetzung mit Aristoteles und Kant und schließlich überhaupt mit einer Vielzahl von *Denkern* der seinsgeschichtlichen Tradition sowie mit ausgewählten *Dichtern*, bis hin zur intensiven Arbeit seiner letzten Jahrzehnte an dem, was heute *ist* und was er einerseits als das Wesen der Technik, andererseits als das Zusammenspiel von Welt und Dingen bedacht hat. Daß Heidegger einen Weg des Denkens gegangen ist, ist keine bloße Metapher. Er selbst hat häufig auf das Weitergehen seines Denkens reflektiert. Es hat ihn zu immer neuen Aussichten und Perspektiven geführt und ist im strengen Sinne auch zu keinem Ende gekommen, sondern weist über sich selbst hinaus" (Guzzoni 7).

4. My translation; the original German reads: "einer gewissen Bedeutungsverschiebung" (Guzzoni 13) and "er also . . . implizit auf Fragen geantwortet und in Bahnen gedacht hat, deren Relevanz und Tragweite er selbst nicht mehr ganz realisiert hat" (16).

5. In this way, the argument also builds upon James Edwards's conviction that "in order to find value in (some of) what Heidegger says, one doesn't need to accept the implausible and totalitarian myths to which his most interesting claims are usually joined" (107).

6. Richard Wolin outlines what he perceives as the problematically paradoxical impact of Heidegger's philosophy: "Die Poststrukturalisten, die sich in den 1960er Jahren mit ominösen Behauptungen über den 'Tod des Menschen'—nach Ansicht ihrer Verfechter ein Anlass zum *Feiern*—hervortaten, fanden verlässlichen philosophischen Beistand in den Deutungsmustern der heideggerschen Vernunftkritik. Auf diese Weise fand die generelle Demokratiefeindlichkeit der europäischen Rechten vor dem Zweiten Weltkrieg dank einer gespenstischen Ideenwanderung über nationale Grenzen hinweg eine neue Heimat ausgerechnet bei den bekennenden linken Akademikern und Kulturvertretern" (411). Considering these insights, a renewed critical engagement with Heidegger's work is vital if one is not content to disavow his influence also on contemporary cultural studies via figures like Foucault, Derrida, Levinas, and also Agamben, to name but a few.

7. As Barbara Bolt explains, Bhabha's work is more compatible with Heidegger's thinking than even *The Location of Culture* makes clear. She describes how the former's interpretation of a sculpture by Anish Kapoor mirrors Heidegger's conceptualization of the work(ings) of art as a struggle between earth and world (which is, as will become apparent, also central for this part's argument) and translates it into an entirely different cultural context: "In recounting his encounter with Anish Kapoor's *Ghost*, Bhabha also reveals the dynamic between earth and world when he makes the distinction between *svyambhuv* ('self-born' aesthetic) and *rupa* (man-made form imposed through human

artifice)" (46). Bolt adds that "Bhabha is no longer the critic or observer looking at an artwork but has found himself in the middle of the work, caught up by its torqued ambivalent movement" (47). Bhabha also conceives of art beyond the Cartesian paradigm in a manner strikingly reminiscent of the German philosopher.

8. Ondaatje's work lends itself to pairing with Heidegger's thinking even more when considering that one of the writer's teachers, George Walley, who exerted a tremendous influence on Ondaatje, was very Heidegger-affine. Hillger explains that particularly Heidegger's unconventional understanding of *Dichtung* (usually translated as "poetry), with its deconstruction of subject/object logic, influenced Ondaatje's literature decisively (cf. 61, 63).

Chapter 5: Ab-Usive Deviations

1. According to Gumbrecht, it was in nineteenth century Germany and Wilhelm Dilthey's realization of the humanities' institutional separation from the methodology of the exact sciences—then primarily the methods of psychology—which resulted in the establishment of the hermeneutic paradigm as the solely valid approach within these newly separated fields: "The (in the end successful) secession was the beginning of the institutional independence of the *Geisteswissenschaften* as a cluster of disciplines that, following Dilthey's programmatic proposal, was supposed to be centered around interpretation as its core practice and hermeneutics as its reflexive space" (43). Gumbrecht adds that "[t]he price that the humanities had to pay for this move was obvious: it was the loss of any non-Cartesian, any non-experience-based type of world-reference" (ibid.).

2. In fact, some Romantics in Germany (and elsewhere) were more sensitive to issues of gender than Gumbrecht is now. Friedrich Schlegel's thought, for instance, "also inflects development toward social and cultural wholeness by insisting on gender, and the sexual component in the emergence of a complete humanity" (Phelan 42). Similarly, Schlegel ridicules Schiller's cult of domesticity when it comes to the status of the female sex, as Elizabeth Millán-Zaibert remarks in a footnote (c.f. 181); Schlegel claims that women are the only interesting and inspiring human beings still fruitfully contributing to early nineteenth century discourse (c.f. Beutin 210). Even if, as Ricarda Schmidt writes, "many patriarchal structures . . . prevailed on a psychological and social level", there were "some remarkable changes to gender roles" (28) underway in early Romantic circles in Germany. In other words—unlike Gumbrecht, as it would seem—Schlegel realized that the criticism of the European *ratio* must include a re-evaluation of gender politics.

3. One may acknowledge Gumbrecht's pointing out that that the ivory tower "certainly has windows and doors" (127). However, this does not serve to alleviate his classist tendencies. As his further argumentation illustrates, these openings do not constitute channels for sincere dialogue, but rather function as check-valves which assist in maintaining academic superiority.

4. Hajduk elaborates: "Allerdings können literarische Stimmungen auch nicht gänzlich ohne ihre Übergängigkeit in symbolische Prozesse 'gelesen', ihr unmittelbarer Bezug zur materialen Präsenz von Literatur keinesfalls als bedeutungsneutral gedacht werden, wie Gumbrecht annimmt. Wird nicht gerade im psychophysischen Selbstvollzug von Stimmungen bereits ein ästhetisches Verstehenspotential freigesetzt? Konnte nicht eben aufgrund dieses Welterschließungscharakters Heidegger die Stimmung als existentiale Befindlichkeit seiner ontologischen Systematisierung einfügen? Die kognitive Dimension der Stimmung blendet

Gumbrecht jedoch aus, wenn er ein bloß affektives Sich-einlassen auf ihre Textpräsenz fordert" (2012: 143).

5. However, it is important to note, as Clark points out, that, consequently, unconcealment applies only to world, whereas hiding only pertains to earth. Both exhibit these forces, albeit in different modes entangled in a continuous struggle: the earth's self-seclusion is also a mode of unconcealment, just as world's self-opening can also appear as a form of hiding (cf. 2002: 53).

6. It is correct to point out earth's relatedness to material substance. *Erde* includes the materiality of nature (cf. Harries 115), but it is also more than that, namely the ground on which *Dasein* bases its existence (cf. Inwood 119), which is inextricably bound to *Welt* as the totality of understanding in the *conditio humana* (cf. Young 39).

7. In fact, Gumbrecht seems to be heading in the exact opposite direction when he writes: "It is no accident that we have witnessed a return to the most canonized and classical literary works. Now, without sacrificing academic honor, one can finally admit to reading them for their own sake" (2012: 2). It appears that, to Gumbrecht, the revision of the canon seems, at best, a phase that has been concluded or, at worst, a nuisance which has kept him from indulging in Eurocentric literature.

8. For a more thorough account of the historical developments of the term *Stimmung* within European literary studies since the eighteenth century, see Hajduk (2011: 77ff.).

9. Friedrich-Wilhelm von Hermann elaborates on Heidegger's critical understanding of aesthetics as an objectifying philosophical discipline as follows: "Die Ästhetik in all ihren Erscheinungsformen ist die verfestigte Meinung, daß die Blickbahn auf die Kunst und alles, was zu ihr gehört, das ästhetische Erleben des Subjekts ist, das durch das Kunstwerk als ästhetisches Objekt und Träger des Schönen in den ästhetischen Erlebniszustand versetzt wird. In dieser ästhetischen Subjekt-Objekt-Beziehung hat sich das Wesende der Kunst, das werkmäßige Entbergungsgeschehen, völlig entzogen und verhüllt" (56).

10. My translation; the original German reads: "der Mut, die Wahrheit der eignen Voraussetzungen und den Raum der eigenen Ziele zum Fragwürdigsten zu machen" (Heidegger 2003: 75).

11. In fact, Heidegger describes his notion of *Stimmung* as defying simply inside-outside-logic: "It is not at all 'inside' in some interiority, only to appear in the flash of an eye; but for this reason it is not at all outside either" (1995: 66). This already hints toward a further possible connection to Waldenfels and Mignolo's border gnosis, which will be elaborated throughout what follows.

12. My translation; the original German reads: "Auch das Selbstgefühl hat an dieser materiellen Körperlichkeit teil, die zu uns gehört, ohne daß wir sie uns je völlig aneignen können. Die Fremdheit des eigenen Leibes macht uns empfänglich für die Fremdheit des Anderen. Ansprechbar, anrührbar, affizierbar sind wir nur, sofern wie nie ganz und gar bei uns selbst sind" (Waldenfels 2010: 326).

13. My translation; the original German reads: "Der Leib fungiert mithin nicht nur als 'Umschlagstelle' zwischen Geist und Natur, zwischen Eigenheit und Fremdheit, sondern auch als Knotenpunkt, an dem die verschiedenen Fäden der Aisthesis, der Kinesis und der Poiesis zusammenlaufen" (Waldenfels 2010: 11).

14. Particularly the insights attained through the negotiation of language, iterability, and singularity in the context of reading Anna Lee Walters's novel *Ghost Singer* with

Diana Taylor's *The Archive and the Repertoire* are helpful if kept in mind throughout what follows.

15. Readers familiar with the work of Heidegger might want to interject that, in the context of his essay on poetic dwelling, the philosopher further develops the *counterturning* of strife of world and earth into what he calls the fourfold (cf. Clark 2002: 99). However, taking this problematic term into account is not necessary for pursuing this chapter's line of argument and to move beyond its scope. Nevertheless, particularly regarding the role of religion and belief as important fields which also need to be addressed beyond representationalism within transnational approaches (cf. Phillips 398), returning to the fourfold elsewhere might prove fruitful.

16. It is in the context of this existential homelessness that Heidegger writes the following infamous passage: "The proper dwelling plight lies in this, that mortals ever search anew for the essence of dwelling, that they *must ever learn to dwell.* What if man's homelessness consisted in this, that man still does not even think of the *proper* plight of dwelling as *the* plight? Yet as soon as man *gives thought* to his homelessness, it is a misery no longer. Rightly considered and kept well in mind, it is the sole summons that *calls* mortals into their dwelling" (2011: 254f.). In the light of his reading of *Antigone*, this statement attains an altogether different character than the nostalgic nationalist inclinations often attributed to it.

17. For a critical discussion of Heidegger's *Antigone* interpretation and its problems, see O'Donoghue (149ff).

18. Heidegger's evocation of "sparing" or "care" (*Sorge*) as the proper relationship toward earth is derived from the Greek Goddess Cura who formed humanity out of clay (*humus*) and, therefore, expects a certain form of human epistemological *humility*: a *careful* treatment of earth as existential space (cf. Harrison 6, 28).

19. Generally, it needs to be added, here, that Heidegger conceives of the relationship between place, humans, and space according to the same holistic principles that characterize his thought in its entirety. Guzzoni explains: "Raum, Mensch und Ort sind nicht getrennt voneinander zu behandeln,—so wenig, wie Sein, Mensch und Seiendes bzw. Welt, Mensch und Dinge getrennt voneinander zu verstehen sind" (2009: 109). She adds: "Raum und Mensch sind nicht zwei unabhängige Entitäten, von denen die eine der anderen vorgängig oder umgekehrt von ihr abhängig wäre" (ibid. 111).

20. Just as earth is not just a substantive geological or geographical term here, planet does not imply the calculated entity of astronomy (cf. Barbaza 47). Like earth, it is related to notions of an ontological ground(ing).

21. Tracy Colony underscores the potential relevance of the concept of dwelling to the overall project of transnational aesthetics and the *presencing* of otherness when she describes mortal dwelling as "Heidegger's rethinking of the human as preserving an essential alterity within our relation to nature and living beings" (38).

22. My translation; the original German reads: "geheimnisvolle Zueinandergehörigkeit von Eigenem und Fremdem" (Gorgone 130).

23. My translation, the original German reads: "*a limine* als Zwischenwelt" (Waldenfels 1997: 66).

24. My translation; the original German reads: "sinnliches Zur-Erscheinung-kommen" (Guzzoni 2009: 149).

25. Another—even explicit—link between corporeality in relation to the motion of

counterturning appears in Heidegger's description of a poetic rendering of the athletics in an ancient Greek wrestling match in his volume on Hölderlin's poetry. There, he identifies a reciprocal relationship of spirit (*Geist*) and body (*Körper*) that mirrors the strife of world and earth (cf. 2012: 160f.).

26. This means that so as not to reproduce the subject/object paradigm through a one-sided lauding of the corporeal and implicitly stylizing the body again as the opposite of the mind, the aspect of embodiment regarding the poetic requires thinking these aspects from within the motion of *counterturning* as *figuring* at the same time.

27. Lyotard, here, does not describe ever-removed aesthetic phenomena, but potentially everyday occurrences.

28. My translation; the original German reads: "Ein-Bildungen als erblickbare Einschlüsse des Fremden" (Guzzoni 2009: 125).

29. Lyotard alludes to this connection between sensuous attunement, the withdrawal of earth, and language's figurality when he writes that "one observes that in sensory certainty language encounters an order it cannot exhaust, but from which it itself draws, and endlessly, its dimension of depth" (2011: 34).

30. My translation; the original German reads: "Die Sprache ist bei Heidegger etwas *Stationäres*" (Thomä 311).

31. My translation; the original German reads: "Unklar bleibt, inwiefern in der Vorgeschichte oder Entstehung des 'Hauses des Seins' Bewegung mitzudenken ist" (Thomä 312).

32. My translation, the original German reads: "eine spezifische Anordnung der Dinge, die sich in ihm [the house] befinden (etwa in der Zuteilung zu Stockwerken und Räumen)" (Thomä 314).

33. My translation; the original German reads: "Wohnen als Weise der Wanderung" (Guzzoni 2009: 122).

34. Guzzoni confirms the dynamism of this "house" when she writes that the *Bezirk* does not outline a fixed territory, but an affective "Gegend, die so heißt, weil sie gegnet" (2009: 131) and to which one needs to respond.

Chapter 6: Counterturning the Life-Wheel

1. John Clifford Holt elaborates on the historical context in which the plot takes place: "Since the early 1980s, Sri Lanka endured what amounted to a protracted civil war between its Sinhala majority and elements of its Tamil minority [Liberation Tigers of Tamil Eelam]. While some observers have sought the roots of this conflict within the deep recesses of ancient or medieval history, the fundamental causes of the current conflict are more recent, causes that have more to do with competition for the relatively scarce economic resources in this comparatively poor South Asian nation (per capita income is roughly two thousand dollars per year). Secondarily, however, the causes of Sri Lanka's social and political conflict are also a byproduct of awakened modern and nationalistic ethnic identities fostered, ironically, by democratic enfranchisement that leads to a majoritarian rule" (2). For a more detailed account of the Sri Lankan civil war linked to Ondaatje's novel, see Spinks (207ff.) and Holt (4ff.).

2. Sculpting faces around skeletal remains is also a procedure well-known in Western science. Although widely debated, this is also done in anthropology to recreate the faces of the dead in processes of forensic facial reconstruction; processes which amalgamate

such different methodologies as artistry, forensic science, anthropology, osteology, and anatomy (cf. Wilkinson 35ff.).

3. The text's motion of *counterturning* is also further underscored by the integration of two elements framing the narrative, namely the Author's Note introducing the plot, where Ondaatje comments on the historical context of the novel (cf. 1), and the Acknowledgments in the back, which give an overview over the research conducted throughout the writing of *Anil's Ghost* (cf. 309ff.). Both contribute to the dehierarchization of art and science enacted throughout the narrative.

4. In this conversation, Palipana also dismisses another of Anil's Western(ized) views: while Anil (naïvely) believes in the redemptive quality of stable truth—which she believes to be expressed in the Johannine Christian dictum "'The truth shall set you free'"—Palipana insists that there is no redemption in her notion of truth. In her review of the novel, Rachel Cusk describes Anil as "schooled in the redemptive mythology of the west" (55). Throughout the entire narrative, the Christian tradition and its symbolism—here in particular the crucifix and the pieta—is challenged by its confrontation with the realities of postcoloniality (cf. Knowles 434).

5. Scanlan's reading of *madanaraga* is also curious as the two characters she attributes it to, Sarath and Gamini, are entirely absent from the scene itself.

6. Haptic sensuousness stands in stark contrast to Anil's prior impulse to break things apart to acknowledge their complexity: "to open—to touch—is not to tear, dismember, destroy" (Nancy 2008: 122).

7. Suggesting that the civil war in Sri Lanka is also fuelled by "state-of-the-art weapons from the West" (Ondaatje 17), the novel further underlines this insufficiency and exposes the hypocrisy of Western humanitarian efforts.

8. My translation; the original German reads: "Das A-politische heißt folglich, daß *in* der Politik selber sich etwas den politischen Maßstäben und Maßnahmen entzieht" (Waldenfels 2001: 444f.). Waldenfels, however, explicitly states that this nontion of relational outside-ness is not to be idealized: "Das griechische Alpha Privativum ist wie das 'in' im Lateinischen doppeldeutig. Es kann eine Negation anzeigen—und ich nehme es als Ausdruck eines Entzugs. Man muß sehr aufpassen, daß man nicht vom einen in das andere gerät und dann eben den Außenseiter auch romantisiert: Wie schön es doch da draußen ist" (2001: 446). Strictly speaking, this is even impossible, since, according to this logic, nothing is ever entirely outside but always remains linked to that which it simultaneously exceeds.

9. My translation; the original German reads: "Ich bin ihr [the political order] also nie völlig mit Leib und Seele verhaftet. Das wäre also die Grenze: das Politische, das sich nicht selber in sich zusammenschließt, ohne von außen negiert zu werden" (Waldenfels 2001: 445).

10. Samuel Moyn clarifies that "[w]hen the history of human rights is told beyond myths of deep origins, it illustrates the persistence of the nation-state as the aspirational forum for humanity until recently [as non-Western voices are now increasingly being heard]. The state was the incubator for rights claims, both in the rise of the absolutist state, with its well-disciplined interior order and colonialist exterior expansion, then in the creation of the modern nation, in which citizenship and rights, identification and contestation, were always bound up with each other" (212).

11. My translation; the original German reads: "Wir stehen nicht einfach auf dem

Boden eines Gemeinwesens oder kosmopolitisch auf dem eines Reichs der Menschheit" (Waldenfels 2001: 444f.).

12. This contention certainly does not sit well with the new utopian strain currently developing in the humanities. For its supporters, as Mike Marais writes, "[u]topianism . . . is an exercise in agency. To trivialise it by suggesting that it is idealistic and unrealistic is therefore simply to suspend disbelief in the status quo, to accept the argument that there is no alternative, and so to deny oneself the possibility of agency" (13). This chapter has shown that this must not necessarily be the case. The agument's emphasis on the (a-)*topos*, instead of offering one more utopian vision, gestures toward an elsewhere that ever-*figures* (from) within bleak systematicity as an-other possibility which does not, once again, merely envision a better future, but that rather draws onto the always already *presencing* potentials for societal change.

Part Four: Precarious In-Dividuality and the Other: Negotiating Simulation and Presence with Jean Baudrillard and Richard Powers's Plowing the Dark

1. Especially considering multiple passages from the so-called *Black Notebooks*, as Johannes Fritsche argues, even Heidegger's onging critique of occidental culculative reasoning (which he connects to the Jewish people) and modern technology is exposed as highly problematic (cf. 189ff.). It needs to be stressed again that this project engages with Heidegger by way of ab-use. This book does not simply reflect Heidegger's thought, but playfully sabotages it. Thereby, this book turns it into "Heidegger's thought," and has the philosopher say things in his own words, he himself would never have uttered, but has, in a way—an (*Ab-*)*Weg*.

Chapter 7: Trans-Figuring Technology

1. Grace elaborates that "[t]he structural assumptions about the construction of the meaning of 'objects' remain the same whether our meaning is assumed to be the same as, or different from, that of 'others'; assumed to be fixed or floating and fluid"; what remains intact throughout all the orders is "a binary structure that designates *the same* or *not the same*. This structure is assumed and naturalized within political economy and within Sausurrian linguistics" (10). In line with Lyotard's emphasis on the irruption of the figural (from) within language, Grace also draws attention to the fact that "Baudrillard is critical of Saussure's theory of the relationship between the Sr [signifier] and the Sd [signified], as idealist. The Sd/Referent is an effect of the ontological assumption of the representational code; a code that splits the Sr and Sd and in doing so effects a real that has a meaning that is pre-empted and controlled by the code. Far from being idealist himself, Baudrillard uses this critique to expose the reductionist nature of the semiological code and creates a space to wander about the real" (24f.).

2. The difference between simulation and representation, according to Baudrillard, can be described as follows: "Whereas representation attempts to absorb simulation by interpreting as a false representation, simulation envelops the whole edifice of representation itself as a simulacrum" (1994: 6). That is why elsewhere he, somewhat drastically, writes of "the vertiginous death of representation within the confines of representation" (1993: 72).

3. Baudrillard elaborates that "[w]ith Virtual Reality and all its consequences, we have passed over in the extreme of technology, into technology as an extreme phenomenon. . . .

This hypothesis is much graver than that of technological alienation or Heidegger's *Gestell*" (2008: 35).

4. For Baudrillard, within this levelling systematicity—all media-technological enhancements notwithstanding—communication becomes a mere farce, borders on schizophrenia, or even begins to cease altogether, despite its apparently exponential increase (cf. Blask 34; Hart n.pag.; Rodriguez n.pag.).

5. Several other scholars also have identified in Baudrillard's work a radical critique of a closed, one-dimensional, and monolithic global system (cf. Hart n.pag.; Zietek n.pag.; Mendoza n.pag.). This section's argument constitutes a critical supplement to these previous insights.

6. Stiegler also writes of "globalatinization [*mondialatinisation*]" as that which "has enabled the West to wage its war on spirits [*esprits*]—a war where it assures its control of spirits *through the control of their symbols*" (2014: 55). This also refers to the eradication of Native pictography throughout the Conquest of the Americas mentioned in chapter two.

7. Just as Baudrillard, Stiegler extends Heidegger's idea on technics and technology: "Heidegger envisages a kind of poeticised technics that gives more truthful expression to the kind of finite beings that we are, but he does not see that we *are*—that we exist as humans—*only through technics*" (Howells and Moore 3).

8. It is, consequently, misleading to accuse Stiegler and his insistence on technogenesis "of unilateral technological determinism" (Beardsworth 217). Stiegler's re-reading does not remain within the epistemological framework that is imposed on his thought with this accusation. His philosophy rather (r)evolves around the irreducible ambivalence of the "technogenetic spiral" (Hayles 86)—always already involving human and technics in a mutual embrace—and must not be reduced to unilateral deterministic technophilia.

9. Gary Genosko further describes art and aesthetics' complicity in Baudrillard's thought as follows: "What Baudrillard did ostensibly for the art world was to provide a poetico-theoretical language with which to describe a state of affairs that certain of its members sensed and sought to render critically: the art world had become no more than the exchange of sign-commodities and these signs no longer signified anything other than their own exchange value" (154). And, as Douglas Kellner writes, it is certainly correct that, in Baudrillard's thought, "[a]rt is subject to the same rules and system of signification as other commodities" (95). Still, it is this very system of signification and its epistemological impact on the aesthetic that his critique targets and not simply the reduction to commodification itself.

10. Baudrillard elaborates on the museological character of aesthetic sensibility: "The general aesthetization of thing should be feared more. Much more than market speculation, we should fear the transcription of every thing in cultural, aesthetic terms, into museographic signs. That is culture, that is our dominant culture: the vast enterprise of aesthetic storage, re-simulation and aesthetic reprinting of all the forms that surround us" (2005: 105). The connection to the epistemological issues raised by Anna Lee Walters's novel *Ghost Singer* becomes even more apparent, when Baudrillard explicitly refers to the cultural extermination of indigenous peoples by way of museumification, (cf. Lane 46).

11. Stiegler does not opt for nostalgic returns. The renewal of sense-sensitivity needs to be worked toward "*without calling for a return to an earlier situation*: without becoming reactive, without mythologizing a past that is over and done with" (2015: 58), or never even existed at all.

12. Butler (tellingly) further elaborates on the iterability of normative structures: "they can only circulate by virtue of their reproducibility, and that very reproducibility introduces a structural risk for the identity of the frame. The frame breaks with itself in order to reproduce itself, and its reproduction becomes the site where a politically consequential break is possible" (2010: 24).

13. As already clarified prior to the discussion of Luce Irigaray's work in relation to Theresa Cha's *Dictée*, Butler's notion of performativity, too, insists on the (figural) corporeal qualities of language and "the very capacity of language to mean more and differently than it appears, a certain possibility for semantic excess that exceeds the formal or syntactic appearance" (2015b: 169).

14. Ryan further bolsters this argument through quoting Pierre Lévy's *Becoming Virtual*: "The virtual is by no means the opposite of the real. On the contrary, it is a fecund and powerful mode of being that expands the process of creation, opens up the future, injects a core of meaning beneath the platitude of immediate physical presence" (Lévy in Ryan 26).

15. Ryan here hints at what Baudrillard calls hyperreality's fractal force: to him, the fourth order of simulacra is fractal (*i.e. curved*) in nature. This *figure* of the fractal is borrowed from the natural sciences. Alex Wade explains concerning its functioning principle that also "the fractal cannot leave its Moebius [sic] strip"; he elaborates that "[c]onsisting of mathematical code and only reaching true representation through the medium of electrified silicon" fractals "are in orbit, constantly circulating and replicating. When they are provided an escape route through a computer they produce a *kaleidoscopic image* that mirrors nature" (n.pag.; my emphasis); albeit in a *curved mirror* that does not simply fix but rather draws attention to the *figural* workings at the fringes of the centralized Western foveal zone.

16. However, one also needs to bear in mind that this reversibility itself can never be fully instrumentalized; it always resists appropriation, or, as Baudrillard writes: "This is the weakness of our historical radicality. All the philosophies of change, the revolutionary, nihilistic, futurist utopias, all this poetics of subversion and transgression so characteristic of modernity, will appear naive when compared with the instability and natural reversibility of the world" (2008: 11).

17. The process of reversibility, or poetic turnabout, is, of course, also tied to a *reconfiguring* of the Cartesian paradigm and the hierarchical ascriptions of activity and passivity it has installed. Baudrillard elaborates on this—again nicely referring back to the analysis of Walters's novel *Ghost Singer*—as follows: "We always thought that things were passively waiting to be discovered, in much the same way that America is imagined to have been waiting for Columbus. But it is not so. At the moment when the subject discovers the object—whether it is an 'Indian' or a virus—the object makes a reversible, but never innocent, discovery of the subject. More—it is actually a sort of invention of the subject by the invented object" (2000: 76). This dynamic of reversibility forms the core of Gerald Vizenor's trickster concept of simulating *native* presences or active *survivance*.

18. In fact, Baudrillard once himself explicitly refers to his particular form of relating to the world in the terms of the project at hand as "an *other* thought (2000: 5); that is to say "a kind of thought that would instead reproblematize all the old solutions and help to hold the world in enigmatic tension" (ibid.).

19. William Pawlett further underscores this when he writes that "writing theory becomes, for Baudrillard, *an act, a gesture and a symbolic relation*" (107). Furthermore,

outlining the deictic aspects of Baudrillard's radical/poetic thought, Pawlett draws attention to what can be perceived as a profound sensibility for the *figural* workings of language characterizing this type of thinking.

20. Baudrillard, again, shares this concern with Stiegler, who argues that hyperindustrialization entails a homogeneous levelling of individuals into its techno-logical framework (cf. Barker 264).

21. Picking up on the argumentation of the previous chapter, Baudrillard asserts: "In his postmodern avatar, however, the individual is a self-referential and self-operating unit. Under such circumstances the human-rights system becomes totally inadequate and illusory. The flexible, mobile individual of variable geometric form is no longer a subject with rights but has become, rather, a tactician and promoter of his own existence whose point of reference is not some agency of law but merely the efficiency of his own functioning or performance." (Baudrillard 1993b: 99). Make Gane builds on this and elaborates in line with the argument at hand: "Western culture cannot tolerate the radical alterity of other cultures. Humanism, the doctrine of universal human rights with its assumption of human equality . . . seeks to form the world after its own image and thus reduces radical otherness to domesticated 'differences'" (18).

22. For Butler, this disavowal of bodily vulnerability stems from the phallogocentric bent of the Western frame-work. It is a certain kind of "masculine position . . . [which] is effectively built through a denial of its own constitutive vulnerability" (2015a:145). Elsewhere she reiterates that "[she is] also suggesting that certain ideals of independence are masculinist and that a feminist account exposes the disavowed dependency at the heart of the masculinist idea of the body (2016: 21), and, then, elaborates: "By theorizing the human body as a certain kind of dependency on infrastructure, understood complexly as environment, social relations, and networks of support and sustenance by which the human itself proves not to be divided from the animal or from the technical world, we foreground ways in which we are vulnerable to decimated or disappearing infrastructures, economic supports, and predictable and well-compensated labor. Not only are we then vulnerable to one another—an invariable feature of social relations—but, in addition, this very vulnerability indicates a broader condition of dependency and interdependency that challenges the dominant ontological understanding of the embodied subject" (ibid.). It functions other-wise: "it characterizes a relation to a field of objects, forces, and passions that impinge on or affect us in some way. As a way of being related to what is not me and not fully masterable, vulnerability is a kind of relationship that belongs to that ambiguous region in which receptivity and responsiveness are not clearly separable from one another, and not distinguished as separate moments in a sequence; indeed, where receptivity and responsiveness become the basis for mobilizing vulnerability rather than engaging in its destructive denial" (2016: 25).

23. In this context, Butler elaborates: "we assume that those who seek to expose others to a vulnerable position—or to install them there—as well as those who seek to posit and maintain a position of vulnerability for themselves all seek to deny a vulnerability by virtue of which they are obstinately, if not unbearably, bound to the others thy seek to subjugate. If one is tied to another against one's will, even when, precisely when, a contract is the means of subjugation, the tie can be quite literally maddening, a form of unacceptably enforced dependency, as happens in slave labor and other forms of coercive contract. The problem is not dependency as such, but its tactical exploitation" (2015a: 147).

24. However, Butler further clarifies: "if we accept that part of what a body is (and this is for the moment an ontological claim) Is its dependency on other bodies and networks of support, then we are suggesting that it is not altogether right to conceive of individual bodies as completely distinct from one another. Of course, neither are they blended into some amorphous social body, but if we conceptualize the political meaning of the human body without understanding those relations in which it lives and thrives, we fail to make the best possible case for the various political ends we seek to achieve" (16).

25. Butler, again, adds: "What grief displays, in contrast, is the thrall in which our relations with others hold us, in ways that we cannot always recount or explain, in ways that often interrupt the self-conscious account of ourselves we might try to provide, in ways that challenge the very notion of ourselves as autonomous and in control" (2006: 23).

26. However, it needs to be emphasized that what is here described as a new form of essentialism does not seek to reestablish a problematic Western foundationalism. Butler herself also stresses this by posing the following set of questions: "Does a turn to vulnerability seek to reintroduce those foundationalist or essentialist modalities of thinking and valuing back into public discourse? — is it smuggling in discounted paradigms for reconsideration? Does the idea of vulnerability work to the detriment of women? Or does that very question presuppose that any concession made to vulnerability will lead to a vulnerability as (a) a foundational premise for politics (which it is not), (b) an essential identity (which it is not), or (c) an identification of women with injurability (which is not necessary)?" (2016: 22).

27. Butler is not outlining an existential utopia, as she herself makes explicit: "Of course, relationality is no utopian term, but a framework (the work of a new frame) for the consideration of those affects invariably articulated within the political field" (2010: 184).

28. Baudrillard writes that "[b]ehind every reflection, every resemblance, every representation a defeated enemy lies concealed. The Other vanquished, and condemned merely to be the Same" (2008: 150) — defeated, however, only from the angle of systemic closure. Baudrillard goes on that the other ever-resists its eradication and always remains as a subversive (*figural*) force: "a being which will one day rebel, and then our whole system of representation and values is destined to perish in that revolt. This slavery of the same, the slavery of resemblance, will one day be smashed by the violent resurgence of otherness" (ibid.).

29. On this equivocality Butler elsewhere elaborates, in a radical manner, as follows: "something about who we are is revealed, something that delineates the ties we have to others, that shows us that these ties constitute what we are, ties or bonds that compose us. It is not as if an 'I' exists independently over here and then simply loses a 'you' over there, especially if the attachment to 'you' is part of what composes who 'I' am. If I lose you, under these conditions, then I not only mourn the loss, but I become inscrutable to myself" (2006: 22).

Chapter 8: The View from Now Here

1. Thomas Nagel elaborates on Western scientism: "At its most myopic it assumes that everything there is must be understandable by the employment of scientific theories like those we have developed to date" (9).

2. Some of the coders even with to "*make the Cavern into a giant ark*" (Powers 2000: 137).

3. According to Kley, *Plowing the Dark*'s discussion of creativity and imagination draws on the taboo of humanity's appropriation of divine creative agency and the full control over the parameters of existence (2009: 437).

4. In the narrative, the programmer Ronan O'Reilly describes this situation as follows: "*Every modern mind is out there with a yardstick, a stop-watch, and a chi-square*" (Powers 2000: 82).

5. Charles Levin clarifies this perversely paradoxical logic: "Digital utopianism, though attractive in many ways, seems to be vitiated philosophically by a disingenuous rationalism which tries to evade the problem of the heterotopic *semantic* dimension of the body. By conflating the latter tendentiously with the 'Cartesian subject', egalitarian thought can simply cancel it out of the equation, whilst seeming radical and 'postmodern'. Down with Descartes! Death to the 'unitary bourgeois subject'—through computers!'" (178).

6. Catherine Keller elaborates: "To be a finite human body being interconnected with others . . . will necessarily involve pain. Masculinity has evolved into one great defense against that pain, which therefore makes others—especially women, people of color, animals, and the earth—feel men's pain for them. Men in the context of male supremacy are the bodies who are able to defer the suffering of finitude, displacing it onto the bodies of the others who cannot" (2005: 179).

7. Baudrillard elaborates: "Intelligence is not the intelligence of the whole human being, but a functional, cerebral version of ideation, and through it you can liberate an ideality of the human being restricted to the brain alone. Making a radical break between calculation and the body and, on that basis, inventing for yourself a definitive, spectral body, an exoteric body, free of any fleshly, sexual uncertainty, a body without depth, re-invented from the screen as skin, as tactile film, far removed from any organic sensibility. This is the perspective of the immaterial machine" (2001: 153).

8. Taimur Martin's blindfolding already alludes to a deeper reversibility which will be further unfolded in the next section of this chapter: "'You hear me, you cover your eyes. You understand?'"; "'You look, you die'" (Powers 2000: 74); While the coders of the RL are not able to see beyond their scientific vision, Taimur is not allowed to see beyond his restricted vision. As will be shown throughout what follows, there is more to this juxtaposition than first meets the eye.

9. The novel aptly reflects Richard Lane's description of the figure of the hostage as a mirror of an entire society held hostage by its own violent epistemology (cf. 102).

10. As Benny Pock explains, "[t]he notion that books are ultimately independent of their material carrier, meanwhile, is countered by the way in which Taimur remembers the stories of literary classics. As concrete books are withheld from Taimur in the beginning, the materiality of reading comes to function as a servomechanism of memory" (127).

11. It is only after Taimur's realization of his need for others that the novel recounts his own family background: "You spend a lifetime, another afternoon, trying to recall what it meant, growing up, to say you were half Persian" (Powers 2000: 234).

12. As Philipp Löffler explains: "For Lukács, the novel as a genre marks a crucial cultural watershed at the beginnings of European modernity. The novel presents a new type of literary format that—unlike the epic—showcases the human individual as a problematic being, as a being who still has to find its place in the world and who has to deal with the fact there are no guiding faculties" (94).

13. The novel per-formatively, and in reverse, implements the experience of precariousness

as described by Butler: "paradoxically, our responsibility is heightened once we have been subjected to the violence of others. We are acted upon, violently, and it appears that our capacity to set our own course at such instances is fully undermined. Only once we have suffered that violence are we compelled, ethically, to ask how we will respond to violent injury" (2006: 16). Butler's line of reasoning is reminiscent of Scarry's argument concerning torture: "If his attention begins to slip down the weapon toward the vulnerable end, if the severed attributes of pain begin to slip back to their origin in the prisoner's sentience" (59), then the inflictor of pain would "allow the reality of the other's suffering to enter his own consciousness [and that, again,] would immediately compel him to stop the torture" (57). The novel harbors such a compelling potential.

14. The rooms resemble the Cavern not due to their specific content, but rather because they reflect the "nature" of simulation that the novel unfolds. Heil reads the text as forming a Borromean Knot (three circles meshed into each other) but, as will become apparent below, it makes sense to stick to the image of the Mobius strip or the double helix.

15. Bradley Smith affirms this: "The cave becomes a guiding trope that helps the reader make connections between the different narrative strains throughout the novel, and as a result of the placement of this trope, realities and fictions (shadows) appear in places where we would normally never place them. The trope functions as an introduction into the blurring of reality and virtual reality in the text; the virtual reality of the cave can at times be real and at other times be imaginative" (99).

16. This question is also reflected in another interstitial moment of the narrative: "In common usage, Virtual Reality (VR) is contrasted with Real Life (RL); by naming the research facility the Realization Lab—RL—Powers scrambles this neat opposition and obscures the line separating the real and the virtual" (Taylor 2013: 84).

17. Baudrillard himself elaborates on poetic transference as follows: "There can still be, as in other worlds, singularities on a backdrop of a virtually flat 'aesthetic encephalogram.' These singularities are unpredictable and could very well be ephemeral, not entering History, in short events that arise against, just as in politics the real events today are singularities that come from beyond and take place against politics and history. There can no doubt be trans-aesthetic singularities, things that emerge from an alterity and are therefore unpredictable" (2005: 58f.).

18. This pun is owed to the ingenuity of Wolfgang Schoberth, who in his introductory lecture to systematic theology draws on Thomas Nagel's work to outline the guiding parameters of the modern (Western) scientific world view.

BIBLIOGRAPHY

Adorno, Theodor W. *Ästhetische Theorie*. Ed. Gretel Adorno and Rolf Tiedemann. Frankfurt /M.: Suhrkamp, 2010[19]. Print.

Aigner-Alvarez, Erika. "Artifact and Written History: Freeing the Terminal Indian in Anna Lee Walters' *Ghost Singer*." *Studies in American Indian Literatures* 2.8 (1996): 45–59. Print.

Akinwumi, Akinbola E. "Within/Without the Locus of Otherness Europe, Societal (In)security and the New Topicalities of Fear." *International Journal of Baudrillard Studies* 4.1 (2007): n.pag. Web.

Altman, Megan. "Heidegger and Aristotle on Contemplating Contemplation." *Schreiben Dichten Denken: Zu Heideggers Sprachbegriff*. Ed. David Espinet. Frankfurt/M.: Vittorio Klostermann, 2011. 227–40. Print.

Archambault, JoAllyn. "Indians and American Museums." *Zeitschrift für Ethnologie* 118.1 (1993): 7–22. Print.

Arendt, Hannah. *The Life of the Mind*. San Diego: Harcourt, Inc. 1978. Print.

Athanasiou, Athena, and Elena Tzelepis. "Mourning (as) Woman: Event, Catachresis, and 'That Other Face of Discourse.'" *Rewriting Difference: Luce Irigaray and "the Greeks."* Ed. Elena Tzelepis and Athena Athanasiou. Albany: State University of New York Press, 2008a. 105–18. Print.

——. "Thinking Difference as Different Thinking in Luce Irigaray's Deconstructive Genealogies." *Rewriting Difference: Luce Irigaray and "the Greeks."* Ed. Elena Tzelepis and Athena Athanasiou. Albany: State University of New York Press, 2008b. 1–14. Print.

Athanassakis, Yanoula. "Transnational American Studies in the Digital Age." *Journal of Transnational American Studies* 2.1 (2010): 1–8. Web.

Attridge, Derek. "Introduction: Derrida and the Questioning of Literature." *Acts of Literature*. Ed. Derek Attridge. New York: Routledge, 1992. 1–29. Print.

——. *The Singularity of Literature*. London: Routledge, 2004. Print.

Babcock, David. "Professional Intimacies: Human Rights and Specialized Bodies in Michael Ondaatje's *Anil's Ghost*." *Cultural Critique* 87.1 (2014): 60–83. Print.

Baldwin, Jon. "Exacerbation, Singularity, Indifference: Baudrillard and Politics." *International Journal of Baudrillard Studies* 9.3 (2012): n.pag. Web.

Ball, Karyn. "Diaspora without Resistance? Theresa Hak Kyung Cha's *DICTEE* and the Law of Genre." *Psychoanalysis and the Image*. Ed. Griselda Pollock. Malden, MA: Blackwell Publishing 2006. 161–93. Print.

Bamford, Kiff. *Lyotard and the Figural in Performance, Art, and Writing*. New York: Continuum, 2012. Print.

Barbaza, Remmon E. *Heidegger and a New Possibility of Dwelling*. Frankfurt/M.: Peter Lang, 2003. Print.

Barison, Marcello. "Seynsgeschichte und Erdgeschichte." *Schreiben Dichten Denken: Zu Heideggers Sprachbegriff*. Ed. David Espinet. Frankfurt/M.: Vittorio Klostermann, 2011. 145–59. Print.

Barker, Stephen. "Techno-pharmaco-genealogy." *Stiegler and Technics*. Ed. Christina Howells and Gerald Moore. Edinburgh: Edinburgh University Press, 2013. 259–75. Print.

Bass, Alan. *Interpretation and Difference: The Strangeness of Care*. Stanford, CA: Stanford University Press, 2006. Print.

Bataille, Gretchen M. Introduction. *Native American Representations: First Encounters, Distorted Images, and Literary Appropriations*. Ed. Gretchen M. Bataille. Lincoln: University of Nebraska Press, 2001. 1–7. Print.

Baudrillard, Jean. 2005. *The Conspiracy of Art: Manifestos, Interviews, Essays*. Trans. Ames Hodges. Ed. Sylvère Lotringer. New York: Semiotext(e), 2005. Print.

———. *Impossible Exchange*. Trans. Chris Turner. London: Verso, 2001. Print.

———. *The Intelligence of Evil or the Lucidity Pact*. London: Bloomsbury, 2013. Print.

———. *The Perfect Crime*. Trans. Chris Turner. London: Verso, 2008. Print.

———. *Simulacra and Simulation*. Trans. Sheila Faria Glaser. Ann Arbor: University of Michigan Press, 1994. Print.

———. *The Spirit of Terrorism and Other Essays*. Trans. Chris Turner. London: Verso, 2003². Print.

———. *Symbolic Exchange and Death*. Trans. Iain Hamilton Grant. London: Sage Publications, 1993a. Print.

———. *The Transparency of Evil: Essays on Extreme Phenomena*. Trans. James Benedict. London: Verso, 1993b. Print.

———. *The Vital Illusion*. Ed. Julia Witwer. New York: Columbia University Press, 2000. Print.

Beardsworth, Richard. "Technology and Politics: A Response to Bernard Stiegler." *Stiegler and Technics*. Ed. Christina Howells and Gerald Moore. Edinburgh: Edinburgh University Press, 2013. 208–24. Print.

Beistegui, Miguel de. "The New Critique of Political Economy." *Stiegler and Technics*. Ed. Christina Howells and Gerald Moore. Edinburgh: Edinburgh University Press, 2013. 181–91. Print.

Benesch, Klaus, Helmbrecht Breinig, Shelley Fisher Fishkin, Kristin Hoganson, Alfred Hornung, Barry Shank, and Ian Tyrell. "Transnational American Studies Whereto?" *Transnational American Studies*. Ed. Udo J. Hebel. Heidelberg, DE: Winter, 2012. 615–34. Print.

Bennington, Geoffrey. *Lyotard: Writing the Event*. Manchester, UK: Manchester University Press, 1988. Print.

———. "Opening up." *Cultural Politics* 9.2 (2013): 203–11. Print.

Berg, Maggie. "Luce Irigaray's 'Contradictions': Poststructuralism and Feminism." *Signs* 17.1 (1991): 50–70. Print.

Bergoffen, Debra. "Irigaray's Couples." *Returning to Irigaray: Feminist Philosophy, Politics, and the Question of Unity*. Ed. Maria C. Cimitile and Elaine P. Miller. Albany: State University of New York Press, 2007. 151–72. Print.

Berila, Elizabeth. "Unsettling Calls for National Unity: The Pedagogy of Experimental Multiethnic Literatures." *MELUS* 30.2 (2005): 31–47. Print.

Berry, Philippa. "The Burning Glass: Paradoxes of Feminist Revelation in *Speculum*." *Engaging with Irigaray: Feminist Philosophy and Modern European Thought.* Ed. Carolyn Burke, Naomi Schor, and Margaret Whitford. New York: Columbia University Press, 1994. 229–46. Print.

Best, Stephen, and Sharon Marcus. "Surface Reading: An Introduction." *Representations* 108 (2009): 1–21. Print.

Beutin, Wolfgang et al., ed. *Deutsche Literaturgeschichte: Von den Anfängen bis zur Gegenwart.* Stuttgart, DE: Metzler, 2007[7]. Print.

Bhabha, Homi K. *The Location of Culture.* New York: Routledge, 2004. Print.

Blask, Falco. *Jean Baudrillard zur Einführung.* Hamburg, DE: Junius, 1995. Print.

Bloom, Harold. *The Western Canon: The Books and School of the Ages.* New York: Harcourt Brace & Company, 1994. Print.

Bolland, John. "Michael Ondaatje's *Anil's Ghost*: Civil Wars, Mystics, and Rationalists." *SLC/ÉLC* 29.2 (2004): 102–21. Print.

Bolt, Barabara. *Heidegger Reframed.* London: I.B. Tauris, 2011. Print.

Bloodsworth, Mary K. "Embodiment and Ambiguity: Luce Irigaray, Sexual Difference, and 'Race.'" *International Studies in Philosophy* 31.2 (1999): 69–90. Print.

Bourne, Randolph. "Trans-National America." *The American Intellectual Tradition. Vol. 2, 1865 to the Present.* Ed. David A. Hollinger and Charles Capper. New York: Oxford UP, 1989. 153–63. Print.

Broders, Simone, Susanne Gruß, and Stephanie Waldow. "Phänomene der Fremdheit. Fremdheit als Phänomen: Einleitung." *Phänomene der Fremdheit. Fremdheit als Phänomen.* Ed. Simone Broders et al. Würzburg, DE: Königshausen & Neumann, 2012. 9–24. Print.

Brosig, Carmen. "'Branches of the Same Tree': Chicano/a Vietnam Solidarity and the Making of Aztlán." *Critical Regionalism.* Ed. Klaus Lösch et al. Heidelberg, DE: Winter, 2016. 79–101. Print.

Brusasco, Paola. *Writing Within/Without/About Sri Lanka: Discourses of Cartography, History and Translation in Selected Works by Michael Ondaatje and Carl Muller.* Stuttgart, DE: ibidem, 2010. Print.

Burn, Stephen J., and Richard Powers. "An Interview with Richard Powers." *Contemporary Literature* 49.2 (2008): 163–79. Print.

Burrows, Victoria. "The Heterotopic Spaces of Postcolonial Trauma in Michael Ondaatje's *Anil's Ghost*." *Studies in the Novel* 40.1–2 (2008): 161–77. Print.

Butler, Judith. *Frames of War: When Is Life Grievable?.* London: Verso, 2010. Print.

———. *Gender Trouble: Feminism and the Subversion of Identity.* New York: Routledge, 2007. Print.

———. *Notes Toward a Performative Theory of Assembly.* Cambridge, MA: Harvard University Press, 2015. Print.

———. *Precarious Life: The Powers of Mourning and Violence.* London: Verso, 2006. Print.

———. "Rethinking Vulnerability and Resistance." *Vulnerability in Resistance.* Ed. Judith Butler et al. Durham, NC: Duke University Press, 2016. 12–27. Print.

———. *Senses of the Subject.* New York: Fordham University Press, 2015. Print.

Callan, Guy, and James Williams. "A Return to Jean-François Lyotard's *Discourse, Figure*." *Parrhesia* 12 (2011): 41–51. Print.

Canters, Hanneke, and Grace M. Jantzen. *Forever Fluid: A Reading of Luce Irigaray's Elemental Passions*. Manchester, UK: Manchester University Press, 2005. Print.

Carroll, Rhoda, and Anna Lee Walters. "The Values of a Collective Past: An Interview with Anna Lee Walters." *American Indian Quarterly* 16.2 (1992): 63–73. Print.

Casanova, Pascale. *The World Republic of Letters*. Trans. M.B. Denevoise. Cambridge, MA: Harvard University Press, 2004. Print.

Cha, Theresa Hak Kyung. *Dictée*. Berkeley, CA: University of California Press, 2001. Print.

Chakravorty, Mrinalini. "The Dead That Haunt *Anil's Ghost*: Subaltern Difference and Postcolonial Melancholia." *PMLA* 128.3 (2013): 542–58. Print.

Chambers, Evan. "Re-Opening *Dictée*: Interpreting the Void in Theresa Cha's Representations of Christianity." *Religion & Literature* 44.2 (2012): 123–46. Print.

Chanter, Tina. "Irigaray's Challenge to the Fetishistic Hegemony of the Platonic One and Many." *Rewriting Difference: Luce Irigaray and "the Greeks."* Ed. Elena Tzelepis and Athena Athanasiou. Albany: State University of New York Press, 2010. 217–29. Print.

Cheah, Pheng, and Elizabeth Grosz. "Of Being-Two: Introduction." *Diacritics* 28.1 (1998): 2–18. Print.

Cheng, Anne Anlin. *The Melancholy of Race: Psychoanalysis, Assimilation, and Hidden Grief*. Oxford, UK: Oxford University Press, 2001. Print.

———. "Memory and Anti-Documentary Desire in Theresa Hak Kyung Cha's *Dictée*." *MELUS* 23.4 (1998): 199–33. Print.

Chew, Kristina. "What Does *E Pluribus Unum* Mean?: Reading the Classics and Multicultural Literature Together." *The Classical Journal* 93.1 (1997): 55–81. Print.

Cheyfitz, Eric. "Savage Law: The Plot against American Indians in *Jonson and Graham's Lessee v. M'Intosh* and *The Pioneers*." *Cultures of United States Imperialism*. Ed. Amy Kaplan and Donald E. Pease. Durham, NC: Duke University Press, 1993. 109–28.

Cho, Jennifer. "Mel-*han*-cholia as Political Practice in Theresa Hak Kyung Cha's *Dictée*." *Meridians* 11.1 (2011): 36–61. Print.

Clark, Timothy. *Derrida, Heidegger, Blanchot: Sources of Derrida's Notion and Practice of Literature*. Cambridge, UK: Cambridge University Press, 1992. Print.

———. *Martin Heidegger*. New York: Routledge, 2002. Print.

———. *The Poetics of Singularity: The Counter-Culturalist Turn in Heidegger, Derrida, Blanchot and the later Gadamer*. Edinburgh: Edinburgh University Press, 2005. Print.

Claviez, Thomas. *Aesthetics & Ethics: Otherness and Moral Imagination from Aristotle to Levinas and From* Uncle Tom's Cabin *to* House Made of Dawn. Heidelberg, DE: Winter, 2008. Print.

Colony, Tracy. "Dwelling in the Biosphere? Heidegger's Critique of Humanism and its Relevance for Ecological Thought." *International Studies in Philosophy* 31.1 (1999): 37–45. Print.

Cook, Victoria. "Exploring Transnational Identities in Ondaatje's *Anil's Ghost*." *Comparative Cultural Studies and Michael Ondaatje's Writing*. Ed. Steven Tötösy de Zepetnek. West Lafayette, IN: Purdue University Press, 2005. 6–15. Print.

Coulter, Gerry. "Jean Baudrillard's Writing about Writing." *International Journal of Baudrillard Studies* 4.3 (2007): n.pag. Web.

Coulter-Smith, Graham. "Between Marx and Derrida: Baudrillard, Art and Technology." *Jean Baudrillard, Art and Artefact*. Ed. Nicholas Zurbrugg. London: Sage, 1997. 91–103. Print.

Crowley, Martin. "The Artist and the Amateur, from Misery to Invention." *Stiegler and Technics*. Ed. Christina Howells and Gerald Moore. Edinburgh: Edinburgh University Press, 2013. 119–43. Print.

Cryne, Julia A. "NAGPRA Revisited: A Twenty-Year Review of Repatriation Efforts." *American Indian Law Review* 34.1 (2009–2010): 99–122. Print.

Culler, Jonathan. "The Most Interesting Thing in the World." *Diacritics* 38.1/2 (2008): 7–16. Print.

Cusk, Rachel. "Sri Lankan Skeletons." *New Statesman* (2000): 55. Print.

Damrosch, David. "The Semiotics of Conquest." *American Literary History* 8.3 (1996): 516–32. Print.

Davis, Steven. "The Path of a Thinking, Poeticizing Building: The Strange Uncanniness of Human Being on Earth." *Heidegger and the Earth: Essays in Environmental Philosophy*. Ed. Ladelle McWhorter and Gail Stenstad. Toronto: University of Toronto Press, 2009². 169–85. Print.

Denetdale, Jennifer Nez. *Reclaiming Diné History: The Legacies of Navajo Chief Manuelito and Juanita*. Tucson: University of Arizona Press, 2007. Print.

Derrida, Jacques. *Archive Fever: A Freudian Impression*. Trans. Eric Prenowitz. Chicago: University of Chicago Press, 1996. Print.

———. *Limited Inc*. Trans. Samuel Weber et al. Evanston, IL: Northwestern University Press, 1988. Print.

———. *Of Grammatology*. Trans. Gayatri Chakravorty Spivak. Baltimore: Johns Hopkins University Press, 1974. Print.

———. *Points . . . —. Interviews, 1974–1994*. Ed. Elisabeth Weber. Trans. Peggy Kamuf et al. Stanford, CA: Stanford University Press, 1995. Print.

———. *Positions*. Trans. Alan Bass. Chicago: University of Chicago Press, 1981. Print.

———. *The Post Card (From Socrates to Freud and Beyond)*. Trans. Alan Bass. Chicago: University of Chicago Press, 1987. Print.

———. *Sovereignties in Question: The Poetics of Paul Celan*. Ed. Thomas Dutoit and Outi Pasanen. New York: Fordham University Press, 2005. Print.

———. *Specters of Marx: The State of Debt, the Work of Mourning and the New International*. Trans. Peggy Kamuf. New York: Routledge, 2006. Print.

Derrida, Jacques, and Derek Attridge. "'This Strange Institution Called Literature'—An Interview with Jacques Derrida." *Acts of Literature*. Ed. Derek Attridge. New York: Routledge, 1992. 33–75. Print.

Derrida, Jacques, and Richard Kearney. "Deconstruction and the Other." *Dialogues with Contemporary Continental Thinkers: The Phenomenological Heritage*. Ed. Richard Kearney. Manchester, UK: Manchester University Press, 1984. 107–25. Print.

Deutscher, Penelope. "*Between East and West* and the Politics of Cultural *Ingénuité*: Irigaray on Cultural Difference." *Returning to Irigaray: Feminist Philosophy, Politics, and the Question of Unity*. Ed. Maria C. Cimitile and Elaine P. Miller. Albany: State University of New York Press, 2007. 137–50. Print.

Dewey, Joseph. *Understanding Richard Powers*. Columbia: University of South Carolina Press, 2002. Print.

Dimock, Wai Chee. "Introduction: Planet and America, Set and Subset." *Shades of the Planet: American Literature as World Literature*. Ed. Wai Chee Dimock and Lawrence Buell. Princeton, NJ: Princeton University Press, 2007. 1–16. Print.

———. *Through Other Continents: American Literature across Deep Time*. Princeton, NJ: Princeton University Press, 2006. Print.

Dreyfus, Hubert L. *Being-in-the-World: A Commentary on Heidegger's Being and Time, Division I*. Cambridge, MA: MIT Press, 1991. Print.

———. "Heidegger on the Connection Between Nihilism, Art, Technology, and Politics." *The Cambridge Companion to Heidegger*. Ed. Charles B. Guignon. Cambridge, UK: Cambridge University Press, 2006². 345–72. Print.

Duncan, Patti. *Tell This Silence: Asian American Women Writers and the Politics of Speech*. Iowa City: University of Iowa Press, 2004. Print.

Dungey, Nicholas. "The Ethics and Politics of Dwelling." *Polity* 39.2 (2007): 234–58. Print.

Eaglestone, Robert. "Postmodernism and Ethics against the Metaphysics of Comprehension." *The Cambridge Companion to Postmodernism*. Ed. Steven Connor. Cambridge, UK: Cambridge University Press, 2004. 182–95. Print.

Edwards, Brian T. "American Studies in Motion: Tehran, Hyderabad, Cairo." *Globalizing American Studies*. Ed. Brian T. Edwards and Dilip Parameshwar Gaonkar. Chicago: University of Chicago Press, 2010. 300–21. Print.

Edwards, Brian T. and Dilip Paramashwar Gaonkar. "Introduction: Globalizing American Studies." *Globalizing American Studies*. Ed. Brian T. Edwards and Dilip Parameshwar Gaonkar. Chicago: University of Chicago Press, 2010. 1–44. Print.

Edwards, James C. *The Plain Sense of Things*. University Park: Pennsylvania State University Press, 1997. Print.

Eid, Haidar. *"Worlding" (Post)modernism: Interpretive Possibilities of Critical Theory*. London: Quintus, 2014. Print.

Eileraas, Karina. *Between Image and Identity: Transnational Fantasy, Symbolic Violence, and Feminist Misrecognition*. Plymouth, UK: Lexington Books, 2007. Print.

Elliott, Emory. "Introduction: Cultural Diversity and the Problem of Aesthetics." *Aesthetics in a Multicultural Age*. Ed. Emory Elliott et al. Oxford, UK: Oxford University Press, 2002. 3–27. Print.

Ernst, Christoph, and Heike Paul. "Präsenz und implizites Wissen: Zur Interdependenz zweier Schlüsselbegriffe der Kultur- und Sozialwissenschaften." *Präsenz und implizites Wissen: Zur Interdependenz zweier Schlüsselbegriffe der Kultur- und Sozialwissenschaften*. Ed. Christoph Ernst and Heike Paul. Bielefeld, DE: transcript, 2013. 9–32. Print.

Eubanks, Cecil L., and David J. Gauthier. "The Politics of the Homeless Spirit: Heidegger and Levinas on Dwelling and Hospitality." *History of Political Thought* 32.1 (2011): 125–46. Print.

Fell, Joseph P. "The Crisis of Reason: A Reading of Heidegger's *Zur Seinsfrage*." *Heidegger Studies* 2 (1986): 41–65.

Fermon, Nicole. "Women on the Global Market: Irigaray and the Democratic State." *Diacritics* 28.1 (1998): 120–37. Print.

Ferreira, Boris. *Stimmung bei Heidegger: Das Phänomen der Stimmung im Kontext von Heideggers Existenzialanalyse des Daseins*. Dodrecht, NL: Kluwer Academic Publishers, 2002. Print.

Fiesta, Melissa J. "Solving Mysteries of Culture and Self: Anita and Naspah in Anna Lee Walters's *Ghost Singer*." *American Indian Quarterly* 17.3 (1993): 370–78. Print.

Fisher Fishkin, Shelley. "Crossroads of Cultures: The Transnational Turn in American Studies: Presidential Address to the American Studies Association, November 12, 2004." *American Quarterly* 57.1 (2005): 17–57. Print.

Fluck, Winfried. "Aesthetics and Cultural Studies." *Aesthetics in a Multicultural Age*. Ed. Emory Elliott et al. Oxford, UK: Oxford University Press, 2002.79–103. Print.

———. "Inside and Outside: What Kind of Knowledge Do We Need? A Response to the Presidential Address." *American Quarterly* 59.1 (2007): 23–32. Print.

———. "Men in Boats and Flaming Skies: American Painting and National Self-Recognition." *Re-Framing the Transnational Turn in American Studies*. Ed. Winfried Fluck et al. Hanover, NH: Dartmouth College Press, 2011. 141–63. Print.

Fontein, Joost. "Die Politik der Toten in Simbabwe." Trans. Lou-Salomé Heer. *Biohistorische Anthropologie: Knochen, Körper und DNA in Erinnerungskulturen*. Ed. Marianne Sommer and Gesine Krüger. Berlin: Kadmos, 2011. 200–30. Print.

Freud, Sigmund. "The Uncanny." Trans. James Strachey. *The Standard Edition of the Complete Psychological Works of Sigmund Freud, Vol. XVII (1917–1919)*. Ed. James Strachey et al. London: The Hogart Press, 1955. 217–52. Print.

Fried, Gregory. "Nach den *Schwarzen Heften* mit und gegen Heidegger Denken." Trans. Larissa Berger and Gertrud Lüdenbach. *Martin Heideggers* Schwarze Hefte*: Eine Philosophisch-Politische Debatte*. Ed. Marion Heinz and Sidonie Kellerer. Berlin: Suhrkamp, 2016. 366–82. Print.

Fritsche, Johannes. "Jüdisches und griechisch-deutsches Rechnen bei Heidegger." *Martin Heidegger* Schwarze Hefte: *Eine Philosophisch-Poltische Debatte*. Ed. Marion Heinz and Sidonie Kellerer. Berlin: Suhrkamp, 2016. 189–210. Print.

Frost, Elisabeth A. "'In Another Tongue: Body, Image, Text in Theresa Hak Kyung Cha's *Dictée*." *We Who Love to Be Astonished: Experimental Women's Writing and Performance Poetics*. Ed. Laura Hinton and Cynthia Hogue. Tuscaloosa: University of Alabama Press, 2002. 181–92. Print.

Fusco, Serena. "'You See Only Her Traces': Theresa Hak Kyung Cha's *Dictée*, or the Performance of a Voice." *"Contact Zones": Rewriting Genre Across the East-West Border*. Ed. Donatella Izzo and Elena Spandri. Naples, IT: Liguori Editore, 2003. 175–96. Print.

Fuss, Diana. "'Essentially Speaking': Luce Irigaray's Language of Essence." *French Feminists: Critical Evaluations in Cultural Theory. Vol. III Luce Irigaray*. Ed. Ann J. Cahill and Jennifer L. Hansen. London: Routledge, 2008. 101–20. Print.

Ganapathy-Doré, Geetha. "Fathoming Private Woes in a Public Story—A Study of Michael Ondaatje's *Anil's Ghost*." *Jouvert: A Journal of Postcolonial Studies* 6.3 (2002): n.pag. Web.

Gane, Mike. *Jean Baudrillard: In Radical Uncertainty*. London: Pluto, 2000. Print.

Garber, Marjorie. *The Use and Abuse of Literature*. New York: Anchor Books, 2011. Print.

Genosko, Gary. *Baudrillard and Signs: Signification Ablaze*. London: Routledge 1994. Print.

Glissant, Édouard. *Poetics of Relation*. Trans. Betsy Wing. Ann Arbor: University of Michigan Press, 1997. Print.

Gorgone, Sandro. "Entwurzelung und Verwüstung: Heidegger und die Dichtung der Heimat." *Schreiben Dichten Denken: Zu Heideggers Sprachbegriff*. Ed. David Espinet. Frankfurt/M.: Vittorio Klostermann, 2011. 127–44. Print.

Goux, Jean-Joseph. "Luce Irigaray versus the Utopia of the Neutral Sex." Trans. Margaret Whitford. *Engaging with Irigaray: Feminist Philosophy and Modern European Thought*. Ed. Carolyn Burke, Naomi Schor, and Margaret Whitford. New York: Columbia University Press, 1994. 175–90. Print.

Graber, Dorothy J. "Anna Lee Walters's *Ghost Singer* Links Native Diasporas in Time and Space." *Wizcazo Sa Review* 15.2 (2000): 7–16. Print.

Grace, Victoria. *Baudrillard's Challenge: A Feminist Reading*. London: Routledge, 2000. Print.

Greenblatt, Stephen. *Marvelous Possessions: The Wonder of the New World*. Chicago: University of Chicago Press, 1991. Print.

Grosz, Elizabeth. "The Hetero and the Homo: The Sexual Ethics of Luce Irigaray." *Engaging with Irigaray: Feminist Philosophy and Modern European Thought*. Ed. Carolyn Burke, Naomi Schor, and Margaret Whitford. New York: Columbia University Press, 1994. 335–50. Print.

Guignon, Charles. "Truth as Disclosure: Art, Language, History." *The Southern Journal of Philosophy* 28 (1989): 105–20. Print.

Gumbrecht, Hans Ulrich. *Atmosphere, Mood, Stimmung: On a Hidden Potential of Literature*. Trans. Erik Butler. Stanford, CA: Stanford University Press, 2012. Print.

———. *Production of Presence: What Meaning Cannot Convey*. Stanford, CA: Stanford University Press, 2004. Print.

Guzzoni, Ute. *Der Andere Heidegger: Überlegungen zu seinem Späteren Denken*. Freiburg, DE: Karl Alber. 2009. Print.

Guzzoni, Ute. *erstaunlich und fremd: Erfahrungen und Reflexionen*. Freiburg, DE: Karl Alber, 2012. Print.

Haar, Michel. "Attunement and Thinking." *Heidegger: A Critical Reader*. Ed. Hubert L. Dreyfus and Harrison Hall. Chichester, UK: Wiley-Blackwell, 1992. 159–72. Print.

Hackel, Steven W., and Hilary E. Wyss. "Print Culture and the Power of Native Literacy in California and New England Missions." *Native Americans, Christianity, and the Reshaping of the American Religious Landscape*. Ed. Joel W. Martin and Mark A. Nicholas. Chapel Hill: University of North Carolina Press, 2010. 201–22. Print.

Hajduk, Stefan. "Stimmungsorientiertes Lesen und seine verdeckte Theorie." *KulturPoetik* 12.1 (2012): 142–46. Print.

———. "Vom Reden über Stimmungen: Ihre Geschichte in der Literaturwissenschaft, ihre Aktuelle Erforschung und ihre Medialität." *KulturPoetik* 11.1 (2011): 76–96. Print.

Han, Byung-Chul. *Heideggers Herz: Zum Begriff der Stimmung bei Martin Heidegger*. München: Wilhelm Fink, 1996. Print.

Harries, Karsten. *Art Matters: A Critical Commentary on Heidegger's* "The Origin of the Work of Art." Heidelberg, DE: Springer, 2009. Print.

Harris, Charles B. "Technoromanticism and the Limits of Representationalism: Richard Powers's *Plowing the Dark*." *Science, Technology, and the Humanities in Recent American Fiction*. Ed. Peter Freese and Charles B. Harris. 249–78. Print.

Harrison, Robert P. *Gardens: An Essay on the Human Condition*. Chicago: University of Chicago Press, 2008. Print.

Hart, David Bentley. *Atheist Delusions: The Christian Revolution and its Fashionable Enemies*. New Haven, CT: Yale University Press, 2008.

Hart, Sally. "Jean Baudrillard and Jacques Derrida: At the Limits of Thought." *International Journal of Baudrillard Studies* 5.1 (2008): n.pag. Web.

Hayles, Katherine N. *How We Think: Digital Media and Contemporary Technogenesis*. Chicago: University of Chicago Press, 2012. Print.

Hayot, Eric. "Immigrating Fictions: Unfailing Mediation in *Dictée* and *Becoming Madame Mao*." *Contemporary Literature* 47.4 (2006): 601–35. Print.

Hebel, Udo J. *Einführung in die Amerikanistik / American Studies*. Stuttgart, DE: Metzler, 2008. Print.

Hegarty, Paul. *Jean Baudrillard: Live Theory*. London: Continuum, 2004. Print.

Heidegger, Martin. *Basic Writings*. Ed. David Farrell Krell. London: Routledge, 2011. Print.

———. *Erläuterungen zu Hölderlins Dichtung*. Frankfurt/M.: Vittorio Klostermann, 2012[7]. Print.

———. *The Fundamental Concepts of Metaphysics: World, Finitude, Solitude*. Trans. William McNeill and Nicholas Walker. Bloomington: Indiana University Press, 1995. Print.

———. *Holzwege*. Frankfurt/M.: Vittorio Klostermann, 2003[8]. Print.

———. *Introduction to Metaphysics*. Trans. Gregory Fried and Richard Polt. New Haven, CT: Yale University Press, 2000. Print.

———. *Poetry, Language, Thought*. Trans. Albert Hofstadter. New York: Harper Perennial, 2001. Print.

———. *The Question Concerning Technology and Other Essays*. Trans. William Lovitt. New York: Harper & Row, 1977. Print.

———. *Sein und Zeit*. Tübingen: Max Niemayer, 2006[19]. Print.

———. *Vorträge und Aufsätze*. Stuttgart, DE: Klett-Cotta, 2009[11]. Print.

Heil, Johanna. "Narrative Strands, Lacanian Orders, and the Borromean Knot: Reading Richard Powers's *Plowing the Dark*." *Ideas of Order: Narrative Patterns in the Novels of Richard Powers*. Ed. Antje Kley and Jan D. Kucharzewski. Heidelberg, DE: Winter, 2012. 143–74. Print.

———. *Walking the Möbius Strip: An Inquiry into Knowing in Richard Powers's Fiction*. Heidelberg, DE: Winter, 2016. Print.

Heinz, Marion. "Einleitung: Die Neue Heidegger-Debatte." *Martin Heideggers Schwarze Hefte: Eine Philosophisch-Politische Debatte*. Ed. Marion Heinz and Sidonie Kellerer. Berlin: Suhrkamp, 2016. 9–39. Print.

Heinze, Rüdiger. "Gazpacho & Tomato Soup: What we Talk about when we Talk about (Post) Multicultural U.S.-American Literature." *Transnational Americas: Envisioning Inter-American Area Studies in Globalization Processes*. Ed. Olaf Kaltmeier. Trier: WVT, 2013. 255–64. Print.

Heise, Ursula K. *Sense of Place and Sense of Planet: The Environmental Imagination of the Global*. Oxford, UK: Oxford University Press, 2008. Print.

Henry, Michel. *Barbarism*. Trans. Scott Davidson. London: Continuum, 2012. Print.

Hermann, Friedrich Wilhelm von. "Kunst und Technik." *Heidegger Studies* 1 (1985): 25–62. Print.

Hiller, Marion. "Heidegger und die Literatur, oder: *Der Ursprung des Kunstwerks* in seinsgeschichtlicher Dimension." *Heidegger und die Literatur.* Ed. Günter Figal and Ulrich Raulff. Frankfurt/M.: Vittorio Klostermann, 2012. 55–72. Print.

Hillger, Annick. *Not Needing All the Words: Michael Ondaatje's Literature of Silence.* Montreal: McGill-Queen's University Press, 2006. Print.

Hirsch, Marianne. "Editor's Column: What's Wrong with these Terms? A Conversation with Barbara Kirshenblatt-Gimblett and Diana Taylor." PMLA 120.5 (2005): 1497–1508. Print.

Holt, John Clifford. Introduction. *The Sri Lanka Reader: History, Culture, Politics.* Ed. John Clifford Holt. Durham, NC: Duke University Press, 2011. 1–7. Print.

Hong, Grace Kyungwon. "The Ghosts of Transnational American Studies: A Response to the Presidential Address." *American Quarterly* 59.1 (2007): 33–9. Print.

Hornung, Alfred. "ChinAmerica: Intercultural Relations for a Transnational World." *Transnational American Studies.* Ed. Udo J. Hebel. Heidelberg, DE: Winter, 2012. 13–30. Print.

Howells, Christina and Gerald Moore. "Introduction: Philosophy—The Repression of Technics." *Stiegler and Technics.* Ed. Christina Howells and Gerald Moore. Edinburgh: Edinburgh University Press, 2013. 1–14. Print.

Huang, Hsinya et al. "Charting Transnational Native American Studies." *Journal of Transnational American Studies* 4.1 (2012): 1–15. Print.

Huhndorf, Shari M. *Mapping the Americas: The Transnational Politics of Contemporary Native Culture.* Ithaca, NY: Cornell University Press, 2009. Print.

Hutcheon, Linda. *A Poetics of Postmodernism: History, Theory, Fiction.* New York: Routledge, 1988. Print.

Huyssen, Andreas. "In the Shadow of McLuhan: Jean Baudrillard's Theory of Simulation." *Assemblage* 10 (1989): 6–17. Print.

Ickstadt, Heinz. "'Asynchronous Messaging': The Multiple Functions of Richard Powers' Fictions." *Ideas of Order: Narrative Patterns in the Novels of Richard Powers.* Ed. Antje Kley and Jan D. Kucharzewski. Heidelberg, DE: Winter, 2012. 23–43. Print.

———. "Aesthetic Experience and the Collective Life: An Introduction." *Aesthetic Innovation and the Democratic Principle: Essays on Twentieth-Century American Poetry and Fiction.* Ed. Susanne Rohr et al. Heidelberg, DE: Winter, 2016. 11–28. Print.

———. "Toward a Pluralist Aesthetics." *Aesthetics in a Multicultural Age.* Ed. Emory Elliott et al. Oxford, UK: Oxford University Press, 2002. 263–78. Print.

Ingram, Penelope. *The Signifying Body: Toward an Ethics of Sexual and Racial Difference.* Albany: State Universtiy of New York Press, 2008. Print.

Inoue, Mayumo. Theresa Hak Kyung Cha's 'Phantomnation': Cinematic Specters and Spectral Collectivity in *Dictée* and *Apparatus.*" *Criticism* 56.1 (2014): 63–87. Print.

Inwood, Michael. *Heidegger: A Very Short Introduction.* Oxford, UK: Oxford University Press, 2000. Print.

Ionescu, Vlad. "Figural Aesthetics: Lyotard, Valéry, Deleuze." *Cultural Politics* 9.2 (2013): 144–57. Print.

———. "The Spectrum of the Figural: Aesthetics in the Eyes of Jean-François Lyotard." *Art History Supplement* 4.1 (2014): 46–73. Print.

Irigaray, Luce. "Being Two, How Many Eyes Have We?" Trans. Luce Irigaray, Catherine

Busson, Jim Mooney, Heidi Bostic, and Stephen Pluháček. *Paragraph* 25.3 (2002a): 143–51. Print.

———. *An Ethics of Sexual Difference*. Trans. Carolyn Burke and Gillian C. Gill. Ithaca, NY: Cornell University Press, 1993. Print.

———. "How Can We Meet the Other?" *Otherness: A Multilateral Perspective*. Ed. Susan Yi Sencindiver et al. Frankfurt/M.: Peter Lang, 2011. 107–20. Print.

———. *I Love to You*. Trans. Alison Martin. New York: Routledge, 1996. Print.

———. *Marine Lover: Of Friedrich Nietzsche*. Trans. Gillian C. Gill. New York: Columbia University Press, 1991. Print.

———. "The Question of the Other." Trans. Noah Guynn. *Yale French Studies* 87 (1995): 7–19. Print.

———. *Speculum of the Other Woman*. Trans. Gillian C. Gill. Ithaca, NY: Cornell University Press, 1985a. Print.

———. *This Sex Which Is Not One*. Trans. Catherine Porter. Ithaca, NY: Cornell University Press, 1985b. Print.

Irigaray, Luce. *To Be Two*. Trans. Monique M. Rhodes and Marco F. Cocito-Monoc. London: The Athlone P, 2000a. Print.

———. *The Way of Love*. Trans. Heide Bostic and Stephen Pluháček. London: Continuum, 2002b. Print.

———. *Why Different? A Culture of Two Subjects: Interviews with Luce Irigaray*. Trans. Camille Collins. New York: Semiotext(e), 2000b. Print.

Izzo, Donatella. "Outside Where? Comparing Notes on Comparative American Studies and American Comparative Studies." *American Studies: An Anthology*. Ed. Janice A. Radway et al. Chichester, UK: Wiley-Blackwell, 2009. 588–604. Print.

Jameson, Fredric. *Postmodernism or, the Cultural Logic of Late Capitalism*. Durham, NC: Duke University Press, 1991. Print.

Jay, Paul. *Global Matters: The Transnational Turn in Literary Studies*. Ithaca, NY: Cornell University Press, 2010. Print.

Johnson, Christopher. "The Prehistory of Technology: On the Contribution of Leroi-Gourhan." *Stiegler and Technics*. Ed. Christina Howells and Gerald Moore. Edinburgh: Edinburgh University Press, 2013. 34–52. Print.

Jones, Rachel. *Irigaray: Towards a Sexuate Philosophy*. Malden, MA: Polity, 2011. Print.

———. "Irigaray and Lyotard: Birth, Infancy, and Metaphysics." *Hypatia* 27.1 (2012): 139–62. Print.

Joy, Morny. *Divine Love: Luce Irigaray, Women, Gender and Religion*. Manchester, UK: Manchester University Press, 2006. Print.

Joyce, Stephen. *A River of Han: Eastern Tragedy in a Western Land: A Study of Korean American Literature*. Heidelberg, DE: Winter, 2015. Print.

June, Pamela B. *The Fragmented Female Body and Identity: The Postmodern, Feminist, and Multiethnic Writings of Toni Morrison, Theresa Hak Kyung Cha, Phyllis Alesia Perry, Gayl Jones, Emma Pérez, Paula Gunn Allen, and Kathy Acker*. New York: Peter Lang, 2010. Print.

Kaltmeier, Olaf. "Transnational Americas: Envisioning Inter-American Area Studies in Globalization Processes." *Transnational Americas: Envisioning Inter-American Area*

Studies in Globalization Processes. Ed. Olaf Kaltmeier. Trier, DE: WVT, 2013. 1–14. Print.

Kang, Laura Hyun Yi. *Compositional Subjects: Enfiguring Asian/American Women*. Durham, NC: Duke University Press, 2002. Print.

———. "The 'Liberatory Voice' of Theresa Hay Kyung Cha's *Dictée*." *Writing Self / Writing Nation: A Collection of Essays on DICTEE by Theresa Hak Kyung Cha*. Ed. Elaine H. Kim and Norma Alarcón. Berkeley, CA: Third Woman, 1994. 73–99. Print.

Keller, Catherine. *Apocalypse Now and Then: A Feminist Guide to the End of the World*. Minneapolis: Fortress P, 2005². Print.

Kellner, Douglas. "Baudrillard and the Art Conspiracy." *Jean Baudrillard: Fatal Theories*. Ed. David B. Clarke et al. London: Routledge, 2009. 91–104. Print.

Kennedy, Liam. "Spectres of Comparison: American Studies and the United States of the West." *American Studies: An Anthology*. Ed. Janice A. Radway et al. Chichster, UK: Wiley-Blackwell, 2009. 569–77. Print.

Kern, Andrea. "'Der Ursprung des Kunstwerks'—Kunst und Wahrheit zwischen Stiftung und Streit." *Heidegger Handbuch: Leben—Werk—Wirkung*. Ed. Dieter Thomä. Stuttgart, DE: Metzler, 2003. 162–74. Print.

Kertzer, Jon. "Justice and the Pathos of Understanding in Michael Ondaatje's Anil's Ghost." *ESC* 29.3–4 (2003): 116–38. Print.

Kim, Elaine H. "Poised on the In-Between: A Korean American's Reflections on Theresa Hak Kyung Cha's *Dictée*." *Writing Self / Writing Nation: A Collection of Essays on DICTEE by Theresa Hak Kyung Cha*. Ed. Elaine H. Kim and Norma Alarcón. Berkeley, CA: Third Woman P, 1994. 3–30. Print.

Kim, Grace Ji-Sun. *Embracing the Other: The Transformative Spirit of Love*. Grand Rapids, MI: William B. Eerdmans Publishing Company, 2015. Print.

Kim, Hyo K. "Embodying the In-Between: Theresa Hak Kyung Cha's *Dictee*." *Mosaic* 46.4 (2013): 127–43. Print.

Kim, Sue J. "Author, Reader: Equivocation in Theresa Hak Kyung Cha's *Dictee*." *Narrative* 16.2 (2008): 163–77. Print.

Knopf, Kerstin. "The Turn Toward the Indigenous: Knowledge Systems and Practices in the Academy." *Amerikastudien/American Studies* 60.2/3 (2015): 179–200. Print.

Knowles, Sam. "Sri Lankan 'Gates of Fire': Michael Ondaatje's Transnational Literature, from *Running in the Family* to *Anil's Ghost*." *The Journal of Commonwealth Literature* 45 (2010): 429–41. Print.

Kley, Antje. *Ethik medialer Repräsentation im britischen und US-amerikanischen Roman, 1741–2000*. Heidelberg, DE: Winter, 2009. Print.

———. "Literatur als Präsentifikation impliziten Wissens: Kulturkontakt in Mary Rowlandsons *captivity narrative* (1682) und Toni Morrisons Kurzgeschichte 'Recitatif' (1983)." *Präsenz und implizites Wissen: Zur Interdependenz zweier Schlüsselbegriffe der Kultur- und Sozialwissenschaften*. Ed. Christoph Ernst and Heike Paul. Bielefeld, DE: transcript, 2013. 211–37. Print.

Kockelmans, Joseph J. *Heidegger on Art and Art Works*. Dordrecht, NL: Martinus Nijhoff Publishers, 1985. Print.

Kristeva, Julia. *Revolution in Poetic Language*. Trans. Margaret Waller. New York: Columbia University Press, 1984. Print.

———. *Strangers to Ourselves*. Trans. Leon S. Roudiez. New York: Columbia University Press, 1991. Print.

Krüger, Gesine. "Knochen im Transfer—Zur Restitution sterblicher Überreste in historischer Perspektive." *Sammeln, Erforschen, Zurückgeben?—Menschliche Gebeine aus der Kolonialzeit in akademischen und musealen Sammlungen*. Ed. Holger Stoecker et al. Berlin: Ch. Links, 2013. 477–92. Print.

Lane, Richard J. *Jean Baudrillard*. London: Routledge, 2009². Print.

Latour, Bruno. "Powers of the Facsimile: A Turing Test on Science and Literature." *Intersections: Essays on Richard Powers*. Ed. Stephen J. Burn and Peter Dempsey. Champaign, IL: Dalkey Archive Press, 2008. 263–91. Print.

LeClair, Tom. "The Sri Lankan Patients." *The Nation* (2000): n.pag. Web.

Lee, Kun Jong. "Rewriting Hesiod, Revisioning Korea: Theresa Hak Kyung Cha's *Dictee* as a Subversive *Hesiodic Catalogue of Women*." *College Literature*. 33.3 (2006): 77–99. Print.

Lee, Sue-Im. "Suspicious Characters: Realism, Asian American Identity, and Theresa Hak Kyung Cha's *Dictee*." *Journal of Narrative Theory* 32.2 (2002): 227–58. Print.

van Leeuwen, Anne. "Sexuate Difference, Ontological Difference: Between Irigaray and Heidegger." *Continental Philosophy Review* 43 (2010): 111–26. Print.

Lehtinen, Virpi. *Luce Irigaray's Phenomenology of Feminine Being*. Albany: State University of New York Press, 2014. Print.

Lemke, Sieglinde. "Liberty: A Transnational Icon." *Re-Framing the Transnational Turn in American Studies*. Ed. Winfried Fluck et al. Hanover, NH: Dartmouth College Press, 2011. 193–218. Print.

Levin, Charles. *Jean Baudrillard: A Study in Cultural Metaphysics*. London: Prentice Hall, 1996. Print.

Lienhard, Martin. "Writing and Power in the Conquest of America." Trans. Carlos Perez. *Latin American Perspectives* 19.3 (1992): 79–85. Print.

Lonetree, Amy. *Decolonizing Museums: Representing Native America in National and Tribal Museums*. Chapel Hill: University of North Carolina Press, 2012. Print.

———. "Museums as Sites of Decolonization: Truth Telling in National and Tribal Museums." *Contesting Knowledge: Museums and Indigenous Perspectives*. Ed. Susan Sleeper-Smith. Lincoln: University of Nebraska Press, 2009. 322–37. Print.

Lorde, Audre. *Sister Outsider: Essays and Speeches*. Berkeley, CA: Crossing Press, 1984. Print.

Lotringer, Sylvère. Introduction: The Piracy of Art." *The Conspiracy of Art: Manifestos, Interviews, Essays*. Trans. Ames Hodges. Ed. Sylvère Lotringer. New York: Semiotext(e): 2005. 9–21. Print.

Love, Heather. "Close but not Deep: Literary Ethics and the Descriptive Turn." *New Literary History* 41 (2010): 371–91. Print.

Lowe, Lisa. "History Hesitant." *Social Text* 33.4 (2015): 85–107. Print.

———. "Unfaithful to the Original: The Subject of *Dictée*." *Writing Self / Writing Nation: A Collection of Essays on DICTEE by Theresa Hak Kyung Cha*. Ed. Elaine H. Kim and Norma Alarcón. Berkeley, CA: Third Woman Press, 1994. 35–69. Print.

Löffler, Philipp. "'The Ability to Make Worlds': Lukácsean Aesthetics, Self-Creation, and Richard Powers' *Plowing the Dark*." *Ideas of Order: Narrative Patterns in the*

Novels of Richard Powers. Ed. Antje Kley and Jan D. Kucharzewski. Heidelberg, DE: Winter, 2012. 91–117. Print.

Lösch, Klaus. "Das Fremde und seine Beschreibung." *Phänomene der Fremdheit— Fremdheit als Phänomen*. Ed. Simone Broders et al. Würzburg, DE: Königshausen & Neumann, 2012. 25–49. Print.

Lösch, Klaus, and Heike Paul. "Präsenz, implizites Wissen und Fremdheit aus kulturwissenschaftlicher Perspektive." *Präsenz und implizites Wissen: Zur Interdependenz zweier Schlüsselbegriffe der Kultur- und Sozialwissenschaften*. Ed. Christoph Ernst and Heike Paul. Bielefeld, DE: transcript, 2013. 151–83. Print.

Lösch, Klaus, and Heike Paul. "Präsenz, implizites Wissen und Fremdheit aus kulturwissenschaftlicher Perspektive." *Crossroads in American Studies: Transnational and Biocultural Encoutners—Essays in Honor of Rüdiger Kunow*. Ed. Frederike Offizier et al. Heidelberg, DE: Winter, 2016. 325–60. Print.

Lydon, Mary. "Veduta on *Discourse, Figure*." *Yale French Studies* 99 (2001): 10–26. Print.

Lyotard, Jean-François. *Discourse, Figure*. Trans. Antony Hudek and Mary Lydon. Minneapolis: University of Minnesota Press, 2011. Print.

Lyotard, Jean-François, and Bernard Marcadé. "What to Paint?" Trans. Kent Still and Peter W: Milne. *Cultural Politics* 9.2 (2013): 212–18. Print.

Lyotard, Jean-François, and Jean-Loup Thébaud. *Just Gaming*. Trans. Brian Massumi. Manchester, UK: Manchester University Press, 1985. Print.

Magrini, J.M. "Worlds Apart in the Curriculum: Heidegger, Technology, and the *Poietic* Attunement of Literature." *Educational Philosophy and Theory* 44.5 (2012): 500–21. Print.

Marais, Mike. Preface. *"Worlding" (Post)modernism: Interpretive Possibilities of Critical Theory*. London: Quintus, 2014. 9–16. Print.

Marinkova, Milena. *Michael Ondaatje: Haptic Aesthetics and Micropolitical Writing*. New York: Continuum, 2011. Print.

Martin, Stephen-Paul. *Open Form and the Feminine Imagination: The Politics of Reading in Twentieth-Century Innovative Writing*. Washington, DC: Maisonneuve Press, 1988. Print.

McDaniel, Nicole. "'The Remnant is the Whole': Collage, Serial Self-Representation, and Recovering Fragments in Theresa Hak Kyung Cha's *Dictée*." *Ariel* 40.4 (2009): 69–88. Print.

Mendoza, Daryl Y. "Baudrillard and the Malaise in the Global Village: Can There Be a Global Community in an Era of Hyper-Communication without Communion?" *International Journal of Baudrillard Studies* 10.1 (2013): n.pag. Web.

Mersch, Dieter. *Was sich zeigt: Materialität, Präsenz, Ereignis*. München, DE: Wilhelm Fink, 2002. Print.

Mignolo, Walter D. *The Darker Side of Western Modernity: Global Futures, Decolonial Options*. Durham, NC: Duke University Press, 2011a. Print.

———. "Geopolitics of Sensing and Knowing: On (De)Coloniality, Border Thinking, and Epistemic Disobedience." *Transversal* (2011b): n. pag. Web.

———. *Local Histories/Global Designs: Coloniality, Subaltern Knowledges, and Border Thinking*. Princeton, NJ: Princeton University Press, 2000. Print.

———. "Re:emerging, Decentring and Delinking: Shifting the Geographies of Sensing, Believing and Knowing." *IBRAAZ* (2013a): 1–15. Web.

Mignolo, Walter D., and Rolando Vázquez. "Decolonial AestheSis: Colonial Wounds/ Decolonial Healings." *Social Text* (2013b): n.pag. Web.

Mihăilă, Rodica. "Cultural Translation and the Discourse of Transnationalism in American Studies." *Journal of Transnational American Studies* 3.1 (2011): 1–13. Web.

Millán-Zaibert, Elizabeth. *Friedrich Schlegel and the Emergence of Romantic Philosophy.* Albany: State University of New York Press, 2007. Print.

Miller, Angela, Janet Berlo, Bryan J. Wolf, and Jennifer L. Roberts. *American Encounters, Art, History, and Cultural Identity.* Upper Saddle River, NJ: Pearson, 2008. Print.

Miller, Elaine P. "Beyond the Madonna: Revisiting Luce Irigaray's Aesthetics." *Thinking with Irigaray.* Ed. Mary C. Rawlinson et al. Albany: State Universtiy of New York Press, 2011. 39–53. Print.

———. "Reconsidering Irigaray's Aesthetics." *Returning to Irigaray: Feminist Philosophy, Politics, and the Question of Unity.* Ed. Maria C. Cimitile and Elaine P. Miller. Albany: State University of New York Press, 2007. 93–119. Print.

Minh-ha, Trinh T. *Elsewhere, Within Here: Immigration, Refugeeism and the Boundary Event.* New York: Routledge, 2011. Print.

Miroković, Nikola. "Ästhetischer Zustand als Grundstimmung: Eine Fußnote zu Heideggers Schiller-Seminar (1936)." *Schreiben Dichten Denken: Zu Heideggers Sprachbegriff.* Ed. David Espinet. Frankfurt/M.: Vittorio Klostermann, 2011. 99–112. Print.

Mitchell, Andrew, J. *Heidegger among the Sculptors: Body, Space, and the Art of Dwelling.* Stanford, CA: Stanford University Press, 2010. Print.

Moi, Toril. "Patriarchal Reflections: Luce Irigaray's Looking-Glass." *French Feminists: Critical Evaluations in Cultural Theory. Vol. III Luce Irigaray.* Ed. Ann J. Cahill and Jennifer L. Hansen. London: Routledge, 2008. 58- 77. Print.

Moslund, Sten Pultz. "Difference, Otherness and Speeds of Becoming in Transcultural and Migration Literature and Theory." *Otherness: A Multilateral Perspective.* Ed. Susan Yi Sencindiver et al. Frankfurt/M.: Peter Lang, 2011. 183–98. Print.

Moyn, Samuel. *The Last Utopia: Human Rights in History.* Cambridge, MA: The Belknap Press of Harvard University Press, 2010. Print.

Mugerauer, Robert. "Call of the Earth: Endowment and (Delayed) Response." *Heidegger and the Earth: Essays in Environmental Philosophy.* Ed. Ladelle McWhorter and Gail Stenstad. Toronto: University of Toronto Press, 2009². 70–99. Print.

Nagel, Thomas. *The View from Nowhere.* New York: Oxford University Press, 1986. Print.

Nancy, Jean-Luc. *Corpus.* Trans. Richard A. Rand. New York: Fordham University Press, 2008. Print.

———. *Corpus II: Writings on Sexuality.* Trans. Anne O'Bryne. New York: Fordham University Press, 2013. Print.

———. *The Birth to Presence.* Trans. Brian Holmes. Stanford, CA: Stanford University Press, 1993. Print.

Ngai, Mae M. "Transnationalism and the Transformation of the 'Other': Response to the Presidential Address." *American Quarterly* 57.1 (2005): 59–65. Print.

Nguyen, Viet Thanh. *Race and Resistance: Literature and Politics in Asian America.* Oxford, UK: Oxford University Press, 2002. Print.

Nordin, Astrid. "Radical Exoticism: Baudrillard and Others' Wars." *International Journal of Baudrillard Studies* 11.2 (2014): n.pag. Web.

O'Donoghue, Brendan. *A Poetics of Homecoming: Heidegger, Homelessness and the Homecoming Venture.* Newcastle upon Tyne, UK: Cambridge Scholars Publishing, 2011. Print.

Oh, Stella. "The Enunciation of the Tenth Muse in Theresa Hak Kyung Cha's *DICTEE*." *Literature Interpretation Theory* 13.1 (2002): 1–20. Print.

Ondaatje, Michael. *Anil's Ghost.* London: Bloomsbury Publishing, 2000. Print.

Ortega, Mariana. *In-Between: Latina Feminist Phenomenology, Multiplicity, and the Self.* Albany: State University of New York Press, 2016. Print.

Ostendorf, Berndt. "Transnationalism or the Fading of Borders?" *Transnational America: The Fading of Borders in the Western Hemisphere.* Ed. Berndt Ostendorf. Heidelberg, DE: Winter, 2002. 1–21. Print.

Pada, Roland Theuas S. "Iterability and Différance: Re-Tracing the Context of the Text." *Kritike* 3.2 (2009): 68–89. Print.

Park, Josephine Nock-Hee. "'What of the Partition': *Dictée*'s Boundaries and the American Epic." *Contemporary Literature* 46.2 (2005): 213–42. Print.

Pasco, Marc Oliver D. "From Objects to Being and Beyond: Situating the Crisis of Reason Within the Bounds of a Hyperreal Interpretation of Contemporary Media Society." *International Journal of Baudrillard Studies* 13.1 (2016): n.pag. Web.

Paul, Heike. "Das Unheimliche und die Präsenz: Fremdheit in der amerikanischen Gegenwartsliteratur und -kultur." *Phänomene der Fremdheit—Fremdheit als Phänomen.* Ed. Simone Broders et al. Würzburg, DE: Königshausen & Neumann, 2012. 95–116. Print.

———. *The Myths That Made America: An Introduction to American Studies.* Bielefeld, DE: transcript, 2014. Print.

Pawlett, William. *Jean Baudrillard: Against Banality.* London: Routledge, 2007. Print.

Pease, Donald E. "Introduction: Re-Mapping the Transnational Turn." *Re-Framing the Transnational Turn in American Studies.* Ed. Winfried Fluck et al. Hanover, NH: Dartmouth College Press, 2011. 1–46. Print.

Peebles, Catherine. "Knowing the Other: Ethics and the Future of Psychoanalysis." *Returning to Irigaray: Feminist Philosophy, Politics, and the Question of Unity.* Ed. Maria C. Cimitile and Elaine P. Miller. Albany: State University of New York Press, 2007. 223–41. Print.

Pensley, D.S. "The Native American Graves Protection and Repatriation Act (1990): Where the Native Voice is Missing." *Wicazo Sa Review* 20.2 (2005): 37–64. Print.

Pfister, Joel. "Transnational American Studies for What?" *Comparative American Studies* 6.1 (2008): 13–36. Print.

Phelan, Anthony. "Prose Fiction of the German Romantics." *The Cambridge Companion to German Romanticism.* Ed. Nicholas Saul. Cambridge, UK: Cambridge University Press, 2009. 41–65. Print.

Phillips, Christopher N. "The United States from Inside Out: Transnational American

Studies—American Studies Association Conference, 12–15 October 2006, Oakland, California." *Early American Literature* 42.2 (2007): 397–99. Print.

Phillips, John. "Humanity's End." *Baudrillard Now: Current Perspectives in Baudrillard Studies*. Ed. Ryan Bishop. Cambridge, UK: Polity, 2009. 159–71. Print.

Pock, Benny. "'The Fabulous Persian Machine': The Function of Narrative Patterns in the Age of Networked Media and in Richard Powers' *Plowing the Dark*." *Ideas of Order: Narrative Patterns in the Novels of Richard Powers*. Ed. Antje Kley and Jan D. Kucharzewski. Heidelberg, DE: Winter, 2012. 119–42. Print.

Porter, Joy. "Historical and Cultural Contexts to Native American Literature." *The Cambridge Companion to Native American Literature*. Ed. Joy Porter and Kenneth M. Roemer. Cambridge, UK: Cambridge University Press, 2005. 39–68. Print.

Powers, Richard. *Plowing the Dark*. New York: Picador, 2000. Print.

Rabasa, José. "Writing Violence." *A Companion to Latin American Literature and Culture*. Ed. Sara Castro-Klaren. Chichester, UK: Wiley-Blackwell, 2013. 49–67. Print.

Rainwater, Catherine. *Dreams of Fiery Stars: The Transformations of Native American Fiction*. Philadelphia: University of Pennsylvania Press, 1999. Print.

Ratti, Manav. "Michael Ondaatje's *Anil's Ghost* and the Aestheticization of Human Rights." *Ariel* 35.1–2 (2004): 121–39. Print.

Reinfandt, Christoph. "Literatur im Digitalen Zeitalter: Zur Gegenwartsdiagnose in Richard Powers' Roman *Plowing the Dark*." *Literatur in Wissenschaft und Unterricht* 35.4 (2002): 359–79. Print.

Rigal-Cellard, Bernadette. "Plotting History: The Function of History in Native North American Literature." *Transnational Voices: Interpretations of Native North American Literatures*. Ed. Elvira Pulitano. Lincoln: University of Nebraska Press, 2007. 24–43. Print.

Riquelme, J.P. "Location and Home in Beckett, Bhabha, Fanon, and Heidegger." *The Centennial Review* 52.3 (1998): 541–68. Print.

Rodowick, D.N. *Reading the Figural, or, Philosophy after the New Media*. Durham, NC: Duke University Press, 2001. Print.

Rooney, Ellen. "Foreword: *An Aesthetic of Bad Objects*." *Reading in Detail: Aesthetics in the Feminine*. Naomi Schor. New York: Routledge 2007. xiii–xlvii. Print.

Root, Deborah. "The Imperial Signifier: Todorov and the Conquest of Mexico." *Cultural Critique* 9 (1988): 197–219. Print.

Roth, Julia. "Changing the *Terms* of the Conversation: Reflecting Translationality in American Studies." *Crossroads in American Studies: Transnational and Biocultural Encounters—Essays in Honor of Rüdiger Kunow*. Ed. Frederike Offizier et al. Heidelberg, DE: Winter, 2016. 243–64. Print.

Rowe, John Carlos. Introduction. *Post-Nationalist American Studies*. Ed. John Carlos Rowe. Berkeley, CA: University of California Press, 2000. 1–22. Print.

Ryan, Marie-Laure. *Narrative as Virtual Reality 2: Revisiting Immersion and Interactivity in Literature and Electronic Media*. Baltimore: Johns Hopkins University Press, 2015. Print.

Sakai, Naoki. *Translation and Subjectivity: On "Japan" and Cultural Nationalism*. Minneapolis: University of Minnesota Press, 1997. Print.

Saldívar, José David. *Trans-Americanity: Subaltern Modernities, Global Coloniality, and the Cultures of Greater Mexico*. Durham, NC: Duke University Press, 2012. Print.

Sanghera, Sandeep. "Touching the Language of Citizenship in Ondaatje's *Anil's Ghost*." *Comparative Cultural Studies and Michael Ondaatje's Writing*. Ed. Steven Tötösy de Zepetnek. West Lafayette: Purdue University Press, 2005. 3–91. Print.

Scanlan, Margaret. "*Anil's Ghost* and Terrorism's Time." *Studies in the Novel* 36.3 (2004): 302–17. Print.

Scarry, Elaine. *The Body in Pain: The Making and Unmaking of the World*. New York: Oxford University Press, 1985. Print.

Schmidt, Ricarda. "From Early to Late Romanticism." *The Cambridge Companion to German Romanticism*. Ed. Nicholas Saul. Cambridge, UK: Cambridge University Press, 2009. 21–39. Print.

Schoberth, Wolfgang. *Das Jenseits der Kunst: Beiträge zu einer wissenssoziologischen Rekonstruktion der ästhetischen Theorie Theodor W. Adornos*. Frankfurt/M.: Peter Lang, 1988. Print.

Schor, Naomi. "This Essentialism Which Is Not One: Coming to Grips with Irigaray." *Engaging with Irigaray: Feminist Philosophy and Modern European Thought*. Ed. Carolyn Burke, Naomi Schor, and Margaret Whitford. New York: Columbia University Press, 1994. 57–78. Print.

Schubnell, Matthias., ed. *Conversations with N. Scott Momaday*. Jackson: University of Mississippi Press, 1997. Print.

Schwab, Gail M. "Sexual Difference as Model: An Ethics for the Global Future." *Diacritics* 28.1 (1998): 76–92. Print.

Seel, Martin. *Ästhetik des Erscheinens*. Frankfurt/M.: Suhrkamp, 2003. Print.

Seubold, Günter. "Stichwort: Ereignis—Was immer schon geschehen ist, bevor wir etwas tun." *Heidegger Handbuch: Leben—Werk—Wirkung*. Ed. Dieter Thomä. Stuttgart, DE: Metzler, 2003. 302–06. Print.

Shotwell, Alexis. *Knowing Otherwise: Race, Gender, and Implicit Understanding*. University Park: Pennsylvania State University Press, 2011. Print.

Siegle, Robert. *Suburban Ambush: Downtown Writing and the Fiction of Insurgency*. Baltimore: Johns Hopkins University Press, 1989. Print.

Sielke, Sabine. "The Subject of Literature, or: (Re-)Cognition in Richard Powers' (Science) Fiction." *Ideas of Order: Narrative Patterns in the Novels of Richard Powers*. Ed. Antje Kley and Jan D. Kucharzewski. Heidelberg, DE: Winter, 2012. 239–61. Print.

Simpson, Moira G. "A Grave Dilemma: Native Americans and Museums in the USA." *Journal of Museum Ethnography* 6 (1994): 25–37. Print.

Slaughter, Joseph R. *Human Rights, Inc.: The World Novel, Narrative Form, and International Law*. New York: Fordham University Press, 2007. Print.

Slotkin, Richard. *Regeneration through Violence: The Mythology of the American Frontier 1600–1860*. Norman: University of Oklahoma Press, 1973. Print.

Smith, Bradley. "On Reality and Virtuality: A Study of Time-Spaces in *Plowing the Dark*." *Mosaic* 42.3 (2009): 95–108. Print.

Sommer, Marianne, and Gesine Krüger. "Biohistorische Anthropologie. Knochen, Körper und DNA in Erinnerungskulturen." *Biohistorische Anthropologie: Knochen,*

Körper und DNA in Erinnerungskulturen. Ed. Marianne Sommer and Gesine Krüger. Berlin: Kadmos, 2011. 7–32. Print.

Sonderegger, Ruth M. "Stichwort: Welt—Ihre Erschlossenheit und ihr Entzug." *Heidegger Handbuch: Leben-Werk-Wirkung.* Ed. Dieter Thomä. Stuttgart, DE: Metzler, 2003. 92–98. Print.

Sophocles. *Antigone.* Trans. David Grene. *Sophocles I: Oedipus the King, Oedipus at Colonus, Antigone.* Ed. David Grene and Richmond Lattimore. Chicago: University of Chicago Press, 1991². 159–212. Print.

Soppa, Sebastian. *Scheiternde Subjektivität: Das unglückliche Bewusstsein bei Hegel und Kierkegaard.* Berlin: Logos, 2010. Print.

Spahr, Juliana M. "Postmodernism, Readers, and Theresa Hak Kyung Cha's *Dictee*." *College Literature* 23.3 (1996): 23–43. Print.

Spandri, Elena. "Introduction: 'The Speech that Cannot be Silenced.'" *"Contact Zones": Rewriting Genre Across the East-West Border.* Ed. Donatella Izzo and Elena Spandri. Naples, IT: Liguori Editore, 2003. 17–44. Print.

Spinks, Lee. *Michael Ondaatje.* Manchester, UK: Manchester University Press, 2009. Print.

Spivak, Gayatri Chakravorty. *An Aesthetic Education in the Era of Globalization.* Cambridge, MA: Harvard University Press, 2012. Print.

———. Foreword. *Rewriting Difference: Luce Irigaray and "the Greeks."* Ed. Elena Tzelepis and Athena Athanasiou. Albany: State University of New York Press, 2008. ix–xii. Print.

———. "French Feminism in an International Frame." *Yale French Studies* 62 (1981): 154–84. Print.

Spivak, Gayatri Chakravorty and Cathy Caruth. "Interview with Gayatri Chakravorty Spivak." *PMLA* 125.4 (2010): 1020–25. Print.

Staels, Hilde. "A Poetic Encounter with Otherness: The Ethics of Affect in Michael Ondaatje's *Anil's Ghost*." *University of Toronto Quarterly* 76.3 (2007): 977–89. Print.

Stein, Wayne. "Theresa Hay Kyung Cha's *Dictee*, Exorcisms from Demons: A Reunification with the Korean Spirit." Korea and Regional Geopolitics. Ed. Walter Jung and Xiao-bing Li. Lanham, MD: University Press of America, 1998. 117–27. Print.

Stephens, Michael. *The Dramaturgy of Style: Vice in Short Fiction.* Carbondale: Southern Illinois University Press, 1986. Print.

Stiegler, Bernard. *Symbolic Misery, Volume 1: The Hyperindustrial Epoch.* Trans. Barnaby Norman. Cambridge, UK: Polity, 2014. Print.

———. *Symbolic Misery, Volume 2: The Katastrophē of the Sensible.* Trans. Barnaby Norman. Cambridge, UK: Polity, 2015. Print.

———. *Technics and Time, 1: The Fault of Epimetheus.* Stanford, CA: Stanford University Press, 1998. Print.

Stoler, Ann Laura. *Duress: Imperial Durabilities in Our Times.* Durham, NC: Duke University Press, 2016. Print.

Stone, Alison. *Luce Irigaray and the Philosophy of Sexual Difference.* Cambridge, UK: Cambridge University Press, 2006. Print.

Stone, Alison. "The Sex of Nature: A Reinterpretation of Irigaray's Metaphysics and Po-
    litical Thought." *Hypatia* 18.3 (2003): 60–84. Print.
Storolow, Robert D. "Heidegger, Mood and the Lived Body: The Ontical and the
    Ontological." *Janus Head* 13.2 (2013): 5–11. Print.
Strehle, Samuel. "A Poetic Anthropology of War: Jean Baudrillard and the 1991 Gulf
    War." *International Journal of Baudrillard Studies* 11.2 (2014): n.pag. Web.
Sutcliffe, F.E. Introduction. *Discourse on Method and The Meditations*. Trans F.E.
    Sutcliffe. London: Penguin Books, 1968. 7–23. Print.
Szadziewicz, Katherine. "Novel Realities and Simulates Structures: The Posthuman
    Fusion of Forms and Simulacra in Richard Powers's *Plowing the Dark*." *aspeers* 7
    (2014): 89–113. Print.
Talbert, Laura Ruth. "Native American Graves Protection and Repatriation Act:
    Requiring Federal Recognition Digs its Own Grave." *American Indian Law Review*
    37.1 (2012–2013): 171–202. Print.
Tayeb, Lamia. *The Transformation of Political Identity from Commonwealth through
    Postcolonial Literature: The Cases of Nadine Gordimer, David Malouf, and Michael
    Ondaatje*. Lewiston, NY: The Edwin Mellen Press, 2006. Print.
Taylor, Diana. *The Archive and the Repertoire: Performing Cultural Memory in the
    Americas*. Durham, NC: Duke University Press, 2003. Print.
———. "Performance and/as History." *TDR (1988-)* 50.1 (2006): 67–86. Print.
———. "Scenes of Cognition: Performance and Conquest." *Theatre Journal* 56.3
    (2004): 353–72. Print.
Taylor, Mark C. *Rewiring the Real: In Conversation with William Gaddis, Richard
    Powers, Mark Danielewski, and Don DeLillo*. New York: Columbia University
    Press, 2013. Print.
Thomä, Dieter. "Sprache: Von der 'Bewandnisganzheit' zum 'Haus des Seins.'"
    Heidegger Handbuch: Leben-Werk-Wirkung. Ed. Dieter Thomä. Stuttgart, DE:
    Metzler, 2013². 295–304. Print.
Thomson, Iain D. *Heidegger, Art, and Postmodernity*. Cambridge, UK: Cambridge
    University Press, 2011. Print.
Tillett, Rebecca. "'Resting in Peace, not in Pieces:' The Concerns of the Living Dead
    in Anna Lee Walters's *Ghost Singer*." *American Indian Literatures* 2.17 (2005):
    85–114. Print.
Todorov, Tzvetan. *The Conquest of America: The Question of the Other*. Trans.
    Richard Howard. New York: HarperCollins Publishers Inc., 1984. Print.
Toffoletti, Kim. *Baudrillard Reframed*. London: I.B. Tauris, 2011. Print.
Tomiche, Anne. "Lyotard and/on Literature." *Yale French Studies* 99 (2001): 149–63. Print.
Torikian, Garen J. "Against a Perpetuating Fiction: Disentangling Art from
    Hyperreality." *International Journal of Baudrillard Studies* 6.2 (2009): n.pag. Web.
Traister, Bryce. "Everything Old Is New Again: Transnationalism and American Literary
    History." *Transnational American Studies*. Ed. Udo J. Hebel. Heidelberg, DE: Winter,
    2012. 147–64. Print.
———. "The Object of Study; or, Are We Being Transnational Yet?" *Journal of
    Transnational American Studies* 2.1 (2010): 1–28. Print.
Trawny, Peter. *Heidegger und der Mythos der Jüdischen Weltverschwörung*.
    Frankfurt/M.: Vittorio Klostermann, 2014². Print.

Turner, Chris. "The Intelligence of Evil: An Introduction." *The Intelligence of Evil or the Lucidity Pact*. London: Bloomsbury, 2013. 1–12. Print.

Vasseleu, Cathryn. *Textures of Light: Vision and Touch in Irigaray, Levinas and Merleau-Ponty*. London: Routledge, 1998. Print.

Vattimo, Gianni. "Aesthetics and the End of Epistemology." *The Reasons of Art*. Ed. Peter McCormick. Ottawa: University of Ottawa Press, 1985: 287–94. Print.

Vedder, Ben. "The Notion of Dwelling in Heidegger." *Archivio di Filosofia: Incarnazione*. Ed. Marco M. Olivetti. Padova: Cedam, 1999. 737–46. Print.

Vizenor, Gerald. *Fugitive Poses: Native American Indian Scenes of Absence and Presence*. Lincoln: University of Nebraska Press, 1998. Print.

———. *Manifest Manners: Narratives on Postindian Survivance*. Lincoln: University of Nebraska Press, 1999. Print.

———. *Native Liberty: Natural Reason and Cultural Survivance*. Lincoln: University of Nebraska Press, 2009. Print.

Wade, Alex. "Social Metaphors and Meaning in Fourth Order Simulacra." *International Journal of Baudrillard Studies* 11.1 (2014): n.pag. Web.

Wald, Priscilla. "Minefields and Meeting Grounds: Transnational Analyses and American Studies." *American Literary History* 10.1 (1998): 199–218. Print.

Waldenfels, Bernhard. "Fremdheit des anderen Geschlechts." *Phänomenologie und Geschlechter differenz*. Ed. Silvia Stoller and Helmut Vetter. Wien, AT: WUV, 1997a. 61–86. Print.

———. *Grenzen der Normalisierung: Studien zur Phänomenologie des Fremden 2*. Frankfurt/M.: Suhrkamp 2008². Print.

———. *Grundmotive einer Phänomenologie des Fremden*. Frankfurt/M.: Suhrkamp, 2006. Print.

———. *Das Leibliche Selbst: Vorlesungen zur Phänomenologie des Leibes*. Frankfurt/M.: Suhrkamp, 2000. Print.

———. *Phenomenology of the Alien: Basic Concepts*. Trans. Alexander Kozin and Tanja Stähler. Evanston, IL: Northwestern University Press, 2011. Print.

———. *Sinnesschwellen: Studien zur Phänomenologie des Fremden 3*. Frankfurt/M.: Suhrkamp 1999a. Print.

———. *Sinne und Künste im Wechselspiel: Modi Ästhetischer Erfahrung*. Frankfurt/M.: Suhrkamp, 2010. Print.

———. *Topografie des Fremden: Studien zur Phänomenologie des Fremden 1*. Frankfurt/M.: Suhrkamp, 1997b. Print.

———. *Vielstimmigkeit der Rede: Studien zur Phänomenologie des Fremden 4*. Frankfurt/M.: Suhrkamp, 1999b. Print.

Waldenfels, Bernhard, Petra Gehring, and Matthias Fischer. "*Gespräch mit Bernhard Waldenfels*: '. . . jeder philosophische Satz ist eigentlich in Unordnung, Bewegung.'" *Vernunft im Zeichen des Fremden: Zur Philosophie Bernhard Waldenfels*. Ed. Matthias Fischer et al. Frankfurt/M.: Suhrkamp, 2001. 408–59. Print.

Walker, Nicholas. "Adorno and Heidegger on the Question of Art: Countering Hegel?." *Adorno and Heidegger: Philosophical Questions*. Ed. Iain Macdonald and Krzysztof Ziarek. Stanford, CA: Stanford University Press, 2008. 87–104. Print.

Walters, Anna Lee. *Ghost Singer*. Albuquerque: University of New Mexico Press, 1988. Print.

Warrior, Robert. "A Room of One's Own at the ASA: An Indigenous Provocation." *American Quarterly* 55.4 (2003): 681–87. Print.

———. "Native American Scholarship and the Transnational Turn." *Cultural Studies Review* 15.2 (2009): 119–30. Print.

Weinbrot, Joel. "The Baudrillardean Object." *International Journal of Baudrillard Studies* 9.2 (2012): n.pag. Web.

Weiss, Martin G. "Reality, Simulation and Hyperreality." *International Journal of Baudrillard Studies* 8.2 (2011): n.pag. Web.

Whitford, Margaret. *Luce Irigaray: Philosophy in the Feminine*. London: Routledge, 1991. Print.

———. "Rereading Irigaray." *French Feminists: Critical Evaluations in Cultural Theory. Vol. III Luce Irigaray*. Ed. Ann J. Cahill and Jennifer L. Hansen. London: Routledge, 2008. 78–98. Print.

Wiegman, Robyn. "Romancing the Future: Internationalization as Symptom and Wish." *American Studies: An Anthology*. Ed. Janice A. Radway et al. Chichester, UK: Wiley-Blackwell, 2009. 578–87. Print.

Wilden, Andrea. *Die Konstruktion von Fremdheit: Eine interaktionistisch-konstruktivistische Perspektive*. Münster, DE: Waxmann, 2013. Print.

Wilkinson, Caroline. *Forensic Facial Reconstruction*. Cambridge, UK: Cambridge University Press, 2009. Print.

Wolin, Richard. "Vernunftkritik nach den *Schwarzen Heften*." Trans. Pieke Biermann. *Martin Heideggers* Schwarze Hefte: *Eine Philosophisch-Politische Debatte*. Ed. Marion Heinz and Sidonie Kellerer. Berlin: Suhrkamp, 2016. 397–425. Print.

Wong, Shelley Sunn. "Unnaming the Same: Theresa Hak Kyung Cha's *Dictée*." *Writing Self / Writing Nation: A Collection of Essays on DICTEE by Theresa Hak Kyung Cha*. Ed. Elaine H. Kim and Norma Alarcón. Berkeley, CA: Third Woman Press, 1994. 103–40. Print.

Worthen, W.B. "Antigone's Bones." *TDR (1988-)* 52.3 (2008): 10–33. Print.

Xu, Ping. "Irigaray's Mimicry and the Problem of Essentialism." *Hypatia* 10.4 (1995): 76–89. Print.

Young, Julian. *Heidegger's Philosophy of Art*. Cambridge, UK: Cambridge University Press, 2001. Print.

Zakin, Emily. "Between Two: Civil Identity and the Sexed Subject of Democracy." *Returning to Irigaray: Feminist Philosophy, Politics, and the Question of Unity*. Ed. Maria C. Cimitile and Elaine P. Miller. Albany: State University of New York Press, 2007. 173–203. Print.

Ziarek, Krzysztof. *The Force of Art*. Stanford, NY: Stanford University Press, 2004. Print.

———. *Language after Heidegger*. Bloomington: Indiana University Press, 2013. Print.

Ziarek, Krzysztof. "A New Economy of Relations." *Returning to Irigaray: Feminist Philosophy, Politics, and the Question of Unity*. Ed. Maria C. Cimitile and Elaine P. Miller. Albany: State University of New York Press, 2007. 51–75. Print.

Zurier, Rebecca. "Newness, Flatness, and Other Myths: Looking for National Identity in European (and a Few British) Histories of American Art." *Internationalizing the History of American Art*. Ed. Barbara Groseclose and Jochen Wierich. University Park: Pennsylvania State Press, 2009. 19–40. Print.